C000151619

GOVERNING HIGHER EDUCATION:
NATIONAL PERSPECTIVES ON INSTITUTIONAL GOVERNANCE

HIGHER EDUCATION DYNAMICS

VOLUME 2

Series Editor

Peter Maassen, *University of Oslo, Norway, and University of Twente, Enschede, The Netherlands*

Editorial Board
Alberto Amaral, *Universidade dò Porto, Portugal*
Akira Arimoto, *Hiroshima University, Japan*
Nico Cloete, *CHET, Pretoria, South Africa*
David Dill, *University of North Carolina at Chapel Hill, USA*
Jürgen Enders, *University of Twente, Enschede, The Netherlands*
Oliver Fulton, *University of Lancaster, United Kingdom*
Patricia Gumport, *Stanford University, USA*
Glenn Jones, *University of Toronto, Canada*

SCOPE OF THE SERIES

Higher Education Dynamics is a bookseries intending to study adaptation processes and their outcomes in higher education at all relevant levels. In addition it wants to examine the way interactions between these levels affect adaptation processes. It aims at applying general social science concepts and theories as well as testing theories in the field of higher education research. It wants to do so in a manner that is of relevance to all those professionally involved in higher education, be it as ministers, policy-makers, politicians, institutional leaders or administrators, higher education researchers, members of the academic staff of universities and colleges, or students. It will include both mature and developing systems of higher education, covering public as well as private institutions.

GOVERNING HIGHER EDUCATION: NATIONAL PERSPECTIVES ON INSTITUTIONAL GOVERNANCE

Edited by

ALBERTO AMARAL

*Center for Higher Education Policy Studies,
Matosinhos, Portugal*

GLEN A. JONES

*University of Toronto,
Toronto, Canada*

and

BERIT KARSETH

*University of Oslo,
Oslo, Norway*

KLUWER ACADEMIC PUBLISHERS
DORDRECHT / BOSTON / LONDON

A C.I.P. Catalogue record for this book is available from the Library of Congress.

ISBN 1-4020-1078-8

Published by Kluwer Academic Publishers,
P.O. Box 17, 3300 AA Dordrecht, The Netherlands.

Sold and distributed in North, Central and South America
by Kluwer Academic Publishers,
101 Philip Drive, Norwell, MA 02061, U.S.A.

In all other countries, sold and distributed
by Kluwer Academic Publishers,
P.O. Box 322, 3300 AH Dordrecht, The Netherlands.

Printed on acid-free paper

All Rights Reserved
© 2002 Kluwer Academic Publishers
No part of this work may be reproduced, stored in a retrieval system, or transmitted
in any form or by any means, electronic, mechanical, photocopying, microfilming, recording
or otherwise, without written permission from the Publisher, with the exception
of any material supplied specifically for the purpose of being entered
and executed on a computer system, for exclusive use by the purchaser of the work.

Printed in the Netherlands.

TABLE OF CONTENTS

LIST OF CONTRIBUTORS

ALBERTO AMARAL is professor at the University of Porto and director of CIPES. He is chair of the Board of CHER, vice-chair of EUA´s steering committee on institutional evaluation, life member of IAUP, and a member of EAIR. Recent publications include: "Private Higher Education and Diversity: An Exploratory Survey." *Higher Education Quarterly* 55.4 (2001), 357 – 393 (with Pedro Teixeira); "Higher education in the process of European integration, globalizing economies and mobility of students and staff." In Huisman, J. and Maassen, P. (eds), *Higher Education and the Nation State.* London: Pergamon, 2001; and "The rise and fall of the private sector in Portuguese higher education." *Higher Education Policy,* 13.3 (2002): 245 – 266 (with Pedro Teixeira).

HARRY F. DE BOER is a senior research associate at the Centre for Higher Education Policy Studies (CHEPS) of the University of Twente in the Netherlands. His research interests include university-government relations, steering models, institutional governance, management styles, leadership, strategic planning and models of decision-making. He has been a frequent contributor to the literature on these topics during the last few years, including recent articles in *Higher Education Policy*, *European Journal of Education*, and *Tertiary Education and Management*. He has also been lecturing and tutoring in courses in higher education management.

THIERRY CHEVAILLIER is senior lecturer in economics at the University of Bourgogne (Dijon, France) and a member of IREDU (Institute for Research on the Economics of Education). He has been vice-president for resources in his university and head of the Institute for Educational Management. His research interests are higher education finance and human resources. He has been involved in several international comparative studies on various aspects of higher education in Europe and is an expert to Eurydice. He is a member of the Consortium of Higher Education Researchers (CHER).

GEERT DEVOS is professor of organisational behaviour at the Vlerick Leuven Gent Management School, Belgium and professor of educational administration at the University of Antwerp, Belgium. His research interests include management of change, organizational development and educational administration. He has published in *Educational Administration Quarterly* and is co-author, with Jef C. Verhoeven, of several publications on higher education policy, communication of educational policy, and school-based review.

ELAINE EL-KHAWAS is professor of education policy at George Washington University. She previously served as professor of higher education at the University of California, Los Angeles and as vice president for policy analysis and research at the American Council on Education. A sociologist who earned her master's and doctoral degree at the University of Chicago, she is a former president of the Association for the Study of Higher Education, a member of the board of trustees of

Emmanuel College, and currently serves on the editorial boards of *The Review of Higher Education, Higher Education Management*, and other academic journals.

OLIVER FULTON is professor of higher education in the Centre for the Study of Education and Training at Lancaster University, where he is also dean for the Associated Institutions. He has researched and published on many aspects of higher education policy and practice, including admissions and access, the academic profession and the organisation of academic work, implementing curriculum change, and policy formation and implementation at both governmental and institutional levels. From 1996 – 97 he was chair of the Society for Research into Higher Education and from 1998 – 2001 he was chair of the Board of the Consortium for Higher Education Researchers (CHER).

GLEN A. JONES is an associate professor in the Higher Education Group, Department of Theory and Policy Studies in Education, Ontario Institute for Studies in Education of the University of Toronto, Canada. His research focuses on systems and politics of higher education in Canada. He is a former president of the Canadian Society for the Study of Higher Education and a former editor of the *Canadian Journal of Higher Education*. In 2001 he received the Distinguished Research Award from the Canadian Society for the Study of Higher Education. He is the author of over fifty papers and reports on various aspects of Canadian higher education.

BERIT KARSETH is an associate professor at the Institute for Educational Research, University of Oslo in Norway. Her main research interests are curriculum studies and changes in higher education. Her publications include "The Emergence of New Educational Programs in the University." *The Review of Higher Education* 18.2 (1995): 195–216, "Didaktik in Forschung, Lehrerausbildung und Lehrplanentwicklung in Norwegen." *Zeitschrift Für Pädagogigik* 33 Beiheft (1995): 249 – 259, and "International mobility among Nordic doctoral students." *Higher Education* 38 (1999): 379 – 400, with S.Kyvik, J.A. Remme and S. Blume.

INGVILD MARHEIM LARSEN is a senior researcher at the Norwegian Institute for Studies in Research and Higher Education. Her main research interests are on reforms and change processes in higher education. Among her publications are "University Research Policy in Norway – Walking the Tightrope between Internal and External Interests." *European Journal of Education,* 35.4 (2000), "The Bureaucratisation of Universities." *Minerva* 36.1 (1996) together with Å. Gornitzka and S. Kyvik), "New Management System at Norwegian Universities: the interface between Reform and Institutional Understanding." *European Journal of Education* 30 (1995), together with Å. Gornitzka.

PETER MAASSEN is senior fellow at the Centre for Higher Education Policy Studies (CHEPS), University of Twente, the Netherlands. He was the director of CHEPS from January 1997 to March 2000. He specializes at CHEPS in the public governance (including policy reform and institutional change) of higher education. He has published numerous books, book chapters and articles (in 6 languages) in journals of higher education, political science, management studies, and policy analysis. In 1998 he was awarded a fellowship by the Society for Research on Higher Education (SRHE).

ANTÓNIO MAGALHÃES is assistant professor at the University of Porto, and a senior researcher at CIPES. His main research interests are the regulation mechanisms of higher education and the relationships between the state and higher education. His recent publications include "The Transformation of State Regulation and the Educational Systems." *Revista Crítica de Ciências Sociais* 59 (2001): 125 – 143 (in Portuguese); "On Markets, Autonomy and Regulation: the Janus Head Revisited." *Higher Education Policy* 14 (2001): 7 – 20 (with Alberto Amaral); and "Portuguese Higher Education and the Imaginary Friend: the Stakeholders role in Institutional Governance." *European Journal of Education* 35.4 (2000): 437 – 446, (with Alberto Amaral).

V. LYNN MEEK is professor and director of the Centre for Higher Education Management and Policy at University of New England, Australia. Trained in sociology of higher education at University of Cambridge, specific research interests include governance and management, research management, diversification of higher education institutions and systems, institutional amalgamations, organisational change, and comparative study of higher education systems. Professor Meek has published 24 books and monographs and numerous scholarly articles and book chapters. He is on the editorial board of several international journals and book series, and has worked with such international agencies as UNESCO and the OECD.

STÉPHANIE MIGNOT-GÉRARD is a doctoral student at the Centre de Sociologie des Organisations (FNSP-CNRS) in Paris. She is finishing her dissertation on the government of French universities. With Christine Musselin, she recently conducted in-depth qualitative fieldwork in four French universities and a quantitative study in 37 French universities.

CHRISTINE MUSSELIN is a senior researcher at the Centre de Sociologie des Organisations (FNSP-CNRS) and lecturer at the Institut d'Etudes Politiques de Paris. She conducted comparative studies on the French and German university systems focusing on university government, state-university relationships and everyday policy making by public authorities in charge of higher education. She is now finishing a comparative study on German, French and US academic labour markets for historians and mathematicians. With E. Friedberg, she wrote *l'Etat face aux universités* (Anthropos 1993) and *En quête d'universités* (L'Harmattan, 1989). In 2001 she published *La longue marche des universités françaises* (P.U.F.).

MICHAEL I. REED is professor of organization theory and associate dean for Research, Lancaster University Management School, UK. His research interests include theoretical development in organisation studies, the study of expert labour, the emergence of new organisational forms, and public sector management. He has published three sole-authored books and jointly edited two books. He has also published extensively in major international journals such as *Organisation Studies*, *Journal of Management Studies*, and *Theory, Culture and Society*. He is one of the senior editors of the journal *Organisation*, published by Sage. He is currently working on a new book on organisational control to be published by Sage.

JEF C. VERHOEVEN is professor of sociology at the KU Leuven (Belgium) and head of the Centre for Sociology of Education of the same university. He publishes in the field of theoretical sociology, and sociology of education. He recently conducted several projects on higher education in Belgium, some of them in collaboration with Geert Devos. He has published several books, and articles in, among others, the *European Journal of Education*, *Journal of Education Policy*, *Educational Management and Administration*, and *Research on Language and Social Interaction*. He recently published (with Kurt de Wit) a paper on "The Higher Education Policy of the European Union: With or Against the member States?" in *Higher Education and the Nation State* (Pergamon, 2001), edited by J. Huisman, P. Maassen and G. Neave.

PREFACE

Over the last decades higher education has gone through an unprecedented growth period, and as a result the average university or college has now more students and a larger output than ever before. At the same time, the socio-economic and political demands with respect to higher education have grown dramatically. These developments have taken place without a proportional increase of the budgets and facilities of the higher education institutions. This has created an imbalance between the expectations with respect to higher education and the institutional capacities in the sector. One of the underlying trends is that the traditional pact between higher education and society has become problematic. Society no longer accepts the rather special and protected position that universities have had for a very long time in our societies. The knowledge-based social and cultural missions of higher education institutions are no longer taken for granted as the main legitimacy bases for public investments in higher education. Universities and colleges are at present expected to function efficiently, to contribute to sustainable economic growth at various levels, and to add to national and even supranational trade balances. On top of this they have to prove that they maintain a high level of quality in their primary activities, i.e. teaching, research and services, while adapting and responding to the expectations expressed so vehemently in their environments, and to a decreasing per capita funding basis. All of this fits the current so-called period of transition, in which our societies are moving from being manufacturing based to being information or knowledge driven. Higher education institutions are argued to be core organizations in the emerging knowledge society, but the exact nature and role of these institutions, and therefore the exact adaptations they have to go through, are not clear yet. Many scenarios have been developed and predictions formulated, but the knowledge needed to make better-founded, valid interpretations of the change processes that currently characterize higher education is often lacking.

Here is where the field of higher education research comes in. This is a relatively young field that has developed rapidly over the last 30 years, resulting in a growing body of knowledge on higher education. However, many of the basic questions on higher education, related to our knowledge on which policies, instruments and approaches work and which do not work, still remain largely unanswered. An example of such a question concerns the contribution of higher education to economic development. Another example is the question on the most effective institutional governance structures for universities and colleges. The relative lack of research funding for these types of questions and the limited research capacity, amongst other things, as a result of the rather fragmented organizational basis of the field, are the main reasons why these kinds of questions have so far not been addressed in an adequate way. In order to use the available funds and capacity more

xi

effectively various initiatives have been taken within the field. One of these initiatives in Europe was the establishment on 1 January 2001 of *Hedda*, a consortium of 7 research centres and institutes on higher education (see webpage: www.uv.uio.no/hedda). The mission of *Hedda* includes strengthening the field of higher education research through stimulating and structuring the research cooperation between the *Hedda* partners and between *Hedda* and other research groups. For this purpose one of the *Hedda* partners, Cipes, has taken the initiative to organize an annual seminar for discussing the state-of-the-art with respect to one specific research area in the field. These discussions take place on the basis of research-based papers that are written within an overall conceptual framework. To make these discussions and the body of knowledge behind it accessible for a larger audience, Cipes and *Hedda* have agreed with Kluwer Academic Publishers to include the manuscripts that are the result of the seminars in the new Kluwer book series called Higher Education Dynamics (HEDY). In order to make these annual books recognizable within the HEDY series Cipes, *Hedda* and Kluwer have decided to start a 'series in the series' called the Douro Seminars on Higher Education Research (DOSHER). The name is inspired by the wonderful location in Portugal where the annual seminars take place.

This is the first of the so-called Douro books. It is edited by three of the colleagues who participated in the first Douro seminar that took place 13-17 October 2001. The seminar topic *Governance structures in higher education* refers to all relevant dimensions of the way higher education institutions are governed, for example, developments concerning the formal and informal institutional decision-making procedures and structures; changes in the composition, tasks and functioning of institutional governance bodies; and the growing involvement of external stakeholders in institutional governance issues. The book reflects this diversity. However, the first and last chapter provide the framework and comparative reflections that give this book the necessary coherence. We are very pleased to start the Douro series with this valuable collection and we are confident that the high scholarly quality level of this book will set the standard for the Douro books to be produced in the coming years, to start with in 2002/2003 on 'Managerialism in higher education; institutional autonomy and the professionalisation of institutional management and administration', and in 2003/2004 on 'Markets in higher education'.

We want to express our gratitude to all who have made the first Douro seminar and this book and the subsequent series possible, to begin with Amélia Veiga at Cipes and Therese Marie Uppstrøm at *Hedda*, without whom the seminar could never have been organised. We are obviously impressed by and grateful for the contributions of our colleagues to the seminar and this book. Not only did they put a lot of effort in the production of the basic paper, but all of them were also willing to take the comments and editorial suggestions received from the others seriously enough to integrate them into the edited version of their paper that you will find in this book. The energy put in this process and the speed with which the papers were developed into edited book chapters is an indication of the commitment of these scholars to their field and their profession. Finally, we want to acknowledge the financial support from *Fundação para a Ciência e Tecnologia*, of the Portuguese

Ministry for Science and Technology that has made possible the organisation of the first Douro seminar.

Alberto Amaral
Peter Maassen
Matosinhos
Oslo

October, 2002

MICHAEL I. REED, V. LYNN MEEK AND GLEN A. JONES

INTRODUCTION

A common theme in the dramatic restructuring of higher education throughout much of the world over the past few decades has been a shift in the relationships between universities, and other institutions of higher education, and the state. These new relationships have received considerable attention in the scholarly literature, in large part because they imply significant changes in the role of higher education in light of new or evolving social and economic demands for knowledge and educated labour, and new mechanisms for steering higher education, often involving a new regulatory environment and the introduction of instruments designed to create market-like competition within the sector. The implications of these reforms are broad and far-reaching, and include changes in how institutions of higher education are defined and understood, their role in society, their relationship to the communities in which they function, the nature and status of academic work, and the ways in which these institutions are funded and supported.

The restructuring of higher education in many jurisdictions has also led to fundamental changes in how institutions decide what they do and how they do it. The objective of this volume is to further our understanding of how institutions of higher education are governed, and how these processes, and the assumptions and discourses that underscore these processes, have evolved. Changes in institutional governance have received far less attention in the research literature than broad system-level reforms of higher education, and most of the studies that have been published have focused on the experience of institutions in a single jurisdiction. The contributors to this volume share a common view that institutional governance is a central issue in higher education; changes in the relationship between higher education and the state have direct implications for institutional governance, and have frequently involved state-imposed reforms of governance arrangements, and these governance structures provide the central forum for the struggle over what these institutions are or should be, and the complex and evolving relationships between academics, students, and external interests. They also share a common view that institutional governance has become an international issue in higher education, and that much can be learned by sharing research findings across national boundaries in order to identify common themes and important differences.

The thirteen core chapters of this volume were written by national experts in the study of higher education governance, and each presents a critical analysis of governance in a particular jurisdiction. The authors address key research questions on governance issues, but given the immense differences between systems there has been no attempt to create a homogeneous framework or a common research template. Instead, the papers focus on specific issues that are relevant to these

Alberto Amaral, Glen A. Jones and Berit Karseth (eds.), Governing Higher Education:
National Perspectives on Institutional Governance, xv—xxxi.
© 2002 *Kluwer Academic Publishers. Printed in the Netherlands.*

jurisdictions, ranging from system-level reforms and influences, to the impact of institutional changes in governance arrangements on the organisational life of the institution or on component parts of the institutions. The authors also draw on a wealth of empirical evidence and a diverse range of theoretical approaches to analyse these issues.

The objective of this chapter is to provide a theoretical roadmap of the concepts and perspectives that provide a foundation for the analyses. We begin by mapping the social science disciplines, perspectives, themes and concepts that are employed by our authors in the analysis of governance issues. This section is followed by a brief review of definitions and concepts from scholarship focusing on university governance that frames these discussions. We conclude the chapter by providing an overview of the volume.

1. THEORETICAL ISSUES AND PERSPECTIVES

A range of theoretical issues and perspectives are highlighted and developed in this book. Research and analysis of the institutional changes and organisational innovations associated with new forms of governance and management within contemporary higher education and universities cannot proceed in an intellectual vacuum. Each of our authors draws on an extensive range of conceptual, analytical and methodological resources to articulate and elaborate their respective analyses of the current situation in university governance and management. The purpose of this section of the chapter is to provide a broad overview and evaluation of the range of intellectual resources that our authors deploy. In this way, the potential reader may be better placed to make his/her own assessments of 'where our authors are coming from' and how their theoretical and methodological preferences influence their substantive analyses and conclusions. We will begin by looking at the range of social science **disciplines** that inform the detailed studies and analyses provided between these two covers. In turn, this will lead into a more focussed discussion of the specific theoretical **perspectives** utilised by our contributors and the ways in which these perspectives necessarily embody certain core ontological, epistemological and methodological commitments. Finally, we will move on to discuss the generic research **themes** that have shaped our authors' analyses and the key sensitising **concepts** they have selected to articulate and advance the former.

Three foundational social science disciplines underpin the substantive analyses developed within this book – organisation/management theory, policy studies/decision-making theory, and the sociology of occupations/professions. Each of these disciplinary matrices provides our contributors with a cluster of interrelated assumptions, categories and propositions that frame and legitimate their empirical studies and the various ways in which they are theoretically interpreted. Most of our contributors draw, in various ways, on organisation/management theory to understand and explain the dynamics of institutional restructuring and its longer-term impact on organisational design and behaviour within contemporary universities. In particular, several authors (Musselin and Mignot-Gérard, Reed, De Boer, Amaral and Magalhães, Meek, Fulton, Jones, Verhoeven and Devos) develop analyses that draw extensively on contemporary organisation/management theory in order to better appreciate the complex interplay between 'structure' and 'agency' over time. They see the latter as being of crucial explanatory significance, given its strategic role in shaping and reshaping the organisational trajectories and outcomes of institutional transformation in a range of higher education systems. We can only begin to understand, much less explain, the strategic re-orientation of higher education systems in different countries and its implications for everyday life in contemporary universities, if we confront the 'structure/agency' dilemma. The latter necessarily entails the development of theoretical approaches that directly engage with the complex ways in which 'structural constraints' and 'action choices' interact across different spatial, temporal and cultural contexts to generate various 'logics' and 'packages' of organisational change that actors then selectively appropriate for their own purposes. In this respect, our contributors tend to draw on the 'non-deterministic' streams of thinking and analysis within contemporary organisation/management studies insofar as they individually and collectively reject approaches that assume a universal direct 'cause and effect' relationship between environmental and organisational change. Instead, the majority of our contributors insist that new forms of university governance and management are emerging out of ongoing power struggles between various policy-making and implementing groups located within material, cultural and structural networks that differentially equip them to engage in 'institution building'. Any attempt to impose a deterministic mode of analysis on this highly complex, uncertain and unpredictable process of change – such as that entailed in the 'adaptive or selective paradigm' favoured by structural contingency theorists, population ecologists and resource-dependency theorists – is firmly rejected. In place of deterministically-inclined approaches, our contributors offer a more subtle and nuanced appreciation of the relatively 'open' and 'contestable' nature of institutional and organisational restructuring.

Policy studies and decision-making theory also provides a major source of disciplinary inspiration to a number of our contributors (Maassen, Jones, Verhoeven and Devos, Karseth, Meek, Fulton, Chevaillier, El-Khawas, and Larsen). This ranges across internal resource allocation decision-making (Chevaillier) and inter-organisational policy decision-making networks (Jones) where a form of structural analysis is deployed to explain the interaction between different levels of policy formulation and implementation. Various formulations of stakeholder theory are also developed and applied by our authors (Amaral and Magalhães, Maassen, De Boer, Meek, and Larsen). These are intended to clarify the impact of both 'internal' and 'external' interest groups on the historical and comparative trajectories of institutional change followed by universities and their implications for strategic steering and operational management. Such stakeholder models also challenge unitary and linear conceptions of policy formulation and implementation in higher education. Instead, they focus on the several competing and legitimate centres of authority and control that characterise and define the policy-making arena within higher education as it struggles to accommodate the plethora of structured alliances, interests and resources that clamour for attention. Finally, a number of contributors (Musselin, Verhoeven and Devos, Reed) develop a model of collective action decision-making as a disciplinary/theoretical basis for their substantive analyses. In this theoretical context, the explanatory focus is directed to the 'loosely-coupled' hierarchy of collective decision-making that shapes the emergence and development of new organisational forms as alternative ways of regulating and managing academic work. The latter have come more forcefully into play as national higher education systems come under increasing pressure to adapt to global policy drivers and trends that seem to push ineluctably in the direction of massification, commodification and rationalisation. These studies also highlight the wider institutional and policy context within which operational innovations at the organisational level – such as the widespread implementation of much more explicit and detailed performance management and control systems across a swathe of public sector service organisations, including universities – have to be understood and explained.

The final disciplinary base that provides a significant source of intellectual inspiration for a number of our contributors is the sociology of the occupations/professions. Several of the chapters in this book (Reed, Fulton, Musselin and Mignot-Gérard, De Boer, Karseth, Meek, and Verhoeven and Devos) are centrally concerned with the longer-term impact of institutional and organisational restructuring on the content, process and practice of academic labour. They are also interested in the political and organisational tactics followed by the academic labourers in the face of the challenges presented by restructuring. Academics seem to have little or no choice but to try and cope with the inevitable discontinuities and dislocations that rapid and deep-seated institutional change necessarily produces. These radical or 'disjunctive' changes also inevitably raise difficult questions about the future prospects for the identity, status and moral authority of academic work/workers as a vocation or profession within a cultural and political context that seems increasingly suspicious of the 'donnish dominion'. These questions are likely to become especially acute when the occupational ideologies and discourses that are conventionally taken to embody and exemplify these core values seem to be under direct attack from an increasingly powerful and pervasive 'managerialism'. Universities may be regarded as the prototypical 'knowledge-intensive organisations' and university academics may likewise be treated as the prototypical 'knowledge workers'. As key institutionalised sites of and settings for core 'knowledge production, dissemination and evaluation' in modern societies, universities are supposed to be exemplars of the high-trust, collegiate, open and dialogical cultures typical of a post-industrial, knowledge-based economy and society (Fuller 2002). However, the evidence and analysis of trends and trajectories that emerge from the chapters in this book suggest something very different is happening. At the very least, they indicate that an ongoing cultural and political struggle for legitimacy and control within higher education is occurring that will have fateful consequences for the nature, organisation and regulation of academic work. Concepts, theories and findings extracted from the sociology of occupations/professions can help us to understand what this might mean for the future of the academic profession. In particular, this body of work and literature can provide a more systematic and rigorous explanation of the competing 'regulative logics' through which expert or specialist – including academic/intellectual – work can be ordered and controlled in much more fluid, not to say contradictory and

chaotic, institutional environments (Freidson 2001). They can also help us to begin
to answer the central question of how the identity, development and practice of
academic work should be redefined and legitimated today. This seems to be a
particularly pertinent question to pose in a political and cultural environment that
seems much less supportive of, if not downright hostile to, the 'academic state' and
its wider social legitimacy. Within this sort of institutional context, the politics and
sociology of expert work and organisation take on a particular analytical and
explanatory relevance for the present situation in which higher education finds itself.
This is true to the extent that they can help us to define and assess a number of
possible 'future scenarios' for academic knowledge workers as they struggle to
defend their 'jurisdictional domains and boundaries' from penetration and incursion
by competitor groups. Will we see academics slowly but surely transformed into a
group of relatively privileged, but deprofessionalised, technical workers (Freidson
2001) or will they be able to retain substantial elements of their professional
autonomy, status and power?

Having previously outlined the disciplinary foundations for much of the analysis
that is provided in this book, we can now move on to a more detailed consideration
of the specific theoretical and methodological positions that emerge from the core
intellectual commitments embodied within the former. We can identify a broad
cluster of theoretical positions developed within this book that have been drawn
primarily from organisation/management theory. Several of our contributors call on
relatively   new   and   innovative   theoretical   approaches   within
organisation/management studies to provide the conceptual tools and analytical
frameworks needed to map, describe, interpret and explain the new governance
structures and organisational forms taking shape in increasingly globalised higher
education systems. Thus, approaches such as neo-institutionalism, organisation
learning theory, strategic management theory, control theory and neo-Foucauldian
discourse analysis (Fulton, Musselin and Mignot-Gérard, Meek, Amaral and
Magalhães, Verhoeven and Devos, De Boer, Reed, and Karseth) are outlined and
deployed by our authors. Their overarching explanatory 'mission' is to provide
greater insight into the political and cultural power struggles that are reshaping the
governance structures and management systems through which contemporary
university education and research is being reformed and reordered. Many of our
authors identify an inexorable blurring of the previously separate and distinctive
decision-making domains or institutional arenas (e.g. the traditional separation
between 'academic' and 'financial' decision-making arenas) that once defined the
system of higher education and everyday university life. This 'de-differentiation' of
previously separate and autonomous institutional spheres within higher education
can be interpreted as a strategic and operational response to the continuous political
demand for more integrative, efficient and effective managerial control within a
sector well-known for its profligacy, indulgency and inertia. However, our authors
suggest that this response often generates and reproduces as many problems as it
solves. In particular, the loss of, or at least significant reduction in, high-trust
relations and the innate flexibility and adaptability that they once provided seems to
create a whole raft of new problems for university managers, administrators and
governors alike. Insofar as the process of institutional and organisational 'de-

differentiation' encourages the widespread adoption of more intrusive, intensive and invasive performance management and control systems, then the more likely that this will produce various forms of 'dysfunctional adaptive behaviour' on the part of students, staff, local communities and elites. In all of these respects, universities seem to be experiencing a loss, perhaps partial or perhaps not, of their cultural, ideological and political distinctiveness as exemplified in their rapidly changing codes of governance and management structures. They lose their innate cultural mystery and legitimacy to become just another cluster of organisational sites or locations for knowledge production and dissemination vying even more intensely with many others – such as corporate universities or privately-funded institutions (Levy 2001) – for economic viability and political validity. Universities may be coming to look and feel like just any other form of collectively organised activity in 'late modernity' (Delanty 2001). If they are, then they need to be subjected to very similar forms of institutional and organisational analysis in which generic research themes of power, conflict, authority, control and trust lie at the very centre of intellectual and practical concern (Calas and Smircich 2001).

Our authors who draw mainly on a policy science/decision-making tradition (Jones, Maassen, Meek, Amaral and Magalhães, Chevaillier) have selected a wide range of conceptual tools and theoretical frameworks to go about their descriptive and explanatory business. Thus, policy network theory, neo-rational market theory, bureaucratic theory, stakeholder theory, resource/path-dependency theory and state control theory figure prominently in their substantive research and analysis. Most of our authors focus on institutional-level policy networks and their impact on the interplay between the formal structures of university governance and the more informal management processes and practices that emerge over time within these governance structures. Stakeholder theory also figures quite prominently in the various national studies developed in this book, often alongside alternative theoretical perspectives, such as neo-rational market decision-making theory, that seem rather odd 'intellectual bedfellows' to say the least! However, our authors' intellectual ingenuity is considerable; they pull out the complementary aspects of these diverse theoretical approaches and recombine them in creative and innovative ways. Thus, micro-level focused models of rational/bureaucratic resource allocation decision-making within individual universities (Chevaillier) are combined with more macro-level focused stakeholder models of strategic policy 'steering' and implementation at the system-wide level (Maassen, Meek). Again, both of these theoretical approaches dovetail rather well with the extensive use made of neo-institutional theory and analysis by a number of our contributors (Maassen, Meek, Fulton, Amaral and Magalhães). The latter is repeatedly drawn on as a key theoretical resource by our authors as they attempt to understand and explain the tensions, if not contradictions, between environmental pressures to conform and the need to retain significant elements of national difference and diversity within an increasingly globalised higher education system. The implication of these institutional contradictions/tensions for the development of organisational strategy, design and management practice within individual universities also emerges as a central theme throughout the pages of this book.

The detailed content and impact of broader 'discourses' of institutional and managerial restructuring across a range of national higher education systems also establishes a pivotal explanatory problematic for our authors. In this context, various theoretical perspectives located within the sociology of work, occupations and professions are deployed to explore the condition of the 'post-Mertonian professions' in general and of the academic profession in particular (Musselin and Mignot-Gérard, Fulton, Reed). A neo-Weberian sociology of the 'professionalisation project' and of changing forms of professional work organisation and regulation figures quite prominently in relation to these issues. By focusing on the exclusionary strategies and tactics followed by various expert or specialist groups, as they struggle to retain monopoly control over their respective jurisdictional domains (Larson 1990; Freidson 2001), our authors strive to develop greater insight into the dynamics and trajectories of contemporary academic restructuring. These neo-Weberian analyses seem to suggest that the conventional model of professionalisation and of the professional, at least within academia, began to be called into question long before globalisation, rationalisation and managerialism began to dominate the higher education policy agenda. Indeed, a number of our authors (Musselin and Mignot-Gérard, Fulton) suggest that by the late 1960's/early 1970's the first significant signs of a decline in the 'donnish dominion' emerged as national governments and their various agencies moved to reduce the discipline-based power and control of the academic profession. This incipient weakening of academic power coincided with reductions in the institutional autonomy of individual universities – through enhanced central government monitoring and control – and a widening social critique of the reality and relevance of academic collegiality as a guiding principle of academic life. These developments opened the door to the 'new managerialist' ideology and practice that would come to dominate the higher education policy making and implementing agenda in the 1980's and 1990's. Thus, several of our authors suggest that the undermining and erosion of academic autonomy, status and power has its historical and political roots in structural changes that emerged at least two decades before the full ideological and practical force of 'new managerialism' began to be experienced on a system-wide basis.

The theoretical perspectives favoured by our authors also have important implications for their ontological, epistemological and methodological preferences as they emerge and take shape within their substantive analyses. On the whole, the majority of our contributors are quite catholic, not to say eclectic, in their methodological tastes and choices. However, there does seem to be a clear and sustained collective preference for research approaches and designs that combine historical, comparative, ethnographic and discursive methods focused on the internal dynamics of academic decision-taking and its complex interplay with wider institutional and societal structures. In this way, our authors contend we may be better placed to understand the shifting combinations – indeed increasingly 'hybridised' forms – of alliances, problems, solutions and discourses that characterise the present condition of and future prospects for higher education on a global scale. Individual universities and systems are struggling to align and adjust themselves to the 'new realities' that these global changes generate. Consequently, our investigative designs and approaches must attempt to access and account for these innovative processes of institutional re-alignment and organisational re-adjustment through a judicious mix of multi-level qualitative and quantitative methodologies that remain sensitive to historical and cultural diversity. Thus, all of our authors strive to analyse the emergence and evolution of strategic (governance) and operational (managerial) restructuring within universities across a wide range of national, cultural and political contexts by combining rich historical and institutional description with in-depth organisational analysis. In the course of their research they also focus on the inevitable gaps, breaks and contradictions within the rationalisation, commercialisation and managerialisation strategies that most systems and institutions seem to be following. The latter seems to exemplify general policy imperatives and political pressures driving in the direction of enhanced central co-ordination and control but through organisational mechanisms and managerial practices that putatively celebrate flexibility, decentralisation and enterprise. These developments and their longer-term implications, our authors argue, can only be understood through engagement with a range of complementary research methodologies such as questionnaire surveys, in-depth semi-structured interviews, focus group interviews, textual and discourse analysis, longitudinal case-studies and network analysis. We will only be able to map and interpret the increasingly complex decision-making and taking patterns evident in higher education systems and universities if we follow this path of methodological pluralism. The nature and functioning of the new institutional, organisational and managerial forms that are emerging as alternative ways of regulating academic work and the academic profession constitute the major explanatory problematic for our authors. They insist that the latter can only be properly confronted if we construct and sustain a research approach that remains sensitive to the complexities of sector-wide and institutional change. In turn, this change has to be contextually embedded within a larger cultural and political environment that is much less sympathetic to and supportive of higher education. This is a contemporary policy environment in which dominant elite networks no longer assume – as an axiomatic assumption or principle guiding policy formulation and implementation – that higher education is necessarily a 'public good' to be invested in and protected for the long-term benefit of society as whole. Indeed, higher education simply becomes yet another demand on the public purse that has to justify its claims in competition with those of many others.

This brings us to the key research themes and sensitising concepts that are pivotal to our contributors in their explanation of the changing relationship between 'governance' and 'management' across a wide range of higher education systems, sectors and institutions. For our authors, the key theme of restructuring governance arrangements, organisational forms and managerial practices in contemporary higher education has to be explained in terms of the complex and dynamic interaction between three 'logics of regulation' - market-based contracts, bureaucratically-based rules and professionally-based norms. To account for the dynamics of the changing relationship between these three regulatory modes and their impact on university structures, cultures and practices our authors suggest that concepts such as 'power', 'control' and 'trust' are of central explanatory importance. In particular, they suggest that the sustained movement towards a managerialist ideology and practice, as the dominant discursive and material reality in contemporary higher education systems and institutions, is generating a fragmenting and hybridising dynamic. They also contend that the latter is unlikely to be contained or stabilised within the current strategic policy orientation and the organisational modes and mechanisms through which it is to be implemented as a politically coherent and economically viable reform strategy.

Most, if not all, of our authors detect a substantial decline in the role of academics in university governance and management as a consequence of the 'rise of managerialism' and its impact on the structures, cultures and practices through which the work of the university is done. The incessant pressure to maximise and exploit 'academic surplus value', combined with the withdrawal of academics from sustained engagement with the day-to-day administrative life of the university, has produced a situation in which the organisational separation between 'professional academics' and 'professional academic managers/administrators' becomes more pronounced and fateful. Although our authors consistently emphasise the role of national history, culture and politics in shaping the meaning, and mediating the impact, of 'managerialism' in particular higher education systems, they all identify a common pattern and trajectory of change associated with it. Consequently, the ideology of 'new managerialism', and its more operational, even pragmatic (Ferlie et al., 1996), organisational offspring, 'new public management', are seen to entail a shared cultural re-orientation and structural redesign that inexorably drives in the direction of commodification, rationalisation and control. Thus, new managerialism/new public management comprise an innovative configuration of institutional, organisational and operational reforms that, collectively, push universities towards governance structures and practices characterised by a 'low trust/high control' syndrome. This shift towards 'regulated or earned autonomy', as the ideological and practical basis of governance and management within contemporary universities, is most clearly and dramatically exemplified in the simultaneously strategically centralised and operationally devolved performance audit and control systems that have come to dominate everyday academic life. While the actual operation of these new performance regimes is unavoidably mediated and modified by the intricate micro-politics of academic institutional and professional life, the former have dominated, and continue to dominate, the decision-making agenda to which others are forced to respond.

However, this, managerialist-inspired and driven, imposition of a new discourse as to what 'higher education' is and what it is for, and of the network of performance audits and controls through which this discourse is meant to be realised in practice, generate all sorts of unintended consequences. The latter eventually come to frame the current agenda for institutional change and organisational management within universities.

Once higher education is redefined as a marketable commodity to be bought and sold through market exchanges like any other commodity, then certain consequences tend to flow from this 'ontological metamorphosis'. It begins to lose its status, and mystique, as a 'public good' that must be collectively nurtured and protected because of its strategic contribution to the social good of the community at large. It is transformed into a 'private good', subject to the unforgiving logic and discipline of market exchange, and no longer requiring the cultural and institutional protections that it previously enjoyed (Trowler 2001; Fuller 2002). Yet, at the same time, the transformation of higher education from a 'public good' into a 'private good' also entails that it has to be strategically managed and regulated in various ways. If the economic, rather than the cultural, status and significance of higher education are to be accorded priority over all other considerations, then they become far too important to be left to the academics. The institutional patina of implicit understandings and relationships through which they traditionally 'administered', rather than 'managed', its content and delivery has to be removed and replaced with a putatively transparent regime of performance audit and control. All economic commodities, like higher education, require an extensive and detailed managerial control system through which their sale and purchase can be properly regulated to ensure conformity with nationally determined policy and legal requirements.

But the discursive processes and institutional practices through which higher education becomes reduced to commodity status and subject to a much tighter and intrusive regime of managerial surveillance and control generate a whole swathe of contradictions and tensions. The latter require further phases or cycles of organisational change and innovation, if they are to be 'fixed' in some way or another. Yet, in the very act of trying to fix the problems that the implementation of the new managerial control systems have created, universities and their constituent stakeholder groups find themselves in a highly uncertain and risky situation. On the one hand, they find themselves being forced to combine and contain opposing principles and practices within increasingly unstable governance and organisation structures. On the other hand, they also discover that whatever direction they may move in to satisfy, or at least to placate, pressing economic, political and cultural demands, incurs substantial risks and costs that are very difficult, if not impossible, to anticipate in advance. In short, like many other public sector service organisations across the globe, universities are acting, or being forced to act, like 'organisational hybrids' as they struggle to respond to powerful cross, indeed contradictory, pressures in their environments (Ferlie et al., 1996; Flynn 1999; Pollitt and Bouckaert 2000).

It might be quite reasonably argued that universities, along with many other complex organisations, have always been hybrids. That is, organisational forms embodying competing logics of action producing endemic tensions and contradictions which have to be somehow contained through unstable assemblages of principles and practices. In turn, the latter can be seen to create even more problems than they solve. Nevertheless, it can also be equally argued that this 'hybridising dynamic and trajectory' has become even more marked over the last 25/30 years as universities and the academic profession alike have been faced with potentially 'life-threatening' challenges to their institutional and occupational authority. Indeed, the contradictory pressures and demands that universities and academics are now forced to face may have become so extreme and threatening as to produce re-active strategies and tactics that make a difficult situation even worse. The move towards a 'low trust/high control' syndrome may lead to an intensification of power struggles and status conflicts between key stakeholder groups, at international, national and institutional levels, that further fragments and divides higher education with all sorts of unpredictable results?

While our authors are very careful in offering any kind of definitive prognostications concerning the longer-term development of and future prospects for higher education systems and their constituent institutions, they share a common perception of increased tension and complexity with increasingly disruptive and destabilising consequences. 'Soft managerialism' may be both cause and consequence of this strengthening hybridising dynamic and its fragmenting impact. If the former entails 'the expansion of liberal management based on decentralisation and 'marketisation' of organisation and autonomy hand in hand with the development of a highly centralised and authoritarian form of government' (Courpasson 2000: 154), then its long-term implications for university governance and management may be very significant indeed. But, as many of our authors also suggest, these longer-term institutional consequences may run along lines very different from, even at odds with, the intentions of those who instigated the 'managerialist revolution' within higher education in the first place.

Rather than achieve a more coherently integrated relationship between resource allocation, performance management and work organisation, under the aegis of a strategic focus shaped by evolving market demand and political needs, universities may be moving, or drifting, towards a developmental path characterised by indecision, de-alignment and isolationism. New managerialism, in practice as opposed to theory, may result in a 'reverse convergence' in national higher education systems that returns universities to a much more contextually-contingent and locally-dependent pattern of change within a global policy environment that formally pushes in the opposite direction of universal conformity and homogeneity. Initially defined and legitimated as the ideological and organisational progenitor of a more rational, yet flexible, conception of higher education and its delivery, new managerialism may usher in an epoch of institutional change in which fragmentation and diversification become the dominant developmental leitmotifs. Considered in these terms, the hybridising dynamic released, or at least reinforced, by new managerialism has the potential to falsify the very universalising, rationalising and standardising presuppositions on which it was originally based. But we should not, as our authors repeatedly warn us, underestimate the very significant changes that it will engender, whatever its eventual fate as a harbinger of paradigm transformation within higher education and beyond.

2. GOVERNANCE IN HIGHER EDUCATION

Before turning to an outline of the remaining chapters of the book, a few more words on higher education governance *per se* are worthwhile. This volume is about change in the governance and management of higher education. But in order to examine change, we first need to understand the existing (or pre-existing) state of affairs upon which change is being imposed. This complicates the analysis considerably, for over time and in different places, multiple models of higher education governance prevail.

What we mean by governance in higher education often depends on the level of analysis: e.g. national, local, institutional, sub-unit or discipline level. Clark (1983: 205–206) directs attention to three primary authority levels: the understructure (basic academic or disciplinary units), the middle or enterprise structure (individual organizations in their entirety), and the superstructure (the vast array of government and other system regulatory mechanisms that relate organizations to one another). The dynamics within each level and the interaction between levels, differ according to context. The context, according to Clark, depends on where higher education institutions are located within a triangular field of governance/coordination constituted by academic oligarchy, state authority and the market.

Explanations with respect to the ability of higher education institutions to exercise initiative in the context of system-wide authority structures have often been organised on a continuum. At one end of the continuum is the 'bottom-up' type of system where government policy follows rather than leads a change process initiated at the departmental, faculty or institutional level; at the other end of the continuum is the 'top-down' type of system where institutions merely respond to government inspired policy initiatives which are enforced by the power of the state. 'Bottom-up' systems are characterised by high institutional autonomy; 'top-down' systems are characterised by the opposite.

National systems differ substantially in the ways in which they have organised the governance of higher education. Harman (1992: 2) identifies three main types of national authority structures: the continental mode; the United Kingdom mode; and the United States mode. In the continental mode of governance, authority is shared by faculty guilds and state bureaucracy; while the United Kingdom mode shares authority between faculty guilds and institutional trustees and administrators. The United States mode, while similar to that in the United Kingdom, is characterised by weaker faculty governance and stronger trustees and administrators rule.

The literature on higher education also throws up a number of different conceptual models of governance: collegial (Millett 1962, 1978); bureaucratic (Stroup 1966); political (Baldridge 1971); organised anarchy (Cohen and March 1974) and professional (Mintzberg 1979). The more recent literature adds to this list the entrepreneurial university (Clark 1998), the service university (Tjeldvoll 1998); the enterprise university (Marginson and Considine 2000) and the corporate/managerial university (Deem 1998), to name but a few.

A central question in research on higher education governance is whether the university is an exceptional institution that has retained its core authority structures over the centuries, or is it to be understood the same as any other modern corporation. Some empirical research on the governance of higher education points to the resilience of higher education institutions and asks whether the changes we are now witnessing are a categorical break with the past or are they merely the codification of existing practices (De Boer, Goedegebuure and Meek 1998). Clark (1998) in his analysis of the entrepreneurial university, while recognising the importance of strengthening the central steering core, nonetheless returns to what he terms the "stimulated academic heartland" as the fundamental ingredient of success. Others, such as Askling and Henkel (2000: 113) see the move of the university to corporate enterprise undermining the claim of exceptionality, where the challenges facing them are "broadly similar to those of a range of public service agencies in the late twentieth century".

The various models and conceptualisations of higher education governance just outlined should be treated mainly as 'ideal types', which is the approach adopted by the contributors to this volume. For example, whether the corporate university is colonising all of the higher education terrain is treated as a heuristic question, the answer to which varies greatly from circumstance to circumstance and country to country. But what our authors would agree with is the following statement from Henkel and Vabø (2000: 165): higher education institutions, universities in particular, are increasingly becoming "sites of struggle for academics competing for authority and resources, and mediators of external mechanisms of control".

There has been no attempt to impose a single definition of higher education governance on our authors. Nonetheless, 'governance' does need to be distinguished from related terms, such as management, administration and leadership. Edwards (2000) offers a simple working definition of 'governance' as meaning "not so much what organisations do but how they do it; governance is about how an organisation steers itself and the processes and structures used to achieve its goal". According to Gallagher (2001: 1),

> *Governance* is the structure of relationships that brings about organisational coherence, authorised policies, plans and decisions, and accounts for their probity, responsiveness and cost-effectiveness. *Leadership* is seeing opportunities and setting strategic directions ... *Management* is achieving intended outcomes through the allocation of responsibilities and resources, and monitoring their efficiency and effectiveness. *Administration* is the implementation of authorised procedures and the application of systems to achieve agreed results.

Governance then seen as a relational concept can be considered to incorporate leadership, management and administration. Marginson and Considine (2000: 7) argue that university governance:

> is concerned with the determination of values inside universities, their systems of decision making and resource allocation, their mission and purposes, the patterns of authority and hierarchy, and the relationship of universities as institutions to the different academic worlds within and the worlds of government, business and community without.

While much of the current writing on higher education assumes a movement away from traditional models of governance (themselves varied and complex), as discussed above, our authors demonstrate that the direction of this movement is far from clear and varies considerably in both content and intensity from country to country and over time. And while change in governance appears ubiquitous, expectations that higher education will retain traditional functions, particularly with respect to knowledge generation and training the next generation of knowledge workers, remain. In the increasingly complex and turbulent environments in which higher education institutions must operate, a single definition of higher education governance cannot prevail. What is common to our contributors' conceptualisation of governance, however, is the notion of relationship or dynamic interaction of bodies and groups operating at different levels of a higher education system, be it the interaction between the academic guild and institutional management or institutional management and ministerial authority.

3. OUTLINE OF THE VOLUME

The fourteen chapters that follow employ the rich tapestry of theoretical concepts and issues discussed above in the analysis of higher education governance in nine countries. Most of the chapters focus on a single jurisdiction, and for four jurisdictions the book includes paired chapters that provide different analytical perspectives on national governance reforms. We will conclude this chapter by briefly outlining the remainder of the volume.

Alberto Amaral and António Magalhães critically analyse both the theoretical assumptions associated with, and the reality of, the emergence of external stakeholders in European higher education governance. They define two forms of stakeholder and analyse recent experiences in the introduction of these external members in university governance in a number of European countries, with a particular emphasis on recent governance reforms in Portugal.

Two chapters focus on the major reforms to university governance in The Netherlands. Peter Maassen provides an insightful analysis of these reforms by focusing on the strategic organisational response of Dutch universities to the external pressures associated with the new legislation. He reviews two institutional case studies in order to explore how universities responded to the introduction of a new governance model. Harry de Boer focuses on the implications of these changes in terms of the internal organisational life of the university, with a particular emphasis on the notion of trust in the context of the new 'managed university'. Drawing on an analysis of submissions to a national evaluation of the new governance structure, he illuminates some of the serious problems associated with these reforms in terms of the complex relationships inside these institutions.

The Dutch movement towards the 'managed university' stands in sharp contrast to the more modest organisational changes associated with recent reforms in France, though in both cases these changes represent attempts to strengthen institution-level authority. Christine Musselin and Stéphanie Mignot-Gérard describe the evolution of French universities towards an increased capacity for institution-level decision-making through changes in the role and work of the rectors, senior administrators, and participatory councils. Drawing on a wealth of empirical data, including detailed institutional case studies and a national survey of university representatives, they describe how the balance of authority in the French university sector, which was formally dominated by high levels of state regulation and powerful faculties within these institutions, has evolved in favour of stronger university-level authority, though they also note that there continue to be obstacles on the pathway towards even greater institutional autonomy. One of the instruments for change in the French system was the development of multi-year contracts between the state and individual universities, and Thierry Chevaillier analyses the relationship between this new approach to financing French universities and university governance. Drawing on resource dependency theory and a number of other useful concepts, he discusses the very complex relationship between resource allocation and organisational structure.

The two chapters that focus on recent governance reforms in Norway analyse these changes from two very different, but complementary, perspectives. Both papers illuminate aspects of the change in governance arrangements associated with the recently restructured college sector. Ingvild Marheim Larsen focuses on the role and work of college governing boards. Her theoretical framework for analysing data obtained from a major study of college board members employs three perspectives on university governance: the instrumental perspective, the neo-institutional perspective, and the political perspective. Her analysis focuses on the roles of these new governing boards and the way these roles are perceived by board members. While Marheim Larsen focuses on institutional-level decision making, Berit Karseth reminds us that system restructuring and governance reforms can have significant, and often unanticipated, implications when analysed at the level of the local unit or program. Using important concepts drawn from the sociology of knowledge, she provides an insightful critical analysis of changes in power and influence over the curriculum in nursing education in response to system-level reforms. Her analysis of interview data reveals that these changes have important role, status, and power implications for faculty, nursing education programs, and the broader profession.

Jeff Verhoeven and Geert Devos are also interested in governance reforms associated with system-level college restructuring, but in this case the focus in on changes in Flanders, Belgium. Their study analyses data from case studies and a survey of college decision-makers at different organisational levels in order to explore the complex relationships between decentralisation and functional integration in the recently merged colleges within this system.

The next five papers focus on jurisdictions that are historically related to Anglo-Saxon traditions in higher education, with the first two focusing on the United Kingdom. Michael Reed analyses the impact of the ideas and practices associated with 'new managerialism' on higher education. Following a theoretical discussion of this construct, he reviews the impact of new managerialism on the power and autonomy of the academic profession based on the findings of a recent empirical study. Oliver Fulton analyses university governance in the United Kingdom by looking at the implications of system-level reforms for institutional governance and by focusing on important changes in the role and authority of the councils and senates associated with bicameral governance.

Glen A. Jones focuses on university governance in Canada by reviewing the findings of a series of complementary studies of university governing board members, senate members, faculty associations, student associations, and university presidents. He uses a policy network approach to describe the complex interrelationships between the individuals, unions, associations, and formal governance structures that are associated with institutional decision-making processes.

V. Lynn Meek demonstrates that many of the changes associated with higher education management and governance in Australia can be traced to broader public sector reforms and the introduction of new public management. These reforms have had a dramatic impact on higher education, and Meek's insightful policy analysis illuminates the far-reaching implications of these changes.

An analysis of university governance in the United States is presented by Elaine El-Khawas. She assesses recent changes in governance and decision-making in American higher education and focuses on the question of whether the current arrangements allow institutions to adapt to changing circumstances.

The concluding essay, written by Glen Jones, Alberto Amaral, and Berit Karseth takes a step back from the jurisdiction-specific studies to offer a comparative analysis of the major trends associated with university governance. They discuss a number of common themes that emerge from these studies, as well as identifying and contextualising some important differences. They conclude by raising some very important questions and issues for further research.

REFERENCES

Askling, B. and M. Henkel. "Higher Education Institutions." In Kogan, M., M. Bauer, I. Bleiklie and M. Henkel (eds). *Transforming Higher Education: a comparative study*. London: Jessica Kingsley, 2000, 109 – 130.

Baldridge, J. V. *Power and Conflict in the University*. New York: John Wiley and Sons, 1971.

Calas, M. and L. Smircich (eds). "Special Issue on Re-Organising Knowledge, Transforming Institutions: Knowing, Knowledge, and the University in the 21st Century." *Organization* 8.2 (2001): 147 – 454.

Clark, B. R. *The Higher Education System*. Berkeley: University of California Press, 1983.

Clark, B. R. *Creating Entrepreneurial Universities: Organisational Pathways of Transformation*. Oxford: Pergamon, 1998.

Cohen, M.D. and J.G. March. *Leadership and Ambiguity*. New York: McGraw-Hill, 1974.

Courpasson, D. "Managerial Strategies of Domination: Power in Soft Bureaucracies." *Organization Studies* 21.1 (2000): 141 – 62.

De Boer, H., L. Goedegebuure and L. Meek (eds). *New Perspectives on Governance*. Special Issue of *Higher Education Policy* 11.2/3 (1998): 103 – 235.

Deem, R. "'New Managerialism' and Higher Education: The Management of Performances and Cultures in Universities in the United Kingdom." *International Studies in Sociology of Education* 8.1 (1998): 47 – 70.

Delanty, G. "The University in the Knowledge Society." In Calas, M. and L. Smircich (eds). Special Issue on Re-Organising Knowledge, Transforming Institutions: Knowing, Knowledge, and the University in the 21st Century. *Organization* 8.2 (2001): 149 – 153.

Edwards, M. "University Governance: A Mapping and Some Issues." Paper presented at the LifeLong Learning Network National Conference, Canberra, University of Canberra, December, 2001. http://governance.canberra.edu.au

Ferlie, E., L. Ashburner, L. Fitzgerald and A. Pettigrew (eds). *The New Public Management in Action*. London: Sage, 1996.

Flynn, R. "Managerialism, Professionalism and Quasi-Markets." In Exworthy, M. and Halford, S. (eds), *Professionals in the New Managerialism*. Buckingham: Open University Press, 1999, 18 – 36.

Freidson, E. *Professionalism: The Third Logic*. Oxford: Polity, 2001.

Fuller, S. *Knowledge Management Foundations*. Woburn, MA: Butterworth Heinemann, 2002.

Gallagher, M. "Modern university governance - a national perspective." Paper presented at The Idea of a University: Enterprise or Academy?, The Australia Institute and Manning Clark House, Canberra, 26 July, 2001.

Harman, G. "Governance, Administration and Finance." In *The Encyclopedia of Higher Education*. Oxford: Pergamon (CD-ROM version), 1992, 1 – 16.

Henkel, M. and A. Vabø. "Academic Identities." in Kogan, M., M. Bauer, I. Bleiklie and M. Henkel (eds). *Transforming Higher Education: a comparative study*. London: Jessica Kingsley, 2000, 159 – 198.

Larson, M. S. "In the Matter of Experts and Professionals." In Burrage, M. and R. Torstendahl (eds). *The Formation of Professions*. London: Sage, 1990, 24 – 50.

Levy, D. C. "When Private Higher Education does not bring Organizational Diversity." In Altbach, P.G. (ed). *Private Prometheus. Private Higher Education and Development in the 21st Century*. Westport, Connecticut: Greenwood Press, 2001, 15 – 43.

Marginson, S. and M. Considine. *The Enterprise University*. Melbourne: Cambridge University Press, 2000.

Millett, J. D. *The Academic Community: An Essay on Organisation*. New York: McGraw-Hill, 1962.

Millett, J.D. *New Structures of Campus Power: Success and Failure of Emerging Forms of Institutional Governance*. San Francisco: Jossey-Bass, 1978.

Mintzberg, H. *The Structuring of Organisations*. Englewood Cliffs, N.J.: Prentice Hall, 1979.

Pollitt, C. and G. Bouckaert. *Public Management Reform: A Comparative Analysis*. Oxford: Oxford University Press, 2000.

Stroup, H. *Bureaucracy in Higher Education*. New York: The Free Press, 1966.

Tjeldvoll, A. "The Idea of the Service University." *International Higher Education* 13 (Fall, 1998): 9 – 12.

Trowler, P. "Captured by the Discourse?: The Socially Constitutive Power of New Higher Education Discourse in the UK", In Calas, M. and L. Smircich (eds). Special Issue on Re-Organising Knowledge, Transforming Institutions: Knowing, Knowledge, and the University in the 21st Century. *Organization* 8.2 (2001): 183 – 201.

ALBERTO AMARAL AND ANTÓNIO MAGALHÃES

THE EMERGENT ROLE OF EXTERNAL STAKEHOLDERS IN EUROPEAN HIGHER EDUCATION GOVERNANCE

1. INTRODUCTION

Over the last few decades, higher education institutions have been confronted with increasing outside pressures aimed at institutional change. The conceptual frameworks that are used to envision, and to a certain extent legitimise, change are increasingly influenced by organisational sciences and theories. In this type of approach, concepts such as 'adaptiveness', 'environmental awareness', 'responsiveness', etc., become central, both as analytical devices and as values to be pursued.

The combined use of these concepts both as analytical devices and as guiding or legitimating values presents some danger to the institutions and needs to be critically debated. Interpretations and decisions inspired by concepts that are legitimated as guiding principles simply because of their analytical use by organisational theorists are often problematic and should be critically analysed. For instance, the concept of adaptation, inspired by organisational theory, cannot simply be applied to the field of higher education without addressing important questions concerning institutional identity. The assumption that responsiveness to environmental changes and needs should be the key criteria for decision-making and institutional performance has important consequences for higher education that need to be considered.

The same comments are true in terms of the increasing importance given to the concept of 'relevance' in higher education. Representatives of the business sector and government argue that institutions of higher education make an important contribution to national wealth production and to the performance of the nation in the global economy. This discourse of economic legitimisation also seems to be anchored on adaptive values and dynamics. Again, care must be taken in critically analysing the assumptions that underscore this perspective, for higher education cannot be reduced to its functional role with regard to the economy.

This critical exercise is made more urgent because of the emergence of the 'market' as a new ideological competitor whose presence erodes the space for the traditional liberal-humanist discourse that provided the foundation for the development of the modern university.

The objective of this article is to contribute to this discussion by focusing on the concept of 'stakeholder'. The concept of 'stakeholder' was popularised by management theory, mainly following the publication of Freeman's book *Strategic*

1

Alberto Amaral, Glen A. Jones and Berit Karseth (eds.), Governing Higher Education:
National Perspectives on Institutional Governance, 1—21.
© 2002 *Kluwer Academic Publishers. Printed in the Netherlands.*

Management: a Stakeholder Approach. In this book, he defined a stakeholder as "any group or individual who can affect or is affected by the achievement of the organisations objectives" (Freeman 1984: 46). We use a similar, broad definition, in the sense of a person or entity with a legitimate interest in higher education and which, as such, acquires the right to intervene. Examples of stakeholders in higher education are academics, students, parents, employers, the state, the higher education institutions themselves (in their relationship with the system), etc.

We define two categories of stakeholders, internal and external, the former being members of the academic community and the latter coming from outside the university. The concept of (external) stakeholder refers to the presence of representatives of the interests of the 'outside world' in university governance. Their presence is justified by assuming that it is both legitimate (in that those who they represent have a 'legitimate' interest in the social, economic and cultural function of the institution) and useful (in that they enhance the institutions' innovation and responsiveness to the 'real' needs of society).

External stakeholders are assuming a growing prominence relative to internal stakeholders in the rhetoric of change, and their presence is designed to make higher education institutions more responsive to environmental needs and changes. In this chapter we will analyse the case of Portugal and several examples from other European higher education systems in order make some observations on the effectiveness of this new role for external stakeholders in university governance.

Finally, it is important to stress that while we refer to history, our approach is not 'historical' but rather paradigmatic. What we intend to analyse by studying the emergence of the concept of 'stakeholder' in the higher education literature is not the particular links that universities and other higher education institutions have built and developed with industry, commerce and the 'outside' world in general. Our focus, instead, is on the legitimating discourses, and our aim is to identify changes in the way higher education itself is being conceptualised. In this we closely follow Björn Wittrock (1993: 323) who argues that an analytical approach cannot be replaced by "a broad functional-evolutionary account, nor a minute historical account of the peculiarities of individual institutions in different countries and contexts."

2. THE MODERN UNIVERSITY AND THE CONSOLIDATION OF THE NATION STATE

The development of the modern university can be placed at the end of the XVIIIth and the beginning of the XIXth centuries, and it is closely associated with the reforms of von Humboldt in Prussia and of Napoleon in France. The modern university was a fundamental instrument for the construction and reinforcement of the nation-state, being assumed as "an agent of national reconstruction, allied with the overhaul of recruitment to the apparatus of state" (Neave and Van Vught 1994: 268). Besides providing the state bureaucracy with qualified manpower, higher education institutions were supposed to socialise students to become model and active citizens, to promote the social mobility of the most talented, and to be a place of free and independent discussion of the society's critical problems.

On the other hand, universities were also assumed to play a crucial role in the project of forging the national political identity through the preservation and enhancement of the national culture. These multiple goals were seen as coherent and part of the same project of consolidation of the nation-state. This had important consequences both for the state and for universities. Neave considers that:

> The Nation-State had profound consequences for the patterns of control and administration in the university world. In the first place, by setting the university at the apex of those institutions defining national identity, it also placed higher learning firmly within the public domain as a national responsibility. University was thus subjected to the oversight of public administration rather than being the object of regalian privilege. (...) And, no less important, the forging of the nation-state went hand in hand with the incorporation of academia into the ranks of state service, thereby placing upon it the implicit obligation of service to the national community (Neave 2001: 26).

On the one hand, the state's administrative posture was heavily centralising. The state claimed what it viewed as a legitimate role in deciding what was to be considered 'useful knowledge' by centrally defining the curricula of study programmes. For example, the reform of Austrian education by Maria Theresa and her son Josef II (Grueber 1982: 260) clearly placed the higher education system under the firm control of the state in order to ensure that civic virtues and a true national spirit were taken seriously as educational objectives.

The political demand for a uniform system was translated into the adoption of the legal homogeneity principle, enforcing the provision of common higher education programmes throughout the nation. Study programmes and credentials provided by national higher education institutions should be homogeneous in order to ensure that all citizens had equal opportunities when competing for public employment, and, of course, the state was the main employer of higher education's graduates. The state acted as the sole regulator of the higher education system by using traditional mechanisms of public regulation, including legislation, funding, and even, in many cases, the appointment of professors.

On the other hand, universities were not just seen as producers of highly qualified personnel, despite their role as providers of qualified manpower for the state bureaucracy. Some, like Cardinal Newman (1996), fiercely opposed a utilitarian concept of higher education. He argued that "the Philosophy of Utility, you will say, gentlemen has at least done its work...and I grant it – it aimed low and it fulfilled its aim". Instead, he proposed "a pure and clear atmosphere of thought..." which leads to "the true and adequate end of intellectual training... Thought or reason exercised upon knowledge."

The university also had a role in the development of citizenship, in the transmission of values, and in the defence and promotion of the national culture. These roles for the university predated the emergence of the modern university. For example, Harvard College, in its present (23 February 1997) mission statement, reaffirmed the objectives for which the Royal Charter of 1650 was granted (http://www.harvard.edu/help/noframes/faq110_nf.html):

The advancement of all good literature, arts, and sciences; the advancement and
education of youth in all manner of good literature, arts, and sciences; and all other
necessary provisions that may conduce to the education of the youth of this country.

To assist the university in pursuing this mission, the state assumed the
responsibility of protecting academic freedom against outside undesirable
influences. The state acted as a shield against the sometimes-conflicting interests
arising from the professions, the politicians, or religion. According to Neave and
Van Vught (1994: 271), one fundamental characteristic of the state control model
was the state's protection of the individual's academic freedom to teach and to learn
without interference from external interests. Wittrock (1993: 318) refers to this role
in terms of safeguarding the intellectual freedom of teaching and learning from
political incursions and violations. The need for academic freedom has been
articulated throughout the history of higher education. In the late 1940s the Swedish
Myrdal (as cited by Wittrock 1993: 332) made a strong appeal for the protection of
academic freedom to do research with the only objective of searching for truth
without interference from immediate utilitarian interests. And more recently, Frank
Newman (2000) argued that this role of the state in protecting academic freedom is
justified because the university must remain a place of free and open debate about
critical issues, a place where faculty can conduct research on contentious issues to
shed light on momentous societal problems.

This was, in essence, the idea of the modern university, based upon a concept of
individual academic freedom but not on institutional autonomy. Humboldt's idea of
the university was built on a basic assumption concerning the central importance of
knowledge and its institutionalisation, freed from Church or State tutelage, and from
the pressures of social and economic demands. It was in the interests of the state to
protect the university's *Lernfreiheit* and *Lehrfreiheit*, for institutionalised knowledge
granted the unifying force that the state needed to legitimate itself both as the top
national institution and, to use Humboldt's words, as the "State of culture".

While the Humboldtian model considered universities as state partners, acting as
the highest expression of the state itself and of national culture, the Napoleonic
model was more restrictive in terms of academic autonomy, largely because this
model involved more generalised state control. The Humboldtian model and the
Jacobin model, however, are not contradictory. They share the same objective and
both guard against the influence of outside interests in the universities, the
contradiction being only apparent. In both models, the task of the state in its
relationship with the university was not only a matter of protecting academic
freedom,   "it was also a question of protecting the modernising sector of society
against the pressures, claims and special pleading of vested interests and inherited
privilege" (Neave and Van Vught 1994: 271).

The Humboldtian idea of the university, first employed at the University of
Berlin, was to become the undisputed international model for university reform
(Wittrock 1993: 321), and it was extremely influential not only in continental
Europe but also in the United States. This model is still viewed by academics as an
ideal form of the research university. *A propos,* it is interesting to note that a recent
recommendation of the Council of Ministers of the Council of Europe (2000) clearly
advocates a Humboldtian type model for higher education. Teaching and research

should be equally integrated into the universities' organisation and structure, the academic freedom of individual researchers should be protected, and universities should have the freedom to decide their own research priorities.

3. THE SHIFT TO STATE SUPERVISION, MARKET VALUES, AND THE RISE OF MANAGERIALISM

Over the last few decades the relationships between higher education institutions and the state and society have been changing. This transition has been described as a shift from the model of state control to the model of state supervision (Neave and Van Vught 1991). The factors influencing this shift are diverse and complex. Among these factors, the most relevant to this discussion are the following:

a) The replacement of the state by the private sector as the main employer of higher education's graduates, thus offsetting the importance of the legal homogeneity principle.
b) The massification of higher education systems and the increasing difficulty of exclusively financing the institutions with public funds.
c) The political assumption of diversity as an important feature of higher education systems, a feature that until recently was virtually excluded because of the legal homogeneity principle.
d) The political awareness of the increasing difficulty of centrally managing the definition of 'useful knowledge' resulting from such factors as the massification and related growth in complexity of higher education systems. Given the fast pace of knowledge obsolescence, the centralised bureaucracy was unable to cope efficiently and in a timely manner with the almost constant redefinition of 'useful knowledge'.
e) The loss of legitimacy of the welfare state and the emergence of neo-liberal theories associated with the idea that the 'inevitable' lack of efficiency and responsiveness of the public sector could only be solved by market regulation.

Over the last few decades, the idea that the state is overloaded by increasing social demands has become popular in political circles. Neo-liberal and monetarist policy reforms were based on the assumption that government intervention and regulation were excessive, and that this phenomenon was the mother of all the sins of the welfare state (inefficiency, wastage of money, unfair distribution of resources, etc.). The 'market' became the solution to all of these problems (Amaral and Magalhães 2001).

The market emerged as a fundamental character in the political discourse on higher education, not only of politicians but also of some academics, namely those associated with management schools. The market could heal all the wounds inflicted by the inefficiency and ineffectiveness of state regulation, and by the low managerial aptitude of rectors and public servants. Institutions should become more flexible and more autonomous so that they can to adapt to the constant changes taking place in their organisational environment.

In response to these factors and arguments, government strategies changed and progressively embraced the principles of autonomy and self-regulation. Typical examples of this new governmental attitude include the HOAK (Higher education: autonomy and quality) policy document of the Dutch government, the Plan Saint-Ann in Belgium, the 1983 Law of University Reform in Spain and the 1988 University Autonomy Act of Portugal. Other countries, such as Denmark, Sweden and Finland, followed similar trends, and even in France, where centralised state bureaucracy was deeply entrenched, universities benefited from a softening of state regulation. More recently, Italy introduced higher education reforms that allow for increased institutional autonomy. In Norway, the Mjøs report (2000) also favours increased institutional autonomy. All over Europe, governments began to assume that it was not in the best interests of society to maintain centralized, detailed control over mass higher education systems, and they transferred the responsibility for day-to-day management and the detailed implementation of higher education policies to the institutions (Amaral 1994).

Neo-liberal discourse also played a role in the introduction of quasi-market concepts and privatisation as mechanisms to create more efficient and responsive services; the users of public services were seen as clients. These changes had a profound impact on universities. Education is no longer seen as a social right; it has become a service. Universities are increasingly viewed as service providers, and students are seen as clients.

The state, however, did not pursue this strategy to its ultimate end by refraining from regulating the higher education system in favour of full market regulation. On the contrary, despite allowing for some degree of institutional autonomy, the state kept a firm hand on the regulation of the system while making rhetorical use of the market, thus creating what is seen as a hybrid model of regulation (Maassen and Van Vught 1988; Amaral and Magalhães 2001). Another component of this new government strategy was the partial replacement of traditional public regulation mechanisms with market-type mechanisms as the 'best way' to taylorise (meaning to make effective and efficient) higher education institutions; the entrepreneurial university became the organisational model of choice. These mechanisms were designed to induce competition among higher education institutions (for students, for funding, for research projects, etc.) for the purpose of forcing institutions to become more efficient and more responsive to outside demands.

In Western Europe, where the state is the main resource provider – and institutional autonomy depends upon funding – the 'market' can be more accurately characterized as a rhetorical construction and an ideological concept:

> Markets are still a relatively minor factor in Europe, which on the whole does not provide a market for higher education, and whose governments rather dislike the idea of a market for higher education and its potential effects on quality and status (Trow 1996: 310).

And, despite Margaret Thatcher's introduction of the full paraphernalia of market rhetoric – value for money, efficiency gains, students as customers – Trow

(1996) concludes that no real market for higher education has been allowed to emerge. Instead, he suggests that "universities currently operate not in a market but in something like a command economy" (1996: 310). And Neave (1995: 57) argues that pragmatic considerations, rather than ideology, have forced the market to the centre of political regulation. He recognises that "action came first, the ideological justification and the elaboration of ideology came after" but in spite of this *a posteriori* feature, he underlines the legitimisation or mediation role of the 'market' (Neave 1995: 57) as the driving force for higher education.

The overall impact of the government's utilisation of market-type mechanisms as instruments of public policy is not yet fully appreciated. Van Vught (1997: 222–223), referring to the introduction of this approach by the Dutch government, offers a positive perspective by suggesting that this strategy represents a means of addressing both market and non-market failures. In contrast, David Dill (1997: 178) is more cautious and argues that the superiority of market-type regulatory mechanisms over traditional public policy mechanisms has not yet been demonstrated.

Some researchers[1] analysed the extensive use of quasi-markets by the Margaret Thatcher government and concluded that the results fell short of expectations. Lindsay and Rodgers (1998) question the use of quasi-markets as a means for introducing a market-strategic orientation in higher education since the 'customer' (the student) is not the same individual who pays for the product (the taxpayer). It is the taxpayer who has delegated the task of determining what is to be consumed, and at what price, to government. The student has no control over the money the university receives for the student's education, and he or she has only imperfect information as to the quality of each university. Consequently, students tend to make choices in terms of an institution's reputation, which is determined mainly by research reputation rather than the quality of teaching. As a result, resources have been shifted away from teaching and towards administration, while the increase in the amount of time dedicated to research has more to do with academic ambition than with customer satisfaction (Lindsay and Rogers 1998).

The movement towards a market orientation, and the financial uncertainty created by this movement, has led to the development of a more bureaucratic organisation[2] that is oriented towards attracting resources, and to appointed Presidents, selected because of their management abilities, replacing elected academics at the rudder of the university vessel. The movement has gained momentum as more and more "the Ship of Learning has to plot its course within financial straits, in both senses – nautical and financial – of that word" (Neave 1995a: 9). This process has led the emergence of a new university stereotype or model: the entrepreneurial university.

In this new environment, traditional university governance became the target of fierce criticism, being diversely, or simultaneously, branded as inefficient, corporative, non-responsive to society's needs and unable to address the declining quality standards of teaching and research. The invasion of university governance by new managerial concepts and attitudes is taking place in many countries and is associated with the neo-liberal credo. Philip Altbach states that:

> Worldwide, the traditional control of the central elements of the university by the
> faculty is being diminished. In the name of efficiency and accountability, business
> practices imported from the corporate sector are coming to dominate the universities.
> Governance, the traditional term used to describe the unique participatory way that
> universities work, is being replaced by management (Altbach 2000: 9).

It is interesting to observe two convergent effects. Universities were given more
autonomy, which can be seen as a repatriation of authority to a sphere closer to the
academics, while financial uncertainty created a more bureaucratic organisation. It is
no wonder that many academics claim today that they are confronted with increasing
attacks on their freedom and with closer control of their work by their own
institution. This clearly demonstrates that institutional autonomy is different from –
and perhaps even functions in opposition to – individual academic freedom, and
provides support for Humboldt's decision to protect individual academics from
narrow guild-like interests within academia by having the state retain the
responsibility for appointing university professors (Wittrock 1993: 318).

> Another obvious manifestation of this trend has been the rapid growth in peer review
> and other quality assessment activities. Ulrich Teichler considers that "the academic
> freedom concept of Humboldt is completely incompatible with peer control of any
> evaluation/accreditation kind (according to Humboldt, the quality control rested with
> the government appointment and resource provisions, and the individual scholar had
> academic freedom which no peer was allowed to interfere).[3]

4. RELEVANCE AND THE EMERGENCE OF THE EXTERNAL STAKEHOLDER

Until a few decades ago, the university was seen as an institution whose essence was
to rise above immediacy. Or, in Neave's words, "the university was, to revert to the
earlier religious analogy – a concept once used by the sociologists of the XVIth
century religious movements to describe the self-perception of certain Protestant
sects – in the world, but not of it" (Neave 1995: 10). He argues that "the prime
feature of the university was not its relevance to society, so much as its detachment
from society. Through its detachment came its ability naturally to entertain a view
on society and its own part in it, *sub specie aeternitatis* – that is, from a long-term
perspective" (ibid: 10). This allowed the university to hold a mirror to society so that
it could see itself in a long-term perspective.

This conception of the university is under stress. There is now considerable
pressure on the university to become 'relevant' in response to state financial
stringency and the related demands that these institutions address the economic
needs of their environment. In the society of the future, where knowledge will have
increased importance and where globalisation cannot be avoided, the university will
face another challenge in the contradiction between external pressures to be relevant
and its tradition of long-term vision.

There has been a shift with respect to the socio-economic functions of the
university. During the period of the "secondary" welfare state, when political, social
and educational institutions were mobilized to promote democracy and encourage
social mobility (Peter Scott 1995: 15), universities were asked primarily to satisfy
rising social expectations and only secondarily to meet the increasing demand for

skilled labour (ibid: 123). During the last two decades this balance has clearly shifted in favour of the economic function of the university, and this new perspective has had a strong influence on the governance models of higher education institutions.

The state wants to ensure that universities become relevant and that they increase their responsiveness to the 'external world', but these notions are only discussed in economic terms and they essentially focus on the economic function of the university. Instead of protecting institutions from external intervention and influence, the state has taken steps (including, where necessary, new laws) to guarantee that 'third parties' intervene. The new 'Babel tower' model, in which national interest is supposed to be protected and enhanced by representatives of the outside world acting within the academic institutions themselves, now challenges the 'Ivory tower' model. The state, in this new model, assumes that the best protection to give to institutions is to provide no protection at all, and it therefore frequently modifies university governing structures so that they become more open to external influence. Examples of this new trend are not difficult to find. They include, for instance, the 'Raad van Toezicht' of the Dutch universities, the 'Board of Social Institutions' of the Italian universities, and the 'Social Council' of the Spanish universities.

The consequences of this shift are far from clear. However, there are already signs of change related to knowledge production, diffusion and preservation associated with the much greater emphasis being placed on Mode 2 knowledge production (emphasizing problem-focused, applied, interdisciplinary research) over Mode 1 (investigator-initiated, discipline-based research) (Gibbons 1997). Other trends include the separation of the research and the teaching functions, and the entrepreneurial selling of services to the community.

It is in this context that the concept of 'stakeholder' needs to be analysed. The term stakeholder traditionally implies a third party; this is the individual who holds the 'stake' or bet for those wagering on an event, such as a horse race. Since the betting process, by its very nature, involves risk because money is being wagered on an uncertain event, the stakeholder should be a trustworthy party, someone of unimpeachable probity, someone who is impartial because he does not bet.

The concept of stakeholder was introduced in the management research literature as a heuristic device designed to help a firm understand its environment and embrace a level of social responsibility that goes beyond the mere maximisation of profits. The concept represents a means of including the interests and claims of non-stockholding parties in corporate decision making, and recognizing "that corporations have an obligation to constituent groups in society other than stockholders and beyond that prescribed by law or union contract, indicating that a stake may go beyond mere ownership" (Jones 1980: 59-60).

Freeman, in his classic book *Strategic Management: A Stakeholder Approach,* presents a very broad definition of stakeholder: "A stakeholder in an organisation is (by definition) any group or individual who can affect or is affected by the achievement of the organisation's objectives" (Freeman 1984: 46).

Mitchell, Agle and Wood (1997), in their work towards a theory of stakeholder identification and salience, suggest that this very broad definition does not help managers identify to whom and to what they should pay attention. To provide a basis for giving priority to competing stakeholder claims, these authors introduced the idea of stakeholder salience based upon a set of three attributes: legitimacy, power and urgency. The concept of salience may be quite useful in terms of explaining the conditions under which managers do consider or should consider certain classes of entities as stakeholders. However, we believe that it is important to recognize that in order to make the concept of stakeholder salience useful, the authors essentially created a much narrower definition of stakeholder where the legitimacy of the stakeholder is linked to power.

Most of the literature on stakeholder theory employs a narrow definition of legitimacy based on some notion of risk, property rights or moral claims. The basis for stakeholder legitimacy includes contractual relationships, legal or moral claims, ownership or legal title to the company's assets or property, and some form of risk resulting from capital, human or financial investments, etc. We would like to see a broader definition of stakeholder legitimacy based on desirable social outcomes.

It is the emphasis on legitimacy issues, rather than on risk, that allowed the concept to travel from the corporate world to public institutions. In the corporate world, the legitimate 'interests' of groups, individuals or organisations could be narrowly defined. The use of risk to denote 'stake' appears to be a way to further narrow the stakeholder field to those with direct interests, regardless of their power to influence the firm or the legitimacy of their relationship with the institution.

What confers legitimacy to a claim? Does the Green Peace movement have legitimacy when acting against activities that may endanger the environment? Do taxpayers have legitimacy when they question the quality of health services or public educational services? Does the press have legitimacy when it brings public attention to the activities of some multinationals that fire employees to increase the level of profit? Does a local population have legitimacy when it contests the location of a new chemical plant?

These kinds of questions become extremely important in the case of higher education, because higher education is a public good. Despite several studies that challenged the existence of strong social returns from higher education, especially when compared with those associated with lower levels of education, or with the private returns resulting from higher education degrees (see among others Psacharopoulos 1994), higher education is still considered a public good. Joseph Stiglitz[4], former senior vice-president of the World Bank, provided unexpected but important support for this conclusion by arguing that knowledge is, in central ways, a public good and that there are important externalities. More recently, the European Ministers of Education, assembled in Prague for debates on the implementation of the Bologna Declaration, publicly supported the idea that higher education should be considered a public good, and that it is, and will remain, a public responsibility.

For these reasons we employ Freeman's broad definition of stakeholder, as well as Suchman's definition of legitimacy as "a generalised perception or assumption that the actions of an entity are desirable, proper or appropriate within some socially constructed system of norms, values, beliefs, and definitions" (Suchman 1995: 574).

One can define two categories of stakeholders of institutions of higher education: internal stakeholders and external stakeholders. Internal stakeholders are all those who participate in the daily life of the institutions, and this includes the academic staff, the non-academic staff and the students. Until the last few decades, internal stakeholders played an important role in university governance, though the importance assigned to students as internal stakeholders has varied over the centuries. For instance, the medieval university was a community of professors and students. In some cases, as in the University of Bologna, the *alma mater studiorum,* the students, hired the professors on an annual basis and ruled the university. Groups of students monitored the activities of professors and the quality of teaching, and they could impose fines based on poor performance (Verger 1996). The role of students in university governance became less important in the modern university, but the May 1968 uprising led to higher education reforms in many European countries that provided students with a more visible presence on the governing bodies of universities.

This means that we consider students as members of the academic community, and not as clients or customers. This was assumed by the European Ministers of Education assembled in Prague[5] and is clearly stated in the Student Goteborg Declaration[6]:

> Students are not consumers of a tradable service. The social and civic contributions must be present as the primary functions of the higher education institutions. Higher education institutions are important actors in civic society; therefore all members of the higher education community should be involved.

External stakeholders are groups or individuals that have an interest in higher education even though they are not members of the higher education community. These include parents, taxpayers, employers, the state, and nowadays even international organisations, such as the European Commission, or international organisations of employers, such as the ERT and the IRDAC.

It is important to define two different categories of stakeholders since recent changes taking place in higher education indicate a loss of influence by internal stakeholders and an increasing role for external stakeholders. Philip Altbach (2000: 10) concludes that academics are loosing their once dominating power over the university.

5. A CHANGE OF PARADIGM

Recent changes involve a major shift in the concept of higher education, at least in terms of its modern configuration. The assumption underlying the Humboldtian-Newmanian model was that there was a direct relationship between the university's independence from the material – economic, social and political – interests of the society in which the institution was integrated, and the university's ability to accomplish its mission: the pursuit of knowledge for its own sake, and the preservation and dissemination of knowledge. According to this model, the state furthered the national interest and protected national culture by preserving the independence of its universities.

Under the new paradigm, the social and economic environments are no longer seen as a set of interests, sometimes even conflicting interests, from which universities should be protected by state. Instead, these interests form a network and higher education institutions must – and not merely 'should' – interact and respond to the interests articulated within this network if they want to survive. It is in this context that the concept of external stakeholder, as an entity representing the interests of this broader environment, assumes an increasing role, and this role is legitimised by the political discourse on higher education.

The concept of 'external stakeholder' refers to a third party acting between the two main parties, the community of scholars and the society, and it is anti-Humboldtian by nature. The state, in the Humboldtian tradition, was not viewed as a party in the strict sense, but rather as an entity guaranteeing that third parties could not interfere with the institutions' pursuit of its mission. This third party, as it is presently defined, is supposed to articulate the interests of society within the institution. This third party ensures that the institution is 'relevant' by making sure that the university community is aware of, and responds to, its environment. In extreme cases 'external stakeholders' are present as members of a Board of Trustees, with some similarity to the administration board of commercial enterprises.

The concept of 'external stakeholder' is complex and open to different interpretations. In what we name Form 1, 'external stakeholders' are narrowly defined and represent outside interests in the same way that stockholders have a role in the management of firms and companies[7]. For instance, external stakeholders representing industry and employers are there to tell the university about their human resource needs and their research interests. Form 1 corresponds to the growing presence of market rhetoric in the political discourse and to a vision of the university, and of higher education institutions in general, as service providers. Form 1 stakeholders may induce quick-fix attitudes from the institutions or may result in what Cardinal Newman called 'utilitarism'.

In what we call Form 2, the role of external stakeholders is opposite to the Form 1 role. It is unwise to view the market as a good regulator of higher education, since market regulation may lead to ethically or socially unacceptable distribution outcomes in terms of equity, or even result in the loss of the university's soul (Newman 2000). The role of Form 2 external stakeholders is to represent the broader and long-term interests of society and this role corresponds to the notion of higher education as a public good. Their role is not to promote market values à outrance, but to ensure that externalities and the core values of the university are not jeopardised by institutional attitudes that emphasize short-term market values while ignoring the university's social role. This is the traditional ideal role of the trustees of American universities: to represent the interest of society but at the same time to uphold the core values of the institution as seen by society and defined in the institution's statutes and mission statement.

Form 2 makes sense provided that external stakeholders are chosen judiciously. At a time when universities play an increasing role as providers of services and look for alternative sources of financing, it may be advantageous to have outside participation from society to scrutinise which activities are not compatible with the institution's core value, despite offering fat profits. But if external stakeholders are to provide this kind of moral oversight, their appointment needs to be carefully considered.

Core values that characterise the university's mission include being a place of free debate of ideas and critical thinking – and this includes a critical view of society itself – independence from outside interests, and educating students to respect ideas and their free expression. Frank Newman (2000) argues that any challenge to those values was traditionally assumed to come from the outside, and this was one of the main reasons why, in the modern university, the state protected the institution from outside interests. Today, as universities become more involved with for-profit activities, challenges to the university's mission can originate from inside the institution itself.

Some of the problems facing the traditional role of the university can be found in academic anecdotes. Laurie Taylor, the witty columnist of the *Times Higher Education Supplement* created a fictional story at the chimerical University of Poppleton based on the true information that a company made a donation of a substantial number of mobile phones to a well-known university whose vice-chancellor held a well-paid position as a non-executive director in the company. Laurie Taylor (2000) describes the contents of a circular letter addressed by the University of Poppleton's vice-chancellor to the academic staff, stressing the importance of stronger links with industry as part of the institution's overall plan to get money from any source whatsoever. He announces that an agreement has been signed with the firm Poppleton Pork Products plc where he holds an extraordinarily well-paid job as non-executive director. Under the terms of the agreement, the company will provide all academics above the level of senior lecturer with a medium size pork pie every week. The pies are free of charge, but recipients are asked to ensure that their personal free pie is displayed in a prominent position during all seminars, tutorials and undergraduate interviews. A modest change in the university crest will be made. While the lion and the unicorn and the open Latin tome will remain central features of the crest, a pig couchant will replace the leaping dolphin.

This example of caustic British humour offers an exaggerated picture of some of the dangers that can originate from inside an institution of higher education that is fully immersed in the market. These dangers often take a form that is more subtle or insidious than the one presented by Lewis Taylor. For instance, they may take the form of the low morale of academics working in research areas where outside funding is more difficult to obtain, especially when they compare their salaries with those of colleagues more fortunate or more 'entrepreneurial'.

Form 1 is completely anti-Humboldtian, both because it represents an outside intervention into the affairs of the university, and because its objective is to increase the influence of external interests. On the other hand, while Form 2 is also anti-Humboldtian because it involves outside intervention, it assumes a Humboldtian character in its objective of protecting academic freedom, in this case from attacks coming from inside the institutions themselves.

6. SOME EUROPEAN EXAMPLES

Examples of the increasing role of 'external stakeholders' are abundant in Europe. In some cases 'external stakeholders' are members of a Board of Trustees or of a university Board.

The 1993 reforms led to the creation of a Council of Directors in every Swedish university. The government appoints most of the members of the Council which is chaired by the rector, though more recently the number of members elected by academics has increased. Trade unions have a right to participate in the Council's meetings and may voice their opinions. In Denmark, the 1993 reform made the presence of representatives of outside interests mandatory on both the Senate and the Faculty Council. In Norway, the report of the Mjøs Commission on the reform of higher education has been released for public debate. This report proposes the creation a university council as the highest governing body. The rector will answer to this council, and the Minister of Education will appoint the majority of its members.

In the Netherlands, new legislation enacted in 1999 established a 'Raad van Toezicht', similar to a Board of Trustees, in each university. All five members are appointed by the Minister of Education after consultation with the universities. This board is responsible for defining the general orientation of the university's management and for appointing the rector. The reform corresponds to a movement away from traditional university governance models by eliminating collective decision making bodies and replacing them with a more managerial organisational structure. The formal participation of the students has disappeared. It is too early to draw conclusions about the consequences of this reform. In some cases, students have taken the university to court in order to contest the decision of eliminating their formal participation in governing bodies. There are also cases of newly appointed deans[8] who, sensing a loss of legitimacy under the new governance arrangement, now consult their colleagues far more frequently than when they were elected. And there are also some interesting academic anecdotes, such as the case of a university where one of the appointed members of the Raad van Toezicht was an executive director of a well-known Dutch coffee company. One of the first decisions of the Board was to replace the brand of coffee served in the university bars and canteens.

In Spain, the 1983 Ley de Reforma Universitaria established a 'Social Council' at each university. This governing body, with a majority members recruited from outside the university, has very important functions such as approving the institution's budget. In Italy, a very similar decision was taken by establishing the 'Council of Social Institutions' with membership and functions similar to their Spanish counterparts. In both cases, the rationale behind the establishment of these bodies was to increase the universities' responsiveness to societal demands and to the needs of the labour market. On the other hand, the universities, taking into account the common practice on the other side of the Atlantic, hoped to receive generous financial support from the wealthy industrialists participating in these councils.

Some institutional audits of Spanish and Italian universities[9] have demonstrated that the practical results of this policy change fell very short of even the more conservative expectations. Fund raising and requests for donations have resulted in only token contributions, the participation of external stakeholders in debating weighty university problems has been of little interest, and the anticipated contribution to better public knowledge of the universities has proven to be ineffective. This means that universities have to cope with an additional governing body without any significant benefit. It is important to realise that trying to copy parts of a model that is associated with good results in another country – in this case the United States – may result in disaster because of differences in culture and tradition. It is also important to note that differences in legal frameworks may favour or deter the generosity of the mighty and wealthy.

We can conclude that, in general, there has been an increase in the role of external stakeholders at the expense of internal stakeholders. In Spain and Italy, for example, external stakeholders have acquired an important role in approving budgets and in shaping the development plans of institutions. In the Netherlands, traditional collective decision making bodies that included internal stakeholders were disbanded in favour of the Raad van Toezicht. In Norway, the report of the Mjøs Commission recommends the establishment of institutional boards with the power to establish long-term institution priorities. The Minister will appoint the majority of board members.

It is also apparent that external stakeholders, in general, assume that their role is the one that we have defined as Form 1. In the Netherlands, members of one university's Raad van Toezicht considered that their first task was to tell the institution what kind of graduates were necessary for the Dutch economy. In Spain, some universities complained that lay members of the councils did not use their influence to promote institutional interests with the regional government or the local society, while some examples of gross interference by regional authorities were noted. In Italy, regional authorities and representatives of regional interests are increasingly intervening in the development plans of universities.

Nico Cloete and Ian Bunting (2000), referring to the South African situation, report that a number of external stakeholders do not have a clear idea of their role on the governing bodies of institutions. Universities are complex organisations and it is not easy for a lay member of a governing body to fully understand the culture and the norms and values that create the institutional ethos. In many cases, they cannot fully appreciate the nature of the problems being debated from an institutional perspective. As such, external stakeholders tend to see themselves more as representatives of outside interests (Form 1) than as upholding the core values of the institution as seen by society and defined in the institution's statutes and mission statement (Form 2).

7. THE PORTUGUESE CASE

In Portugal one can also see the rise and political deployment of the concept of stakeholder. However, since the Portuguese higher education system is differentiated along two dimensions – the polytechnic-university dimension and private-public dimension – the concept of stakeholder assumes different meanings and weights in different parts of the system.

Portuguese legislation allows for the participation of external stakeholders in the governing bodies of public universities, but this participation is mandatory for public polytechnics, while there are no legal rules concerning their participation in private institutions. The University Autonomy Act (Law 108/88) allows for the presence of representatives of external interests in the Senate (up to 15% of total membership), and for the establishment of advisory boards. The reaction of the 14 public universities has been very diverse and can be interpreted by means of neo-institutional theories. Six universities, including the old universities where academic values and traditions are more deeply rooted, do not allow for the participation of external stakeholders in the Senate, while another six, including some of the newer universities, have taken the opposite decision. Two other universities have not made a clear on the participation of external stakeholders. Ten universities have created advisory boards. Advisory boards, however, have no power at all, they meet very seldom, and in most cases the members have never actually been appointed.

The situation of polytechnics is very different because from the start these institutions were considered to have closer connections with the Portuguese economic and industrial situation, as well as a strong regional emphasis. Consequently their autonomy act (Law 54/90, 5th September, 1990) takes a more forceful position vis-à-vis the participation of external stakeholders in institutional governance. The participation of external stakeholders is mandatory in the election of the President of the Polytechnic Institutes and in their General Councils (equivalent to the university's senate), and it is optional in the Scientific Council.

As a result, the presence of external stakeholders should be more evident in the governance of Polytechnics, where they even participate in the election of the presidents. However, in general, Portuguese industry does not play any significant role as a stakeholder in higher education, and, with a few exceptions, has not demonstrated any interest in developing partnerships with higher education institutions, probably because the industrial sector is mainly composed of small and micro enterprises. In all of our case studies[10] informants reported difficulties in obtaining the effective participation of external stakeholders.

In one of the case studies, it was noted that the participation of outside stakeholders in the General Council was more active when strategic issues were on the table and less active when internal administrative problems were being debated. Several important actors indicated that the participation of external stakeholders in institutional governance was valuable, but suggested that it less significant that it should be, due to the reduced number of delegates from the outside community (the number is limited by the law of autonomy). Moreover, the internal dynamics and affairs of the institution tended to attract more attention in the General Council than the institution's relationship with the surrounding community. This was made even more evident by the fact that the statutes refer to Advisory Councils, both at the central level and at the school level, but so far not a single council has been established even if institutions apparently recognise that they are a priority.

In another case study, it was felt that although the law prescribes the presence of outside stakeholders in some governing bodies, their influence had been very weak and did not have the impact intended by the legislation. This participation was only formal, and it was generally characterised by the delegates' absence. The presence of the academic staff in cultural and professional activities in the town and their participation in many local organisations probably had more influence in creating links with the outside community than the formal, generally ineffective participation of external stakeholders in institutional governance. To some extent the limited participation of external stakeholders at this institution was the result of a very weak, regional entrepreneurial network, and of people having other more urgent problems to solve than participating in the election of the president of the local polytechnic[11]. Our informants believed that, in most cases, participation was the result of relationships developed by people responsible for running the institutions and not the result of any legislated reforms. This does not mean that they would like to limit outside participation by changing the statutes, but they believed that new ways of making this participation more effective were needed.

It is somewhat surprising that external stakeholders are not formally involved in the internal processes of private institutions. The legislation, however, requires that in the private sector, the university must be separated from the owner (the co-operative)[12]. Yet there are serious doubts both about whether these interests are actually separated, and about the independence of academic interests given that there are internal stakeholders who, in fact, own the university. The governing bodies of the university are defined in purely academic terms, rejecting, in general, any role for external participation in these bodies, but there are serious concerns about the undisclosed influence of those who hold a financial interest in the business.

At one private university our interviewees were quite articulate in stressing the importance of securing strong academic leadership for the institution, and, in their view, the presence of a strong external representation could upset the balance of that leadership. This university's mission statement, however, is based on the assumption that the political perspective behind a private university's project should give strong attention to labour market demands and to the employability of graduates. To solve this apparent contradiction, this university has assumed that the Advisory Council of an associated Foundation plays an important role in opening the institution to the views, perspectives and demands of the outside community. This means that the university has avoided the direct influence of external stakeholders over internal governance by limiting their participation to membership on an Advisory Council without any decisive influence on institutional governance.

At a private polytechnic, the participation of outside stakeholders in the design of the activities of the institution has so far been rather informal. In order to review study programs, the Institute collects the opinions of students and alumni, and uses expert opinions from professionals who are also members of the teaching staff. The institute is trying to change this situation by developing protocols with the City Council and local industries, and by allowing external stakeholders to participate in some governing bodies of the Institute, but the impact of these measures is not yet known. So far the results have not been very positive; problems have emerged because of the lack of a tradition co-operation, and because the City Council, unlike other towns, has never demonstrated an interest in having an institution of higher education.

In Portugal, most private higher education institutions are owned by an individual or group of individuals, despite the fact that under law these institutions are technically owned by co-operative societies. It is clear from our research that the decisions of the governing bodies of private higher education institutions are generally submitted to the owning society for review. It is only natural that the owners will protect their domination over the institution by avoiding the presence of Form 1 stakeholders, and the law does not require the participation of outside representatives in the governing bodies of private higher education institutions. This is probably the reason why the owners prefer to invite outside stakeholders to participate on advisory boards, sometimes even for organisations lying outside the higher education institution, as this will promote a Form 2 behaviour.

The Polytechnic Public Institutes are located all over the country and many of have been established in small towns. This fact, combined with the reality of a Portuguese industrial sector composed mainly of small and micro enterprises, helps to explain the low level of effective industry participation in institute governance. On the other hand, there are no regional governments in Portugal and this confines the power of local authorities to the level of city council. This explains why outside stakeholders are, in general, not very effective and do not assume Form 1 behaviour. Generally speaking, local authorities will become active only when they support the promotion of the local Polytechnic to become a university, or when they support proposals of the local Polytechnic to create new schools, activities that may be viewed positively by the electorate. We wonder if this can be classified as a pure Form 2 behaviour.

Neo-institutional theories explain why the more traditional universities have avoided the presence of external stakeholders on governing bodies, confining their participation to advisory boards. This restricts external stakeholders either to Form 2 behaviour, or to a very weak and ineffective position within institutional governance. Newer universities were established with a stronger emphasis on regional or local demands for qualified manpower and in some cases they have decided to enlist the assistance of external stakeholders as a form of political and social support. Since the law does not require the participation of external stakeholders, they are selected and appointed by the university and will generally exhibit Form 2 behaviour. This is not, however, an absolute rule since have been exceptions, for example there was the case of a local mayor, representing the city council on the senate, who favoured real estate developments that were not in the best interests of the university campus.

8. CONCLUSION

Outside pressure on universities to become more relevant and responsive, more elaborate mechanisms of accountability – even when these mechanisms assume a more civilised form as the by-product of quality improvement – and the emergence of practices imported from the business world (managerialism), are all assuming an increasing role in higher education.

The replacement of elected rectors by appointed presidents/managers, the increased salience of external stakeholders, the dismissal of traditional governance mechanisms, and the proliferation of 'boards of trustees' and 'social councils' are some of the most visible signs of the changes that are taking place in higher education. In Europe, these changes are too recent for us to be able to reach definitive conclusions. However, we would suggest that the changes taking place could result in negative consequences for the institutions insofar as core academic values may be replaced by short-term views and criteria focusing on the needs of the economy. It is well known that even in a very liberal environment the market will focus on the short-term needs of people and not on long-term strategies. And there is a clear danger that Form 1 external stakeholders will not view protecting the core values of the university as a priority.

It is also interesting to note that the traditional idea of the stakeholder – the independent third-party who did not have a direct interest in the result of the game – has been replaced by someone who has a stake or an interest. A stakeholder may no longer be the independent party entrusted with the money from the bets, but someone who has taken a risk and has a vested interest in the result.

The preliminary analysis presented here is necessarily incomplete. The European examples and the Portuguese case, however, reveal some problems with these new external stakeholders, and their role to-date has certainly been less effective than was hoped for. For example there is evidence that some external stakeholders are unwilling to devote the time and energy necessary to play a relevant role in the management of higher education institutions.

The analysis also seems to suggest these individuals are more likely to assume the role of Form 2 stakeholders when they are chosen and appointed by the university instead of being appointed by an external constituency or by the government. This behaviour is reinforced if external stakeholders only participate in advisory boards, but in these situations their role can be easily disregarded by academics.

We believe that the concept of stakeholder and the participation of external representatives in university governance are important topics for further study and critical analysis, especially since they can help us understand some of the broader changes taking place in higher education.

NOTES

[1] See for instance Gewirtz et al. (1993), Le Grand and Bartlett (1995), and Kursten et al. (2001).

[2] The movement towards a selling orientation has created new administrative functions such as marketing and fund raising and led to the emergence of new administrative positions. This is also observed in secondary schools in a competitive environment. See for instance Gewirtz et al. (1993).

[3] Ulrich Teichler (2000), private communication.

[4] See for instance *Times Higher Education Supplement* 2001 (July 13): 19.

[5] In the communiqué of the Ministers assembled in Prague on May 19th 2001 it is stated that *"students are full members of the higher education community."*

[6] Declaration produced by ESIB – The National Union of Students in Europe – on March 25th, 2001.

[7] In Form 1 external stakeholders protects investments made for instance by society trough public funds, or the investments made by students and their parents through payment of tuition fees and profit deferral of an earlier employment.

[8] Academic peers no longer elect their deans. The rector appoints them after consultation with the Faculty.

[9] We refer to the CRE (Association of European Universities) quality audit programme.

[10] We refer to the EU funded TSER–HEINE project. Cipes has run six case studies, including four public HEIs (1 classical university, 1 new university, 2 public polytechnics) and two private institutions (1 university and 1 polytechnic).

[11] For the second and more recent election, only one out of 15 delegates of the local municipalities has voted, and only two out of 12 delegates from the regional economic activities has been present.

[12] The intention of the legislation is to protect academic decisions made by the university from the interference of the owner. This is difficult to guarantee insofar as those decisions can only be implemented if the owner provides the necessary funds.

REFERENCES

Altbach, P. "Academic Freedom in Hong Kong – Threats Inside and Out." *International Higher Education* 21 (2000): 9 –10.
Amaral, A. "Sistemas de Avaliação." *Educação Brasileira* 16 (1994): 221 – 232.
Amaral, A. and A. Magalhães. "On Markets, Autonomy and Regulation. The Janus Head Revisited." *Higher Education Policy* XIV.1 (2001): 1 –14.
Cloete, N. and I. Bunting. *Higher Education Transformation. Assessing performance in South Africa.* Pretoria: CHET, 2000.
Council of Europe, *Recommendation No. R (2000) 8, of the Committee of Ministers to member states on the research mission of universities.* Strasbourg, 2000.
Dill, D.D. "Higher Education Markets and Public Policy." *Higher Education Policy* 10.3/4 (1997): 167 – 185.
Freeman, R.E. *Strategic management: A stakeholder approach.* Boston: Pitman, 1984.
Gewirtz, S., S.J. Ball and R. Bowe. *Markets, Choice and Equity in Education.* Buckingham: Oxford University Press, 1993.
Gibbons, M. et al. *The New Production of Knowledge: The Dynamics of Science and Research in Contemporary Societies.* London: Sage, 1997.
Gruber, K.H. "The State and higher education in Austria: an historical and institutional approach." *European Journal of Education* 17.2 (1982).
Jones, T.M. "Corporate social responsibility revisited, redefined." *California Management Review* 22.2 (1980): 59 – 67.
Kursten, S., et al. "Another Side of the Coin: the unintended effects of the publication of school performance data in England and France." *Comparative Education* 37.2 (2001): 231 – 242.
Le Grand, J., and W. Bartlett (eds). *Quasi-Markets and Social Policy.* London: McMillan, 1995.
Lindsay, G. and T. Rodgers. "Market Orientation in the UK Higher Education Sector: the influence of the education reform process 1979-1993." *Quality in Higher Education* 4.2 (1988): 159 – 171.
Maassen, P.A.M., and Van Vught, F. "An Intriguing Janus-Head: The two faces of the new government strategy towards higher education in the Netherlands." *European Journal of Education* 23.1/2 (1988): 65 – 77.
Mitchell, R.K., B.R. Agle and D.J. Wood. "Toward a Theory of Stakeholder Identification and Salience: Defining the Principle of Who and What Really Counts." *Academy of Management Review* 22.4 (1997): 853 – 896.
Mjøs Commission Report. *Oslo, Ministry of Church Affairs, Education and Research, 2000.*
Neave, G., and van Vught, F. (eds). *Prometheus Bound: The Changing Relationship Between Government and Higher Education in Western Europe.* London: Pergamon Press, 1991.
Neave, G. and Van Vught, F. "Conclusion." In Neave, G. and Van Vught, F (eds). *Government and Higher Education Relationships Across Three Continents: The Winds of Change.* London: Pergamon Press, 1994, 264 – 319.

Neave, G. "The Stirring of the Prince and the Silence of the Lambs: The Changing Assumptions Beneath Higher Education Policy, Reform and Society." In Dill, D. and B. Sporn (eds). *Emerging Patterns of Social Demand and University Reform: Through a Glass Darkly.* Oxford: Pergamon Press, 1995, 54 – 71.

Neave, G. "On Visions, Short and Long." *Higher Education Policy* 8.4 (1995a): 9 - 10.

Neave, G. "Homogenization, Integration and Convergence: The Cheshire Cats of Higher Education Analysis." In Meek, V.L., L. Goedegebuure, O. Kivinen and R. Rinne (eds). *The Mockers and Mocked: Comparative Perspectives on Differentiation, Convergence and Diversity in Higher Education.* London: Pergamon, 1996, 26 – 41.

Neave, G. "The European Dimension in Higher Education: An Excursion into the Modern Use of Historical Analogues." In Huisman, J., P.A.M. Maassen and G. Neave (eds). *Higher Education and the Nation State: The Institutional Dimension of Higher Education.* London: Pergamon, 2001, 13 – 73.

Newman, F. "Saving Higher Education's Soul." *Change* (2000, September/October): 16 – 23.

Newman, J.H. *The Idea of the University, Defined and Illustrated,* Turner, F. (ed). New Haven: Yale University Press, 1996.

Psacharopoulos (1994), "Returns to Investment in Education: a Global Update." *World Development* 22.9 (1994).

Santos, B.S. *O Estado e a Sociedade em Portugal (1975-1986).* Porto: Edições Afrontamento, 1992.

Santos, B.S. *Portugal, um retrato singular.* Porto: Edições Afrontamento, Porto, 1993.

Scott, P. *The Meanings of Mass Higher Education.* Buckingham: SHRE and Open University Press, 1995.

Suchman, M.C. "Managing legitimacy: Strategic and institutional approaches." *Academy of Management Review.* 20 (1995): 571-610.

Taylor, L. "Chronicle." *Times Higher Education Supplement,* 3rd September (2000): 60.

Trow, M. "Trust, Markets and Accountability in Higher Education: a Comparative Perspective." *Higher Education Policy* 9.4 (1996): 309 – 324.

Van Vught, F. "Combining planning and the market: an analysis of the Government strategy towards higher education in the Netherlands." *Higher Education Policy* 10.3/4 (1997): 211 – 224.

Verger, J. "Os Professores." in Ridder-Symoens, H. (ed). *As Universidades na Idade Média.* Lisboa: Imprensa Nacional, 1996, 33 – 63.

Von Humboldt, W. "Über die Innere und Äussere Organisation der Höberen Wissenschaftlichen Ansalten." in E. Anrich (ed). *Die Idee der Deutschen Universität.* Darmstadt,1959.

Wittrock, B. "The modern university: the three transformations." In *The European and American university since 1800. Historical and sociological essays.* Rothblatt, S. and B. Wittrock (eds). Cambridge: Cambridge University Press (1993), 303 – 362.

PETER MAASSEN

ORGANISATIONAL STRATEGIES AND GOVERNANCE STRUCTURES IN DUTCH UNIVERSITIES

1. INTRODUCTION

The focus of this chapter is on the interaction in higher education systems between environmental pressures and organisational strategies for responding to these pressures. This general focus will be exemplified by a discussion of the way in which Dutch universities have responded to a new law on university governance structures.

An important frame of reference for examining changes in university governance structures can be found in the nature of the relationship between society and higher education. The university has contributed in many ways to the social, cultural, technological and economic development of modern societies. As such it can be regarded as a key social institution. However, as argued, for example, by Gumport (2000) and Olsen (2000), the traditional contract or pact[1] between society and higher education has come under serious pressure. The discussion on the role of social institutions is not limited to higher education only. Many societies are in a period of transformation (Castells 1996) in which attempts are made to adapt key social, political and economic structures and institutions. A core issue is the redistribution of authority and power in society (Olsen 2000), which also leads to the search for appropriate new forms of governance, organisation and steering at all relevant levels, including new university governance structures.

In the first decades of the nineteenth century the Continental European states took upon themselves the regulatory and funding responsibilities for higher education. This 'state-control' governmental steering strategy has continued for almost 200 years. It was only in the 1980s that this strategy was seriously questioned and gradually replaced by alternative approaches. While in the USA, Canada, Australia, and the UK the relationship between society and higher education is driven more and more by a form of academic capitalism (Slaughter and Leslie, 1997) relying on market-type interactions, in Continental Europe the emerging new relationships between higher education and society can be characterised as network-types of relationships with the state continuing to be an important actor. Market elements have also been introduced in the steering of higher education in Continental Europe, but they are not as radical and far-reaching as in the Anglo-Saxon countries.

Alberto Amaral, Glen A. Jones and Berit Karseth (eds.), Governing Higher Education: National Perspectives on Institutional Governance, 23—41.
© 2002 *Kluwer Academic Publishers. Printed in the Netherlands.*

The Netherlands is often regarded as offering an interesting example for the adaptations of other national higher education systems in Continental Europe. This view is mainly based on the higher education reforms of the first half of the 1980s. They have led to major adaptations of the policy arrangements for, and the social institutional contexts of, Dutch higher education (Maassen 1996; Jongbloed et al., 1999). Important innovations, such as a new governmental steering approach, a new comprehensive higher education law, new quality assessment mechanisms, a new structure for the teaching programmes of the universities, a new institutional landscape for the higher vocational education sector, etc., have been realised over a relatively short time period. The Netherlands was the first Continental European country to translate the changing social expectations with respect to higher education into reform initiatives. As such the reforms have given the Netherlands a major advantage over other European countries in making its higher education system more effective, efficient, and responsive.

The comprehensive framework law for higher education, passed by Parliament in 1993, neither included a new funding structure for higher education, nor a new governance structure for the universities. These two topics were too complicated, too sensitive and to some extent too controversial to be dealt with satisfactorily in the time frame between the launching of the new governmental steering strategy (1985) and the acceptance of the new law by Parliament in 1993. More time, consultation, discussion, reflection, and experimentation was needed before the Minister of Education was able to propose major innovations with respect to these two areas. Of course, this was not a unique position to be in given that in any higher education reform the issues of how the allocation of public funds to higher education relates to the aims of the reform and who is going to be responsible for the main academic and administrative decisions within the higher education institutions are crucial.

While the discussion on the innovation of the allocation model is still going on[2], in 1997 the Dutch Parliament accepted the new act on university governance[3]. The new act addressed many of the criticisms of the democratic, internally oriented university governance structure introduced at the beginning of the 1970s (De Boer et al., 1998). Compared to the old structure, the new structure is less democratic, more managerially driven, more centralised, and more externally oriented (De Boer et al., 1999).

Even though the 1997 act was rather prescriptive, it did offer the universities a number of choices in terms of some of the core elements of the new governance structure. The responses of the institutions to these choice options will be discussed in this chapter. In doing so, also the underlying rationale of the new governance structure will be analysed, as well as the way in which institutional realities played a role in the change process, and the extent to which dominant patterns can be observed in the introduction of the new governance structure. First an important contextual aspect will be discussed, i.e. the way in which the Dutch governmental steering approach with respect to higher education changed in the 1980s and 1990s.

2. THE CHANGING STEERING APPROACH

In Continental Europe, universities were traditionally allowed to steer themselves in academic matters. Academic self-steering was part of a large democratic social order, with partly autonomous institutions. Constitutional regulations specified these institutions and their roles, competence, social and political relationships, and responsibilities. From this perspective institutional autonomy in higher education is a condition for legitimate governmental steering and a peaceful co-existence with other institutions (Olsen 2000).

National debates about social institutions are not new. They have regularly taken place and have led to many threats concerning the autonomy of universities and other social institutions in the national context. However, currently the notion of institutional self-steering in higher education is challenged by the effects of international reform ideologies. According to the underlying ideas and assumptions associated with these reform ideologies, universities and colleges should be externally controlled, their activities should be formally evaluated, they should be held accountable for their performance, they should be steered by market forces and not by governmental or state mechanisms, they should be included as service industries in regional and global trade agreements, and they should be run by professional leaders and managers instead of by academic *primus-inter-pares*. In a world were institutional success is more and more assumed to be dependent upon the institution's competitive power, representatives of the academic staff are in general regarded as being poorly equipped for running their own institutions (Olsen 2000; Maassen and Cloete 2002).

The reforms resulting from the acceptance and application of these ideas and assumptions at the national level differ from country to country. While the reform agendas in general include the goals of efficiency, effectiveness, responsiveness and competition, the way in which national authorities transform their public higher education systems in practice depends to a large extent on national institutional realities and social expectations. In the USA and Australia current reforms are, for example, characterised by the underlying assumption that the role of the state should be minimized, while Continental European reform efforts aim at changing the role of the state instead of minimizing it. In the latter case a government steering 'at a distance' is not the same as an absent or minimal government role (Maassen 1996). This can be illustrated by referring to the way in which the Dutch Ministry of Education has adapted since the mid-1980s its steering strategy with respect to higher education.

In 1985 the Dutch government introduced a new governmental higher education steering strategy (Maassen and Van Vught, 1989). This approach implied more freedom, but also more responsibilities for the institutions. Until that time the steering approach could be characterised as being dominated by the government and academia, with a rather weak position for the central institutional leaders (Maassen 1996: 107). The new steering approach assumed that the best position for the government in the steering of higher education is 'at a distance'. The government's role should consist of developing a framework within which the institutions can operate rather autonomously. The main conditions for granting this freedom to the higher education system were that the institutions would become more effective and more efficient, would introduce a formal quality assessment system, and would become more responsive to social needs. In order to make it possible for the universities to live up to the expectations underlying the new steering approach, it was necessary to adapt the (intra-) university governance structure. This adaptation was aimed at stimulating more direct interactions between university and society.

Some authors have pointed to the inconsistencies and ambivalences of the new steering approach (Kickert 1986; Maassen and Van Vught 1988; Gornitzka and Maassen 2000b). Nevertheless, the changes introduced since 1985 in the relationship between the government and higher education have altered the formal governance structure as well as the governance practice in Dutch universities. How can the ways in which the universities reacted to the external pressures to increase their responsiveness to society by, among other things, innovating their governance structures, be interpreted? How did the universities balance the internal and external pressures for change *and* stability? In what way did the role of external stakeholders change and how can this change be explained?

3. ORGANISATIONAL STRATEGIES FOR DEALING WITH INSTITUTIONAL PRESSURES

According to the neo-institutional literature, organisational structures are shaped by institutional environments (Meyer and Rowan, 1977). Early studies applying neo-institutional approaches were based on the assumption that organisations react passively to institutional pressures from their environment. The notion of varied strategic organisational behaviour was not explicitly included in these studies. Only gradually differences between organisations concerning the way they responded to environmental pressures were recognised in neo-institutional studies (Zucker 1988). It has been suggested that a neo-institutional perspective can "readily accommodate a variety of strategic responses [of organisations] to the institutional environment" (Oliver 1991: 173). By combining neo-institutional and resource dependence theories, Oliver identifies five organisational strategies for dealing with environmental pressures: acquiescing, compromising, avoiding, defying, and manipulating (Oliver 1991: 152).

Scott (1995) has interpreted and elaborated Oliver's typology of organisational strategies on the basis of a conditionalisation and amplification of her arguments. Scott's condition for using Oliver's typology consists of the recognition that organisational strategies are shaped by the environment of institutions: "institutional environments influence and delimit what strategies organisations can use" (Scott 1995: 124). He amplifies Oliver's arguments by indicating that they are limited to individual organisations, while responses made by groups of organisations can be equally important (Scott 1995: 125). Since the discussion in this chapter is focused mainly on the level of individual organisations, Scott's *condition* is particularly important.

Taking Scott's interpretations as a starting-point, the five strategies can be described as follows:

Acquiesce: refers to extreme forms of conformity to institutional pressures in the form of habit, imitation and compliance. According to Scott (1995: 128), this strategy is emphasised by most institutional theorists.

Compromise: involves balancing, pacifying, or bargaining with external stakeholders. This strategy is very common in conflicting environments, and in situations where there is an inconsistency between external expectations and internal organisational objectives.

Avoidance: can be defined as an organisation's attempt to disguise its non-conformity, buffer itself from institutional pressures, or escape from institutional rules and expectations (Oliver 1991: 154). Scott (1987; 1995: 130) suggests that the question of whether various forms of avoidance are used as a response to institutional pressures stemming from legitimate sources of authority or from sources exercising unauthorised power should be evaluated empirically.

Defiance: refers to organisations that resist institutional pressures in a very public manner. This strategy will be used when the norms and interests of an organisation are very different from those incorporated in the requirements that are imposed on it (Scott 1995: 130). The tactics of defiance are dismissal, challenge and attack.

Manipulation: is the most active strategic response to environmental pressures. It consists of co-opting, influencing or controlling the environment (Oliver 1991: 157).

Organisations are not purely reactive. Rather they "are creatures of their institutional environments, but most modern organisations are constituted as active players, not passive pawns" (Scott 1995: 132). They can and will use one or more of the above strategies in dealing with environmental pressures.

The five strategies described by Oliver offer an interesting frame for analysing the ways in which Dutch universities have responded to the introduction by the Dutch Minister of Education of a new governance structure in which both external interests and internal values and objectives should be represented. In the next sections a modest attempt at analysing the university responses is presented. The scope of analysis is modest since the empirical evidence available is limited.

4. INNOVATIONS IN THE DUTCH GOVERNANCE STRUCTURE[4]

While in the 1960s and early 1970s all over Europe university structures were adapted in response to student revolts, no country went as far as the Netherlands in democratising university governance (De Boer et al., 1999). Dutch Parliament accepted the Act on University Governance in 1970, thereby introducing a system of *representative leadership*. This system was modelled after the representative governance structure of Dutch counties. For universities, this implied a governance system that gave academics, non-academic support staff and students the right to elect their representatives to university and faculty councils (De Boer et al., 1998). University councils could also include external laymen, expected to represent the general public. It is striking that not all universities used this opportunity provided by the 1970 Act to include such 'promoters of public interests' on their council.

In 1986 a new Law on University Education was enacted in which the powers of university and faculty boards and councils were redistributed. This led to a form of *mixed leadership* in which the powers of the board were strengthened. However, the foundational role of the councils was not altered. They remained representative control bodies with a considerable power in the university governance structure.

As part of the framework of the governmental steering approach towards higher education, introduced in 1985, the government wanted to stimulate the universities to become more responsive to social needs by, among other things, adapting the university governance structure. In the new comprehensive framework Law on Higher Education accepted by Parliament in 1993, the university governance structure was largely left untouched. In the consultations at the beginning of the 1990s between the Minister of Education and the universities concerning the governance structure, a clear difference in perception came to the fore. The Minister wanted to fundamentally alter the nature of the governance structure from a system of *mixed leadership* to a form of *executive leadership* (De Boer et al., 1998: 154, 162 – 163). He felt that the *mixed leadership* system of university governance introduced in 1986 hindered the universities in developing more direct interactions with society.

The universities opposed this view by claiming that, in practice, the governance structure had already been modified. These adaptations had streamlined the internal procedures, thereby strengthening the decisiveness of the universities. Nonetheless, the Minister proposed a new bill on university governance in 1995, accepted by Parliament in 1997, in which the formal balance of power was tilted in favour of the boards. The new Act introduced a system of *executive leadership* both for the university as a whole and for the faculties (De Boer et al., 1998). The role of the councils changed from being control bodies to being advisory bodies. In addition, the Act provided for the formal inclusion of a strong, separate body for external stakeholders in the university governance structure.

The main changes associated with the 1997 Act can be summarised as follows:

1. The authority and power of the university executive board[5] (in Dutch: *College van Bestuur*) and faculty boards[6] are strengthened. In addition, power is concentrated more by strengthening the position of certain collective or individual actors in the governance structure.
2. The university and faculty councils become advisory bodies (with students and staff as members) instead of control bodies.
3. Academic and management responsibilities are integrated.

4. The department level (in Dutch: *vakgroepen*) looses its legal basis.
5. A new governing body, the *Raad van Toezicht* (a Supervisory Board comparable to a Board of Trustees) is introduced. (De Boer et al., 1998: 163).

Two elements are of interest. The first concerns the developments that occurred between the launching of the Act in 1995 and its enactment in 1997. To understand the nature and importance of these developments, one must be aware of a specific characteristic of the Netherlands, i.e. "the Dutch consultation society" (Maassen 2000: 450 – 451). Even before the introduction of the Act of 1995, the Minister and the university representatives discussed the Minister's wish to adapt the university governance structures. The Minister of Education was very much in favour of replacing the university councils by a structure based on the *Ondernemingsraad*. This *Ondernemingsraad* (abbreviated as OR) is a body included in the law on business firms. Every Dutch firm is obliged to create a *Raad* (in English: council) composed of employees. This council is advisory. The Minister wanted the universities to opt for a governance structure with an 'OR' for staff members and a separate council for students. Given the reactions of the universities to this proposal, it became clear in the Dutch consultation and lawmaking tradition that the Minister had to look for a compromise. As a consequence, the Law of 1997 gave the universities a certain amount of freedom concerning the development of their governance structure. This implied, for example, that they had the ability to choose between a structure of separated councils for staff and students, and a joint council. The latter would be, in practice, a continuation of the existing structure where all internal parties are represented on a university council. The 1997 Law was also modified in other ways after the consultations between Minister and universities.

Second, the *Raad van Toezicht* (Supervisory Board), introduced by the 1997 Act, cannot be compared as a formal body in the university governance structure to the inclusion of lay members on university councils provided for by the 1970 Act. The latter involved individuals who did not necessarily directly represent external sectors or interests. These lay members were individuals functioning as a member of a council in a private capacity (see also the case of University A below). The new Supervisory Board is a body intended to represent external interests and stakeholders in the intra-university governance processes. It is a body positioned between the Minister and the Executive Board of a university. Each university nominates the members of its own Supervisory Board, but the Minister of Education appoints the members. The Supervisory Board is also accountable to the Minister and not to its university.

An important question[7] with respect to the functioning of this Supervisory Board is whether it represents the interests of the university in terms of being composed of *trustees* for the institution in question, or a specific point of view with an obligation to report back to the constituency, implying that the Board members are *delegates*. While this question can be raised with respect to university Supervisory Boards in general, a specific Dutch question is whether this Board interpret its role as a ministerial body, or as a body that should protect the university from outside influences, including the Minister. Unfortunately there are no empirical data available at this time that would make it possible to answer this question in a valid way.

5. THE RESPONSES OF THE UNIVERSITIES TO THE 1997 ACT ON UNIVERSITY GOVERNANCE

The 1997 Act on University Governance provides the universities room to develop their own governance structure within the frame offered by the Act. How did the universities respond to this room to manoeuvre in implementing the provisions of the Act?

This question will be addressed by first discussing the responses of all the universities. Case study material from the TSER/HEINE study (Gornitzka and Maassen 2000a) will then be used to reflect in more detail on the responses of two universities to these external institutional pressures. These universities are presented here as University A and University B[8].

5.1. General university responses

The new bill on University Governance was launched in 1995 and enacted in 1997. In the Dutch tradition of allowing the main actors involved the possibility of starting innovative experiments before a new law is actually enacted, the universities were allowed to experiment with new elements in their governance structure. It is striking that none of the universities seriously initiated such experiments. There are a number of reasons for this. The most important can be argued to be the position of the University Councils. The nature and functioning of the Councils was one of the main elements in the external criticism of the university governance structures. However, given their control function, any experiment had to be approved of by the University Council. It did not come as a surprise that none of the councils were very eager to co-operate in orchestrating their demise.

Another reason was that the Executive Boards of the universities had already started to adapt some functions of, and procedures concerning the internal governance practice. Therefore, the external criticism on the functioning of the university governance structure was not necessarily shared inside the universities.

Finally, concerning strengthening the involvement of external stakeholders in university governance, the universities were not able or willing to adapt their governance structures.

Before and immediately after the launching of the 1995 bill, the Minister consulted with the universities about the proposed university governance structure. In line with some "collective responses studies" presented by Scott (1995: 125 – 128), the Dutch universities were able, in the period 1995–1997, to respond collectively to the proposed regulatory regime in such a way that the regime was redefined. Instead of being a rather prescriptive and strict regulative structure, the 1997 Act allowed the universities a large amount of autonomy in the adaptations of their governance structures.

An important option provided for in the 1997 Act was the choice between a separate or joint council structure. The separate council structure is closer to a business-like management structure than the joint structure. Of the thirteen Dutch universities, three have private status, even though they generally come under the same regulations, and are publicly funded in the same way and at the same level as the other ten universities. The private status of the universities is related to their denominational background. One area where a difference occurs is in the governance structure. In line with their private status, two of the three denominational universities have chosen a structure with a separate university council for staff members. Of the ten non-denominational universities, four originally chose a separate university staff council. Six non-denominational institutions and one private university decided to stick to the undivided council for staff and students. Recently, one of the four 'public' universities with a separate council structure decided to integrate staff and student councils. Hence, only three 'regular' public universities are left with the more business-like, divided university council structure.

5.2. Two individual university's responses

University A

At the central level of University A, the main bodies in the governance structure are the Supervisory Board (*Raad van Toezicht*), the Executive Board (*College van Bestuur*), the University Council (*Universiteitsraad*), and the Board of Deans (*College van Decanen*). The Supervisory Board consists of five external members, appointed by and accountable to the Minister of Education. The most important policy plans are submitted for approval to this Board. Furthermore, the Board arbitrates in cases of disputes between Executive board and the University council. The Executive Board consists of three persons, appointed by the Supervisory Board. One of the members of the Executive Board is the *Rector Magnificus*, chosen from among the current and former deans of the university by the Supervisory Board on recommendation of the Executive Board, which has already received advice from the Council of Deans.

Figure 1 shows the main actors and groups involved in the governance structure of University A.

The Council of Deans consists of the Deans of the faculties. It has the power to award the doctorate and it advises the Executive Board. The *rector* is both a member of the Executive board and the chair of the Council of Deans.

The current University Council is, to a large extent, a representative advisory body, consisting of students and staff members chosen by their respective communities. University A has chosen to adopt the so-called undivided or combined option of governance for the university council. This implies that the board has brought the powers of the students and staff members together in one body (consisting of 12 students appointed for one year and 12 staff members appointed for two years).

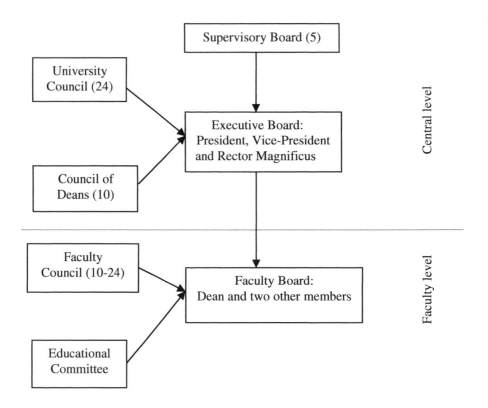

Figure 1. Governance structure University A (including number of members).

At the faculty level, the Dean is responsible for governance issues with respect to education and research. The Dean is part of the Faculty Board (*Faculteitsbestuur*), consisting of two other members, one of these being the *opleidingsdirecteur* (Educational Director). A student with advisory power (nominated by the students in the Faculty Council) also participates in the Faculty Board. The responsibilities of the Dean can be delegated or mandated to other members of the Faculty Board, especially the Educational Director. While the Dean also has an advisory role concerning the Executive Board, it is the Executive Board that appoints the Dean.

The Faculty Council (*Faculteitsraad*), chosen by staff members and students, is a body comparable to the University Council at the central level. At the faculty level, this university also chose the undivided structure for the Faculty Council. The size of the Faculty Council varies from 10 to 24 members, depending on the size of the faculty in question. The Educational Committee (*Opleidingscommissie*) is required by law, and half of its members are students. Each study programme within the faculty has such a committee, advising the Dean and evaluating the implementation of the regulations with respect to education and examinations.

A point of debate at University A during the implementation of the new governance structure was whether the Deans should be part of a central management team. Most faculties preferred to continue the situation at that time in which Deans were members of the Council of Deans. Integrating the Deans into a central management team was expected to lead to 'collegial problems' at the faculty level. Another point of debate related to the reallocation of responsibilities. The former University Council wanted to adhere to the 'model of harmony', in force for two decades, in which staff members and students were accepted as equal partners in the policy discussions at the central level. In that situation, delegates from three sections of the then University Council (students, academic staff, support staff) participated in the regular meetings of the Executive Board. They did not have official responsibilities, but the structure allowed for some input in the debates and decision-making by the university's Board. With the introduction of the new structure, the Council claimed that it should have additional powers to those included in the regulations. The Executive Board, however, would only grant the formal legislative powers to the new University Council. As a compromise, a two-year covenant has been drawn up in which 'rules of conduct' for all parties were laid down.

Involvement of external stakeholders in internal processes at University A
The relationship between the university and society has been on the agenda for a long period. As early as the 1960s the then *Rector Magnificus* reported that the university community should improve its relationship with the society. Most of the activities proposed to address this point were intended to make the university more visible to society, while they did not relate (yet) to active participation of stakeholders in university affairs.

The 1970 Act on University Governance allowed for the inclusion of external members in the University Council. These members were to be appointed for two years, but could opt for continuation. When the new governance structure was implemented at University A in 1972, the Council had to develop a procedure for selecting and nominating external members. The first Executive Board developed a procedure to select external members for the University Council. Suggestions for the characteristics of external members (based on suggestions from the Minister of Education) were: representatives from regional or local government, business, education and science, and higher professional education, as well as former students and those involved in post-initial higher education. In fact, the university was looking for individuals representing important societal groups who had administrative skills and, while not members of the academic community, were not unfamiliar with university life. Candidates were recruited using advertisements in local and regional newspapers. In contrast to the other parties on the University Council that acted mostly as a coalition, the external members acted mostly on an individual basis.

An analysis of the background of external members over time does not reveal specific patterns, apart from the fact that most fulfilled the criteria set by the

University Council. During application procedures in the 1980s, it was stressed that the candidate should be living in the region of the university, should add to the activities of the university because of his/her societal position, and should have some insight into the university's main processes. The distribution across the types of positions was quite regular.

The present governance structure appears to have, at first glance, similar patterns of societal representation. However, it is important to note, first, that the Supervisory Board is a separate, powerful body with no internal members. Second, the current members of the Supervisory Board have, generally speaking, more prestige than the former external members of the University Council. Most members of the Supervisory Board have held more than one position. In terms of the present Supervisory Board, three members have a background in both administration and (higher) education, and two members have held various positions in business organisations.

Two issues concerning external representation in internal university affairs that arose the period in question are interesting to mention here. First the problem of finding external representatives for the University Council who combined three qualities. First, the external members were to be representative of a specific group outside the university. Second, the members were supposed to be familiar with university affairs. Third, the members were to have administrative skills. At times, these three qualities could not be found in one person or, even worse, the junction of these qualities led to role ambiguity. Also, the external members were often criticised for their lack of knowledge of academic affairs.

Second, compared to the formal position and role of the Supervisory Board, the power of the external members of the former University Council was relatively weak. First, the external members were confronted with ambiguity in terms of their roles. Second, the external members quite often had very different backgrounds (from business to education to administration). Third, the external group of members was always the smallest group on the Council. From the mid-1980s on, this group consisted of four or five members; the internal groups consisted of eight members each. Fourth, the external members did not have – by definition – intrinsic motivations for their points of view, in contrast to the internal members who often had much more at stake.

University B

This University has a long history of experimenting with its governance structure. It had, by Dutch standards, a rather unique governance structure at the beginning of the 1970s that disappeared when the new national Act on University Governance was put into effect in 1970. The new Act did not meet the most radical 'one person, one vote' demands for direct democracy, but it ensured the participation of all university community members in university decision making. The law introduced representative democracy at both the central and the faculty level. Distinct groups (students, academics, support staff, and the 'general public') could directly select or elect their representatives to an assembly or council. These university and faculty councils had important powers regarding the budget, staffing, the curricula and the research programmes.

This democratic structure existed at University B until 1998. At the central level, the main decision making bodies were the Executive Board and the University Council. They ruled the university together ('co-determination'). The Executive Board consisted of three members[9]: the *Rector Magnificus,* who was a member *ex officio,* and two appointed members. The Minister of Education appointed all three members, and the Board reported directly to the Minister. The university community had the right to submit nominations to the Minister. The main powers of the Board concerned policy design, financial advice, building and grounds, personnel matters, and policy execution. The University Council consisted of 25 members from the university community: at least one-third were academics, a maximum of one-third were support staff, and a maximum of one-third were students. The number of council members could be increased by including a maximum of five external lay members. All members, except the lay members, were elected by and from the university community. Members served for at least a two-year term, except for students who served for one year. The University Council had the final say with respect to the budget, institutional plans, annual reports, academic procedures, and the university's rules and regulations. At the faculty level, the main bodies – besides two standing committees (the research committee and the education committee) – were the Faculty Board and the Faculty Council. The roles of the Faculty Board and the Faculty Council, as well as the relationship between them, were analogous to the board and council at the central level. At the basic unit level – the third level of the pre-1998 governance structure in the university – the *vakgroep* (department) was the most important governing body. *Vakgroepen* were small clusters of professors and staff working in the same discipline area (they also included non-academic staff and students). The main function of the *vakgroep* was the management of study and research programmes.

Beginning in 1989, the Executive Board of University B took steps to improve the working of the governance structure of the university. The Board asked the minister to give it permission to develop a 'status aparte': a governance structure that would deviate from the national law in certain respects. The minister refused this request because at that time he was working on alternative designs for all universities' governance structures. In the following years the Executive Board made various proposals to change the governance structure of University B, but the University Council, who had the final say over these kinds of changes, turned down all proposals.

The 1997 Act incorporated a fundamental change in university governance. Many elements of the new Act were in line with ideas expressed by the Executive Board of University B in the early 1990s. The University Council, however, strongly opposed the new Act. Consequently, from the start of the introduction of the new governance structure at University B, the Executive Board and the University Council had very different views on this subject, creating many conflict situations.

After the turmoil caused by the implementation of the 1997 Act, the main governing bodies at the central level of University B include, first, the *Raad van Toezicht* (Supervisory Board or 'Board of Trustees'), consisting of five external members appointed by the minister. Its main functions are the supervision of governance and administration matters, and the approval of strategic documents. It is accountable to the Minister. The second body is the *College van Bestuur* (Executive Board), consisting of three members including the *Rector Magnificus*. The Supervisory Board appoints all members of the Executive Board following consultation with the Deans. The third body is the *College van Promoties* ('Doctoral Degree Board'), consisting of the Deans and the Rector, who is the chair. This board has legal authority with respect to the right to grant doctoral degrees. Fourth, the *Raad van Advies* (Advisory Council) is an advisory body to the Executive Board with respect to strategic issues. This Advisory Council consists of approximately ten members from outside the university, appointed by the Executive Board. The fifth body is the powerful University Management-team. Unlike University A, University B decided to form a Management-team consisting of all Deans and the members of the Executive Board. This team, where central and faculty level actors meet on a monthly basis, is important because most of the main decisions are discussed here. Though it has no formal decision-making powers, the 'code of conduct' at University B is that both the Executive Board and the Deans are committed to the outcomes of the Management-team discussions.

In 1998, University B introduced the divided system of participation in decision-making for students and employees. This meant that, at the central level, there was a representative Advisory Council for Students (*Centrale Studentenraad* / CSR) and a representative 'Works Council' for employees (*Centrale Ondernemingsraad* / COR). These two advisory bodies met together every now and then in the so-called Joint Meeting (*Gezamenlijke Vergadering*). The CSR had nine student members; the COR had thirteen members (more or less one per faculty). The CSR and COR had the right to make proposals, the right to provide advice with respect to the budget and any proposed reorganisation, and the right of approval over the strategic plan, the system of quality assurance, labour conditions (COR only), personnel policies (COR only), and student ordinances (CSR only). In 1999 University B made the surprising decision to change its participation system from a divided council structure into an undivided or unified structure.

The most powerful officeholder at the faculty level is the Dean who is appointed by the Executive Board for what is normally a fixed, five-year term. In comparison to the old situation at University B, the new arrangement involves the professionalisation of the dean-function. The Dean is responsible for all faculty matters. He or she has far-reaching authority with respect to teaching, research, and administrative matters. The Dean is accountable to the Executive Board.

Every Dean appoints an *Opleidingsdirecteur* (education director), whose appointment has to be approved by the Executive Board. This education director co-ordinates all activities related to the teaching programmes (e.g. evaluation of courses, curriculum development). In addition, there are the Programme Committees (one for each programme) at the faculty level, consisting of 50 % students and 50 % academics with all members appointed by the Dean. These standing committees advise (and negotiate with) the Dean on curricula and examination regulations, and the implementation of these regulations.

Each Dean at University B has created a faculty management-team. The composition and tasks of these management-teams differ by faculty. Most of these teams consist of the Dean, the education director, a research director and an administrative director. These management-teams rarely include student members.

Involvement of external stakeholders in internal processes at University B
Over the years, individuals from outside the university participated in the decision-making processes at University B in a number of ways. However, the introduction of the Supervisory Board represented the first direct, formal involvement of external stakeholders in the internal governance of the university. Until 1998, external stakeholders did not directly interfere in the university's affairs. Generally speaking, they had an advisory role, discussing strategic issues from a distance. This was certainly not a structure that involved some form of 'lay dominion'.

The regime of the University Governance Acts from 1971 to 1997 allowed for lay members on the University Councils. In the period from 1980 till 1997, about five of the total of 30 seats on the University Council of University B were held by lay members. Additionally, individuals from outside the university participated in Governing Boards of research institutes and in Advisory Councils at the faculty level with respect to research.

An 'Advisory Council' was created at the central level in 1996. This Council offers advice to the Executive Board with respect to strategic issues, and consists of 10–14 members (representatives from multinationals, politicians, and senior civil servants).

As mentioned above, the new Act on university governance introduced the Supervisory Board (*Raad van Toezicht*). This Board, whose members represent external stakeholders, consists of five individuals coming from industry or the public sector (for example, former politicians). Since this board was only created in 1997, it is not yet possible to provide a detailed assessment of its function and role in the university's policy-making process.

What is interesting is that at University B the adaptation of the governance structure was not an attempt to continue the governance tradition of the institution developed since the 1960s in the framework of the new Act, as was the approach of University A. Instead University B tried to introduce rather fundamental innovations in its governance structure. This process, that confronted internal resistance, still continues.

6. ORGANISATIONAL CHANGE STRATEGIES OF THE DUTCH UNIVERSITIES

While the universities collectively managed to have the proposed regulative regime concerning their governance structures redefined in the period 1995–1997, this did not imply that the individual institutional responses were identical. As illustrated by the two case studies, individual universities have dealt differently with the choices provided for by the 1997 Law. While the 1997 Law created the same institutional pressures on all universities (at least on the ten public universities), the university strategies for responding to these pressures differed.

The Dutch social context and traditions (Maassen 2000: 450 – 451) provide a frame within which the *defiance* and *manipulation* strategies, as well as the *acquiescence* strategy are rare for universities to use in any case of changing regulative regimes. Establishing a period for experimentation and consultation, built into most lawmaking processes, takes away the sharp edges of possibly differing views and positions in the interactions between the lawmaker and (in this case) the universities. Therefore, it comes as no surprise that the strategies used most by Dutch universities are *compromising* and *avoiding*. The Dutch practice of experimentation and consultation stimulates the reaching of compromises, both with external lawmakers as well as internally, through the implementation of externally reached compromises, to which, in general, all parties involved feel committed. This commitment implies that passively conforming to external pressure is unusual and rare.

In situations of (serious) conflict between the reached compromise and internal objectives and expectations, the strategy of avoidance seems to be preferred over openly defying or manipulating the compromise position. This implies, in the case of Dutch universities, blocking parts of the organisation from the impact of external pressure, or engaging in symbolic behaviour, for example, by creating new bodies or structures that are supposed to deal with the external pressures or demands, without affecting the rest of the organisation.

The university cases presented above offer interesting examples of both strategies. How do institutions balance the external pressures and demands with the internal expectations and objectives? University A has a strong tradition of internal democracy. It is a university with a relatively limited history of involving external stakeholders in internal governance affairs. The 'harmony model' that allowed the various internal interest groups to participate in the discussions, and to some extent the decision-making, of the Executive Board is an example of this. When it was introduced, the internal groups decided to exclude the external stakeholders. This model created an internal conflict when the university had to balance the external demands concerning the 'new-style University Council' with the internal expectations of continuing the harmony model. The strategy this university utilized was a combination of internal compromise (two-year covenant) and external avoidance. The latter implies disguising non-conformity by not openly formalising or continuing the harmony model, but, by creating a covenant, allowing democratic participation to continue by blocking it from the impact of the 1997 Act demands.

University B has a tradition of involving external stakeholders in its internal affairs. While it has, like all Dutch universities, a thirty year democratic history, its internal expectations and objectives were somewhat different compared to those at University A. Therefore, unlike University A, University B could introduce a university management-team, initially introduce a divided central council structure, and install a Supervisory Board with a strong business orientation. However, University B is also part of the Dutch higher education system and it carefully monitors the decisions and developments at the other Dutch universities. The desire to be in line with the other universities was one of the reasons for deciding to integrate the two separate central councils, in addition to the need to seek internally for compromises in the introduction of governance innovations. As such, the strategy employed by this university can be interpreted as a combination of internal compromise and external conforming and compromising.

Oliver's five strategies offer a useful tool for analysing the responses of organisations that operate in one organisational field when it comes to understanding how they deal with changes in regulative regimes that apply to the field as a whole. More research is needed to further investigate these kinds of responses. In addition to regulative changes, normative and cognitive changes leading to institutional pressures for organisations in one field, e.g. universities, should also be examined. It would be interesting to see empirically in what ways Oliver's strategies also apply to institutional changes other than regulative ones.

7. CONCLUSION

The attempts of the Dutch Ministry of Education to modify the university governance structures were based on the conviction that the universities should be more responsive to the needs of society. How better to do that than to involve society more directly into the university's internal affairs? The 1997 Law on University Governance provided for a stronger involvement of external stakeholders. The universities' responses to the Law did not initially consist of conforming to these provisions, nor did it involve defying or manipulating these provisions. The Law itself can be seen as a compromise between the collective body of universities and the minister of Education, while the universities' implementation of the Law can be regarded as consisting of internal compromise and external compromise and avoidance.

The two case studies provide examples of how university realities interact with external pressures in organisational change processes. As was indicated by the universities in their reaction to the 1995 Law proposal, institutional governance practices had already changed in the preceding years. The changes were in-line with the direction that the minister wanted the institutional governance structures to move. However, factors such as the history and culture(s) of the institution, the governance traditions, the size and complexity of the institutions, as well as the personalities of the main individual leaders in charge at that time, all played a role in shaping the new institutional governance structures before 1995 (before the Law proposal was introduced), in the period 1995–1997 (before the Act on University Governance was passed by Parliament), and after 1997 (during the implementation of the 1997 Act). Analysed at the institutional level, this resulted in a diversified pattern of new governance structures. For example, the degree to which the democratic nature of the governance structures has been altered is not the same in all universities. Some, such as University A presented in this chapter, have managed to largely continue their democratic practices and traditions through, among other things, avoidance strategies. Others, such as University B, have changed much more in-line with the intentions of the Law. They have attempted to introduce strong decision-making bodies, dominated by new-style managers, such as professional deans, and provided for the involvement of students and staff in decision-making mainly through advisory bodies.

However, when analysed at the system level, there is also an overall pattern. The outcome of these changes to-date is that, in general, institutional governance has become more centralised, implying that in a number of respects the democratic nature of the internal university governance structures has decreased. The University Councils have changed from control to advisory bodies; the involvement of support staff and students in university decision-making is reduced; and the position of some individual actors, especially Deans, has been strengthened.

The governance of universities has been an issue of discussion since their establishment. Throughout the centuries there have been smaller and larger shifts between emphasising internal academic interests and external socio-economic and political interests in university governance structures. Universities have been very successful in handling these shifts. Even in cases of rather radical external pressure for change, like in the 1960s, universities have managed to handle the external pressures in such a way that the governance structure could continue to act as a buffer between internal and external interests. The above case studies provide a glimpse of how two Dutch universities responded to external pressures and adapted their governance structures in the direction of the external interests. It is too early to tell whether these adaptations are merely examples of the wave-like adaptive power of the university when it comes to governance matters, or whether the university, as many observers suggest, must now make the revolutionary change of having internal academic interests subservient to external interests.

NOTES

[1] Olsen (2000) prefers to use the term pact over contract because pact refers to a long-term relationship that is based on general principles while contract is argued to refer to a short-term assessment of self-interests.

[2] For an analytical reflection on the underlying issues, see, for example, CPB/CHEPS, 2001.

[3] For an overview of the developments since the 1960s with respect to the Dutch university governance structure, see the chapter by De Boer in this volume.

[4] In this section I have focused mainly on the notion of extra-university involvement in intra-university governance structures. For a more general reflection on the development of the university governance structure see the chapter by De Boer in this volume.

[5] This Board continues in practice to exist of three members appointed by the new *Raad van Toezicht* (Supervisory Board). The members are the president, the *Rector Magnificus*, and a third member sometimes referred to as vice-president. However, the 1997 Act prescribes only that the university executive board should consist of a maximum of three people. It is up to the Supervisory Board to decide whether they want to appoint three persons or less. There is even an experimental provision in the 1997 Act allowing universities to have executive boards of more than three persons. However, if a Supervisory Board intends to create an executive board of more than three persons it needs to obtain permission from the minister of Education.

[6] The position of the dean is strengthening. In practice it can be argued that the 1997 Act introduced professional deans in Dutch universities. While the Act allows the selection of external candidates for a dean position, in practice nearly all deans are internal candidates.

[7] This question was raised by Lynn Meek at the seminar in Pinhão (14 – 16 October 2001) during which the papers forming the basis for the chapters in this volume were discussed.

[8] The sections on University A and B are based on internal CHEPS case study reports produced for the TSER/HEINE project. The report on University A was written by J. Huisman, the report on University B by H. de Boer.
[9] In fact, this was the situation after the introduction of the 1986 Act. Until 1986 the executive board of University B had five members.

REFERENCES

Castells, M. *The rise of the network society*. Oxford: Blackwell, 1996.
Clark, B.R. *Creating Entrepreneurial Universities. Organizational Pathways to Transformation*. Oxford: Pergamon, 1998.
CPB/CHEPS. *Higher education reform; getting the incentives right*. SDU: Den Haag, 2001.
De Boer, H., B. Denters and L. Goedegebuure. "On boards and councils; shaky balances considered. The governance of Dutch universities." *Higher Education Policy* 11 (1998): 153 – 164.
De Boer, H., P. Maassen and E. de Weert. "The troublesome Dutch university and its Route 66 towards a new governance structure." *Higher Education Policy* 12 (1999): 329 – 342.
Gornitzka, Å. and P. Maassen. "The economy, higher education, and European integration: an introduction." *Higher Education Policy* 13 (2000a): 217 – 225.
Gornitzka, Å. and P. Maassen. "Hybrid steering approaches with respect to European higher education." *Higher Education Policy* 13 (2000b): 267 – 285.
Gumport, P. "Academic restructuring: Organizational change and institutional imperatives." *Higher Education* 39 (2000): 67 – 91.
Jongbloed, B., P. Maassen, and G. Neave (eds). *From the Eye of the Storm. Higher Education's Changing Institution*. Dordrecht: Kluwer Academic Publishers, 1999.
Kickert, W. "Afstandelijker besturing van het wetenschappelijk onderwijs?" *Universiteit en Hogeschool* 32 (1986): 185 – 202.
Maassen, P. *Governmental steering and the academic culture. The intangibility of the human factor in Dutch and German universities*. Utrecht: De Tijdstroom, 1996.
Maassen, P. "The Changing Roles of Stakeholders in Dutch University Governance." *European Journal of Education* 35 (2000): 449 – 464.
Maassen, P. and N. Cloete. "Global reform trends in higher education." In: N. Cloete et al. (eds). *Transformation in Higher Education. Global Pressures and Local Realities in South Africa*. Lansdowne, S.A.: Juta and Company (2002): 13 – 58.
Maassen, P. and F. van Vught. "An intriguing Janus-head. The two faces of the new governmental strategy for higher education in the Netherlands." *European Journal of Education* 23 (1988): 65 – 76.
Maassen, P. and F. van Vught (eds). *Dutch higher education in transition*. Culemborg: LEMMA, 1989.
Meyer, J.W. and B. Rowan. "Institutionalized organizations: formal structure as myth and ceremony." *American Journal of Sociology* 83 (1977): 340 – 363.
Oliver, C. "Strategic responses to institutional processes." *Academy of Management Review* 16 (1991): 145 – 179.
Olsen, J. *Organisering og styring av universiteter. En kommentar til Mjøs-utvalgets reformforslag*. Oslo: ARENA Working Paper WP 00/20, 2000. (www.arena.uio.no/nor_publications/wp00_20.htm)
Scott, W.R. "The adolescence of institutional theory." *Administrative Science Quarterly* 32 (1987): 493 – 511.
Scott, W.R. *Institutions and Organizations*. Thousand Oaks, CA: Sage Publications, 1995.
Slaughter, S. and L. Leslie. *Academic Capitalism*. Baltimore: John Hopkins, 1997.
Zucker, L. (ed). *Institutional Patterns and Organizations: Culture and environment*. Cambridge, MA: Ballinger, 1988.

HARRY DE BOER

TRUST, THE ESSENCE OF GOVERNANCE?

1. MANAGED UNIVERSITIES?

In this first decade of the twenty-first century, universities seem to be caught up in grand contradictions (Clark 1998: 146). They have, for instance, to do more and more with less money, to maintain the expanding cultural heritage with the best of the past and at the same time quickly and flexibly develop new fields of study and modes of thought, and to respond to everyone's demands because all are 'stakeholders'. It is, however, not only the 'angry world outside' that puts pressure on universities, but also the dynamics of science itself, with its accelerating pace of knowledge growth, specialization and reconfiguration. To deal with these contradictions, problems and tensions, or if one likes to dramatize, to survive in the increasingly tight and competitive world of higher education, universities should have an organisational structure that is able to swiftly respond to this rapidly changing environment. Most of us would tend to agree with this conclusion, but then what should the university decision making structure look like? There are, and have always been, significant differences of opinion on the answer to this question.

Advocates of what might be broadly termed neo-liberal ideologies towards the public sector (new public management, managerialism and the like), argue that responsiveness, adaptiveness, entrepreneurialism and flexibility are essential strategies for organisations, both public and private, to survive in turbulent times and situations. They believe that traditional models of university governance, such as the British and Continental models (Clark 1983), have become obsolete and unfit for rapidly changing environments. They believe that a fundamental change is needed in the way universities are run.

In several Continental and Anglo-Saxon countries, these ideologies actually took root.[1] The new rules of institutional governance and management differ, of course, from one country to another, but most reforms amounted to strengthening the executive leadership at the central institutional and faculty levels vis-à-vis a diminishing of powers of senates, councils and assemblies where elected members usually represent staff and students. Broadly speaking, these changes have been based on the assumption that decision making authority within universities should be less dispersed and should be in the hands of those who are 'qualified to rule' (see De Boer and Denters 1999). In terms of the new public management rhetoric, university executives should have the 'right to manage'.

It goes without saying that these kinds of developments create tensions within universities. Some, particularly executives and managers, have welcomed the changes, assuming that they gain power. Others, mainly academics and students,

Alberto Amaral, Glen A. Jones and Berit Karseth (eds.), Governing Higher Education: National Perspectives on Institutional Governance, 43—61.
© 2002 *Kluwer Academic Publishers. Printed in the Netherlands.*

have been less enthusiastic. They argue that the centralization and concentration of power reduces their opportunity to participate in (strategic) decision-making, which may have negative implications for the university's viability. Bypassing academics and students may impact on both the quality of decisions and the university's capacity to implement of policy. Are they right? And if so, what are the implications?

In this chapter I will address the governing structure of the 'managed university', a structure that, compared to previous university regimes, is characterized by executive leadership and the concentration of authority (at the expense of the professional's role in decision-making), by instrumental rationality, stressing the 3 E-s of efficiency, effectiveness and economy, and by top-down decision-making (or centralization). A university governance structure, as such, is regarded as a set of rules concerning authority and power related to the performance of a university's activities directed towards a set of common goals. It reflects the ways in which an organisation divides and integrates responsibility and authority. The rules refer to prescriptions commonly known and used by organisational members to bring about an orderly set of repetitive, interdependent relationships inside an organisation.

The concept of hierarchy will be used to reflect on the new internal order of universities in many Western European and Anglo-Saxon countries that exude an atmosphere of tight forms of surveillance and control in which self-management, at the various levels, is significantly reduced. Following Miller's insightful line of reasoning in his book *Managerial Dilemmas, The Political Economy of Hierarchy*, I will use this concept to elucidate some of the managerial dilemmas that universities will encounter if they rush towards a model of governance and management that the more advanced and enlightened business corporations are rejecting and moving away from. The core managerial problems that are discussed in the next section evolve out of tensions between the individual self-interest of organisational members and collective efficiency (Miller 1992).

University governance and management in the Netherlands will serve as an example of a 'managed university'. In 1997, the Dutch government enforced a new organisational design for universities in which appointed executives seem to have 'the right to manage' without many opportunities for staff and students to play a decisive and effective role in university decision-making. Recent experiences with this new structure will be analysed in terms of the managerial dilemmas described below.

2. MANAGERIAL DILEMMAS

Coase, in his famous 1937 article "The Nature of the Firm," argued that transaction costs determine the degree of efficiency of an organising principle. Transaction costs are those costs associated with negotiating, monitoring and enforcing agreements, and rational actors will try to reduce such costs. In the ideal market the price of a good or service functions as a perfect carrier of information and, consequently, transaction costs are marginal. In a perfect market these costs only happen when conflicts arise, and an arbiter is needed to solve the dispute. However, market imperfections like externalities, information asymmetries or market concentrations increase the transaction costs and this leads to a loss of efficiency. By introducing new lines of authority the transaction costs can be reduced and, consequently, a hierarchy may reduce inefficiency. Basically, hierarchies exist because of market failures.

There is, however, a price associated with hierarchy (Miller 1992). In a hierarchy there is a tension between individual freedom and liberty on the one hand and group efficiency on the other hand. To 'solve' social dilemmas, such as the well-known prisoner's dilemma[2], actors may choose to increase collective efficiency by becoming organised in hierarchies (with 'binding decisions forced upon subordinates'). This is the core tension between efficiency and freedom, and this tension is a central theme in the debate over higher education governance where university executives and managers promote greater efficiency for the university as a whole and academics treasure their academic freedom.

There are also other problems associated with a hierarchical structure; problems that exist because information asymmetries do not simply disappear with the introduction of a hierarchy, a point I will demonstrate below.

Take, for argument's sake[3], the most extreme hierarchy – a dictatorship, where power is centralized and concentrated in one actor – as a point of departure. It seems that such a hierarchy is beneficial in terms of efficiency, coherence and consistency. But, as Machiavelli noted, even an absolute prince needs accurate information and advice from others (Miller 1992: 77). Dictators are also subject to the concept of bounded rationality. Consequently, (benevolent) dictators who want to establish and select the best alternative require advice and information, and this leads to a dependency on those who possess information and expertise.

Suppose that an almighty university president has two advisors, an academic and a student, and that each have a 0.6 probability of making the right decision. Thus, the president has a 0.6 chance of being right, if he does not listen to his advisors. However, if the president is willing to make the decision by majority rule and asks the academic and student to express their true opinions, then the probability of choosing the right answer will increase by nearly 5 percent. A good decision will be made if all three are right ($(0.6)^3 = 0.216$), or if any two are right ($(0.6)^2 (0.4)$ x 3 = 0.432). The probability of making the right decision is then $0.216 + 0.432 = 0.648$, which is 4.8 percent better than the probability of the president making the right decision alone. If the two advisors are real experts and have, for instance, a 0.8 probability of making the right choice – and the president still has a 0.6 chance – then in 83 per cent of the cases the right decision can be made by majority rule, which is an improvement of 23 per cent.

The implications for hierarchies are that those units or individuals that have knowledge and expertise will not only be asked to utilize this expertise, but will increasingly manage to secure a share of the decision-making power. The relationship between the decision-maker and the expert is one of dependence and this dependence is related to power. Dependence is based on two dimensions: 1) the availability of alternatives from which similar outcomes may be obtained, and 2) the importance of the outcomes at stake (Bacharach et al., 1999). Delegation of decision-making becomes inevitable within a hierarchical structure (under the 'rational' assumption that the best alternative should be selected) and, as a consequence of a dependency on expertise, knowledge becomes a political resource or power base. This is obviously a well-known phenomenon within universities. Because of the dependence on the highly specialized knowledge of the 'shop floor' that is required for strategic planning for teaching and research and that is hard to come by elsewhere (thus no alternatives to acquire indispensable information), universities are generally characterized as highly fragmented organisations with significant diffusion of decision-making power.

The delegation of authority to those who possess valuable knowledge is not a problem as long as the experts use their expertise to further the interests of the organisation as a whole. But what happens if experts located throughout the organisation have very different opinions? And why shouldn't experts pursue their own interests, which may be incongruent with the interests of the organisation? If experts have the opportunity to pursue their own interests, then inefficiency for the collective may be the result. Since it is needed in the decision making process, expertise becomes a source of power, but at the same time it is a seedbed for conflicts of interests. One way to deal with these kinds of conflict is to shape and mould the preferences of individual actors into patterns that are mutually consistent. This is what a hierarchy tries to do (Miller 1992: 94).

Selection and socialisation are normally used to establish coherent group preferences, that is, you select or train actors that have compatible preferences in order to avoid, or minimize, conflict. It means that you try to get 'people that are made of the right stuff'. However, this usually addresses only part of the problem, because selection and socialization take place primarily at the lower levels of the organisation. The conflicts between the various units do not disappear, in fact, the danger for tribal warfare is real. Politicisation frequently decreases efficiency, consistency and coherence. This raises the question of whether an organisational structure, or incentive scheme, that reconciles aspects of decentralization, coherence, and efficiency actually exists.

Ideally, one would introduce an 'invisible hand' to stimulate experts to use their knowledge to advance the organisation's goals. But, as in markets, information asymmetries, externalities and power concentrations create problems in terms of efficiency. It is possible, according to Miller (1992), to construct a perfect hierarchical structure in the absence of asymmetries, externalities and monopolies, but this tells us only that hierarchies work well under the same conditions that promote market efficiency!

Agency and related theories have stressed information problems, such as hidden action and hidden information, in relationships between principals and agents. Hidden action, or moral hazard, implies the ability of a relatively risk averse actor to hide risk-increasing action. Some activities cannot be monitored, or are associated with high monitor costs, a situation that obviously decreases efficiency, as the Coase theorem demonstrates. The problem of hidden information is even more serious. Principals need information from agents in order to set goals and expectations for these agents, and this, of course, gives agents a potential source of power that can be used strategically. To elicit valuable information that is hard to get from agents requires substantial effort and resources. This is usually not in the principal's interest.

Theoretically, it is possible to design an incentive structure that restrains agents from shirking. There are 'demand revealing' or 'incentive compliance' systems that represent strategies for inducing agents to reveal true preferences (Miller 1992: 145). However, information and incentive problems are associated with principals as well as agents. Principals may choose inefficient structures because these structures contribute more to their interests than efficient arrangements. Self-interested principals may sacrifice efficiency even if they possess the accurate information necessary to develop 'optimal' solutions. Agents know this, and they have no reason to trust that principals with accurate information will do the right thing. Efficient incentive schemes for agents require superiors who deny their own self-interest. In Miller's elegant words:

> From this perspective, organizational efficiency requires that the manager be a philosopher-king who can be content with an efficient kingdom even though his court is less regal than those of more acquisitive neighboring lords. An attempt by the king to squeeze the last surplus out of the kingdom for his own use will induce his subjects to hide their gold rather than invest it and to shirk rather than work productively to produce revenue that the king will only take away. (Miller 1992: 155).

It is clear that a hierarchy may face the same kinds of problems as a market. However, the advantage of a hierarchy is that it provides an explicit setting for establishing long-term cooperative relationships. Principal-agent relationships in a hierarchy can be seen as a chain of repeated games. Cooperation becomes possible because of this repetition, which creates opportunities to develop common knowledge, social norms and reciprocity based on tit-for-tat strategies (that is, each actor will stop cooperating as soon as the other cheats, even though cooperation is beneficial to both actors in the long run). One way to establish common knowledge, conventions or organisational norms and values is joint decision-making where the principal and (representatives of) agents meet regularly. Joint decision-making can provide a forum for establishing commitment and trust via the exchange of intentions and information. The sharing of centralized decision-making power with employee representatives is, according to Miller (1992: 225), one of the best ways to establish and maintain commitment and trust.

Good management implies, in other words, executives who are able to make credible commitments to resist their own temptation to violate the trust of organisational members. At the same time they must encourage others to transcend self-interested behaviour. Communication, reputation building and the creation of trust are therefore essential. Arrow (1974: 23) sees trust as an important lubricant of social systems. It is extremely efficient, because it means that actors can make decisions that assume a fair degree of reliance on other actors, institutions or systems. It enables transactions to occur more easily and efficiently than if it were absent (Ruscio 1996: 463). In other words, transaction costs are low.

Trust, however, is a complicated concept. It is beyond the scope of this chapter to discuss this multidimensional concept in detail[4], but I will briefly review some aspects of this idea in the next section.

3. TRUST

Trust is a complex phenomenon that is defined and interpreted in different ways (Kramer and Tyler 1996, Misztal 1996, Lane 1998). First, there is calculative or instrumental trust that involves expectations about another, based on a computation of costs and benefits. This way of understanding trust assumes a rational choice perspective. This is, in effect, the perspective used by Miller (1992) that I explored in the previous section. Second, there is norm-based trust. In this view the moral aspect of trust is given primary emphasis. Trust comes out of shared values and norms. Reed (2001: 201), for example, views trust "as a coordinating mechanism based on shared moral values and norms supporting collective action within uncertain environments." Parsons's name is frequently invoked in discussions of this kind of trust. Third, common cognitions are seen as the basis of trust. Here cognitions are regarded as being embodied in the expectations actors hold about the social order in general and about specific interactions with others (Lane 1998: 10). This is a kind of expectations-based trust. Each of these different ways of defining trust can contribute to our understanding of this notion. Trust is, as Misztal (1996) argues, a multidimensional concept that consists of a mixture of interests, reasons and values. No matter how it is defined, trust facilitates stability, cooperation and cohesion.

Zucker (1986), stressing the cognitive content of expectations, makes a different distinction between forms of trust. She speaks of characteristic-based, process-based, and institutional-based trust. Characteristic-based trust rests on social similarity and assumes cultural congruence. The one who trusts and the trustee belong to the same group and have, by and large, the same background. Process-based trust emerges from recurrent transactions ('repeated games'). It entails an incremental process of building trust through the gradual accumulation of knowledge about the other. Institution-based trust relates to formal social structures. This impersonal form of trust generalizes beyond a given transaction and beyond specific sets of exchange partners. It becomes part of the common knowledge of the external world.

Tyler and Degoey (1996) focus on the role of trust in authority relations within managerial settings. Following Barnard's argument in his famous 1938 article "The Functions of the Executive", as Miller (1992) did, they see the willingness of actors to contribute their individual efforts to a co-operative system as an essential element of organisations. This is particularly true if actors are willing to accept decisions more or less voluntarily, because if executives must continually explain and justify their decisions, their ability to manage effectively diminishes. Trust, Tyler and Degoey (1996: 332) argue, plays an important role in facilitating the voluntary acceptance of an executive's decision. The perceived trustworthiness of executives has an impact on the willingness of actors to accept the decisions made by these executives, and it influences whether one feels an obligation to follow organisational rules and laws. This generates what Zucker (1986) calls institution-based trust. Organisational actors are also influenced by the motives attributed to executives. It is not only what they do, but also what they radiate and intend to do that becomes important in this view of trust.

However, Tyler and Degoey (1996) do not deny the instrumental (calculative) concerns of trust. In an organisational setting, the assessment of the decisions taken by the executive in terms of favourability plays an important role in determining trustworthiness. Trustworthiness is linked to each actor's individual beliefs about the likelihood of receiving positive outcomes from interactions with executives. This 'profitability' is based on a belief that an actor will have a reasonable degree of control over outcomes (sharing control) and on the expectation that a desired outcomes will be received. But relational aspects, such as fairness, impartiality and status recognition are also important. In fact, Tyler and Degoey believe that this is the most important dimension of trust. This second model of trust, the relational model, suggests that trust is linked to the sense of identity actors derive from their relationships with executives.

Tyler and Degoey (1996) contrasted the instrumental and relational model of trust in three ways. First, they examined when trust is important. The instrumental model implies that trust is important when one is, or feels, dependent on the organisation. The relational model suggests that trust is important when actors identify with the organisation. Second, they considered how judgements about the behaviour of executives leads to inferences about trustworthiness. The level of satisfaction with the decisions taken by the executives and the actor's assessment of their role in the decision-making process are associated with instrumental trust. If there is relational trust, judgements about the neutrality of executives and the degree to which these authorities treat their subordinates with dignity and respect are considered to be important. Third, they contrasted the way executive competence is understood in each model. The instrumental model suggests simply that performance matters. Trust is related to the capabilities of executives to deal effectively with organisational problems, whereas the relational model stresses the benevolent intentions of the authorities.

The results of Tyler and Degoey's empirical studies on trust in managerial settings are not univocal; they conclude that people's feelings about trust are more social in nature. I would argue that their data suggest that trust is not solely instrumental. In hierarchies, trust has both calculative and relational aspects. One might even push this notion further and argue that relational aspects are part of an actor's calculations, but I will return to the governance and management of universities.

What are the implications of the reforms in university governance given this understanding of hierarchies and trust? In order to address this question I will describe the 'Dutch case' so that it can serve as a good example of a 'modern' university governance reform in the spirit of new public management ideologies.

4. UNIVERSITY GOVERNANCE

4.1. University governance in the Netherlands

The 1960s saw a growing concern in the Netherlands, as elsewhere, about the effectiveness and efficiency of traditional forms of university governance in an era of unprecedented growth of participation in higher education. The academic senates, for instance, were subject to severe criticism. Worries about the effectiveness and efficiency of universities, however, were overshadowed by demands for democratic participation in university decision-making by junior academics, non-academic staff and students. The spirit of this democratic movement left a deep imprint on the new Act of university governance, passed by the Dutch Parliament in 1970 (Daalder 1982).

The new Act – the *Wet op de Universitaire Bestuurshervorming* (WUB) – established powerful councils at the central and faculty level on the basis of functional representation. The University Councils (UC) were composed of a maximum of five-sixths of elected members and a minimum of one-sixth of persons appointed by the Crown to represent the public at large. At least one-third of the elected members were chosen from and by academics (full-time professors and other academics). Students and non-academic staff each held a maximum of one-third of the remaining seats. The maximum total number of seats of a UC was 40.

Members of the UC served for at least two years, except for students who served for only one. The meetings of the councils were public. The chair of the UC was elected by the UC from its members. The UC had a final say in budgetary matters, institutional plans, annual reports, general academic procedures, and the university's internal regulations and rules.

The Executive Board (*college van bestuur* (CvB)) was responsible for the executive function. In most universities, it consisted of five members, one of whom being the rector magnificus. Three members, including the rector, were appointed by the national government for a four-year term (after consultation with deans and the UC). The other two members were elected for a two-year period by the UC. This CvB became responsible for the 'administrative hierarchy' within the university.

The relationship between the UC and the CvB created under the new Act was complicated, and there were many disputes because of a lack of clarity about the authority of the two decision-making bodies and power struggles between them (Polak-Committee 1979; Daalder 1982; De Boer et al., 1998). Basically, the structure in the early 1970s could be typified as a system of representative leadership within which the UC held most of the decision-making power. According to the WUB-Act, the UC had the authority to regulate and administer all matters of the university as a whole, insofar as these were not entrusted by the Act to the CvB. The CvB was in charge of daily management and non-academic matters (buildings, finance, personnel matters, etc.) and had to prepare, publish and execute the decisions taken by the UC.

The WUB-Act was evaluated by the Polak-Committee, which reported in 1979. One of its main concerns was the relationship between the UC and the CvB. For reasons of effectiveness, efficiency and decisiveness, the Committee advised that the powers of the CvB should be increased at the expense of the UC. This advice was followed in the 1980s when the laws concerning the Dutch universities were changed. The new Act on 'university education' (*Wet op het Wetenschappelijk Onderwijs*) in 1986 did not question the raison-d'être of the participatory mode of governance as such, but the balance of powers between the UC and the CvB was shifted to the CvB. Compared with the structure in the 1970s, the formal powers of the elected councils were reduced. From 1986 onwards, all powers were assigned to the CvB, with the exception of those assigned to the UC that were exhaustively detailed in the Act. The governance structure of Dutch universities in the 1980s and early 1990s can be described as a system of 'mixed leadership'; decision-making was supposed to be on the basis of 'co-determination' (De Boer et al., 1998).

There were also changes in the composition of the UC and the CvB. The CvB now consisted of three instead of five persons, i.e. the rector magnificus and two members, all appointed by the minister. A committee of the UC had the right to nominate candidates. The UC had a maximum of 25 members drawn from the university community. Universities with over 20,000 students were allowed to have a UC with 30 seats. The number of seats on the UC could be extended by a maximum of five lay members. Unlike the arrangement in the 1970s, the inclusion of lay members was optional.

This mixed system of university governance was significantly changed in the mid-1990s. In September 1995, the minister sent a preliminary design of a new authority structure to Parliament. In the spring of 1996, the bill was sent to Parliament, which passed it one year later (February/March 1997). The universities had to implement the new governing structure before the end of March 1998.

The 1997 Act (*Modernisering Universitaire Bestuursorganisatie* or "Modernizing universities' governing organisation" referred to as the MUB-Act) implied a fundamental reform in the sense that it changed the pillars of the governance structure. The MUB-Act provided for a form of executive leadership of universities. The system of co-determination by the CvB and the UC was abolished. At the institutional level, nearly all powers regarding both academic and non-academic affairs were assigned to the CvB, which continued to consist of three appointed members (including the rector magnificus). The CvB-members are now appointed by and accountable to a new supervisory body, the *Raad van Toezicht* (a lay body of five persons appointed by, and accountable to the minister).

The representative councils were retained but lost most of their former power and became mainly advisory bodies. 'Mainly' in that, aside from their advisory role, the UCs have some additional powers. The UCs must, for instance, approve 1) the biannual institutional plan (strategic policy document), 2) the university's ordinances, and 3) rules regarding safety, health and well-being. Hence, the UC should be seen as a 'heavily equipped advisory council'; it is more than just an advisory body, but it no longer has decision-making powers. Moreover, the composition of the councils changed. The principle of '*Drittelparität*' was replaced by the notion of fifty-fifty parity. The basic principle is that the new councils equally represent employees (academics and non-academics) and students.

Besides this principle, the MUB-Act offers different options that universities can choose from regarding the 'council structure'. The first is the 'divided structure' in which there are two separate councils: one for employees and one for students. The Employee Council and the Student Council come together in a 'Joint Meeting' with respect to particular issues. The size of the two councils may differ, but in the Joint Meeting parity is obtained by weighting votes. Alternatively, universities may decide to choose a unified structure where there is only one council, made up of employees and students, each having half the seats. Eight universities decided to have a unified structure, while five opted for the dual structure. Soon after the reforms, six universities had a divided structure. One of these, the University of Twente, decided to change its council structure after two years from a divided structure to a unified structure.

De Boer and Denters (1999: 230) conclude that, compared with the previous regime, the contemporary university governance arrangement can be characterized as "a guardianship having a monocentric, monocephalic and 'centralized' constitution." Guardianship resembles many features of a hierarchy (Dahl 1989).

4.2. Experiences with the "managed university"

The minister required each university to submit an evaluative report on the new governance structures resulting from the MUB-Act by July 2001. This relatively light form of evaluation, supervised by the 'Franse-committee', was meant to inform Parliament about the choices made by universities, the current state of governance arrangements, and the experience of the first four years of the MUB-regime. The Franse-committee prescribed a format for the review, and each institution was required to report on at least four main elements of the MUB-Act:

1. The integration of governance and management authority ('comprehensive' management, i.e. a monocephalic instead of a bicephalic structure);
2. Transparency of authority relationships (in terms of responsibility and accountability);
3. Significant participation;
4. Decisiveness and effectiveness of decision-making.[5]

Nearly all parties regard abandoning the separation of responsibilities for academic affairs, on the one hand and non-academic affairs, on the other – the first element – as a clear improvement. A monocephalic or 'one-headed' structure of authority facilitates policy making in several ways. Some problems, however, seem to exist at the department level. The rationale for the integration of academic and administrative matters in the position of the chair of the department is less obvious and more ambiguous than the reasons for integrating authority at higher levels. The general impression is that the implementation of this reform has been more difficult and less clear at the lower levels of the university (Datema-committee 1998; Smit 2001).

The fact that responsibility for policies regarding teaching, research, finance, housing, and personnel are no longer separated, has had, in principle, a positive impact on the transparency (in terms of accountability) of the structure.[6] While not every one is convinced, most of those involved in the evaluation exercise believe that the MUB-reform helped clarify the power relationships inside universities, at least when compared with the previous authority structure. However, some problems still exist.

The first weakness is, once again, found at the department level. The distinction between schools, research institutes and new departments ('capacity groups'), another organisational development facilitated and supported by the MUB-Act, has created ambiguity in the relationships between the heads of schools ('program directors'), the research directors, and the heads of departments. Under the old structure, departments ('*vakgroepen*') could, internally, make decisions on teaching and research matters, programs and the division of labour. Under the new MUB-Act three people – the teaching program director, the scientific research director, and head of the 'new' department – are expected to negotiate with each other regarding the deployment of personnel in relation to teaching and research tasks. In this new setting, frequently referred to as a 'matrix organisation', with new players, not all of the new rules are clear, known, or immediately accepted. In some faculties people act as if traditional departments ('*vakgroepen*') still exist, whereas in other faculties individuals complain and want the old departments back in place.

A second problem regarding the transparency of authority relationships relates to the establishment of so-called "management teams"[7], at both the institutional and the faculty levels. At the institutional level, the CvBs and deans have created management teams (usually consisting of all three CvB-members and all the deans). Management teams were also established at the faculty level, usually comprised of the dean, a vice-dean for teaching matters, a vice-dean for research and sometimes a vice-dean for non-academic matters.[8] The idea is to create a forum to discuss strategic matters, to exchange information, and to create support for institution-wide, or faculty-wide, policies.

Formally, these management teams cannot make decisions, because they lack the legal status to do so. In reality, however, they certainly leave their mark on institutional and faculty decision-making. There are mixed feelings about these informal decision making bodies within the universities. On the positive side, some believe that the management teams at the institutional level have reduced the level of tension between the central administration and the faculties, and, consequently, contributed to greater policy coherence. Communication and cooperation between the institutional level and the faculty level has been a longstanding problem, but it seems that, generally speaking, the establishment of management teams has improved this relationship. There seems to be less of a feeling of 'us' and 'them', though there have been situations that convincingly suggest that these management teams do not guarantee close cooperation between these organisational levels. On the negative side, a frequently expressed complaint is that central management meetings create a 'top-down' atmosphere, whereas two-way communication is desirable. Ideally these meetings were thought of as a place for the mutual exchange of ideas, instead of a place where the executive board unfolds its plans to the deans.

Another consequence of the existence of management teams is that they have obscured the position of councils. Councils seem to be sidelined. It is hard to act firmly in decision-making when important issues have been pre-digested and informally decided upon already in management teams. It takes a real (wo)man to speak out loudly and disagree with policies that are agreed upon by the CvB and all the deans. In other words, executives are seen to present councils with *faits accomplis*. Executives and council-members meet every once in a while as a formal procedural step, while most of the real decision-making has already taken place.

Moreover, management team meetings are not public and they therefore contribute to a political culture where important discussions are perceived to be made in back rooms. The relationship between the *raad van toezicht* ('supervisory board') and the CvB has the same connotation. How these two boards interact and what they discuss with each other is a mystery to the university community. These 'black boxes' do not contribute to the transparency of university decision-making, and do not facilitate or stimulate commitment and involvement from others.

Another point of concern in terms of transparency and efficiency relates to the role and position of the labour unions. Labour unions are represented in a formal standing committee called 'local consultation' (*'lokaal overleg'*).[9] This union committee discusses and negotiates a variety of issues related to conditions of employment with the executive board. The university council[10], however, also has jurisdiction over certain personnel policies and related issues. This means that the executive board may be discussing the same issue twice with representatives of the same constituency, since union members frequently hold seats in the university council. It is obvious that this is an undesirable situation in terms of efficiency and transparency.

The major concern with the new governance structure, however, relates to the third element raised in the evaluation process, that is, the significant participation of the university community in decision-making. It is patently obvious that one of the main problems in contemporary university governance is the lack of involvement and commitment of many constituencies at nearly all levels within the universities. The evaluation reports from the universities suggest that the MUB reform has contributed to this problem. The new modes of participation, or more generally the philosophy of the MUB reform, do not encourage broad involvement and commitment.

The poor turnouts at the elections provide a very clear example of this problem. Participation rates of between 10% and 20% were common in the last student elections. In only a few cases did more than 30% of the students vote. The staff election voting rates were higher, in a range of between 30% and 55%. In several cases, no elections were held because the number of council candidates equalled or was less than the number of seats. In such cases, candidates automatically obtain a position. One of the saddest stories involved a faculty council election held in 2001 where there were more candidates (41, which was exceptionally high) than voters (35, a turnout rate of just under 5%).

Low turnout rates have an impact on the councils' position and image because they cast doubt on the legitimacy of these 'representative' bodies. Whose opinions do they represent? Taking part in decision-making 'on behalf of' the broader community becomes virtually impossible in these circumstances. But there is more at stake than just the issue of legitimacy. Because the level of community interest is low, councils find it difficult to keep their constituencies informed in terms of explaining what they do, what they stand for, and what they achieve.

The problems of communication, interaction and exchange of information are not limited to the relationship between the councils and their constituencies, but also extend to the councils' relationship with the executives (CvB and/or deans). Members of councils frequently complain about poor communication with those that run the university (or faculty), both in a qualitative and a quantitative sense. It is their perception that executives are unwilling to keep councils adequately informed in a timely fashion. It goes without saying that a council is not in the best position to make a useful contribution to university policy-making if communication lines are poor. One of the consequences is that the gap between executives and the university community has grown larger. The distance between staff and students on the one hand, and executives on the other hand, seems to be bigger than ever before.

Another participation issue concerns the composition of the councils, or more precisely, the notion of representation on an equal footing. The fact that, as required by the MUB Act, students have half the seats and all staff (called 'employees') have the other half means that academics normally have fewer seats than students do. And since the academic positions represent all teaching and research staff, it is easy to understand why only a few full professors, for instance, hold a seat on university councils. Perhaps it is surprising that some still do.

Recent data on university council membership illustrate this point. In 2000-2001, the number of seats held by full-time professors varied from zero to three per university. Five of the thirteen universities did not have a single full professor on their university councils, and at another five universities there was only one professor on each council. The number of seats held by professors is around 4% of all the available seats in Dutch university councils (De Boer 2002). According to the MUB Act, a university can theoretically have a university council without academics, but in practice this is not the case. Of a total of 180 'employee seats', 95 are taken by academics (53%). These 95 'academic seats' represent some 31% of all available seats in university councils (compared to students 44%, non-academics 23% and vacancies 4%).

The system of equal representation, together with the reduced powers of councils, seem to mean that academics, and especially senior academics, are not exactly dying to hold a council seat. There are increasing problems in universities in terms of finding and 'recruiting' good candidates for councils and committees. In 2001, thirteen seats on university councils were vacant, which represented 4% of the total. The number of unfilled positions equalled the numbers of seats held by professors! Students also have problems in finding good candidates. Councils seem to enter a 'cycle of frustration' causing a 'cycle of decline' of commitment and involvement; as councils are perceived to be less prestigious, less interesting, and less visible, the more trouble they experience in finding highly qualified representatives, which, in turn, means less prestigious councils, etc.

The final point that I will raise in this section concerns the competencies needed to participate in complex decision-making processes. Are council members adequately equipped to make a useful contribution to university decision-making? There are two types of relevant expertise: specialized knowledge related to the content of the issues, and general knowledge about the art of governing. I believe that academics and students do hold valuable knowledge regarding teaching and research matters. It is the second type of expertise, however, that is frequently referred to in the university evaluation reports on the MUB reform, and the general concern that is raised is that council members, especially students, frequently lack the 'technical' experience and capabilities necessary to contribute to policy discussions with the executives. Given their inexperience and the fact that they serve for a one-year term, this concern may suggest that students are unable to exploit their talents and knowledge without significant orientation and training.

5. THE MANAGED UNIVERSITY AND ITS PROBLEMS

In contrast to the previous governance arrangement, the MUB-structure of universities includes a number of features of a hierarchy, as described in section 4.1. The new chain of responsibility and accountability is a clear illustration of vertical integration. The minister appoints the members of the supervisory board *(raad van toezicht)* who are accountable to the minister. This *raad van toezicht* appoints the members of the CvB, who are accountable to the *raad van toezicht*. The CvB appoints the deans, who are accountable to the CvB. The dean appoints the heads of programs who are accountable to the dean. Coherence, consistency and efficiency should be enhanced by these relationships. But the 'Dutch case' shows that these gains should not be taken for granted.

The frequent meetings of the CvB and the deans to preview institution-wide decisions appear to have contributed to more coherence from the institutional point of view. The CvBs, selecting deans 'of their liking', seem to have succeeded in shaping and moulding the preferences of the deans, who represent the different 'tribes', into patterns that are, by and large, mutually consistent and that facilitate institution-wide policy-making. I do not wish to imply that strategic fights do not take place in this "political power centre" of the managed university. But, the new 'team structure' seems to have created a platform that facilitates mutual understanding and 'corporate' spirit. It is a seedbed for trust.

Deans, however, face new problems. If they cooperate too closely with other deans and the CvB, then the staff will question their legitimacy inside the faculty. In the new structure, deans are in a powerful but delicate position. They must possess a gymnast's sense of balance; in fact, they are always struggling to land safely given their split position! Their position is even more problematic if one realizes that there has never been a clear career track for these positions, or any form of sophisticated training programs for deans in the Netherlands to learn the 'art of governing'.

The 'managed university' – stressing vertical relationships among a minimal number of powerful persons or bodies – has various advantages, which is no surprise since hierarchies have many respected qualities. At the same time, the managerial dilemmas associated with hierarchies described in section 2 cannot be ignored. These dilemmas can only be resolved by establishing 'cultures of trust', in which both executives and employees are willing to abandon the permanent pursuit of self-interest. Based on four years of experience following the reforms of university governance, one is left with the impression that, in general, these 'cultures of trust' do not exist. This is a serious problem because, as I noted in section 3, trust facilitates stability, cooperation and cohesion.

The most striking problem in the 'managed university' concerns the low levels of involvement and commitment of staff and students, and the poor lines of communication and interaction between executives and councils and between councils and their constituencies. Involvement and communication are interrelated, that is, low levels of involvement hamper efficient lines of communication and vice versa, since poor communication does not stimulate participation. As a consequence, valuable information and knowledge may not be available to decision-makers. This decreases the quality of the decision-making process, as I demonstrated in section 2. One can, of course, question the expertise of staff and students in terms of their input to university decision-making. However, it is common knowledge that students and, especially, staff possess valuable knowledge, at least regarding teaching and research. Personnel issues or finance may be different subjects. It is, however, not only expertise in terms of knowledge that counts. Competence is also an important factor, and, as the university evaluation reports suggest, the level of 'technical' expertise in the art of governing possessed by some participants may not always be adequate. This may cause a lack of trust.

Low levels of commitment not only influence the quality of decision-making, but also decrease the level of trust because actors will not have the opportunity to get to know each other. This can easily lead to the emergence of 'different worlds' in which different groups function in isolation from each other, and this, of course, does not increase coherence and consistency. To prevent situations of 'unknown, unloved' in which trust cannot flourish, frequent interaction needs to be established. If not, it will be impossible to create 'characteristic-based trust' or a setting in which shared moral values are important. The risk of increasing incongruence of values and norms, and its consequences for trust building, is serious, especially if we take into account that universities are usually viewed as professional organisations where there are natural tensions between executives and professionals (academics) (Bacharach et al., 1999; Birnbaum 1989)

Low levels of commitment and trust, accompanied by poor lines of communication, do not make it very likely that staff will reveal their true preferences. This means that the agency problems of hidden action and hidden information will be real. The design of tasks and the monitoring of performances will be problematic. The executives remain dependent on the work of academics, no matter what kind of formal structure is in place. One of the unintended consequences of a structure in which the 'see-saw' (Bacharach et al., 1999) gravitates towards executives is that excluded but powerful actors (such as full time professors) will find their way in the informal or grey power structure to protect and pursue their interests.

When one reads the university evaluation reports on the governance reforms, one cannot escape the impression that the executives' intentions and behaviours create suspicion within the universities. Apparently not many 'philosopher-kings' have been spotted among the university executives. It may be that they are around, but I would argue that executives have not succeed in *showing* that they are able and willing to sacrifice 'self-interest' for the sake of the university. In this respect, they did not appear to be too competent. Evidently executives found it difficult to communicate good intentions and proper motives, but considering all the communication problems mentioned in the evaluation reports, this is hardly a surprise. This is problematic, since intentions are as important as outcomes when it comes to building trust (Tyler and Degoey 1996). When their intentions become questioned, the degree to which decisions made by the executives are voluntarily accepted by the university community decreases, and this, in turn, reduces organisational efficiency.

Worries in and around Dutch universities about the lack of trust in the university policy-making process are justified, considering its consequences. A lack of trust may cause agency and legitimacy problems, which are serious problems by themselves. But one of the major concerns is that a lack of trust will lead to exorbitant micromanagement. At the end of the day, a lack of trust "leads to an excessive dependence on rules, formal procedures, regulations, and legalisms". (Ruscio 1996: 463). Flexibility becomes constrained. This is exactly the opposite of what university governance structures should be like if these organisations are to survive in turbulent times (see section 1).

All together, I am not impressed by the efficiency gains of the 'managed university', although the old structure might have been even worse. In assessing efficiency, it is also important to recognize the costs of time and energy that were necessary to implement the new rules of the game. Transaction costs are high in times of transition. In the first year of implementing the MUB-Act a great deal of time was spent on the precise delineation of the authority and responsibility of the various persons and bodies associated with the new structure; there were many meetings, disputes, and negotiations. Moreover, it took a 'bureaucracy' to draft new ordinances and internal procedures. Finally, people obviously needed to invest time getting to know each other in a new, formal setting. They had to learn the new rules of the game, experiencing the teething troubles of new rules-in-action. In other words, it took a substantial amount of time and energy to implement these reforms, and the real efficiency gains will only happen after years, if they happen at all.

6. DISCUSSION

This early snapshot of the 'managed university' in the Netherlands reveals a picture of distrust. The swift and flexible university governance structure remains a sweet dream. However, we must be careful to avoid premature conclusions about the governance reform. There are at least two points that must be made concerning our ability to analyse the picture of reform that emerges from the Dutch case.

The first point is that we need a more accurate understanding of the relationship between the reform and its perceived effects. Is there actually a causal relationship between the MUB and the negative feelings about institutional governance? Is this situation limited to higher education, or is it part of a broader phenomenon? In the Netherlands, for instance, turnout rates in elections for Parliament at the national and other levels have decreased. Low involvement and commitment may be a general 'societal tendency' linked to atomism or consumerism. Did the MUB cause distrust, or was there already distrust within the organisational arrangements of the universities? Elsewhere I argue that several problems related to university governance were also associated with previous governance arrangements (De Boer 2002). This means that we must be cautious in our conclusions about the impact of the governance reforms. However, this observation does not make the problems go away or less real.

The second point is that the degree of actual change may make a difference in how one interprets the outcomes of the reform. There are, as Lanzara (1998) explains, two general strategies to establish new institutions ('rules of the game') when existing ones become obsolete. The first strategy is exploitation and implies the incremental adaptation of an existing structure. It is about learning and fine-tuning. In the world of higher education this strategy is known as 'soft managerialism' (Trow 1994). The second strategy is exploration and means the introduction of a 'complete' new rule structure, referred to in higher education as 'hard managerialism' (Trow 1994). The exploration strategy is more risky, more experimental, more uncertain, and requires patience because outcomes only become clear after the passage of time. Actors tend to favour exploitation strategies because, in Lanzara's words, "people are more willing to do what they know how to do better (...)." In times of uncertainty, unpredictability, insecurity and instability, trust is needed but scarce. Trust may reduce these negative feelings, but at the same time it is extremely hard to establish and maintain it under these circumstances.

The question I want to raise concerns whether the reforms associated with the movement from WUB to MUB actually involved a change in the day-to-day governance practices of the universities. If the reform was really experienced as a big change, then we may hope that the problems will 'solve' as time goes by. A decline in the level of trust could be regarded as a temporary regression. There are, however, indications that the reform may have been a codification of an already existing practice (De Boer et al., 1998). This would mean that the changes were actually less dramatic than they were expected to be. If the reform did not cause much uncertainly or instability, then the distrust discussed above is probably not related to the reform and must have other causes.

The issue of trust in university governance is an important topic for further research. A better understanding of the issue is desirable, as are more empirical studies. In this article, for instance, I attempted to provide a broad picture of university governance reform at all Dutch universities, though it is clear that local differences exist. While they all operate within the same legal framework, some universities, or faculties, have more problems with governance than others. Why? Did some executives succeed in building bridges of trust? How did they do that? A good point of departure to investigate such a topic could be Putnam's famous study *"Making Democracy Work"* in which he analyses why and how one and the same institution functions differently in one country. He reveals patterns of association, trust and cooperation that facilitate good governance and performance. Of course, there are many other intriguing questions regarding the concept of trust. If we want to have a better understanding of 'good governance in higher education', the concept of trust deserves more attention.

NOTES

[1] Changes in the formal governance and management structures of universities have, for instance, taken place in the Scandinavian countries, the United Kingdom, Australia, Austria and the Netherlands (see a special issue of *Higher Education Policy* 11.2/3 (1998))

[2] The key theme in the prisoner's dilemma and related games is that if someone forces the players to not take the alternative that seems individually attractive to each, all players would be better off. Because individual rationality is insufficient, actors try to seek group solutions to their problems – even coercive solutions (Miller 1992: 25 – 6).

[3] I would not dare to suggest that executive officers of universities should be regarded as dictators.

[4] For insightful and comprehensive discussions on this topic see: Kramer and Tyler 1996, Lane and Bachmann 1998, Misztal 1996, and a special issue of *Organization Studies* 22.2 (2001).

[5] It is difficult to present a general overview of this element since opinions differ on how this issue should be understood and defined. This fourth element will be left aside in this paper, just as the minister did when he wrote a letter to Parliament regarding the evaluation in November 2001.

[6] This does not automatically imply that the present structure is perceived as transparent. There are other factors that have an impact on transparency.

[7] These management teams have different names such as 'managerial meeting', 'managerial platform', etc.

[8] There are local variations. Moreover, the MUB-Act provides the opportunity to install a faculty executive board instead of a dean. This board includes the dean (as chair) and has the same powers as the dean when the 'single-headed' option is chosen. The composition of the faculty executive board is by and large comparable with the faculty management teams.

[9] These standing committees are not new; they existed in the previous structure.

[10] Or, in the case of a divided structure, the Employees Council.

REFERENCES

Arrow, K. *The Limits of Organization*. New York: Norton, 1974.

Bacharach, S. B., B. Peter and C.C. Sharon. "Negotiating the 'See-Saw' of Managerial Strategy: A Resurrection of the Study of Professionals in Organizational Study." In *Institutional Management and Change in Higher Education, Unit 2: Management and Decision-Making in Higher Education Institutions*, edited by CHEPS/QSC. Utrecht: Lemma, 1999, 155 – 176.

Barnard, C. I. *The Functions of the Executive*. Cambridge, Mass.: Harvard University Press, 1938.

Birnbaum, R. *How Colleges Work: The Cybernetics of Academic Organization and Leadership*. San Francisco: Jossey-Bass, 1989.

Coase, R. "The Nature of the Firm." *Economica* 4 (1937): 386 – 405.

Daalder, H. "The Netherlands: Universities between the 'New Democracy' and the 'New Management'." in Daalder, H. and E. Shils (eds). *Universities, Politicians and Bureaucrats; Europe and the United States*. Cambridge: University Press, 1982, 173 – 232.

Datema, Committee. "De Kanteling Van Het Universitaire Bestuur (Rapport Van De Klankbordgroep Invoering Mub)." Zoetermeer: Ministerie van Onderwijs, Cultuur en Wetenschappen, 1998.

De Boer, H. "On Nails, Coffins and Councils." *European Journal of Education* 37.1 (2002): 7 – 20.

De Boer, H. and Denters, B. "Analysis of Institutions of University Governance: A Classification Scheme Applied to Postwar Changes in Dutch Higher Education." In Jongbloed, B., P. Maassen and G. Neave. (eds). *From the Eye of the Storm; Higher Education's Changing Institution*. Dordrecht: Kluwer Academic Publishers, 1999, 211 – 233.

De Boer, H., B. Denters and L. Goedegebuure. "On Boards and Councils; Shaky Balances Considered. The Governance of Dutch Universities." *Higher Education Policy* 11.2/3 (1998): 153 - 164.

Dill, D.D and H.K. Peterson. "Faculty Participation in Strategic Policy Making." In Smart, J. C. (ed). *Higher Education: Handbook of Theory and Research*. New York: Agathon Press, 1988, 319 – 355.

Lane, C. "Introduction: Theories and Issues in the Study of Trust." In Lane, C. and R. Bachmann (eds). *Trust within and between Organizations; Conceptual Issues and Empirical Applications*. Oxford: University press, 1998, 1 – 31.

Lane, C. and R. Bachmann (eds). *Trust within and between Organizations: Conceptual Issues and Empirical Applications*. Oxford , New York: Oxford University Press, 1998.

Lanzara, G.F. "Self-Destructive Processes in Institution Building and Some Modest Countervailing Mechanisms." *European Journal of Political Research* 33.1 (1998): 1 – 40.

Polak, Committee. "Gewubd En Gewogen (Tweede Kamer, Zitting 1978-1979, 15 515)." 's-Gravenhage: SDU Uitgeverij, 1979.

Putnam, R.D. *Making Democracy Work; Civic Traditions in Modern Italy.* Princeton, New Jersey: University Press, 1993.

Reed, M.I. "Organization, Trust and Control: A Realist Analysis." *Organization studies* 22.2 (2001): 201 – 228.

Ruscio, K.P. "Trust, Democracy, and Public Management: A Theoretical Argument." *Journal of public administration research and theory* 6.3 (1996): 461 – 477.

Smit, F. (red). *Medezeggenschap Op De Universiteit: Dwangbuis of Maatwerk?* Nijmegen: ITS, 2001.

Trow, M. "Managerialism and the Academic Profession; the Case of England." *Higher Education Policy* 7.2 (1994): 11 – 18.

Tyler, T.R. and P. Degoey. "Trust in Organizational Authorities: The Influence of Motive Attributions on Willingness to Accept Decisions." In Kramer, R. M. and T.R. Tyler (eds). *Trust in Organizations; Frontiers of Theory and Research.* Thousand Oaks: Sage, 1996, 331 – 356.

Zucker, L.G. "Production of Trust: Institutional Resources of Economic Structure, 1840-1920." In Staw, B.M. and L.L. Cummings (eds). *Research in Organizational Behavior.* Greenwich, CT: JAI, 1986, 53 – 111.

CHRISTINE MUSSELIN AND STÉPHANIE MIGNOT-GÉRARD

THE RECENT EVOLUTION OF FRENCH
UNIVERSITIES

1. INTRODUCTION

The French agency for the modernisation of universities[1] (*Agence de Modernisation des Universités et des Etablissements*, AMUE) was created in June 1997 as an expansion of a former structure called GIGUE (*Groupement pour l'Informatique de Gestion des Universités et des Etablissements*). It is in charge of disseminating university management software and offering services to universities in order to improve their management and internal practices. Shortly after its creation, this new agency commissioned a number of research studies aimed at obtaining knowledge of the current state of the French university system. One of these research areas was 'university government' and our centre, the *Centre de Sociologie des Organisations* was chosen to conduct this study. The study involved two large fieldwork projects. In 1998, a qualitative study based on 250 interviews was conducted in four universities with the help of graduate students from Sciences-Po Paris. A comparative report was written (Mignot-Gérard and Musselin 1999) for the AMUE. Drawing on the results of this first study, we designed a questionnaire that was sent to individuals associated with 37 universities in 1999. We received 1660 responses (from 5000 questionnaires sent), about 1100 from academics and 560 from members of the administrative staff (see the methodological appendix at the end of the paper). A second report was written in 2000 and delivered to the AMUE (Mignot-Gérard and Musselin 2000).

These studies provide us with a large body of empirical data on French universities that we can compare with the narrower corpus Friedberg and Musselin (1989) collected on the same topic in the eighties. This comparison clearly reveals that one should not give too much weight to the overwhelming discourse on the 'impossible reform' of French universities[2], on their endemic immovability, and even on the conservative nature of the academic profession. Change has occurred and university government has evolved in France. This does not, of course, mean that all of the problems have been solved, but it does mean that the way we understand change in this system, including the role of various actors and their capacity to influence change, are not the same as they were fifteen years ago. However, before discussing the broader impact of these changes it is important to review the actual changes that have taken place.

In this paper we will briefly describe some of the main changes associated with the French university system in the last decade. We will then highlight the more

Alberto Amaral, Glen A. Jones and Berit Karseth (eds.), Governing Higher Education: National Perspectives on Institutional Governance, 63—85.
© 2002 *Kluwer Academic Publishers. Printed in the Netherlands.*

striking developments in terms of university government by comparing the findings of the qualitative and quantitative studies we recently conducted for AMUE with the results of the study conducted by Friedberg and Musselin in the 1980s. A major conclusion, based on this analysis, is that the previous conception of French universities as a kind of administrative grouping of *facultés* has been modified in favour of a more, cohesive, collective, institutional conception. As in other countries, French reforms have strengthened the university leadership, allowed for the development of strategic plans, and increased the capacity for university self-governance. But, it is important to note that, unlike some other countries, these changes did not result from the implementation of New Public Management or of New Managerialism; there has been no French parallel to the Jarratt report in the United Kingdom, or to the Dutch reforms of university structures designed to foster executive leadership. The process of reform in French higher education is better understood as a transformation of rather anomic universities into institutions with their own identity, perspectives, and dynamics[3]. Given this perspective, we would argue that the level of institutional autonomy of French universities has increased, though there have not been dramatic changes in the relationship between these institutions and the state in terms of their respective responsibilities and functions.

While it is possible to observe evolutionary but profound changes in the French universities, there are still problems that hinder the process of change and limit the capacity of these institutions for self-government, problems that we will discuss in the third and final section of this paper. These are problems that restrain or impede the emergence of more cohesive universities.

2. THE CONTEXT: NO BIG INSTITUTIONAL REFORMS BUT SOME RADICAL CHANGES

The objective of this chapter is to focus on the existence and boundaries of recent evolutionary changes in the French system rather than to provide a detailed explanation of these changes. However, we will highlight three important changes that help to explain the broad evolution of the French university system in the last two decades.

The first involves what has sometimes been described as a 'second massification' (the first one was related to the rising enrolment of students that occurred in the sixties) that French universities experienced between 1988 and 1995, followed by decreasing numbers of entrants. There are about two million students currently enrolled in the French higher education system, 1.5 million of whom are attending university. As Kogan and Hanney (2000) have demonstrated, student expansion is an important factor for change.

The second factor is the increasing role of local authorities. This factor became obvious with the implementation of the University 2000 policy, which was launched at the beginning of the 1990s to improve university facilities and to plan new construction in each region. Local authorities were heavily involved with these initiatives and significantly contributed to the realization of these regional plans. In fact, the role of local authorities in the higher education system was already beginning to shift in the 1980s (Filâtre 1993), despite the fact that the decentralization law of 1982 did not assign any formal responsibility over higher education to the local authorities. Now, with the possible exception of the Parisian region, universities can no longer ignore the communities in which they are located, and they will frequently take steps to strengthen their interactions with and support from their local authorities[4].

The third factor that we will note is that even though no important institutional reforms have been initiated since the 1984 Act, some limited (both in terms of scope and in the public attention they received) policy decisions were made to increase the institutional autonomy of the universities. One of the most important of these changes was the introduction of four-year contracts at the end of the 1980s. In some respects the introduction of contracts was a minor and not very visible change in the university sector, but it led to some radical modifications in terms of weakening the discipline-focused interventions of the ministry and recognizing and strengthening the role of universities as relevant actors within the French higher education system (see Musselin 2001 for a detailed discussion of these changes).

From our point of view, these three developments established the context for changes in French university governance during the last two decades.

3. IMPORTANT CHANGES WITHIN UNIVERSITIES

In comparing the description of French university government provided by Friedberg and Musselin in the 1980s with the findings of our recent work, it is quite obvious that there have been important changes. In fact, most of the characteristics of French university governance stressed in the earlier study are no longer true. In particular, the role of the presidents has evolved, the deliberative bodies no longer prefer to avoid decisions, universities are active in domains they previously ignored or considered 'taboo', and the greater degree of cooperation within the universities allows for the development of collective plans and strategies. Before describing these changes in more detail we will briefly review the structure of French universities under the 1984 act (the Savary Law).

3.1. The structures of French universities according to the 1984 act

Broadly speaking, French universities are organised into *facultés* (called UFR for *Unité de Formation et de Recherche*) that represent part of a discipline (for instance, a UFR of Modern History), a discipline (History) or a set of disciplines (a UFR for Social Sciences).

The university is led by a president. S/he is a an academic, elected for a five year non-renewable term[5] by an assembly composed of all the elected members of the university's three deliberative bodies. The president works with a group (called the *bureau*) whose composition varies by university because it is set by each university's statutes. The president proposes the names of the individuals that she or he would like elected to the bureau.

Each UFR (*faculté*) is led by a dean who is an academic elected by the UFR council for a five-year mandate. The dean's term can be renewed once. The UFRs are frequently subdivided into sections or departments led by section or department heads.

The university's academic leadership interacts with two other structural elements that can be found at both the university and the *facultés* levels.

First, there is an administrative structure led by the *secrétaire général*, an administrator who is a civil servant. There are a number of central administrative units operating at the university level, including units associated with such standard functions as budget, personnel, and pedagogical affairs. In each UFR, there is a UFR administrator, and an administrative staff structure that parallels the central structure (that is, with staff focusing on budget, pedagogical affairs, etc.). There are also administrative staff at the department or section level and in the research institutes.

Second, there is a deliberative structure. There are three deliberative bodies at the university level. Two of these bodies (the *Conseil scientifique*, or Academic Council, and the *Conseil des Etudes et de la Vie Universitaire*, called CEVU or Board of Studies) prepare proposals or recommendations for decisions that are made by the third, the *Conseil d'administration* or Governing board. The CEVU has between 20 and 40 elected members[6]. Academics and students have an equal number of members and, combined, hold between 75 and 80% of CEVU seats. Representatives of the administrative staff hold 10 to 15 % of the seats and the remaining 10 to 15% are filled by 'external personalities'. The CEVU focuses primarily on curricula and issues related to student life on campus. The Academic Council consists of 20 to 40 elected members, with 60 to 80 % being representatives of university staff (with at least half of these seats for professors), and 7.5 to 12.5 % being representatives of the graduate students. External members hold the remaining 10 to 30 % of seats. This body considers policy proposals focusing on research policy and the university budget. The Governing Board is composed of 30 to 60 elected members[7]; 40 to 45% of Board members are academics, 20 to 30 % are external or lay members, 20 to 25 % are students, and 10 to 15 % are administrative staff. The law stipulates that the university statutes must be created with a view to representing all of the disciplines present within the institution. The Governing Board makes policy decisions based on the proposals it receives from the two other bodies, but it primarily focuses on resource issues, especially with budget and position allocations. Each body elects a vice-president (generally proposed by the president, in order to create a cohesive presidential team).

The deliberative body at the faculty level is the *conseil d'UFR* or Faculté council, which includes no more than 40 elected members, 20 to 25 % of which are external members, and the rest of the seats are equally divided between the academics, the students and the administrative staff.

The formal structure of French universities has not been explicitly reformed or modified, but, as we will note below, the way in which this structure functions has changed. Academic leaders are playing a different role, the deliberative bodies are being asked to work together in different ways, and the balance of authority between the various components of this structure appear to be changing. In short, the rules of the game that previously characterized the governance of French universities are being rewritten.

3.2. From reactive to proactive presidents

At the time when Friedberg and Musselin conducted their study on university organisation, the Faure Law of 1968 was about to be replaced by the Savary law (adopted by the French Parliament in 1984). Though it only remained in effect for 16 years, the Faure Law had an important impact on French universities. Before 1968, the French 'university' system was characterized by strong faculties which were led by powerful deans. Most important decisions took place through interactions between the faculties, representing the academics, and the ministry. The central administrative level of the university, a territorial gathering of faculties, under the control of a high-level civil servant called the 'recteur', was relatively weak. The Faure Law abolished the old faculties and favoured the creation of multidisciplinary universities led by an elected president, who was always an academic.

This brief review of the history of the universities demonstrates, first, that the presidential function is quite new in France and, second, while the presidential function is a new creation there is a long tradition of strong deans. Most of the memoirs written by the early presidents (see for instance Rémond 1979 or Merlin 1980) underline the quite difficult time they experienced in the seventies. They simultaneously had to develop this new function while at the same time operate under the Faure Law that required them to employ a participatory decision-making approach that included full professors but also students, non-professor faculty and administrative staff, a major change from the former tradition where only professors participated in decision making bodies. The confusion, occasional conflicts, and political opposition that characterized university governance in the seventies had dissipated by the time Friedberg and Musselin conducted their study. At the same time, their research found that presidents were not playing the decisive role that had been intended under the new structure of the Faure Law. The presidents employed a more traditional style of academic leadership, that is, as mediators of internal conflicts and representatives of university interests outside the university, but not as managers or leaders. Most presidents preferred to stay in the background.

This is no longer the case for most French presidents who are currently in office. First, the way they speak about their function, their conception of their role, suggests that they view themselves as managers who supervise projects, define institutional direction and priorities, and intervene to make decisions. They do not simply define themselves as a reflection of their peers' preferences and but adopt a more interventionist conception of their work. The opinions expressed by the (13) presidents who responded to our questions dealing with the form of institutional autonomy they prefer are different from the majority of the answers we received: 31% of the presidents are in favour of more organisational and more financial autonomy compared with 23% of all respondents; 15% oppose more organisational and more financial autonomy compared with 26% of all respondents. Moreover, 24 of the presidents (65%) of the 37 universities included in our quantitative study were described as being influential or very influential on major decisions made within the university.

Second, the presidents insist that they are not alone in providing institutional leadership but work with a team, which generally includes the vice-presidents, and frequently the leading administrators of the university. They describe their work in terms of delegating responsibility over some activities but also, at the same time, working cooperatively with other members of the team. This collective feature of university management is reflected by the distribution of the 1563 responses (academics and administrative staff) we received to a question on the composition of the president's team (see Table 1).

Table 1. Q132 : Who belongs to the president's team in your university?

President only	President and deans	President, deans, vice-presidents	President, vice-presidents	President, vice-pres., leading administrators	Do not know
4.7 %	4.2 %	19.8 %	21.5 %	45.0 %	4.8 %

Third, the presidents usually consider the job as a full-time position[8] and they stress the professionalisation of the leadership function. They may continue to offer one or two courses to maintain contact with students, but they are, first and foremost, presidents. They all stress that this function now requires more expertise (technical, relational, managerial) than before. While they do not believe that the president should be able to do or know everything, an 'enlightened amateur' can no longer accomplish the requirements of the position; many stressed the importance of having been a vice-president previously.

There is therefore a general trend towards a more active and committed leadership at the presidential level. There is also a general trend for presidents to request more responsibility and autonomy as stated by the recent 'orientation paper' produced by the French Conference of University Presidents, entitled *University Autonomy and Responsibility* (Conférence des Présidents d'Université 2001).

3.3. Deliberative bodies that make decisions

In the eighties, the university's deliberative bodies were defined by two main characteristics. First, they were described as 'rubberstamp chambers' and had a fairly poor reputation within the university. Elected academic members of these bodies were frequently described as 'poor researchers who have nothing else to do'. Second, their main approach to making decisions was 'no decision'. They would monitor decisions made by the ministry and simply replicate these decisions[9], or fail to choose between competing projects initiated by departments and leave the decision to the ministry, or discuss an issue for hours without coming to any final decision.

Once again, the findings of our study suggest that the situation has changed. About 70% of the individuals who participated in our quantitative study, and who were not elected members of one of the deliberative bodies, indicated that they believed that the three councils were working well. In particular, the Governing Board was described as 'a place where decisions are made' by 78% of respondents and as 'an important body by 82% of respondents.

In addition, and perhaps more importantly, the 'no decision' is no longer the favourite response of deliberative bodies. This does not mean that detailed policy decisions are now made by these participatory bodies functioning as a whole; they involve too many members, and so preparatory work is undertaken by small groups before the plenary meeting. These groups develop proposals and positions that are then presented to and discussed by the council as a whole, generally resulting in decisions that receive the agreement of a large majority of members. To explore this process in more detail, it is important to distinguish the situation of the Academic Council and CEVU, on the one hand, with the Governing Board on the other.

Most of the decisions made by the Academic Council and the CEVU consist of evaluating, ranking, or making recommendations on projects initiated by academics. Two kinds of criteria are generally taken into account. First, the council will consider the level of the support that projects received at the faculty level. If a proposal was seen as very controversial within the faculty, or was accepted with only a small majority of votes by the faculty council, the Academic Council or the CEVU will be reluctant to approve it. They will probably send it back to the *faculté* and ask for a different proposal. Second, we observed that the Academic Council and the CEVU frequently developed and articulated their own criteria[10] that they then used to select the projects going to the ministry[11].

We found that the specific criteria used by these councils varied according to the types of policy proposals we were looking at, on whether the deliberative body one was observing was the CEVU or the Academic Council, and according to the preferences of these bodies. We were able to conclude, however, that clear and shared criteria were more likely to be found in situations where the president had articulated an explicit strategic plan. In such cases the strategy was accepted by the deliberative bodies and provided the foundation for the development of decision criteria[12].

It is impossible to discuss precise criteria without considering specific cases, but we were able to draw two general conclusions from the analyses. First, these criteria never deal with the scientific or pedagogical content of the project. Second, some items on our questionnaire provided us with an indication of the sort of issues that are considered in certain types of decisions. We asked respondents to rank the influence of five different criteria (with 1 as the most influential and 5 is the less influential) on decisions about the creation of new program of study. Two items received high rankings in terms of influence: 1) job possibilities for the graduates and 2) evidence of student demand. The ranking of the most influential criteria for a decision to cancel an academic program also stressed two items: 1) diminishing numbers of students and 2) poor job possibilities.

The existence of criteria on which to make decisions is important because it helps the subcommittees do their preparatory work in advance of the meetings of the Academic council or the CEVU; the committees will know what issues should be considered, and what points they need to stress in their reports to the plenary session. But the existence of decision criteria can also facilitate the participation of elected members of councils who are not members of a subcommittee; they have a clearer understanding of the rationale that is being employed to make a recommendation and they can ask questions about how the criteria were applied to a specific case, request modifications if they believe that certain points were not taken into account, participate in the hearings with project leaders, etc. In other words, the existence of decision criteria can provide elected members who are not part of the subcommittee process with a foundation for participating at the plenary level and help create a sense that all members play a role since there is a common understanding of the basis on which decisions are made.

The situation is different for the Governing Board, though not for decisions based on the proposals made by the CEVU or the Academic Council. The Governing Board members trust the opinions offered by these bodies and approve their proposals. But the Governing Board must also make decision on other matters, especially decisions on budget allocations and recommendations on new academic positions. In this respect, it is important to note that the Governing Board is now making decisions that it did not make before. In the 1980s, most universities refused to rank the list of positions they requested, leaving the decision to the ministry. Now, ranking by priority is the norm. Moreover, each faculty provides its ranking and the Governing Board is able to cross-rank and can even depart from the ranking order suggested by the *faculté*; positions qualified as 'low priority' by a *faculté* may be considered 'high priority' by the Governing Board.

The Governing Boards capacity for decision-making, however, may be limited by a number of factors that emerged from our study. Elected members of this body are generally as satisfied as members of the CEVU or the Academic council. 73.5% of these respondents agreed with the item 'the work done in these meetings is satisfying' (compared with 74.9% of the Academic council members about the Academic council meetings and 74.3% of the CEVU members about the CEVU meetings). Decisions are generally approved with a very large majority, but, at the same time, members of the Governing Board often feel 'dispossessed'. Like for the CEVU and the Academic council, recommendations for the Board are prepared in advance, but in many cases this preparatory work is done by the president's team and the administration, not by elected members of the Governing Board. In other words, the Board discusses proposals that members of the Board were not involved in preparing, and Board members may not have the technical expertise to present opposing arguments, let alone alternative positions; Board members feel that they are obligated to rubberstamp proposals that they may not have played a role in developing[13].

Thus, university councils play a greater role in the decision-making process and make decisions in new policy areas compared with the former structure, but this does not imply that they are a major force in terms of actually developing university policy. They provide legitimacy to university policy by reviewing and approving decisions rather than developing policy positions (Mignot-Gérard 2000).

3.4. Developing strategies on issues that were previously ignored[14]

A third point to note is the development of strategies at the university level on issues that were previously ignored. Our research suggests that there are four policy domains or issues where universities have developed institutional strategies that have influenced their activities and led to new forms of internal decision-making.

The first domain involves strategic research plans. The introduction of four-year research contracts[15] between the central authority and each university in 1983 fostered the definition of research priorities at the university level. Three different kinds of initiatives have been developed through these processes: the discipline-based grouping of research centres in the same building (*Maison de l'Economie, Maison des Sciences sociales...*); the creation of interdisciplinary research centres (which are called *fédérations* or *instituts thématiques*, or *ensembles* etc.) aimed at giving more visibility to, and enhancing relationships and cooperation among, these research teams; and finally the creation or development of research offices. These new research offices are generally created to fulfil two objectives: on one hand they are intended to provide some level of financial, technical and legal support to academics who are engaged in research contracts with firms, communities, the European commission etc; on the other, they facilitate a more transparent process for reviewing and approving research contracts within the university and encourage academics to have their contracts managed by the university administration[16] and pay overhead (Mignot-Gérard and Musselin, forthcoming).

The second domain of institutional strategy involves what may be called 'rationalization strategies'. Two different approaches can be observed. First, universities have developed instruments designed to improve the decision-making process. The introduction of management software (Gueissaz 1999)[17] and the construction of indicators reflect this first orientation; figures, standardized information, and comparative data are produced and used to support decisions[18]. Second, there is a general trend towards better control and more effective analysis of expenditures. Most universities have developed strategies to reduce or adjust the budget for overtime (*heures complémentaires*[19]), and some also try to enforce volume-discount procurement policies. A wide range of decisions of these issues have been made by the presidents and their teams.

Teaching is the third domain and strategic decisions on this topic are quite recent. Some universities are trying to change the ways in which curricular decisions are made; instead of adding new courses to a forever growing catalogue, these universities are trying to establish priorities, determine which program areas or diplomas should be expanded, and develop a more coherent set of course offerings. In addition, the assessment of teaching quality and the evaluation of teaching by students is no longer simply taking place on the personal initiative of a few isolated academics, but is increasingly viewed as a matter of university strategy, though formal teaching evaluations continue to be uncommon (see Table 2).

Finally, human resources issues are receiving increasing attention. We have already noted that the deliberative bodies now believe that they must rank-order their recommendations for positions that they forward to the ministry each year[20]. It is also important to note that existing (administrative or academic) positions can now be redeployed within the university, though this would have seemed impossible before[21].

Table 2. Q36. Does some formalized teaching evaluation procedure exist in your faculty?

Yes	22.9%
No	43.9%
There exists no formalized procedure but some teachers developed an evaluation procedure for their own courses	26.7%
I do not know	4.8%

One can now identify a wide range of policy areas where universities did not make decisions in the past but which are now viewed as the responsibility of university management.

3.5. Collective priorities oriented decision-making

Our final point in this section involves the emergence of a more collective conception of universities. As in other countries (Altbach 1996), French academics have dual loyalties: to their discipline and to their institution. The former has almost always existed; the second form of loyalty has been strengthened under the new arrangements. The four-year contracts introduced by the central state administration by the end of the eighties favoured this evolution (Chevaillier 1998).

In order to sign a contract with the French ministry, each university must first prepare a form of 'strategic plan' which describes its priorities and main objectives for the next four years. The first step in this process consists of an analysis of institutional strengths and weaknesses, and this provides a foundation for the development of a collective strategic orientation. The main directive given by the central state administration when it launched this new procedure was that the project should not be conceived as a juxtaposition of faculty projects. It should be an opportunity to stimulate collective reflection within each university, to develop a shared understanding of institutional goals that moves beyond the traditional supremacy of the faculties in French higher education (Musselin 2001).

The impact of these contracts, or more precisely of the process that surrounds them rather than the contracts themselves (one should not forget that they still represent only 10 to 15% of the operating budget – which does not include salaries – of French universities) is important. As demonstrated by the questionnaire responses presented in Table 3, the contracts are viewed positively by the academic and administrative staff.

Contracts are seen as a way to improve the government of the university as shown by items 1, 2 and 5. But they are also viewed as a point of reference for making other decisions. The general opinion reflected in items 3 and 4 of Table 3 was reinforced by responses to a question dealing with criteria for Governing Board decisions (see Table 4).

Table 3. (based on Q114 and Q115) Opinions on four-year contracts.

Would you say that the four-year contracts	No. of answers	Agree (%)	Disagree (%)	Do not know (%)
are positive because universities have to project themselves in the future	1583	78.9	7.5	13.6
are positive because their preparation allows universities to better know themselves	1566	72.2	11.3	16.5
are positive because they help the deliberative bodies to make decisions	1565	67.7	15.4	16.9
serve as a reference to make decisions within the university	1621	65.9	7.1	27.0
enhance university autonomy	1549	60.5	18.8	20.7

Table 4. Q92. In order to rank the need for academic positions, what criteria does the Governing Board first take into account[22] ?

The evolution of the student population or of the students/teacher ratio	90.1%
The priorities set by the four-year contract	75.1%
The research priorities	33.2%
Each faculty is given its turn	17.3%

The impact of the contracts seems quite clear in terms of the ranking of academic positions. However, the contracts seem to have far less impact on the development of annual budgets (only 27.8% of respondents indicated that the contracts influenced these decisions). This suggests that contracts are more influential on the distribution of supplementary resources than on the redistribution of existing resources.

But these are not the only consequences associated with the contract policy. The contracts also facilitate the development of a shared vision of the university. The projects that are part of the strategic plan are more than a collection of individual projects supported by different groups of academics. They have been recognized as projects of the whole university that are directly related to the long term development of the institution. These projects have been approved because of how they relate to the general objectives and future direction of the university.

The four main changes we identified in this second section are particularly striking when we compare our recent findings with the conclusions reached by Friedberg and Musselin in the eighties. Patterns of decision-making within French universities have evolved and reflect the emergence of universities as collective actors and their increasing institutional autonomy (Berdahl 1990). These changes did not occur because the ministry delegated more responsibility to the institutions, but because the universities (i.e. their leadership and the deliberative bodies) began to become involved in areas of policy that they previously ignored.

4. REMAINING OBSTACLES

Despite the evolutionary changes that we have described, governing French universities and enhancing institutional autonomy remain difficult tasks that are constrained by many limitations.

These constraints include a number of external factors, such as the slow, back and forth reforms of the ministry itself. The ministry increasingly recognizes universities as significant actors in the higher education system, but still remains under the influence of the disciplines; the role of the academic experts is still important and the balance between the discipline-based decisions and the university-based decisions is always shifting and has not yet stabilized. The ministry is also always ready to preach about the importance of increasing autonomy but it maintains detailed and constraining rules. One might wonder, for instance, how French universities can be described as autonomous when they have almost no flexibility in terms of dealing with personnel issues: they need the agreement of the ministry to create new positions or to replace vacant positions; they cannot recruit when they need to but must wait for the next national procedure; and the recruitment procedures involve national bodies or even depend on national *concours* (for instance the *agrégation du supérieur*) on which universities have no influence.

But the problems confronting French universities that prevent them from becoming more cohesive, self-governing institutions are not just associated with external factors. There are also internal obstacles.

4.1. An evolution that lacks legitimacy

In the second section of this chapter we noted some of the policy domains that are receiving attention from French universities, policy areas where they are making new decisions and defining institutional strategies. In particular, we stressed the development of strategic research plans, rationalization strategies, interventions on teaching, and human resource management. These initiatives are largely supported by the president's team and the administrators but are not viewed as legitimate by many other actors.

In the qualitative study of four universities, the only non-controversial policy was the follow-up of the *heures supplémentaires'* budget. Policy initiatives on all other matters (research policy, teaching offerings, introduction of software, procurement policy, redistribution of positions, etc.) were severely criticized by most of our interviewees.

This is confirmed by the findings of the quantitative study. In most cases the universities' intervention into a new area of policy is criticized. For example, responses to a question on the preferred objectives of the university research strategy are presented in Table 5.

In terms of research policy, most people expect technical support from the university but they do not believe that the university should make decisions on research themes. The respondents were also very clear in terms of the expected role of the university in recruitment decisions; only 18.7% agreed that search committees should be advisory bodies and that the university should have the final decision on appointments.

Table 5. Q79. What are the priorities for which the research strategy of your university should aim? (answers from academics only)

Constructing new buildings for the research institutes	39.1%
Offering some legal help for the management of research contracts	25.5%
Finding and negotiating new research contracts	20.3%
Defining research themes	9.0%
Others	6.1%

According to our findings, respondents do not believe that a stronger university-level role in many policy areas is desirable. They also do not expect the level of institutional autonomy to increase. Our questionnaire included questions dealing with expectations on the organisational autonomy of the universities (should universities be free to determine their own status, public versus private accounting, etc). We also included questions on financial autonomy (need for a diversification of resources, for more partnerships, etc.). In cross-tabulating responses to these questions, we noted that our respondent population could be divided into four groups:

- a group opposed both to more organisational and to more financial autonomy: 26% of the respondents
- a group opposed to more organisational autonomy but in favour of more financial autonomy: 28% of the respondents
- a group in favour of more organisational autonomy and opposed to more financial autonomy: 23% of the respondents
- a group in favour of both more organisational and more financial autonomy: 23% of the respondents

Less than one-quarter of the respondents wanted to see a significant increase in institutional autonomy, a little more than one-quarter supported the status quo, and the rest of the respondents were in favour of only a limited form of autonomy. There are significant differences of opinion on these issues and it is difficult for university leaders to find consensus and to build legitimacy.

4.2. Decisions are easier to make than to implement

A second type of problem is associated with the fact that while universities are able to define strategies and make decisions that are supported by a large majority of members of the deliberative bodies, these decisions are often difficult to implement. There are three main reasons for this discrepancy between their ability to make decisions and their ability to implement decisions.

The first reason is a high degree of individual resistance. This individual autonomy is enhanced by the fact that universities are loosely coupled organisations

(Cohen, March and Olsen 1972; Weick 1976). Many activities can be continued as before at the individual level because there is to nothing to constrain these activities and because the lack of change at this level does not affect other levels (or cannot be observed by other levels). Institutional autonomy may also be enhanced by the fact that often there are ways to circumvent directives. In our qualitative study, for example, some academics explained that they could circumvent university purchasing policies by buying their furniture with the CNRS budgets that are not managed by the university.

The second reason deals with the presidents and their teams. These leaders are often skilled at initiating participatory processes that lead to collective decisions, or at articulating strategic positions and setting priorities, but they do not give enough attention to the implementation process. In the study that Lipiansky and Musselin (1995) conducted on the preparation, negotiation and implementation of four-year contracts, it was clear that many projects were kept on stand-by because there was a lack of follow-up from the university management that initiated them. For instance, a bureau for 'industry-university relationships' was created, but the administrative staff assigned to it felt abandoned. They expected some 'political' direction from the president as well as support when they encountered resistance from academics, but they did not receive direction or support .

The third reason is linked to the rather difficult relationships between the group composed of the president, his team and the administrators on one hand, and the deans (and the academic and administrative staff within the faculties) on the other. Strategies defined at the university level are thus poorly transmitted within the university. The first group rarely includes the deans and most of the time the deans are not associated with the decisions that are made at the central university level. They are only informed after a decision has been made, or an already-developed proposal is submitted for their review to see how they will react. Most presidents and administrators believe that deans should more strongly support the president's team, but a much smaller majority believe that deans should be part of this team (Table 6). The vast majority of deans believe that they should be members of the central-university decision-making team, but a much smaller majority believe that they should show solidarity with the president's team (Table 6).

The ambiguous nature of this relationship and the poor cooperation between the president's teams and the deans are detrimental to the implementation of university-level policy.

Table 6. (based on Q130) : Opinions on the role and the behaviours deans should have

	Faculties members	Deans	Administrators	Presidents
The deans show solidarity to the president's team	45.6%	62.1%	76.5%	76.9%
The deans should systematically be members of the president's team	72.5%	86.0%	66.7%	61.5%

4.3. Incremental rather than radical decisions

It is also important to note the kinds of decisions made by university management and the deliberative bodies. Most of these decisions are incremental in that they generally build on rather than modify the status quo. There is considerable inertia and little evidence of radical change.

This holds particularly true for budget allocation decisions which generally build on decisions made in previous years (see Table 7).

Table 7. Q50. Upon which criteria is the annual budget for your faculty established ? (see note 12)

The evolution of students numbers	93.5%
The previous years budget	65.8%
The criteria used by the ministry (Sanremo criteria)	48.9%
The priorities developed in the four-year contracts	27.8%
Projects developed by the faculties	10.9%

There are, of course, 'good' reasons for this, and one is the fact that once you have established the budget for utilities, maintenance, etc. there is little room left. But this is too easy an explanation. It is very hard indeed to introduce change, even when the circumstances of the various faculties are changing; increasing (or decreasing) numbers of students, for example, do not automatically lead to a reconsideration of the budget allocation strategy[23]. Even if 'objective criteria' could be used to promote change, it is difficult to know how much could be accomplished in a situation where a president's team wants to develop priorities and intends to reallocate resources in order to reach certain goals. In fact, change only seems to occur through the aggregation of minor transformations, but the only way to assess this would be to conduct a longitudinal study of budget allocations within a number of universities in order to evaluate the degree of change-over-time and whether the marginal changes introduced each year finally produced significant changes in the long run.

The inertia assumption also suggests that the cancellation or termination of existing activities is almost impossible. A good example of this is the development of the course offerings. It is very rare to terminate a course offering even when there are very few students. In their recent study, Kletz and Pallez (2001 and forthcoming) describe the case of a deserted curricula; the faculty was almost ready to cancel this specific curriculum offering, which means that a request to renew the agreement (*habilitation*) would not be forwarded to the ministry. But, just before the decisive vote, the academics teaching in this program of study proposed to modify it, submitted a new proposal, and asked for the renewal of their agreement. The university accepted the proposal. This is not simply an isolated anecdote. Two pieces of quantitative evidence confirm this point. First, the statistical study led by Enaafa and Lefebvre (2001) concluded that most requests for agreement renewals are accepted (over 85%, and the authors note that this is probably understated).

Second, respondents to our questionnaire provided us with data related to the creation and termination of curricula (see Table 8)

Table 8. On the creation and termination of curricula (based on Q11 and Q16)

As far as you know, were...	...new curricula created in your faculty within the past two years	... curricula abolished in your faculty within the past two years
First cycle	29.4 %	4.5%
Second Cycle	43.7%	4.2%
Graduate studies	43.7%	3.8%

It seems much more difficult to terminate courses or programs of study than to create new ones. We also observed that universities which have the highest rate of creating new courses do not have a high rate in terms of terminating courses.

This leads us to a second observation: there is a greater magnitude of change associated with decisions dealing with the allocation of new or additional resources than for the redistribution of existing resources. Our data on the creation of new curricula, for instance, reveals a preference for the development of job-oriented training and for courses of study at the second cycle and graduate studies levels. This should have an impact on the balance between traditional curricula and other kinds of curricula in the middle term.

The same holds true for the creation of new academic positions. As we noted above, the priorities described in the contract play a rather important role in the ranking of requests for new positions, and the rule 'each faculty its turn' is rarely followed.

Our last example is the four-year contracts. These contracts articulate the priorities and direction of the institution. The contracts are not simply a restatement of what currently exists, and they therefore play an important role in terms of stimulating a momentum for change within the university.

Nevertheless, on the whole, most decisions made by the universities involve only incremental change.

4.4. Restricted access to decision-making process

The final point that we would like to make in this section deals with the actors involved in decision-making. The most active participants in the decision-making process are the administrators and academics of each university. The relative indifference of the students elected to the deliberative bodies (as shown by their high absenteeism rates and by their rather weak influence on the decision process), and the low level of participation of the so-called 'outside personalities' (*personnalités extérieures*) who are supposed to represent the interests of the external environment, indicates that the decision-making process remains relatively closed.

The closed nature of these processes may change as a function of the increasing interactions between the universities and their local environment. Universities are under increasing pressure to cooperate with the world around them, especially since these interactions can lead to new sources of resources (essentially for research and for buildings). But, while the universities are ready to develop partnerships with their environment, they are not ready to provide external interests with a greater voice in their internal decision-making structures. For example, 75.4% of the respondents to our questionnaire agreed with the statement: "It is alright to develop partnerships with our socio-economic and institutional environment in order to improve the financial settings of universities." At the same time, a majority did not agree that local leaders should be more involved in university governance (see Table 9).

Table 9. Q134 : Political and economic leaders should be more involved in university government ?

Agree	29.0%
Disagree	64.0%
Do not know	7.0%

Partnerships are acceptable as long as these partners do not interfere within the internal affairs of the university.

5. CONCLUSION

The picture we present of French universities in this article involves two contrasting images. On the one hand, many of the findings we have reported in this paper suggest an image of a university system that has undergone important changes, or at the very least has experienced more change than is normally suggested in the research literature (probably because most studies have focused on higher education reforms in France rather than on in-depth studies of universities). On the other hand, our analysis of internal factors presents an image of the many obstacles and difficulties that have not yet been addressed, and these factors may prevent or slow down progress towards the development of more cohesive institutions.

There are a number of consequences associated with the recent evolution of French universities, and we would like to conclude by focusing on two. The first is the increasing diversity of the French university system. A limited form of diversity within the system had already begun to emerge in the 1960s when the increasing numbers of students allowed for the development of new curricula and the emergence of the so-called 'professionnalised' programmes. These first steps towards diversity, however, remained hidden behind the national rules, national procedures, national diplomas, etc. that were supposed to guarantee a uniform national model. Diversity is now encouraged (universities are asked to develop their priorities, to articulate their institutional identity) and recognized by the ministry. While diversity is encouraged, there continue to be important factors that support uniformity among institutions (for example, the implementation of similar software, the fact that some university strategies are more a translation of the Ministry's national directives than 'locally-developed' strategies, the routinisation of the management of the contractual procedure within the central state administration, etc.). Despite these 'national' forces, there is now a higher level of differentiation within the French university system than before.

The second consequence of the evolution of the French university system is the shift in the balance between ministry and university-level policy development. The role of the ministry is still very important, and one can probably argue that the ministry has less been affected by change than the universities, but the ministry can no longer be described as the principal agent for change and for determining system policies. Again, the recent proposals for more institutional autonomy emerging from the University Presidents Conference confirms the emergence of the latter as a possible forum for articulating system interests. The difference between the scope of the strategic plan of a university and the scope of the contract with the ministry (i.e. the aspects of the strategic plan that will receive financial funding from the ministry) shows that universities have room to define their own priorities and policies.

We, of course, are not able to predict what will happen in the future and what changes will take place, but the level of institutional autonomy for French universities will probably increase in the coming years. Three reasons speak in favour of this hypothesis. First, in order to reverse the present trend, the ministry would need to reassert its legitimacy and find the financial resources that would be necessary to return to the centralized steering of such a large system. Second, university management is enjoying its increased autonomy and asking for more. Third, the recent European agreements on higher education seem to favour decentralized, rather than highly centralized, systems.

This evolution of French universities is, of course, important for the French higher education system. While the universities were once viewed as a rather weak structure, they now are relevant actors within this system with an increased capacity for self-governance.

Our experience in reviewing the French case suggests a need for further theoretical research. We believe that it is important to return to some of the early models and theories that have been used to characterize and explain the organisation of higher education. As El-Khawas noted in a recent paper, there is still much to be learned from this earlier work and it is important to recognize that "the old theories still have something to offer" (2001: 10). But, if we need to revisit these theories and models, we also need to find ways to extend them in order to be able to theoretically analyse the nature and operation of the new organisational forms that are emerging as an alternative, original approach to managing the profession. These new forms and structures challenge our conception of collegial organisations.

NOTES

[1] This agency depends on the French Conference of University Presidents.

[2] This discourse is heavily diffused by the media which always describe the French University as 'in crisis' and which are an open platform for the publication of French intellectuals' critical opinions on the dramatic situation or evolution of French universities (see for instance the paper published by Bourdieu and Charle in April 2000 after the resignation of Claude Allègre, minister of education). But this is also a recurrent diagnosis that is to be found in many publications in the past (Caullery 1920, Colloque de Caen 1956) but also more recently (for instance Lucas 1987, Charle 1994, Renaut 1995, Areser 1997, Compagnon 1998...). The main explanation given by most of these authors is

that French academics never succeeded in developing a common idea (or ideal) of the University and in forming a cohesive academic community.

[3] This is very close to the "constructing organisation" process described by Brunsson and Sahlin-Andersson (2000).

[4] We do not have enough room here to develop this point, but it led to the increasing financial participation of local authorities in the university budget, as well as more normative consequences: for instance some regions are very active in proposing research funding that are allocated through 'call for proposals'. They are thus having an influence on research programmes.

[5] This could change. French presidents could be elected for a four year mandate that could be renewed one time.

[6] They are elected by all the members of the university belonging to the same category or constituency. For instance, students vote for the students representatives and administrative staff members for administrative representatives.

[7] The elections of the bodies and the election of the president do not occur at the same time. It means that a president can be elected by bodies in t, and that the bodies' elections can occur for instance in t+2 leading to constitution of new bodies that may be hostile to the president !

[8] Recently a president who just left his office after a five year period (1996–2001), told us that he worked full time as president, that his predecessor (1991–1996) spent 3 and one-half days each week in the presidential function, and the predecessor of the latter (1986–1991) one to two days a week.

[9] These mainly concerned budget allocation that mostly respected the ministry criteria, not because they were obliged to, but because it was easier to use them than develop new criteria.

[10] They generally pay attention to the relevance of the project in terms of the employment possibilities for the students. As this is also encouraged by the ministry, an expansion of job-oriented curricula is to be observed. In fact, two evolutions are to be observed about the development of curricula in France: first, two levels of regulation (one at the university level and one at the ministry level) instead of one (the ministry); second, curriculum development is less supply driven (what academics think is interesting to propose) and more demand driven (what is needed by the students, the society, the job-market, etc.).

[11] They do not refuse frequently either, and this can be explained by two reasons. First, they generally prefer asking for modifications than just saying 'no'. Second, they are usually dealing with projects that have a good chance of being accepted because project leaders frequently engage in pre-discussions within their faculty and the university to "estimate" the viability of the project, and also because the criteria of the CEVU are known and there exists a kind of auto-censure: one does not lose time preparing a project that has no chance to meet the required criteria

[12] For instance, in one of the three universities studied by Simmonet (1999) in her study on curricula decision-making, the president clearly expressed that job-oriented curricula related to the Bologna declaration would be preferred and this defined the preferences of the CEVU.

[13] H. de Boer (2001) has also observed this 'dispossession' feeling within Dutch bodies. They not only experienced a loss in status but are increasingly confronted with ready-made proposals.

[14] This point is based on the section 1.2. of a contribution to be published (cf. Mignot-Gérard and Musselin, forthcoming).

[15] These four-year contracts are very different from the four-year contracts introduced in 1988 and that deal with the operating budget. The main reason for that is that the former remain a centralised discipline-based procedure leaving little autonomy to the university level, while the latter is a university-based procedure intending to and succeeding in fostering university autonomy. For the last few years now, the two procedures were supposed to be held simultaneously, but they are not really coordinated.

[16] Academics sometimes try to escape this constraint and develop alternative solutions for the management of their research contracts, solutions that the university does not know about or is unable to avoid.

[17] In particular those developed by the GIGUE and then the AMUE: Nabuco for finance and budget, Apogée for the management of students (inscriptions, diplomas, statistics...), Harpège for human resources management...

[18] Such instruments had two pragmatic consequences. First it formalized the fact of belonging to the university: the different parts of the institution are not only linked by the same heating system, but also by the same software, the same way of calculating, counting, etc. Second, it produced information (previously unavailable) that on the one hand have been used to express priorities and to

legitimate them, but that on the other hand are also a kind of reference for accepting or refusing demands.

[19] The *heures complémentaires* is a specific budget that allow adjustment between the needed volume of teaching hours (based on student inscriptions) and the existing volume (depending on the number of teaching positions). This budget is dedicated to the payment of the supplementary hours (called *heures complémentaires*) given by faculty members who have a fixed position (but who should not teach more than twice their official teaching duties) or by teachers on time-limited contracts (*vacataires*).

[20] In France, universities are not free to create or reallocate positions as they wish. The ministry is responsible for such decisions. Each year the faculties are asked about their needs and they provide the ministry with a list of positions ranked by priority. Then the university cross-ranks the demands and produces a list of priorities for the whole university, which is sent to the Ministry. If the latter decides to create four new positions in a university, the first four ranked positions are created.

[21] The point here is, of course, not to plead for redistribution per se, but to outline that it is no more considered to be the responsibility of the ministry and that universities can make such decisions on their own.

[22] Four possibilities were offered and they were to be ranked from 1 to 4, 1 for the most important criteria and 4 for the least important one. The percentage expresses the number of times the item received a '1' compared to the number of times the item was chosen as the more important plus the number of time it was chosen as least important.

[23] It follows the number of students but does not lead to a redefinition of the allocation criteria, or to decisions such as maintaining the faculty budget even if numbers decrease because it is a priority domain for the university. Nevertheless, in the case of a sharp and abrupt increase (as recently occurred in the training of gym teachers), the budget does not strictly follow the number of students in order not to unbalance the global equilibrium among the faculties.

REFERENCES

Altbach, P. G. *The International Academic Profession: Portraits of fourteen Countries*. Princeton N.J.: Carnegie Foundation for the Advancement of Teaching, Ewing N.J.: California, Princeton, Fulfilment Services, 1996.

Berdahl, R. "Academic Freedom, Autonomy and Accountability in British Universities." *Studies in Higher Education* 15.2 (1990): 169 – 180.

Brunsson, N. and S. Kerstin. "Constructing Organizations: The example of Public Sector Reform." *Organization Studies* 21.4 (2000): 721 - 746.

Chevaillier, T. "Moving away from Central Planning : Using Contracts to Steer Higher Education in France." *European Journal of Education* 33.1 (1998): 65 – 76.

Cohen, M. D., J.G. March and P.O. Johan. "A Garbage Can Model of Organizational Choice." *Administrative Science Quarterly* 17.1 (1972): 1 - 25.

Conférence des Présidents d'université. *Autonomie des universités et responsabilité : pour un service public renouvelé*. Texte d'orientation, Paris: CPU, 2001.

De Boer, H. "On the MUB and Bikinis. Impressions on Dutch University Governance." *23rd Annual EAIR Forum*, Porto, 2001.

El-Khawas, E. "Changing Management and Governance Patterns for US Universities : Are Old Theories still Relevant ?", *CHER conference*, Dijon. September 2001.

Enaafa R. and F. Lefebvre. *Evaluation de la capacité d'action des établissements d'enseignement supérieur et de recherché sur la définition et l'évolution de leur offre de formation*. Rapport final, Paris: Evalua-OVE-AMUE, 2001

Filâtre, D. (under the direction of). *Collectivités locales et politiques universitaires. Les enjeux des délocalisations universitaires*. Rapport dans le cadre du programme de recherche-expérimentation "L'université et la ville", Université de Toulouse le Mirail, 1993.

Friedberg, E. and C. Musselin. *En quête d'universités*. Paris: L'Harmattan, 1989.

Gueissaz, A. *Les mondes universitaires et leur informatique - Pratiques de rationalisation*. Paris: CNRS Editions, 1999.

Kletz, F. and F. Pallez. *L'offre de formation des universités: création de diplômes et stratégies d'établissement*, Rapport final, Paris: CGS-AMUE, 2001.

Kletz, F. and F. Pallez. "Taking Decisions on New Curricula in French Universities: Disciplinary Criteria still Prevail?" *European Journal of Education* 37.1 (2002): 57 – 69.

Kogan, M. and S. Hanney. *Reforming Higher Education*. London and Philadelphia: Jessica Kingsley Publishers, 2000.

Lipiansky, S. and C. Musselin. *La démarche de contractualisation dans trois universités françaises: Les effets de la politique contractuelle sur le fonctionnement des établissements universitaires*. Rapport d'enquête, Paris: CSO, 1995.

Merlin, P. *L'université assassinée. Vincennes 1968-1980*. Paris: Editions Ramsay, 1980.

Mignot-Gérard, S. and C. Musselin (forthcoming). "More Leadership for French Universities, but also more Divergences between the Presidents and the Deans" In Dewatripont, M., F. Thys-Clément and L. Wilkin (eds). *The strategic Analysis of Universities: Microeconomic and management Perspectives*. Bruxelles: Editions de l'Université de Bruxelles.

Mignot-Gérard, S. "The Paradoxal Victory of Representative Leadership in Universities – The French Model." *Contribution to the 22nd EAIR Forum*, Berlin, September 2000.

Mignot-Gérard, S. and C. Musselin. *Comparaison des modes de gouvernement de quatre universités françaises*. Paris: Rapport CSO/CAFI, 1999.

Mignot-Gérard, S. and C. Musselin. *Enquête quantitative des modes de gouvernement de 37 établissements*. Paris: CAFI-CSO et Agence de Modernisation des universités, 2000.

Musselin, C. *La longue marche des universités françaises*. Paris: PUF, 2001.

Rémond, R. *La règle et le consentement – Gouverner une société*. Paris: Fayard, 1979.

Simmonet, S. *La politique d'offre de formation de trois universités et son articulation avec la politique ministérielle*. Paris: Mémoire de DEA de l'Institut d'Etudes Politiques de Paris, 1999.

Weick, K.E. "Educational Organization as Loosely Coupled Systems." *Administrative Science Quarterly* 21.1 (1976): 1 – 19.

METHODOLOGICAL APPENDIX

The qualitative study was conducted in four French universities, one in Paris and the three others in the Province. They were chosen in order to consider different situations including their geographical location, their size, their spectrum of disciplines (in France, universities are rarely comprehensive). Some are monodisciplinary, including for instance, only disciplines from the humanities; others are pluridisciplinary and can for instance include a Law and a Medicine Faculty but no Science; some are omnidisciplinary or complete). In each case we led semi-structured interviews with members of the presidential team, the deans, faculty members, administrative members of the university central administration, administrative members at the faculty level and elected members of the university deliberative bodies (Governing board, Academic council and CEVU). Each interview lasted about two hours. The interview subjects were asked about their activity (what it consists of, what is important for them, what is of interest for them, the problems they meet), about their relationships with other actors (who are their principal interlocutors, what do they accomplish with these persons, are these relationships good, difficult, etc.), and, finally, about their perspective of the current situation (are they satisfied about it, what could be improved, their wishes...). In each university, we also chose three faculties in which we led more interviews and that we investigated more in detail. Within the university central administration we also more closely looked at four services : accounting, pedagogical affairs, human resources, budget.

Table A. Global sample

	Uni Centre	Uni Ouest	Uni Est	Uni Sud
Professors	15	26	14	23
Maîtres de conférences	9	16	4	10
Other teachers or researchers	2	1	9	3
Administrative staff	28	32	29	129
Total	54	75	56	64

Table B. Among the global sample, people holding management and/or elected responsibilities

	Uni Centre	Uni Ouest	Uni Est	Uni Sud
Presidential team	7	11	7	6
Deans	7	5	6	8
Directors of research units	1	5	8	4
Governing board (elected)	5	9	7	6
Academic Council (elected)	7	5	5	6
Board of studies (elected)	5	6	8	5
Total	32	41	41	35

A monograph was written for each university and a comparative report was then prepared. We used these results to prepare a questionnaire (including 185 questions with common questions but also specific questions for the administrative staff, for the academic staff and for elected members of the deliberative bodies), organised in three parts: one on the *facultés*, one on the university level, and one on deliberative bodies. It was sent to 5000 individuals associated with 37 universities. The institutions were chosen using the following criteria : geographical location, number of students, students per teachers ratio, number of *facultés*, date of creation, discipline structure (mono, pluri and omni disciplinary). We sent between 110 and 150 questionnaires per institution and the questionnaires were allocated according to the following principles: 10% to members of the presidential team, 13% to administrative staff at the university level, 42% in three selected faculties (2/3 of them to academics – 1/3 to administrative members), 15% to elected members of the Governing board, 10% to elected members of the Academic Council and 10% to elected members of the CEVU.

We received 1660 responses (with a response rate ranging from 20% to 51% and a medium rate of 34%) that were analysed using SPSS. The responses reflect the national distribution of the scientific disciplines as shown here.

But, the sample suffers from three problems :

- a slightly over-representation of the administrative staff (especially those at the university level)
- the discipline distribution, which is respected for the global sample, is not respected at the level of each institution

- in some institutions, we observed a large discrepancy between the number of answers received from the administrative staff compared to the number of answers received from the academic staff.

Table C. Distribution of academic staff by discipline

	Percentage of academic staff by discipline in France (1999)	Percentage of the academic staff by disciplines for respondents
Sciences	42.1 %	38.7%
Humanities	28.8 %	32.6%
Law and economics	13.3%	16.7%
Medicine	15.8%	12.0%

Furthermore, the way we constituted the sample favoured university members that have elective or management responsibilities in their institution: 76.8% of the people who sent the questionnaire back were either members of the presidential team, or deans, or directors of department /research institutes, or elected members of the university deliberative bodies. Such an orientation was voluntary as many of the questions concerned the way decisions are made, the role of the different levels, of the bodies, etc. The aim of the questionnaire was not primarily to obtain the opinions of academic and administrative staff but first of all to elaborate a typology of university government in France.

THIERRY CHEVAILLIER

UNIVERSITY GOVERNANCE AND FINANCE: THE IMPACT OF CHANGES IN RESOURCE ALLOCATION ON DECISION MAKING STRUCTURES

1. INTRODUCTION

When trying to account for changes that take place over time in the structure of any organisation, social scientists often use a conceptual framework known as resource dependency theory. This theory assumes that organisations survive only if they are able to react to changes that occur in the world around them in order to obtain the resources they need to stay in operation. Since they have the capacity for independent action, organisations are not passively shaped by their environment; they sometimes are also able to influence it.

Higher education institutions, like other organisations, depend on resources. Although, as "organised anarchies" (Cohen and March 1974), they are rather resistant to external control, their dependence on external resources means that changes to resource allocation arrangements will impact on their internal modes of organisation. It is not just the amount of resources they control that matters, but also the way these resources are obtained and from whom. As the funding patterns of higher education change, the internal structure of institutions are transformed.

The aim of this paper is to explore the relationship between changes in resource allocation and decision making structures, and to examine how academics and administrators, acting collectively, develop strategies that shape the institutions and the system in which they operate in reaction to what they perceive as changes in their environment. While one cannot assume that all of the transformations that have occurred in higher education are responses to funding matters, it can be argued that resource dependency offers a simple and powerful way of explaining many of the changes that have taken place within institutions and systems.

The main trends in higher education finance over the last decades are, for most countries, a diversification of funding and a change in the financial relations between the universities and the State. These changes are partly a result of the increasing costs of higher education associated with the democratisation of access and the related growth in enrolment They are also, in many countries, a product of new approaches to public policy that attempt to introduce public sector management techniques derived from private sector practices, partly through decentralisation, incentives and increased accountability of public services.

Given these trends, a thorough treatment of the effect of changes in resource allocation on decision making processes and structures in universities would imply a

87

Alberto Amaral, Glen A. Jones and Berit Karseth (eds.), Governing Higher Education:
National Perspectives on Institutional Governance, 87—98.
© 2002 *Kluwer Academic Publishers. Printed in the Netherlands.*

programme of research designed to address a series of complex questions: How (political, social, technical influences) has control been redistributed among the various resource providers and decision makers (for example, the State, students, institutional managers, university committees, etc.)? How have institutions accommodated these shifts in control (resilience, active or passive resistance, etc.)? To what extent have formal or informal decision making processes and structures been altered (for example, devolution, decentralisation)?

As a first step towards addressing these questions, this paper proposes an analytical framework based on the various models of resource allocation in organisations in order to highlight and explore the relationship between decision-making structures and financial arrangements. This framework will also be used to present a brief analysis of the recent evolution of the French Higher Education system towards greater institutional autonomy after centuries of centralisation. This new situation means that in France, like in other jurisdictions where institutions have enjoyed a high level of autonomy such as the United Kingdom, the picture becomes more complicated because there are now two levels of adaptation to change, that of the state and that of the institution. Adaptations at the state level contribute to shaping the new environment of the institutions.

2. ALTERNATIVE RESOURCE ALLOCATION MODELS

2.1. Alternative allocation processes at system level

At the system level, resource allocation models range from central control to markets. Markets are basically a mode of co-ordination of autonomous entities through which goods and services are sold and bought. Central control implies that every action is subordinated to centralized decisions over the allocation of resources in kind to various economic entities.

These definitions correspond to extreme situations or 'ideal' models that are seldom observed in real life. Producers always have some degree of autonomy, even in the most centralised economy. There is usually a degree of central co-ordination in even the most liberal market system.

It is important to recognize that money plays a very different role in resource allocation in each of these two models. In a centralised system, money is used as an accounting device. Institutions receive resources that are measured and expressed in money terms but these resources are specified in terms of their nature and amount: so many square meters of buildings, so many workers of a given type, so many computers, etc. In a centrally planned economy, describing the allocation process in money terms or in the physical amounts of the various resources has the same meaning. In a market context, money is purchasing power. Money can be used to obtain anything that its owner decides to buy. The way in which money is used becomes an expression of the autonomy of the individual who is free to choose whatever physical resource he or she wishes.

In the higher education world, a centralised system is one in which universities are a component of the state administration and they are allocated the resources deemed necessary to produce the education service specified by the political authorities. A market system is one in which independent institutions sell their services to the students or any other body willing to buy them. They freely decide on the amount and the type of resources they need to produce such services. Institutions are financed by tuition fees paid by the individual students or by a lump sum received from the government who purchases education on behalf of the students. In centralised systems, universities are granted resources in kind, or, if in money, with strings attached, i.e. every sum allocated must be used for a specific purpose.

It is hard to see if resources are allocated in a centralised or in a decentralised way by simply looking at budgets or accounts. If it is fairly easy to convey the meaning of centralism (and therefore of centralisation as a process leading to centralism), but decentralisation is far more difficult to define. For Lauglo (1995: 6), "decentralisation refers to a variety of organisational forms which differ in their rationales and in their implications for the distribution of authority on different agencies, groups and stake holders." An OECD study on decision making processes in primary and secondary education, focusing on four levels of decision making and about thirty decision domains, showed how difficult it is to assess the extent of decentralisation within a given system (CERI 1995).

Governments may attempt to create incentives for the various institutions by introducing a market mechanism. This amounts to making institutions compete for resources by selling their services to various customers. In higher education, at least in the European context, complete markets are not feasible. The most that can be done to decentralise the system and reap the benefits associated with the operation of the market is to introduce some of the features of complete markets, thus creating **quasi-markets**. One way to do this is for the funding authority to finance institutions as if they were in a market, competing for students. This can be achieved by funding institutions on the basis of the number of students, paying a 'price' for each student enrolled, or through voucher schemes, where students receive some form of purchasing power that they are able to spend in the institution of their choice. Both methods are equivalent if students are really free to choose their university. Universities can also be made to compete for research money or industrial contracts. What is important is that they compete with one another, thus feeling the need to find new ways to operate in order to be more efficient in attracting funds. However, it is important to note that creating the conditions that are necessary to allow competition among institutions may not be sufficient to bring it about.[1]

When analysing the actual funding arrangements in higher education, one finds that they usually involve a combination of these various techniques. One can imagine a situation where, for example, earned income (that is, monies collected from 'buyers') can be spent freely while the use of some specific grants received from public authorities may be narrowly prescribed. Each country determines the resource allocation model that will be used at the higher education system level, that is, the precise combination of various resource allocation methods, through its political system. This decision may be reconsidered from time to time to accommodate changing circumstances.

2.2. Alternative allocation processes at the institution level

At the level of the individual institution, any resource allocation model creates constraints on some actions and allows for freedom of choice on others. Taking into account the fact that universities are highly complex organisations, a specific funding arrangement will bring about an internal order that will 'fit' with the financial environment of the institution. A change in this environment will create tensions that are resolved with the redistribution of decision-making power within the institution. A better understanding of these complex relationships can be obtained by analysing universities as producers, where one can distinguish different types of interrelated units involved in the production process: operational units, support units and a strategic centre.

Operational units perform tasks directly related to the core activities (missions) of the institution, such as teaching, research, and service to the community. Academic units (faculty, school, department) are indisputably operational units. So are research centres. **Support units** provide services to operational units or to other support units (library, computer centre, various resource centres, personnel office, accounting department, etc.). **A centre** is responsible for the combined operation of all these units.

The distinction between an operational unit and a support unit can become blurred when the mission of the institution is not clearly defined. Support units that are allowed to provide services to the outside world can think of themselves as operational units. Conversely, an operational unit that develops strong internal relations with other similar units can easily be mistaken for a support unit.

Subject to limitations associated with the amount, the quality and the type of information available on how the whole of this interrelated system operates, increased efficiency of production may be pursued in two ways: by co-ordinating allocation decisions taken separately by different units, or by determining, in a consistent manner, all the tasks to be undertaken by the different units and the resources necessary to perform them. Each approach has its own internal logic and its distinctive features. I will briefly describe these two models of internal resource allocation systems. Once again, these are 'ideal' models that are seldom used in their pure form, but they can provide a foundation for the analysis and comparison of systems that are in operation in our universities.

2.2.1. Centralised internal allocation of resources

In a bureaucratic organisation, three processes are controlled by one element of the structure (the centre): decision making (that is, the production of norms and standards), resource allocation, and the gathering of information. Other elements (the periphery) are actually performing the activities of the organisation (for example, producing goods or services). Actors located at intermediate levels between the centre and the periphery are merely transmitters of information, decisions and resources. At the periphery of the organisation, tasks are limited to the programmed, routine implementation of central decisions. Every piece of information must travel up to the centre. Based on this information, rules are created by the centre in the most detailed way possible. Resources allocations are made on the basis of detailed specifications.

This highly centralised allocation of resources employs what may be referred to as a logic of **appropriation**. Resources are basically allocated in kind by the centre to the various units. The production process and the combination of resources required for producing a given service are known exactly, so it is possible to calculate the needs of each unit and of the institution as a whole, once the decisions have on what to produce and in what amount have been made.

All types of units are **cost centres** where the use of physical quantities (working time of staff, square meters of buildings, kilowatt hours of power, tons of paper, etc.) of the various resources is recorded and transformed into costs by the application of some money values. These values are not prices, in the sense that they are do not influence the decision to use them, but they nevertheless reflect the relative scarcity the institution as a whole attaches to the various resources (shadow prices). Units have no purchasing power to spend and are not allowed to substitute one resource for another, because such a substitution would endanger the whole of the process by creating imbalances (deficits or surpluses) in other parts of the organisation.

All the costs incurred when buying resources from the market are borne by the **centre**. Sometimes, the centre itself is partly a cost centre of another wider institution (for example, French universities are allocated staff and buildings by the Ministry of Higher Education). In these circumstances, what is the meaning of a unit's budget? It is merely a list of drawing rights on various physical resources, valued at a price which can be the market price or **any price** calculated by the centre.

The value of the set of resources allocated to a given unit is said to be appropriated, and the value of common resources that the unit is entitled to is withheld from these appropriations by the centre. It is only when units can really choose what to spend their resources on that a clear distinction can be made between withholding and charging. A unit is charged by the centre or by another unit when it has chosen to acquire a resource. Withholding is an accounting device through which the planned use of a resource by a budget unit is recorded. Budgets do not have to be balanced at the level of individual units, but, when required, a balanced budget can be created simply by changing the accounting prices.

When all resources are allocated in this way, a budget is nothing more than a set of figures describing a list of physical items expressed in money terms so that they can be compared and added. There is no incentive for units to make efficient use of the resources allocated to them since transfers between budget lines are not allowed and any savings through under-spending cannot be carried forward. Units will attempt whenever possible to hoard unused amounts of resources to protect themselves from the impact of future budget cuts and other uncertainties. In this centralized model it is quite difficult to create incentives that are likely to promote the efficient use of resources at the unit level.

2.2.2. Decentralised internal allocation of resources

In a decentralised approach to resource allocation, the budget structure of an institution parallels the overall decision making structure; the budget-making process becomes a mechanism through which some of the most important decisions affecting the operation of the institution are made. It is therefore obvious that external forces that have a strong influence on the budget-making process will also have a significant impact on the internal decision making process. Changes in the relationship between a university and an external funder may have an impact on the internal balance of power within the university.

Funders can be viewed as buyers of services. Some purchases of services are quite explicit and obvious (for example, a firm buys a training programme for its executives), while others are not (a government buys future scientific discoveries and technological breakthroughs, or cultural developments, etc.). External funders may purchase for themselves, as employers or as producers, or on behalf of others (a government may pay the tuition of some students on equity grounds, or a charity may finance research without any specific industrial or strategic purpose in mind). The structure of external funding reflects the various demands that society, through stakeholders, places on higher education institutions. In reality, these demands are directed towards different operational units inside the institution.

3. INTERNAL MARKETS

Support units, facilities or activities provide services to the operational units and should be financed by the operational units. A form of **internal market** can be created that is managed, controlled or regulated by the centre of the institution. An internal market is feasible if three basic conditions are met:

1- Units are free to make their own decisions and relate to each other through the sale and purchase of goods and services. Each unit charges for the services it produces and pays for the goods and services it consumes.
2- Units must balance their income and their expenditure. A unit is entitled to spend only if it is able to secure an equivalent income, either by selling the services it produces, by borrowing, or by having another unit's income transferred to it.
3- Every resource has a price as soon as the amount available is limited in relation to the needs of the institution. This principle ensures that unused resources bear a cost for those who 'own' them as well as for those who need them. Efficient allocation means that the highest satisfaction of needs can be obtained with a fixed amount of a given resource. For the university as a whole, a resource allocated to one unit may be used more efficiently if it is sold or rented to another unit or even to an entity outside the institution.

Creating a market for unused resources is the best way to deter units from keeping precautionary holdings. If an academic unit knows it can borrow staff from another unit, it might decide that it does not need to request new permanent staff positions for what may turn out to be a short-term requirement. Even resources that are available free of charge to the institution as a whole ought to be given an internal price in order to improve the efficiency of internal allocation Experiments along this line have been conducted for staff or for office and classroom space.

Organising an internal market raises a few difficult issues, including establishing internal prices and dealing with the relationships between internal and external markets.

3.1. The level of internal prices

The logic of internal prices not only demands that scarce resources be given a price in order to promote greater efficiency of their use, it also requires that the prices of various resources be such that they do not distort the structure of resource utilisation by making one of them more attractive than the others. The structure of internal prices is therefore of the utmost importance. When alternative methods using different resources are available to perform a task, the price of one of these resources relative to the others becomes one of the key factors in the choice of which method to utilize.

Should prices be set at a such a level as to allow units to make a profit? The answer to this question depends on the institutional context: In private institutions, profit made by a unit can be used as an individual incentive for managers and staff involved in the decision making process. In public institutions, an incentive policy (premium, bonuses) often requires legislative assent and must be based on objective criteria that are often inconsistent with efficient management of the units. Generally speaking, when teaching and support staff have statutory rights, developing an effective system of individual incentives can be a daunting task.

3.2. The relations between internal and external markets

Competition can be a powerful device for improving the internal allocation of resources. Some competition can be introduced in the internal market, but, given the relatively small size of universities as organisations, the prospect for significant improvements through internal competition is limited.

Competition between units and outside firms is more likely to occur. In some cases, it can have a positive effect on the allocation of resources. But it can also be devastating for the efficiency of the institution as a whole by disrupting an internal price system devised to ensure consistency of decisions.

This raises the problem of **contracting out** activities (like maintenance, printing, etc.) in decentralised institutions. If units are allowed to contract out at different prices and conditions, the consistency of the internal market prices is threatened and the internal market itself may be destroyed.

There are limits to the internal market. There are cases in which charging for services is impossible or too costly to operate and where the provision of services must be financed by the centre through a levy on the units' income in the form of a compulsory contribution. This levy may not be connected to the amount of services actually consumed by a given unit (it could then be named a tax) or it can be related to it as closely as possible, in which case the units are compelled by the centre to pay a price for a service. In some situations a 'tax' may be levied by the centre on the units on income they earn.

4. DEFINITION OF THE BUDGET STRUCTURE IN A UNIVERSITY

In a decentralised system, each unit is treated as a responsibility centre since it is responsible for its own income and expenditure (see Lang 1999). Its budget is therefore a forecast of its activity. Actual revenue and expenses must be monitored constantly and accurately to prevent unexpected imbalances.

The closer the links between the different units of the same institution, the more interrelated their forecasts and therefore the greater the need to check their consistency. Only the centre can make such checks and make sure that the various forecasts and the decisions based on them are consistent. The centre must also make sure that units have the resources required to produce services that are of interest to the institution as a whole or that cannot be traded on the internal market.

A unit must be created where one type of service is produced using different resources or where a resource is shared among different uses. As many services are produced jointly from several shared resources, it is difficult to devise a clear functional structure. For example, consider the case of buildings shared by several departments each doing teaching, research, and consultancy, sometimes in joint programmes. Tradition often dictates structures, even when the conditions prevailing when they were set up have radically changed. Sometimes different traditions coexist in the same institution, divided into the "tribes and territories" (see Becher and Kogan 1992) of the academic disciplines. It is therefore much easier to introduce new units when a new activity, a new process, or a new field of research emerges.

The budget structure that goes with a centralised system is based on technical decisions and can therefore be considered as the preserve of the technicians. Decisions are made by the centre and budgeting is only a matter of implementing these decisions and accounting for their consequences. A university shifting from a centralised to a decentralised resource allocation process may therefore face problems with its staff; the skills and aptitudes required to operate these systems can be very different and must be distributed differently between the centre and the units.

5. ADAPTING TO CHANGES IN THE FUNDING ENVIRONMENT

Generally speaking, different institutions with different histories will respond to changes in the external funding environment in different ways. Even when they share a common management culture, universities are likely to react differently to new external constraints, according to each university's unique combination of activities, access to various resources, and local environment. Two recent studies, one in the United Kingdom and one in France, illustrate of this diversity of institutional pathways to transformation.

This notion of differences in institutional responses to the external environment was clearly illustrated in a recent study of the relationship between the resource allocation model and the strategic decision making structure of three British higher education institutions (Jarzabkowski 2002). At Warwick University, a centralised resource allocation model made it possible for resources to be reallocated from income generating units to new academic initiatives, based on the decisions of a strategic committee. The resource allocation model included a degree of cross-subsidisation and the centre kept a tight control of internal transformations. The picture that emerged from this case conforms with this institution's reputation as a fast growing "entrepreneurial university"[2]. The decentralised London School of Economics was described as being "more collegial, with loosely defined strategic direction and control". Closer to the professional bureaucracy model of an organisation, it allocated resources among departments according to collegially negotiated criteria. At Oxford Brookes University the departments enjoyed a considerable degree of autonomy, but the centre was found to play a strategic role by setting the overall direction that framed the development plans created at the department level, and by allocating resources in accordance with performance indicators. From these very different institutional cases the author concludes that "all forms of resource allocation models are inherently problematic when carried to extremes" and that the choice of a model is a matter of internal fit.

6. FUNDING AND STRUCTURAL CHANGES IN FRENCH UNIVERSITIES

Until quite recently, the French higher education system exhibited most of the distinctive features of bureaucratic centralism and, despite marked changes, has retained many of these features: the allocation of public resources to universities is still highly centralised; decisions to invest in new buildings or equipment, or to create a new chair or to hire new clerical staff, are still made by the Ministry.

French higher education institutions had a weak management structure. After decades of strict control by the Ministry of Education and centralised allocation of resources, universities found it difficult to devise a policy or a strategy of their own. Information, collected for the purposes of central system-level administration, did not match the management needs of institutions.

In the mid 1980's, when it became obvious that there were problems associated with the central state control of the economy, French politicians were reluctant to abandon an approach that had been so successful for 30 years and to privatise and transfer control to the markets. The 'market solution' was considered unfeasible for most of the public sector. The French approach was to set the conditions for the independence of individual institutions, to help them acquire greater autonomy, and to leave the Ministry of Education with the responsibility for co-ordinating the institutions as they started to develop their own plans, which, over time, became increasingly incompatible.

Central steering of the economy began to evolve towards a focus on medium term contracts[3] (*contrats de Plan* or 'planning contracts') between the central government and various public institutions (Local authorities, public enterprises, autonomous public agencies). First introduced in 1990, contracts with universities became the central tool of higher education policy within a decade. In a nutshell, 'contractual policy' consists of agreements between the Ministry of Education and individual institutions on the basis of the medium-term development plan that institutions have to produce every 4 years (see Chevaillier 1998).

7. THE OUTCOME OF THE CONTRACT POLICY FOR HIGHER EDUCATION

The change in the relationship between Ministry officials and the heads of universities led to the emergence of new internal relationships and transformed the nature of institutional leadership. A new generation of university presidents emerged and the roles of deans of faculties and heads of departments were significantly altered (Musselin 2001).

Recent research on the governance structure of four universities demonstrates how the new French higher education steering policies have impacted different institutions in different ways (Mignot-Gérard and Musselin 1999). Although the governing structure of French universities is rather homogeneous, given the detailed regulations that frame these governance arrangements, the organisation of the decision making process was very different in each of the four institutions surveyed. One change, however, was common to all institutions. According to this study, the introduction of the institutional contracts has led to the emergence of a strong centre: a small group of academics and administrators working closely with the president. This centre controls the senate and the various committees, especially those bodies concerned with resource allocation. There are tensions between the centre and the departments, with those that are least in conflict with the 'president's team' being able to command external resources. Departments are resisting the introduction of the new principles of resource allocation, although there is general agreement in each institution that something should be done to improve institutional management.

8. CONCLUSION

The French higher education system has evolved in response to changes in the government's approach. Universities have changed significantly in the last decade, largely as a result of their changing financial environment. With financial help from the Ministry, universities have developed new information systems (accounting, finance, personnel management, student records, etc.). The contractual policy has also introduced an incentive for the development of internal evaluation systems. With the support of the Ministry, university administrators began to reflect on and obtain training in management techniques.

While the government initially feared that the new policy would translate into a loss of state power, the central system-level administration did not abandon its control over the higher education system. Instead, it can be said that the overall control of the Ministry over the higher education system increased when the focus attention shifted from detailed administration to strategic management (Berrivin and Musselin 1996: 591).

NOTES

[1] Johnes (1992) has described the attitude of British universities colluding to protect themselves against the will of the government to introduce competition.

[2] Warwick was one of the European "entrepreneurial universities" studied by Burton Clark (1998).

[3] In the legal context of the French public administration where the authority of public bodies is founded on a delegation from the state, the idea that contracts could be signed between the state and public agencies seems very odd to lawyers and difficult to accept for a central administration staffed with people trained in public law. The asymmetry of power inherent in such agreements has lead some analysts to call them "negotiated public rules" rather than "contracts". Nevertheless, the term contract had a lot of appeal and gained widespread use.

REFERENCES

Becher, T., and M. Kogan. *Process and Structure in Higher Education*. London: Routledge, 1992

Berrivin R., and C. Musselin. " Les politiques de contractualisation entre centralisation et décentralisation: Le cas de l'équipement et de l'enseignement supérieur ." *Sociologie du Travail* 4 (1996): 575 – 596

Chevaillier T. "Moving Away from Central Planning: Using Contracts to Steer Higher Education in France." *European Journal of Education* 33.1 (1998): 65-76

CERI. *Decision Making in 14 OECD Education System*. Paris: OECD, 1995.

Clark, B.R. *Creating Entrepreneurial Universities. Organisational Pathways of Transformation*. Oxford: Pergamon, 1998

Cohen, M.D. and J.G. March. *Leadership and Ambiguity; the American College President*. MacGraw Hill, 1974.

Eicher J.C. and T. Chevaillier. "Rethinking the Finance of Post-Compulsory Education." *International Journal of Educational Research* 19.5 (1993): 445 – 519.

Frackmann, E. "The Role of Buffer Institutions in Higher Education." *Higher Education Policy* 5 (1992): 14 – 17

James, E. *Decision-making Structures and Incentives at American Higher Educational Institutions*. Erasmus: Universiteit Rotterdam, 1988.

Jarzabkowsky P. "Centralised or Decentralised? Strategic Implications of Resource Allocation Models." *Higher Education Quarterly* 56.1 (2002) (forthcoming) .

Johnes G. "Bidding for Students in Britain: Why the UFC Auction 'Failed'." *Higher Education*, 23.2 (1992): 173-182.

Kogan, M. "Academic and administrative interface", in Henkel, M. and Little, B. (eds). *Changing Relationships between Higher Education and the State*. London: Jessica Kingsley, 1999

Lang D. "Responsibility Center Budgeting and Responsibility Center Management in Theory and Practice." *Higher Education Management* 11.3 (1999): 89 – 124.

Lauglo J. " Forms of Decentralisation and Their Implications for Education. " *Comparative Education* 1 (1995): 5-29.

Mignot-Gérard, S. and C. Musselin. *Comparaison des modes de gouvernement de quatre universités françaises*. Paris: CSO/CAFI, 2000.

Musselin, C. " State/University Relations and How to Change Them: The Case of France and Germany." *European Journal of Education* 32. 2 (1997): 145 – 164

Musselin C. *La longue marche des universities*. Paris: PUF, 2001

Otten, C. " Allocation Models at University Level." *Higher Education Managemen* 8.1 (1996): 71 – 86.

Pfeffer, J. and G.R. Salancik. *The External Control of Organisations*. New York: Harper & Row, 1978.

Thys-Clement, F. and L. Wilkin. "Strategic Management and Universities: Outcomes of a European Survey." *Higher Education Management* 10.1 (1998): 13 – 28.

Williams, G. " State Finance of Higher Education: An Overview of Theoretical and Empirical Issues. " In
    Henkel, M. and B. Little (ed). *Changing Relationships between Higher Education and the State*.
    London: Jessica Kingsley, 1999, 142 – 161.
Williams, G. *Changing Patterns of Finance in Higher Education*, Buckingham: SRHE/Open University,
    1992.

INGVILD MARHEIM LARSEN

BETWEEN CONTROL, RITUALS AND POLITICS: THE GOVERNING BOARD IN HIGHER EDUCATION INSTITUTIONS IN NORWAY

1. INTRODUCTION

Great changes have taken place in the Norwegian higher education sector during the last decade. This chapter focuses on two of these changes. First, a new Act on Universities and Colleges, approved in 1995, provided more autonomy to the institutions by delegating decision-making authority on a number of issues to the individual institutions. This new arrangement places a stronger emphasis on leadership within institutions. Second, there was a reorganisation of the college sector in 1994 that included a reform of governing system in accordance with the principles of the Act. The state colleges represent a newly established institutional context in Norwegian higher education. The merger of 98 regional colleges into 26 state colleges in 1994 resulted in the foundation of a new organisational framework within which decisions are made. Behind this college reform was a clear desire for a change in this sector, and, as the governing body at the institutional level, the college board became the focal point for change.

The elected bodies are important actors in the decision-making process in the colleges, and the governing board is the most important body at the institutional level. The main purpose of this chapter is to focus attention on the manner in which these boards function in practice. The central issue is the degree to which these boards actually govern the colleges. Themes relating to the board's latitude for action and the extent to which boards actually make decisions are central topics in the chapter.

Three perspectives on organisations will be used in order to illustrate the approach to this question. An instrumental perspective focuses on those roles that may be expected given the board's mandate. The point of departure for this approach is the legal foundation of the board. Neo institutional theory focuses attention on the possible decoupling between the formal structure and actual behaviour, and addresses the circumstances under which this arises. In a political model, the board is seen as an arena for the exercise of power and the promotion of interests in an environment where members have preferences that they attempt to advance through negotiation and formation of coalitions.

Alberto Amaral, Glen A. Jones and Berit Karseth (eds.), Governing Higher Education:
National Perspectives on Institutional Governance, 99—119.
© 2002 *Kluwer Academic Publishers. Printed in the Netherlands.*

2. IN BETWEEN TWO REFORMS

The merging process in 1994 was the most comprehensive reorganisation that has ever taken place in Norwegian higher education. The reform encompassed the regional colleges, colleges of teacher training, engineering, health education, social work and other small and specialised colleges. The reorganisation of the college sector affected about half of the students in the higher education system. One of the outcomes of the reform was the development of a formal binary system in Norway.

Today the higher education sector in Norway includes 4 universities, 6 specialised university level institutions, 26 state colleges, and a number of private colleges. The universities and the university-level institutions are responsible for most basic research and research training. The state colleges are responsible for a wide variety of profession and vocation-oriented teaching programmes, and, in addition, have taken on some of the university programmes in basic and undergraduate education. Programmes are normally two to four years in length. In some fields the state colleges also offer graduate and doctoral education. Many students combine courses at the colleges with courses at universities.

The aim of the state college sector is to make higher education more widely available while increasing the amount of academic expertise available to the different regions of Norway.

Even though great changes took place in the Norwegian higher education sector during the nineties, the higher education system in Norway is facing a new comprehensive reform that will take place within the next few years. In the spring of 2001, a White Paper announced a reform of the quality of higher education that encompasses both universities and colleges. These changes will affect the governance structure of higher education institutions. According to the Ministry, the current form of organisation does not provide universities and colleges with sufficient freedom and responsibility to achieve overall objectives. The Ministry therefore proposes that universities and colleges be redefined as administrative bodies with formal competencies, and that educational institutions be allowed greater freedom in academic, financial and organisational issues. By changing the form of association and creating a wider gap between the Ministry and the educational institutions, the Ministry wishes to emphasise the educational institutions' independent responsibility for shaping their own future. This reform will further reinforce the current trend towards greater institutional autonomy. The reform also means a change in the composition of the board; an increase in the number of external board members is proposed, coupled with a reduction in the number of employees on the board.

This study took place after the reform of the college sector, but before the reform of the quality of higher education, which will be implemented in the coming years.

3. THE UNIVERSITY AND COLLEGE SECTOR – A SYSTEM WITH INHERENT TENSIONS

The movement towards mass education and a stronger market orientation have characterized developments in Norwegian higher education over the last decade.

One consequence of these developments has been an intensified debate concerning the governance and management of the system. This led to an expansion of board responsibilities. A similar process, where "governing bodies were thrust into the front line," has also been observed in other western countries (Bargh et al., 1996: 9). In addition to expanding the role of these boards, they have also evolved from being functionally complex representative bodies into smaller executive bodies.

This development has contributed to reinforcing the view of universities and colleges as complex institutions where different organisational and governing models exist side by side. First we have the traditional collegial model where professionals direct and control each other; second, the representative system where the question of participation dominates, and third, the bureaucratic model where line management and hierarchy are central features. In recent years there has also been a change in public policy in a number of areas of the welfare state. Among other things, this change has been marked by the introduction of market-type solutions and quasi markets, increased decentralisation of public control and a more competitive mentality. This change has resulted in the emergence of a new culture in the public sector where elements of the private sector have been incorporated. These elements have come in addition to, rather than as substitutes for, established systems. As public institutions, universities and colleges have also been affected by these changes. This increased market orientation has resulted in a situation where internal academic considerations and democratic values are no longer predominant in the governance of these institutions. The major challenge to the higher education system will be to manage the tensions between these different and somewhat opposing approaches. This change in public policy has meant that the board is regarded as an arena for change and as a means for quality assurance (Bargh et al., 1996: 21,22).

The governing body is playing on a stage with many actors. The question is which role the board should play within the whole system of management. The law defines the board's tasks and its formal place within the college structure. The University and College Act places the board at the top of the pyramid and empowers this body with responsibility for the overall function of the institution. As the institution's highest governing body with overall responsibility for the institution's activities, the board is undoubtedly an important forum.

The various steering principles in the university and college system are in many respects sustained by the law that defines the board's tasks and composition. Professional interests and loyalty are accounted for in that the academic staff has a majority of seats on the board and the rector is elected by, and is a member of, the academic staff. Democratic and representative principles are preserved in that college management involves an elected body and also that various groups have a seat on the formal decision-making bodies. In order to improve the efficiency, the board has relatively few members. The idea of managerialism is reflected in the 'total responsibility' assigned to this body and the introduction of external members on the board.

Since universities and colleges operate with a greater degree of autonomy than other public organisations, the board plays an important role in establishing external support for these institutions. The board can be considered as a response to the demand for external accountability. The presence of external members is an important element in this. The external members can be seen as a means for society to exercise influence on the institutions. As such, the board may be seen as a meeting place for the college and the society.

Even though different principles have been included in the governing system, some are nevertheless more predominant than others. The reason that the previous representative board was replaced by a smaller body with personally elected members was that the former was regarded as an inefficient system that had trouble making strategic decisions. The principle of functional representation is now incorporated into the council structure. The changes in the governing structure for universities and colleges can thus be regarded as an attempt to combine the democratic element – which is embodied in a large council with functional representation – with an approach that attaches primary importance to the function of an executive body. Since the governing board is given considerable authority while the council is intended to function as an advisory body, the changes which have taken place undoubtedly favour 'management ideals', while the democratic values incorporated into a representative system are correspondingly toned down. This development can be found throughout the western world. In many countries the governance system of universities and colleges changed during the 1990s. One consequence of this change is that the democratic approach to university governance has been put under pressure (de Boer, Denters and Goedegebuure 1998). Consideration of the governance capacity and efficiency of the system has displaced power from the representative system, transferring it to an executive body.

The 1996 Act on Universities and Colleges identifies five areas where the board has particular responsibility. First, the board is "responsible for maintaining a high standard of academic quality". Second, the board shall "draw up a strategy for the institution's educational programme, research and other academic activities". Third, the board is responsible for the institution's financial resources. Fourth, it is responsible for ensuring that the internal organisation of activities is appropriate and cost effective, and, fifth, the board is responsible for the budget, accounts and the reporting of results. It is underlined that the board is responsible for all of these tasks and must act in accordance with applicable laws, regulations, rules, limits and targets laid down by the authorities.

Each board has 9, 11 or 13 members and includes the rector in addition to representatives of the academic staff, technical personnel, students and external board members. The rector, elected by the staff, is the chairman of the board. The members are elected for a three-year term (except for the student representatives). The act assumes that both universities and colleges will have between 2 and 4 external representatives on the board. While external members were new to the universities, this was a well-established procedure for some colleges; for others it was new. As I have already noted, the Ministry of Education has proposed that the boards include more external members.

The Act on Universities and Colleges also states that each institution must have an advisory Council at the institutional level. Under the proposed reforms, this advisory Council will no longer be obligatory. The academic activities of the institution are to be organised into faculties. The institutions themselves may establish departments as a third level. There are faculty and department-level boards that are delegated authority from the institution's board. The institution's board determines the size and composition of each faculty and department board, which can include external members; though academic staff must hold the majority of seats.

4. DATA AND METHOD

The study is based on data from several sources. First, the study draws on data from a questionnaire survey. All members of the boards, both internal and external representatives, of the 26 colleges were sent a questionnaire in the spring of 1998. This means that the new structure had been in place almost 4 years at the time the survey was conducted. A total of 230 responses (80%) were received. The response rate was high for all categories of members, but highest for the students (87%) and the rectors (85%), and lowest for the external members (78%). Second, the study draws on data obtained from in-depths interviews that were carried out in eight colleges. These eight colleges vary according to geography, size in terms of number of students and staff, organisational structure, academic profile, and whether they have a unified or multiple-campus physical location. The interviews took place in two phases, first, in 1996 and 1997, and then some additional interviews were conducted in early 1999. Both academic and administrative leaders working at different levels were interviewed. In addition, the study utilizes data obtained written materials, primarily documents prepared by the Ministry of Education and Research. Finally, this study makes reference to an analysis of the minutes of board meetings in the eight colleges for 1997.

5. THE ANALYTICAL FRAMEWORK

The boards were studied using three perspectives: an instrumental, an institutional and a political perspective. Each of these theoretical approaches provides us with a different way of understanding the role of the board.

5.1. Boards as instruments

An instrumental perspective implies that the organisation can be considered as a means for achieving specific goals (Scott 1987). The core assumption in this perspective is that formal structure controls behaviour. Formal structure comprises a stable, impersonal and written set of expectations for persons in a specific position. Further, the formal structure regulates participation and the agenda, both in terms of problems and solutions (March and Olsen, 1976).

Based on this perspective, the board's position in the organisational structure and the board's mandate determine the board's work and its influence on the institution. The expectations with respect to the board are prescribed in the Act of Universities and Colleges, which also defines the board's functions. This implies that the board's legal role and responsibility are central issues. One would expect that the tasks assigned to the board directly influence the roles that the board will play.

The board is required to present an annual report and financial statement in addition to its responsibility for ensuring that activities and the use of resources are carried out in accordance with the aims of the superior authority. This indicates that the board is expected to carry out a *control function*. Since the Act states that the board is responsibility for determining the strategy for the institution's academic activity, the role of *academic strategy body* is also highly relevant for the board.

In addition being the highest level of authority in the institution, boards in state institutions can also be considered as a link in the chain between the state and the institutions. The need for external control of the organisation's internal decisions has often been the basis for establishing a board (Mintzberg 1983: 243). The board is responsible to the Ministry of Education, Research and Church Affairs and the colleges find themselves in an administrative hierarchy with the Ministry as the superior political administrative level. The political authorities do not have direct representation on the board but they do appoint external members. The relationship to public authorities is clearly expressed in the Act of Universities and Colleges. Even though it is emphasised that the board is the college's superior decision-making body, with responsibility for all activities of the college, this responsibility is largely concerned with ensuring that the institution functions "in accordance with those laws, directives and regulations which apply, and the framework and objectives stipulated by the authority." (Universities and Colleges Act, §4). As such, the board's *role as a unit in a state hierarchical system* is highly relevant. Based on this role, the board should act in the interests of the state and fulfil two central tasks. The first task is to receive and interpret signals from the political system to the institution, and ensure that the political system's policies are considered and followed. As such, the board contributes to implementing public policy. The second task is to ensure that the state as 'owner' is informed about the activities of the institution. This role as informant is closely allied to the control function.

The board's advisory functions with respect to the academic and administrative leadership of the college can also be deduced from the instrumental model. The rationale for including external representatives on the board representatives clearly emerged in the preliminary work that led to the Act of Universities and Colleges. According to Bernt (2000), the commission for the new act (NOU 1993: 24), the Ministry (Ot.orp.nr.85, 1993-94) and the parliamentary committee (Innst. O nr. 40 (1994-95)), all emphasised that the reason for including external members was to broaden the expertise of the board. If the board is a resource that shall contributes skills not found internally within the organisation, the board can be described as an *advisory board*. This role also includes forming links with society and exercising control and exerting influence over critical elements in this society.

Studies have shown that public servants are characterised more by their position in organisations than their social background (Lægreid and Olsen 1978: 269). However, there is a strong possibility that social characteristics influence the behaviour of collegial organisations more than hierarchical organisations, where socialisation and discipline are stronger forces. Members of the board are part-time participants in the sense that they only devote part of their time to board functions and have another main occupation. This part-time membership contributes to the fact that collegial bodies do not have the same capacity or social mechanisms to modify member behaviour that are associated with hierarchical organisation. Personal factors are therefore assumed to have a greater effect in collegial, compared with hierarchical, organisations. The individual's main occupation or position within the organisation will be important in understanding that member's views and modes of action.

Given the mandate specified in the Act of Universities and Colleges and the rationale behind the introduction of external members, we can expect, from an instrumental perspective, that the board will fill the roles of an academic strategy body, control body, an agency in the state hierarchy and an advisory body.

5.2. Boards as rituals

The second approach to the study of the college board is inspired by neo institutionalism. Of special interest in this connection is the assumption within neo institutional theory of decoupling the formal structure from actual organisational behaviour. The theory represents a break away from the assumption that structure controls actions. According to the theory, the façade showing an apparent accordance between formal governing and behavioural patterns might conceal the division between formal structures and processes and observed behaviour (Meyer and Rowan 1977). Since external demands are obligatory but are regarded as unsuitable based on existing values, structures and organisational forms are developed that give the appearance of responding to external pressure. These structures function as an empty holster without any influence, other than the symbolic and in terms of establishing legitimacy. Instead of formal structure, culture becomes a central issue in terms of being able to understand actions.

This perspective is particularly relevant for universities and colleges because they have high levels of institutional autonomy but are also, at the same time, part of the state hierarchy. As an administrative agency in a state hierarchical structure of governance, the institutions must follow the line of public policy in their area. This implies that the colleges must adapt to the various strains of public authority. In contrast, the norms of academic freedom and autonomy dominate the internal organisation. The system is characterised by the fact that the academic community is the core element rather than the formal structure. Universities and colleges are often characterised as decentralised organisations where the academic staff have a large degree of independence and where the autonomy of the lower-level units is an obstacle to governance from the top (Mintzberg 1983; Van Vught 1988). The combination of state control on the one hand, and autonomy on the other, implies that we are concerned with complex organisations where there are tensions between the formal and the informal. Problems that arise when different 'logics' meet are solved in that an apparent adjustment takes place, but the formal structural change has no effect.

How would we expect a college board to function as seen from a neo institutional standpoint? The question is whether some of the tasks to be undertaken by the board conflict with the prevailing norms in the college. Regarding the board's responsibility for strategy and quality control of research, there is reason to believe that the board's tasks are on a collision course with traditional values. Academic freedom and loyalty to the field of study suggest that the board will face difficulty in exercising control over academic activities. The board's responsibility within these areas can be restricted to symbolic activity in the form of planning documents without follow-up or control. A board that devotes little attention to its strategic and control responsibilities will retain a symbolic function within the institution as it approves decisions that are made elsewhere. A board of this character can be considered a formal body with *ritual functions*. When the board has the role of a formal body or instrument it retains two functions (Reve 1993). First, the board can legitimise the college's activity within its surroundings. Governance then has a legal construction that meets the legitimate requirements of being headed by a governing board. Conformity with the formal structure is a means of acquiring legitimacy and support from the community. This implies that the focus is on those board activities that establish this legitimacy. Second, the board is a *'rubber-stamp'* in so far as it approves and follows the advice of others. At the same time it is important to point out that the board, as a formal body, has governance authority that is being held in reserve but which it might choose to exercise at some point in time.

The relationships between the board and the governing bodies at the faculty level and between the board and the administration are important when analysing the board as a rubber-stamp. The Act of Universities and Colleges states that there should normally be two organisational levels – the college level and the faculty level with a governing body at each level. The faculty board is delegated authority from the institution's board. In addition, the colleges may choose to create a third level in the form of departments. This implies that a number of matters presented to the college board have been considered at both the faculty and departmental levels. One possible consequence in an organisation with two or more levels is that the board will find it difficult to oppose proposals and decisions that come from lower levels of the organisation. The faculty level will have greater understanding of academic issues, and therefore the faculty board may have more legitimacy as a governing body for academic activity than the college board. Given this situation, the college board may function as a rubber-stamp in terms of approving the recommendations of the faculty board.

The administration can also contribute to undermining the board's role. According to the Act, universities and colleges are organised as two parallel leadership pyramids; one academic, headed by an elected Rector, and one administrative, headed by an administrative director. The administration is important to the board in two respects. The administrative leadership is the most important source of information for the board, including providing the board with background materials and proposals. If the board follows the director's recommendations and remains passive by failing to consider alternative proposals, it will emerge as a formal body where control, in reality, lies in the hands of the administration. In addition, it is important to remember that the administration plays an important role in terms of implementing the board's decisions. Furthermore, the new University and College Act assigned increased powers to the Director compared to the previous arrangement. This suggests a situation where there is some ambiguity in the relationship between the board and the administration. On the one hand, the Director, as the chief administrator, controls the whole administrative structure of the institution in addition to having independent, formal responsibility for financial management. On the other hand, it is the board that is charged with the overall responsibility for the activities of the institution.

5.3. Boards as political arenas

While the instrumental and the neo institutional perspectives presented above primarily focuses on the outcomes of the board's activities, the process aspect of the board's work is a central feature of the political model. The political model focuses on how the board functions as a decision-making arena. While the first two perspectives view the board as an entity, the political model assumes that the board is composed of members with different views, interests and aims, and that the board is an arena for interest promotion and political struggle. The political perspective concentrates on features of difference of interests, values and norms (Middlehurst 1993: 52). These differences give rise to competition and conflict between different actors. Since no single group has a majority position in the organisation, there is a need for various groups to become allied and create coalitions.

Different internal and external interests are represented on the board. This means that the board can function as an interest organisation – an arena for negotiation and struggle for power. Decisions will be made through voting procedures. Furthermore, a political perspective focuses attention on the struggle for representation; what characterises the nomination process and the election of board members, and to what extent do members have a mandate and function as representatives for the various parties? Concern for the institution as a whole may be absent when the board functions as an interest organisation. The Ministry of Education has emphasised that representation on the board is a personal attribute and that "the internal members are not to be regarded as representatives for organisations or for interest groups, but as board members it is assumed that they participate in board activities with a general responsibility for all aspects of the college's function" (Ot.prp.nr.85, 1993 – 94: 41). The Act, however, states that all groups within the institution should be represented on the board and it can be regarded as being interest-group-based. It is therefore possible that the board will function as a *political arena*. As a political arena, processes will be characterised by the promotion of interests, conflict and negotiation. It will become a tool for different interests and alliances, where resolutions are made following negotiation, compromise, bargaining or voting, and where the decisions reflect the dominant coalition on the board.

Given this focus on the college board as a political arena, it is also interesting to see whether the board plays *a lobbyist role* in terms of defending and strengthening the institution's position within the broader political arena. In this respect it will be of particular interest to view the role of the Rector, who is the chairman of the board and is the institution's lawful representative and its spokesperson in relation to the political authorities and the public. For the lobbyist, the main task is to defend and strengthen the institution's position, particularly with respect to finance. By placing pressure on the authorities, the aim is to influence the decision-makers in a specific direction. Research indicates that parliamentary lobbying has increased in Norway during the last twenty years (Espeli 1996: 270). The colleges' attempts to advance their interests must be seen as part of this broader picture.

There are, however, processes that may moderate the character of the board as an arena for different interests and conflict. Though board members may initially have different preferences and interests, studies have shown that representation results in co-optation. The co-optation of external members, for example, can result in these individuals becoming supporters of, rather than opponents to, the institution's traditional norms and values. Board members develop a sense of loyalty towards the institution.

6. THE COLLEGE BOARD AS A GOVERNING ARENA

In the theoretical discussion, three different approaches to analysing the board's work within the college sector were presented. Each perspective, in turn, suggests different roles that the board may exercise. In this section the focus is on the manner in which the college boards play these roles.

6.1. The strategic role and control function

According to an instrumental approach, the mandate provides the guidelines for the board's work. The question is whether the board can influence the institution's activities. A precondition is that the board members actually understand the mandate. Questionnaire data obtained from members of the college boards indicate that the majority of representatives consider the mandate to be relatively clear. A minority, 15 percent, indicated it is fairly unclear. As the vast majority do not report any difficulty in interpreting the mandate, there is little reason to believe that any problems arising in the board's activities are due to an unclear mandate.

According to the mandate, there are two particular tasks that are essential for an active board. The first is control and the second is strategy. If importance is only attached to the first, we are only dealing with a control board, but a board that combines the dimension of control and strategy can be characterised as a strategic board (Reve 1993). The financial responsibility with which the board is charged implies the responsibility of control over the use of resources. A common feature of the college boards is that, to date, considerable time has been spent on financial matters, which suggests that it is a control body. The survey shows that the majority of board members consider supervision and control functions as tasks that the board undertakes (Table 1). An analysis of board minutes at eight colleges also indicates that this category of activity ranks among the highest in board matters (Figure 1).

The board has, in addition, the responsibility for ensuring that the organisation has a strategy. In order to develop a strategy, i.e. to formulate the organisation's aims and objectives, it is necessary to have an overview of the situation. The control function will also be an important input in the strategic work of the board, and, as such, these two functions are closely interwoven. If the college board is to fulfil the intentions of the Act, it will have to fulfil both control and strategic requirements. The board's mandate, as such, implies that the board will have influence over the college. The question is whether the board succeeds in fulfilling its mission.

The college board's strategic responsibility implies, among other things, academic leadership. Given the academic specialisation and freedom that characterises the academic staff in higher educational institutions, one might expect that this is a difficult role for the board. Among board members, there is a somewhat surprisingly large number who indicate that the board largely, or mainly, fulfils this function (Table 1). The interviews data suggest a somewhat more problematic situation. The available data to not indicate the extent to which these strategic plans actually guide academic activity in the colleges. A recurring theme in the interview material is that the board aims to have a strategic role. For example, one interviewee stated "the board is attempting to be more strategic."

Table 1. Board members' evaluation of the various board roles. (Percent response by scale category; N=230)

	To a large extent	To some extent	To a small extent	Not at all	Don't know	Total
Professional strategy body	30	50	18	2	1	101
Supervisory/ control body	15	57	23	2	3	100
Resource allocation body	61	25	12	0	1	99
Link between state and college	23	45	24	6	2	100
Appeals Body	9	26	49	8	7	99
Body for handling single issues	17	47	32	2	2	100
Strengthens college's external position	20	43	28	5	4	100
Advisory body for rector and director	14	52	24	7	4	101
Negotiating body for different internal groups	5	18	48	24	6	101

The minutes of the board meetings are another source of information on how the board copes with academic leadership. Consideration of proposals for new study courses is one of the items in the minutes that might address the question whether the board fulfils its task as professional strategy organ. Naturally, new study courses constitute a large group of items that receive board attention indicating that the board has academic leadership functions. However, it should be noted that the academic units initiate the majority of these proposals; the board gives its approval and passes on its recommendations for implementation to the Ministry. In this connection the board appears to be more of a rubber stamp than a real strategic body for academic activity. Furthermore, the minutes show that the board at each of the eight colleges handled matters in the category 'plan and programme measures' (Figure 1). These are largely matters of strategic character. Each of these eight boards dealt with less than ten matters of this type during the course of a year. In total, these issues represented 5% of all board items at these colleges. Clearly strategic matters do not dominate the minutes of board meetings. However, the degree to which the board focuses on these issues is obviously more important than the number of matters of this type. It is possible that this type of item receives considerable attention when it finally appears on the agenda.

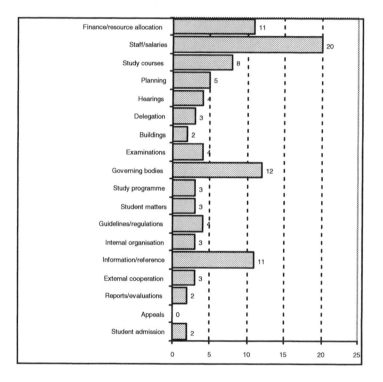

Figure 1. Items raised at board meetings based on an analysis of board minutes of eight colleges. Percent.

The board's strategic function may also come to expression during the preparation of the budget. If strategic plans are to be achieved, they must receive priority in the budget. In times of budget cuts this is an extra challenge, as new activities must be realised through a reallocation of resources. The extent to which the board managed to redistribute resources internally within the college is therefore an important indicator as to whether it has functioned strategically. Only ten percent of the respondents indicated that their board has been successful in its reallocation of resources, while about half suggested that the board has been fairly successful in this task. The interview material supports the impression that the board has not functioned as a strategic body in the matter of resource allocation. The respondents stated that historical data, rather than strategic considerations, have the greatest influence over the distribution of resources in the colleges. Even though the boards at several of the colleges indicated an interest in developing a new model for allocating resources between the various educational courses, the potential for conflict was so great that a cautious approach was necessary. A study of attempts to reallocate resources between the various fields of learning at the University of Oslo found it can be extremely difficult to shift resources from one unit to another (Langfeldt 1991).

One danger for a board that attaches great importance to control, is that it will focus too much attention on controlling details rather than broad policy. What is the situation in the college boards in this respect? It was unanimous among those interviewed that detail-oriented decisions are not the responsibility of the board. The data, however, suggests that the college board, like other types of elected bodies, has a tendency to allow details to dominate. An analysis of the interview data suggests when matters of principle do come on to the agenda the level of involvement is somewhat lower than when matters of detail are under discussion. The board's focus on certain matters can be an indication of whether it is 'detail-oriented' or whether it concentrates on the essential issues. The survey of board members revealed that many of the representatives believed that the board functions as a body for dealing with single issues, that is, matters which board members find difficult to link to a broad category of issues. In fact, some 60 percent agreed that the board, to at least some extent, is a body for handling individual matters (Table 1). The degree of detail in the board's work is a generally recognised problem, but this is taken as the 'price' to be paid for establishing common standards throughout the institution.

6.2. The Board – a bridge for external interests?

As I have already noted, boards in the public sector may be seen as a link between state authority and the institution. This is a view shared by many representatives on college boards. Almost 70 percent of the representatives agreed that the board functions as a link between the state and the college (Table 1). Given this finding, it is important to determine whether the board acts on behalf of the institution in terms of influencing the environment and a buffer against external influence, or whether it is a tool for external interests to exert influence on the organisation. A central question in this connection is whether the college board has the autonomy to play a real governing role and influence the core activities of the organisation. Or does it possess so little freedom for action that the governing function is empty or merely symbolic?

The college reform that led to the merger of 98 educational institutions into 26 partly was, in part, designed to address the increasing workload of the Ministry. The Ministry's problem in terms of its capacity to deal with this large system was solved by reducing the number of institutions and delegating responsibility to the college boards. This arrangement can be regarded as a mechanism for increasing the state's capacity for steering. The boards function under the power granted by the public authorities while, at the same time, they remain responsible to these authorities. When the board takes up this administrative role, the primary function of the board is to preserve the interests of the state within the field of higher education. This role is closely associated to the control function described above.

A board within the public sector may be held hostage by the policies of the state. Given this possibility, it is important to clarify the relationship between the board and the role of the Ministry. The internal organisation of activity is explicitly mentioned in the Act as one of five main areas where the board has a special responsibility. In this light, it is somewhat remarkable that the Ministry must approve changes in the departmental structure when, according to the Act, it is the board which has the responsibility for determining the appropriate internal organisation of the institution! Regarding the colleges, the Ministry, on the recommendation of the board, actually determines the departmental structure. This procedure is followed because the departmental structure is seen as "relevant to national interests" (Bernt 2000: 66). The Ministry must also approve new courses in the colleges. Until quite recently, this applied to all courses of study irrespective of scope or length. The colleges now have the ability to establish programmes of study of up to 30 study points (generally corresponding to the first one and one-half years of university courses) without seeking the approval of the Ministry. In addition, large components of the programmes of study offered in the colleges are controlled by national core curriculum determined by the Ministry. These are examples that illustrate how the boards' management functions can come into conflict with, and restrict, its role as a strategic body with overall responsibility for the college.

Furthermore, it is important to note that the director has an independent financial responsibility in relation to the Ministry. The director's direct relationship with the Ministry concerning the institution's financial management can be interpreted as a break in the steering structure where the board has overall responsibility for the institution. The right to make budgetary proposals remains, however, with the board; the same applies to the right to approve the annual plan. These plans, however, have been found to have a limited effect on higher education institutions (Larsen and Gornitzka 1995), and this responsibility does not necessarily mean that the board can influence the organisation.

Nothing emerges from the data to suggest the direct involvement of the Ministry in the board's activities. However, the majority of board members believe that government regulations and requirements restrict their actions (Table 2). The rectors, in particular, feel that the state authorities restrict the freedom of the board. Since the Rectors have the closest contact with the authorities, there is reason to attach importance to their viewpoint in this area. This theme also emerged in the interviews; participants indicated that the work of the board is restricted because the Ministry holds tight reins on the colleges. Many found that a considerable amount of board activity is bound up in regulations, which, in part, prevent new developments and reorganisation. Some suggest that the board has less influence than might be suggested by the Universities and Colleges Act.

Table 2. Board members' views on the autonomy of the college board (Percent response by scale category; N=230)

	To a large extent	To some extent	To a small extent	Not at all	Don't know	Total
Restricted by regulations and imposition by authorities	41	47	10	0	1	99
Restricted by activities and resistance in the academic fields	12	48	33	6	1	100
Restricted by activities and resistance by the administration	6	25	47	20	2	100

6.3. The Board's advisory role

When one focuses on the consultative role of the board, the main question is whether the board functions as support for the academic and administrative leadership within the institution. The assumption is that external representatives on the board can compensate for the lack of internal expertise within the organisation. As noted in the theoretical section, this was the intention behind the appointment of external representatives to university and college boards.

The selection of external candidates will often pose a dilemma since the best candidates are frequently in great demand and, given their busy schedules, may not have the time necessary to function as advisors to the board. This seems to be a current problem facing the colleges. Even though the arrangement with external representatives has been well received, their absenteeism has been a problem in certain colleges. The absence of external representatives at board meetings is unfortunate, but understandable, since these are busy individuals with important positions in organisations and business.

Prior to the establishment of the Act for Universities and Colleges, many were critical of the notion of including external members on boards. Subsequently, however, the majority of board members have come to regard it as an excellent arrangement. Members pointed out that the external representatives have made constructive contributions to board meetings. Their ability to shift the focus of attention to rise above the different internal interests was considered helpful in terms of the work of the board. The fact that they have raised important questions on a number of issues was described as being extremely useful. The following quotation serves to illustrate how internal members evaluated their external counterparts:

> The corrections we receive from the external members of the board is something we need. We have a need to know what the society expects of us. It is here that we receive strong signals from the external members. We are too frequently contemplating our own

navels, and should be much more oriented towards the needs of society than we are
today. (Interview).

The majority of respondents fully supported the new arrangement of including
external members on the board and indicated that their participation largely met the
objective of supplementing the board with experience beyond that contributed by the
internal representatives. The interviews included many reference to how external
members have made positive contributions and the how the new arrangement has
benefited the colleges. This also implies that the board functions, at least in part, as a
advisory board. The board's advisory role was reinforced by the responses to the
questionnaire; two-thirds of respondents indicated that the board acts as a advisory
body for the leadership. This suggests that the board regards itself as a resource and
a forum for providing advice to the leadership, while at the same time the board can
contribute to establishing contacts both internally and externally.

6.4. The Board and internal relationships

In this section the focus is on the relationship between the board and the
administrative leadership, and the board and the faculty level. The question is
whether the board functions as a rubber-stamp with respect to these internal actors.
If the board functions as at formal body, it is the board's symbolic functions that
stand in focus. Such tasks are important in so far as they are imposed by law and
important to acquiring public funds. In this situation, the board attends to the legally
imposed requirements but does not function as the real governing body. As a formal
body the board focuses on two tasks: 1) approval of decisions, and 2) legitimising
the activities of the institution (Reve 1993). The most important task for a board of
this type is to approve decisions recommended by other internal actors. A board that
restricts its activity to approving the budget and accounts can be regarded as a
'minimum board' that has failed in its essential functions. Formally, the board has
the right to manage and direct, but this only occurs in exceptional circumstance. In
spite of the fact that the real management takes place elsewhere in the organisation,
the board can serve a role in terms of legitimising the internal activities of the
college in terms of the external environment.

When it comes to the relationship between the college board and the
administration, it is clear that the administration is the most important source of
information and the main source of proposals for the board. The leadership presents
an agenda of issues requiring decisions and makes recommendations and proposals
for resolving these issues. In contrast to the board, the administrative leadership
involves full-time employees. The relationship will frequently be characterised by
asymmetric access to information where the administration will be the dominant
player given its role in preparing the background materials for board meetings. The
administration is also important to the board since it implements the decisions of the
board. In this lies the possibility that the college board may function as a formal
body. Certain aspects of the data also point in this direction. Some of the interview
subjects indicated that the board primarily responds to the initiatives of the
administration and infrequently takes the initiative itself. Others were of the opinion

that the college administration works very independently in terms of preparing the agenda for board meetings. The volume of orientation matters on the board's agenda may be another indication that the board merely functions as a rubber-stamp. The analysis of the board minutes at eight colleges found that, in addition to the total number of items under 'orientation/information', there are a number of separate matters under each item. This implies that the number of board matters concerning orientation/information may be greater than suggested in Figure 1.

There are, however, elements of the data that do not support the view that the administration controls the board. First, the rector and director at many colleges cooperate closely. What may appear for many to be an item on the agenda initiated by the director will often be the result of the close liaison with the rector. The Universities and Colleges Act also assumes that board will deal with matters "after consultation with the rector". The board's approval role with respect to proposals prepared by the administration may also be handled in different ways. The formal role will be passive if matters are only accepted as information, but a more active approving role is implied if the board raises critical questions. Further, one cannot assume that all of the administration's proposals are accepted by the board. An examination of the board documents shows that it is not unusual for the representatives to work towards a new proposal at the meeting that then receives board approval. The data from the survey of board members suggests that the relationship between the administration and the board was viewed as good, and that few members perceived that the activities or opposition of the administration limited the autonomy of the board (Table 2). Another factor, which may be worth noting, is that a majority of board representatives in the colleges are not part-time participants in the organisation as is the case with board members of other organisations. The rector is a full-time position and many of the internal members are full-time employees of the college. It is only the external members who have a part-time affiliation with the institution. We might therefore assume that most board members have a good knowledge of the organisation. The internal network in the colleges may also mean that the administration is not the only source of recommendations for board decisions.

The administration is not the only internal body that the board must maintain a relationship with. The faculty level also has to be taken into consideration. It will be difficult for the college board to implement decisions that conflict with decisions taken by the faculty board. The questionnaire data indicates that over fifty percent of members consider that opposition among the academic staff limits the freedom of action of the board to at least some extent (Table 2). Another factor, which supports the view of the board as a formal body with respect to the faculties, is the 'historical argument' when resource allocation decisions are debated. The budget is only modestly influenced by criteria determined by the board.

6.5. The Board as a political arena

According to the Universities and Colleges Act, the board is not intended to be a representative body. It is, nevertheless, structured so as to ensure that various internal and external interests are represented. If these representatives appear with a pre-determined mandate and regard themselves as representatives of the various groups, it can be difficult for the board to function as a cohesive entity. The question is whether the board has the ability to function as a collegium, or whether its work has political elements that become manifest when self-interests are promoted and coalitions are generated.

The interviews revealed that several colleges had experienced certain problems in getting the board to function as one unit. Particularly in the first period following the merger process, the boards at several colleges functioned more as a representative body rather than a governing board for the whole institution. Particularly in connection with the budget, the representatives argued forcefully for faculty interests. In general it appears as though staff representatives have functioned as interest representatives for their academic alliances, showing lesser consideration to advance the broader interests of the institution. This is a problem that has been experienced by many colleges, although it has improved of late. The survey undertaken some eighteen months after the first interviews support the impression that the majority of board members no longer regard this as a general problem (Table 1). It was also noted that students and external members of the board have been engaged in non-partisan solutions. Their ability to disregard the various internal interests is regarded as beneficial to the board's work. The data collected for this study indicates that the board increasingly functions as a collegium that focuses on the college as a whole. This may be interpreted as a process characterised by co-optation where representation leads to joint responsibility and reduced political influence.

The board has attached importance to consensus in its work, not that this means that there has not been any disagreement, but in the sense that the board has worked towards solutions based on general agreement. Decisions are reached through discussion rather than by vote. An examination of the board minutes shows that of those issues that were on the agenda in the eight colleges studied in 1997, there were very few situations where the entire board was not unanimous in reaching its decision. The unanimity associated with these decisions suggests that the board does not function primarily as a political forum characterised by votes, power struggles, alliances and conflict.

According to the law, the rector is the institution's spokesperson in relation to public authorities and the public. Following the reform, the rector, as academic leader, has fewer administrative responsibilities than previously. On the other hand, the 'political' element of the position has greatly increased. Several of the rectors regard their role as that of political leader. Externally this role briefly entails being *primus motor* when approaching politicians to lobby for more funds to the colleges. The interview data suggests that the rectors fulfil a role as 'spokesperson for foreign affairs' for the colleges. The rectors devote considerable time to defending and strengthening the colleges' financial situation and in attempting to persuade the politicians to increase grants to colleges. Many of the rectors have assumed the role of lobbyist in respect to the political authorities. This is not an easy task, but several rectors believed that they had been able to convince politicians with their arguments.

7. SUMMARY

An instrumental perspective of the board focuses on how the board attends to its functions. According to the Universities and Colleges Act, the board has a control function. The data suggests that this is a mandate that the college boards take seriously. The problem with the control function is the temptation to exercise comprehensive control, and the dangers associated with detailed control are widely recognised. Instead, the board's ambition is to be a policy-forming body with importance attached to strategic tasks. In the literature on boards, tasks related to strategy emerge as the most neglected of the board's functions (Reve 1993). There is evidence to suggest that the college boards have taken their role in terms of developing strategy seriously, but that this is a demanding task. The board's role in a new institution is particularly demanding because the board also becomes an arena for change. In a time of budget cuts, new measures are required to focus on resource reallocation. Issues related to the internal reallocation of resources in the colleges are particularly difficult.

Even though the evidence concerning issues of reallocation indicates that, to some extent, the board lacks the ability to steer the institution, the problem is also related to the limited space for action. As an agency in a state hierarchical structure, the institutions in the university and college sector occupy a special position in so far as they are afforded a higher degree of autonomy than other public institutions, but they nevertheless "carry out their functions on behalf of the state and under state supervision." (Bernt 2000: 30). This form of association between the state and the institution has an impact on the board; board members view the rules and requirements of the state authorities as the main restriction on the board's activities. In addition, many state that the board acts as an intermediary between the public authorities and the colleges. This means that, as the instrumental approach suggests, the administrative role is reflected in the board's working pattern. In spite of the fact that the University and College Act gives the board total responsibility for the overall activities of the institution, with particular importance attached to matters of primary and principle character, the same Act requires the board to respond to political signals from the authorities.

The rationale for appointing external members to the board was to provide the board with expertise and experience that was not found within the organisation. In line with an instrumental perspective, the evidence clearly suggests that the external board members fulfil certain service functions in relation to the institution and are regarded as a resource for the colleges. The evidence confirms that the external members do contribute new expertise to the work of the board. While this indicates that the board functions in some ways as a advisory body, the college board can still be considered an internal body in so far as the majority of board members are internally elected by the college staff. But, the external element has increased and become legally institutionalised.

Neo institutional theory focuses on possible differences between the formal structure and actual behaviour, and shifts attention to the board's role as a formal body. From this perspective, the board's relationship to the administration and the faculties becomes very important. According to the data, board members believe that it is the activities and resistance of the academics, rather than of the administration, that restricts the colleges' possibilities for action. The state colleges are relatively new organisations, and the links between the formal and the informal structures can take time to forge, especially in an organisation where established norms and values do not automatically disappear even in the face of substantive change. This does not apply to the same degree for the administration. The central administrative level in the colleges is composed of new units that do not have an established culture to defend.

Reform processes are rarely unproblematic and conflict-free, and no one expected that the merger of the colleges was going to be painless. The colleges represent a new institutional context where different groups have a need to re-establish themselves. Even though the system of representation and the board's mandate are designed to prevent the board from functioning as an interest body, its role as a forum for advancing the interests of various internal groups dominated the boards' work at the beginning of the reform process. The political role of the board has declined over time, and the boards seem to have been successful in moving towards developing a more collegial decision-making environment focusing on furthering the interests of the institution as a whole.

In comparison with the earlier profession-based colleges that had a permanent appointed rectors with ultimate responsibility for administrative as well as academic matters, the new arrangement assigns fewer administrative responsibilities to the rector. On the other hand, the rector now fulfils an important political function. The political aspect of the rector's role is clearly associated with the rector's work as the institution's 'foreign spokesperson' and lobbyist to the political authorities. The board, on the other hand, is not a distinctive political body in the sense that voting procedures and conflict dominate the board meetings. The boards appear to be consensus-oriented as evidenced by the fact that a large majority of decisions are unanimous.

Three theoretical approaches on organisations have been used to study the institutional board in the college sector: the instrumental approach, the neo institutional approach and the political approach. Each approach focuses attention on different aspects of the board's activities and they are intended to be complementary, rather than competing perspectives. The study shows that the college boards combine different functions. In the years to come, we can expect that the instrumental aspects of the board's work will be emphasised while the political and institutional aspects decrease in importance. The decline in the institutional aspects of the role is based on the assumption that the colleges will gradually develop a new identity and the power relationships associated with old unit identities may shift. A new common culture encompassing the whole college could emerge over time, resulting in a stronger association between the formal structure and actual behaviour. There is reason to believe that this process will accelerate as new staff are recruited. A survey at Oslo College showed that staff whose tenure went back to the earlier college system were more critical than those who were appointed subsequent to the merger (Larsen, Kyvik and Dimmen 1997). However, such processes could be reversed.

There is also evidence that the advancement of group interests does not characterise the college board to the same degree as it did in the beginning. However, the same evidence could be interpreted as suggesting that the board is now primarily a rubber-stamp. The instrumental perspective allows us to observe that the board has roles that partly contradict each other. In spite of the fact that the board has been given total responsibility for the college through the Universities and Colleges Act, the same act requires the board to respond to the political signals of the government. The law creates a situation where the board's role as an administrative body may conflict with its responsibility for strategic planning and decision-making.

REFERENCES

Bargh, C., P. Scott and D. Smith. *Governing universities : changing the culture?* Buckingham: Society for Research into Higher Education, 1996.

Bernt, J. F. *Lov om universiteter og høgskoler. Med kommentarer.* Bergen: Alma Mater forlag. Third edition, 2000.

De Boer, H., B. Denters and L. Goedegebuure. "On Board and councils; shaky balances considered. The governance of Dutch universities." *Higher education policy* 11.2/3 (1998): 153 – 164.

Espeli, H. "Lobbyvirksomhet på Stortinget." *Nytt norsk tidsskrift* 3-4 (1996): 265 – 80.

Innst O nr 40 1994 – 95 (1995): *Innstilling fra Kirke,- utdannings- og forskningskomiteen om lov om universiteter og høgskoler.*

Langfeldt, L. *Styringsproblemer i en desentralisert og heterogen institusjon: Forsøk på omfordeling av ressurser ved Universitetet i Oslo.* Oslo: Hovedoppgave, Institutt for statsvitenskap, Universitetet i Oslo, 1991.

Larsen, I. M. and Å. Gornitzka, "New Management Systems in Norwegian Universities: the interface between reform and institutional understanding." *European Journal of Education* 30.3 (1995): 347 – 361.

Larsen, I. M., S. Kyvik and Å. Dimmen. *Administrasjonen ved Høgskolen i Oslo. En evaluering.* Oslo: Høgskolen i Oslo. (HiO-rapport 1997 nr 2.), 1997.

Lægreid, P. and J.P. Olsen. *Byråkrati og beslutninger.* Bergen: Univeristetsforlaget, 1978.

March, J. and J.P. Olsen. *Ambiguity and Choice in Organizations.* Bergen: University Press, 1976.

Meyer, J. W. and B. Rowan. "Institutionalized Organizations: Formal Structure as Myth and Ceremony." *American Journal of Sociology* 83 (1977): 340 – 63.

Middlehurst, R. *Leading Academics.* Buckingham: The Society for Research into Higher Education & Open University Press, 1993.

Mintzberg, H. *Power In and Around Organizations.* Englewood Cliffs: Prentice-Hall, Inc., 1983.

NOU 1993:24 *Lov om universiteter og høgskoler,* Oslo: Kirke-, utdannings- og forskningsdepartementet.

Ot.prp.nr.85 (1993 – 94): *Om lov om høgre utdanning:* Kirke-, utdannings- og forskningsdepartementet.

Reve, T. "Styrets rolle: Passiv sandpåstrøer eller aktivt strategi- og kontrollorgan." in Reve, T. and Grønlie, T. (eds). *Styrets rolle,* Bergen: TANO, 1993: 17-42.

Scott, R. W. *Organizations: rational, natural and open systems.* Englewoods Cliffs: New Jersey, 1987.

Van Vught, F. "A new autonomy in European higher education? An exploration and analysis of the strategy of self-regulation in higher education governance." *Institutional Management in Higher Education* 12 (1988): 16 – 25.

BERIT KARSETH

THE CONSTRUCTION OF CURRICULA IN A NEW EDUCATIONAL CONTEXT

Roles and Responsibilities in Nursing Education in Norway

1. INTRODUCTION

At the heart of every educational enterprise is a curriculum. Questions like what ought to be the aim and content of the education, how should we teach and collaborate with students, and how do we evaluate, constitute the substance of all education.

The curriculum is not, however, a fixed, or given entity. Rather, as Patricia Gumport (1988) notes:

> Curricula may be seen as a part of the cultural life of academic organisation in which faculty, administrators, and students construct and revise their understandings and in which they negotiate about what counts as valid knowledge in particular historical and social settings (Gumport 1988: 50).

Although the curriculum may be viewed as negotiable, the regulation of curriculum may limit or frame these negotiations. The degree of regulation varies between different levels and types of education. In primary, secondary and vocational education the curriculum is often prescribed at the national or state level. These regulations set important parameters for the negotiation and decision-making processes at the local level.

When it comes to higher education, national regulation is often weaker. This pertains in particular to universities, which have a long and strong tradition of autonomy (OECD 1998). Curricular decisions made by individuals who are not intimately engaged in the educational programme are seen by many university teachers as a potential treat to academic freedom (Scott and Watson, 1994: 33). In the non-university sector, however, there is a different tradition. Within this sector there are usually detailed state requirements and regulations.

However, a growing convergence of the traditional university sector and the vocation-oriented college sector has moved higher education toward a more unified system, and raised the question of who is responsible for the making of curriculum in higher education.

In this article I will examine the context of the curriculum making process in higher education by focusing on one case: nursing education in Norway. The aim is to describe how changes in higher education policy and the governing structure effect the process of determining the curriculum. The restructuring of higher

121

*Alberto Amaral, Glen A. Jones and Berit Karseth (eds.), Governing Higher Education:
National Perspectives on Institutional Governance*, 121—140.
© 2002 *Kluwer Academic Publishers. Printed in the Netherlands.*

education has created a new power structure, which implies that new actors come into play in the curriculum process while others are pushed into the background. In this article I will give some examples of these changes. However, as I will argue towards the end of the paper, although the governing structure and a national curriculum set some important parameters on educational practice, students and teachers continue to be the main negotiators of curriculum. The day-to-day educational practices of the classroom are influenced, but not wholly determined, by governance structures and state regulation.

2. PERSPECTIVES ON CURRICULUM IN HIGHER EDUCATION

> The curriculum is avowedly and manifestly a social construction. Why, then, is this central social construct treated as a timeless given in so many studies of schooling? In particular, why have social scientists, who traditionally have been more attuned than most to the ideological and political struggles that underpin social life, largely accepted the "givenness" of the school curriculum? (Goodson 1997: 181)

Curriculum as a field of study has not played a central role in the research literature on higher education in Europe. However, as higher education institutions have expanded and become more complex, the planning process within these institutions, and therefore the management of the curriculum, has come to be seen as rather important. In contrast, the academic staff regard the curriculum in higher education as an internal, or even a private, matter.

Stark and Lattuca (1997) define curriculum as an academic plan. "Viewing curriculum as a plan" they argue:

> implies a deliberate planning process that focuses attention on important educational considerations which can vary by field, student body, institutional goals, instructor and others. Despite these variations, the notion of a plan provides a template – a checklist, if you wish – that encourages a careful process of decision making (ibid: 10).

This perspective represents a rational approach to curriculum development where the curriculum is carefully planned and organised prior to classroom engagement. The position emphasized in this article is nevertheless something different. The curriculum is viewed as a social construction where the process of decision-making is seen as a socio-political and a cultural process. This approach, following Slaughter (2002: 28), "allows us to consider organisational and cultural context as well as power and recourses when theorizing about curricula". Although the restructuring discourse in higher education is usually not discussed in terms of its central influence on curricular formulation, these processes affect the shape of curricula (Slaughter 1997). Changes in the overall governing structure or a single educational programme have important consequences for both the political and the professional questions that are being discussed. According to Slaughter, the dominant view has been that "knowledge makes its way into the curricula as part of a lengthy but rational and linear process" (ibid: 10 – 11). She criticises higher education scholarship on curricular issues for not paying sufficient attention to social movements, the political imperatives of the professional class, or the influence of external entities.

In analysing the curriculum process one must acknowledge a number of the important issues that are at stake in these decisions. First, this process always, explicitly or implicitly, includes a debate over the overall aim of the educational programme. Is the aim, for instance, to educate good citizens for the public sphere, or is it to train people to be skilled for a specific vocation? When focusing on the aims of education we discover the tension between, on the one hand, the commitment to scholarship, academic norms and intellectual life, and, on the other, the commitment to the transmission of distinctly vocational skills and attitudes for professional practice. There is also a tension between equality and efficiency in any discussion of the aim and mission of higher education.

Second, in every educational programme there is a continuing debate over curriculum content, a debate that often focuses on the relevance and value of knowledge. Although this debate is central to different actors within the institution, external stakeholders have strong opinions about what students should learn.

Finally, the third issue concerns the role of the student in the process of learning and how the institution organises its teaching activities. There has been a shift in the rhetoric in higher education from subject-based teaching to student-centred learning (Scott 1995). This interest in changing traditional teaching practices is clearly related to enrolment growth and the increased diversity of students (OECD 1998: 65), and it is particularly noticeable in new educational areas, such as technology. This shift also represents a reaction against the strong tradition of formal and didactic teaching methods in higher education. Although the idea of the active learner as responsible for his or her own learning "is attractive", Young argues that " in practice, there are nevertheless some fundamental problems with the concept of learner centeredness, which are magnified in a political context in which the government distrusts the expertise of teachers as a professional group" (Young 1998: 86).

Making decisions about aims, knowledge and pedagogical structures is not a straightforward process. Actors within and outside the educational programme may use different strategies in order to promote their own interests. Both Goodson and Slaughter argue that the curriculum should be understood as the outcome of negotiation and political struggle on different levels. It is therefore important for researchers to examine the power relations that underlie curriculum issues.

In order to understand the 'battle of the curriculum' I will use Bourdieu's concepts of *field*, *capital* and *habitus*. When studying higher education as a *field*, the focus is on the struggle between contesting agents (individuals or departments) in trying to define what is at stake in the field. In a field, according to Bourdieu in an interview with Wacquant:

There exists a space of positions which cannot be occupied unless one possesses one of a number of forms of capital to a very high degree, and which can only be characterized by grasping them in their mutual relations (Wacquant 1993: 21).

'Field', then, may be understood as field of struggle, as a battlefield or playing field.

The concept of *capital* describes the knowledge that is worthwhile in the field. In addition to economic and cultural capital, Bourdieu introduces other types of capital, including social capital, which refers to social relations and influence, and symbolic capital which is probably the most fundamental. The latter describes what social groups see as worthwhile and of value. In this sense symbolic capital also includes cultural capital.

The third concept is habitus. *Habitus* produces individual and collective practices, and the concept helps us to understand that actors within a field of knowledge are both producers and reproducers of objective meaning. Habitus is a system of disposition of thoughts, perceptions, expressions and actions, which produce practices. These practices must be related to the field.

> These practices can be accounted for only by relating the objective structure defining the social conditions of the production of the habitus which engendered them to the conditions in which this habitus is operating, that is, to the conjuncture which, short of a radical transformation, represents a particular state of this structure (Bourdieu 1979: 78).

I will return to Bourdieu's concepts in the discussion.

3. SOURCES OF DATA

My analysis of contextual changes in nursing education utilized data obtained from a number of different sources. The most important source of data was a major evaluation of the reform of the Norwegian college sector. I was one of a number of researchers from different institutions who participated in this process, which was coordinated by the Norwegian Institute for Studies in Research and Higher Education (NIFU). The project provided the foundation for a number of reports on different topics (see Kyvik 1999). An important source of data for this study was a survey of academic staff in the state colleges conducted in 1997/98. In total, 71 per cent of the faculty members in the relevant staff groups answered the questionnaire. In addition, about 300 interviews were undertaken with academic and administrative leaders in the colleges as well as with key informants in the Ministry of Education and other state agencies.

The Norwegian Nurses' Association (NSF) also asked NIFU to do an evaluation focusing on nursing education. This was a qualitative study and I conducted interviews with 35 faculty members in nursing education from 5 different colleges (Karseth 2000). The interviews were conducted during 1997 and structured around 6 themes:

- The transition from being a independent professional school to being part of a faculty in a college institution
- The relationships between the reform and the aim and profile of the educational programme
- Teaching methods and perspectives on student's learning
- Qualification system and strategies
- Professional autonomy – from the perspective of the individual and the basic unit
- The role of the professional organisation: the Norwegian Nurses' Association (NSF)

In addition to these sources, I also draw on a number of major policy documents.

4. NURSING EDUCATION IN NORWAY – A HISTORICAL VIEW

The first educational programme in nursing was established in 1868. The establishment of formal education in nursing was not initiated by the state. Rather, voluntary religious and humanitarian organisations took on the responsibility for nursing education and most of the schools we have to day were originally established by these organisations (Lerheim 1980). Educating nurses evolved from a broad commitment on the part of these organisations to fight against poverty and illness. Public agencies later took over these tasks (Alvsvåg 1997).

In order to give a picture of what it was like to be a student in the period before the establishment of state regulation, I will quote from Larsen's description of the nursing education school in Bergen called Haukeland:

> The school, the sister house and the hospital – the whole created a unit like a mini society. They got their education here, they worked here and it was the home of the students. Most of their social activities were closely related to the institution, and it was here that the students had their friends. It is obvious that this nearness to the hospital created a sense of belonging and identity. They were Haukeland sisters (Larsen 1998: 38, my translation).

Larsen gives a rich description of an institution of teaching and labour characterized by a close social community and explicit rules of behaviour. The cultural norms of this community emphasized discipline, commitment to humanity, mercy and renunciation.

Until 1948, there was no state regulation of nursing education. However, the Norwegian Nurses' Association (NSF) played an important role in the development of programme standards. Education in an approved school became a condition for membership in the Association.

The first Act that regulated nursing education was passed in 1948, and in 1950 directives governing the public approval of qualified nurses were approved. This decision signalled the national government's interest in governing nursing education in order to control the programme standards. The schools now had to fulfil standardized requirements for the content and length of nursing programmes. Government directives were changed in 1962 in order to give the state even greater control. The new directives regulated both the academic and practical-based components of the curriculum. The government also sought to protect the interests of the students and ensure that their role in the hospital setting was to learn nursing and not to be cheap labour. A model of apprenticeship characterized the nursing curriculum until 1975, when students in nursing education were given the same status as other higher education student. In the 1970s, the government's approach to nursing education was viewed as too controlling and its regulations were strongly criticized. In 1980 the Ministry of Health and Social Affairs responded by relaxing some of its regulations.

Nursing education has had status as a higher education programme since 1977, and in 1981 nursing education became an integrated part of the regional college sector and placed under the authority of the Ministry of Education. This shift implied a greater independence, economically, administratively as well as professionally, for nursing education. The once firm grasp of the hospitals on this educational programme had already begun to relax, however the change of ministry was the final step in detaching nursing education from the vocational field (Heggen 1995).

In 1987 the Ministry of Education provided the first curriculum guidelines for nursing education. These guidelines lasted until 2000 when the Ministry approved a new plan.

As I have already noted, nursing education in Norway has a relatively long history. For more than 50 years the schools of nursing education were the responsibility of private organisations and the schools were closely associated with the hospitals. In addition, the fact that the nurse association has had a strong grasp on the educational programme cannot not be overlooked (Karseth 1994; Melby 1991).

In the 1980s nursing education became more like others educational programmes. It became possible to combine nursing education with educational programmes at others institutions of higher education. Beginning in the 1990s, completing a nursing education programme could serve as the basis for fulfilling the entrance requirements for graduate studies (masters programmes) at universities.

However, while nursing education began to resemble other higher education programmes in important ways, it is extremely important to note the important continuing relationship between this educational programme and the field of practice. Even today, half of the educational time focuses on practical studies outside the educational institution. This relatively strong vocational aspect of this programme is in sharp contrast to the liberal education programmes in the universities.

5. NURSING EDUCATION: A NEW CONTEXT

5.1. College reform

In 1994, as Marheim Larsen describes in her article in this book, the non-university higher education sector in Norway underwent a major reorganisation. The 98 vocationally-oriented colleges were amalgamated into 26 new state colleges encompassing the previous colleges of teacher training (25), engineering (15), health education (including nursing education) (27), and social work (3), as well as the regional colleges (14), and various other institutions offering a range of specialized teaching programmes (14).

The overall objectives of this reform can be described in terms of several sub-goals (Kyvik 1999):

1. To create larger and stronger disciplinary units
2. To enhance contact and collaboration between staff across different teaching programmes
3. To create a common educational culture in the new colleges

4. To offer students possibilities to combine subjects in new ways
5. To create better organisational conditions for adaptation to changes in societal needs and demands and for development of new courses
6. To make the college system more cost efficient
7. To improve library and ICT services
8. To improve the quality of administrative services.

5.2. A new act

In addition to the reforms described above, all universities, university colleges and state colleges have been under the same act since 1996. The act provides a common framework for the organisation and governance of these institutions. Furthermore, the act links the institutions through the 'Norway network'. The purpose of the 'Norway Network' is to strengthen professional environments, provide students with a broader range of choices, make it easier to transfer from one place of learning to another, and ensure that better use is made of resources.

Under the new Act on Universities and Colleges, the universities continue to be responsible for most basic research, graduate education, and research training. The main responsibility of the state colleges is to offer a wide variety of professional and vocational-oriented programmes and, in addition, to take on some of the university programmes for basic and undergraduate education. However, within certain fields, where the universities do not offer similar programmes, the new colleges may offer graduate education. The colleges are also required to do research, preferably connected to practice within specific fields, or to problems particularly relevant to their region. Highly competent research environments in the college sector with adequate depth may also play a role in graduate and postgraduate education in collaboration with a university or a university-level college.

5.3. Changes in career development and reward structures

In 1995 the Ministry approved a new appointments structure that applied to both the university and the college sectors. One of the implications of this change was that it was no longer possible to have a college appointment without at least a masters degree. As a consequence of this decision, a stronger emphasis was placed on academic qualifications in appointment decision.

While approximately 9 percent of college sector faculty members had a doctoral degree at the end of 1997, about 60 percent of university faculty members had a doctorate. Of the 1275 faculty members in nurse and health education, only two percent held the rank of associate professor and there were no professors. In contrast, about one third of faculty in mathematics and natural science were associate professors and 4 percent were professors (n 222) (Kyvik 1999: 94 –95). More than half of the faculty in nursing education did not have a degree at the masters level.

However, the restructuring and new regulations have led to an enormous growth in the formal education of nursing faculty. These changes are having an impact on the educational culture in nursing education.

5.4. New governance structure

The Act on Universities and Colleges also led to significant changes in the governance arrangements within the college sector (Kyvik 1999). Before the reorganisation, all public non-university institutions in each region operated under a regional board. These boards, however, had limited power and the institutions operated rather independently, preferring direct relations with the Ministry instead of going through the regional board. Professional education institutions, including those that offered nursing education, had an appointed rector who was both the academic and administrative leader of the institution. The new act changed the leadership and management structure and required that the college management be divided into two parts: the faculty and the administration.

The highest body in the new governance structure is the institutional board. Members are elected for a term of three years (except for the student representatives). The board is led by an elected rector, and it is composed of elected representatives of the faculty, the students, and the technical/administrative staff. In addition, there are also some external board members. At the institutional level there is also an advisory council. The most powerful body at the faculty-level is the faculty board, which is chaired by an elected dean. At the level of the basic unit there is an elected leader of the unit responsible for the educational programme. A small number of the colleges have also established a board at the unit level and in this way follow the traditional governance structure within the university.

A central issue in higher education has been the relationship and the division of labour between the university sector and the college sector. The educational act underlines the responsibility of the university when it comes to research and graduate education. The colleges, however, believe that there are few differences between the university sector and the state college sector. The colleges are regulated under the same structure and regulations as the universities, and the colleges have, in certain circumstances, the possibility of offering graduate and postgraduate education.

5.5. Nursing education – size, organisation and numbers

Just over 191,600 students were enrolled in higher education in autumn, 1999. This is an increase of almost 7500 students, or about 4 per cent, compared with the year before. The largest increase in enrolment has taken place in the colleges, where the number of students has increased by more than 9 700. On the other hand, the combined enrolment in the four universities declined by 2800 students, or around 4 per cent. (Statistics Norway, Published 26 February 2001).

There are more than 10,000 registered students in nursing education programmes (10,111). This is a larger enrolment more than engineering (9,109) or four-year teacher education (primary to secondary education) (9,508). In terms of undergraduate professional education, nursing is the largest education programme within the colleges. Nursing education is offered by 22 of the 26 state colleges. In addition, there are also 5 private institutions (Aktuell utdanningsstatistikk 7/2000).

Nursing education is organised in different ways in different state colleges. For example, at Ålesund, a relatively small college, nursing education is a component of an academic unit that includes programmes in fishery and aquaculture. Except for medical laboratory technology, nursing is the only undergraduate health education programme at Ålesund. Nursing is also the only educational programme at this college that includes a practice training component. At Bergen, a relatively big college, nursing education is located in a faculty together with 7 different educational programmes in social work and health. At Oslo, the biggest college, nursing education is a faculty of its own.

Differences in organisational arrangements, and college size and programme offerings, mean that nursing education is located in quite different organisational contexts that influence the political and educational discourse. Obviously, the possibilities for building alliances differ, for instance, between the College in Ålesund and the College in Bergen (Karseth 2000). These contextual features have an effect on the local construction of curriculum in nursing education.

5.6. A new national curriculum

In 1992 the Council for Education in Health and Social Work (RHHS) recommended that all seven educational programmes in these fields include a common half-year of study. The Ministry of Education accepted this proposal and developed a curriculum guideline for a half-year of study divided into two main areas: scientific methods, and ethics and social sciences. This decision resulted in a curriculum structure for health and social work education with two parts: a common component and a programme-specific component. In May, 1996, the RHHS provided the Ministry of Education with its recommendations on the programme-specific component of the nursing education curriculum. The Ministry of Health and Social Affairs, however, vetoed this proposal. The Ministry was very critical of the amount of clinical practice time and the coverage of the natural sciences and asked for a new proposal. An ad hoc committee was appointed and it finished its report in December, 1998. In January 2000, the curriculum was approved.

The college reforms, the new act, the new appointment structure, and the new national curriculum involve changes in power relationships and, combined, create a new, challenging context for the construction of curricula in nursing education. These changes affect the discourse on what knowledge is valued, the discourse on how decisions are going to be made, and the discourse on pedagogy in these higher education institutions.

In the next part of the chapter I highlight some of the consequences of the new governance structure on the curriculum making process in nursing education.

6. CONSTRUCTING THE CURRICULUM WITHIN THE NEW GOVERNANCE STRUCTURE

The formal structure of higher education in Norway can be simply described in terms of the following levels:

Central authorities
Individual institution
Faculty level
Basic unit

However, as Marheim Larsen points out in her chapter, universities and colleges are complex institutions. There are also important stakeholders outside the formal governance structure who have strong interests in higher education.

In Figure 1 I describe the new governance framework as viewed from the perspective of nursing education.

The figure shows that from the perspective of the basic unit, both the central authorities and the institutional level represent a superior level of authority in this hierarchical structure. However, the distribution of responsibility between the institutional level and the central authorities is not clear. The figure also captures the relationship between, on the one hand, nursing education and the scientific or academic community, and, on the other hand, nursing education and the field of practice (the hospitals, etc.). In this section of the chapter I will describe some inherent tensions in this structure and provide examples of how they effect the curriculum making process.

6.1. Two ministries – two voices?

Although nursing education is placed under The Ministry of Education (KUF), there is also a strong link to The Ministry of Health and Social Affairs. The latter is responsible for the certification of nurses. The history of the development of the new curriculum illustrates that there are differences of opinion about the aim and content of nursing education between the two ministries.

Through the college reform, the establishment of the Norwegian Network and the new act for universities and colleges, the KUF has clearly emphasised the academic enterprise and the importance of research-based teaching. In contrast, the Ministry of Health and Social Affairs (SHD), in its Plan of Action on Health Personnel 1998-2001 (SHD 1997), emphasises the need to strengthen the practice-oriented nature of the educational programme. Given these different objectives, the SHD vetoed the curriculum guidelines proposed by KUF and asked for revisions that would strengthen the practice component and the coverage of such as subjects as medicine and natural science.

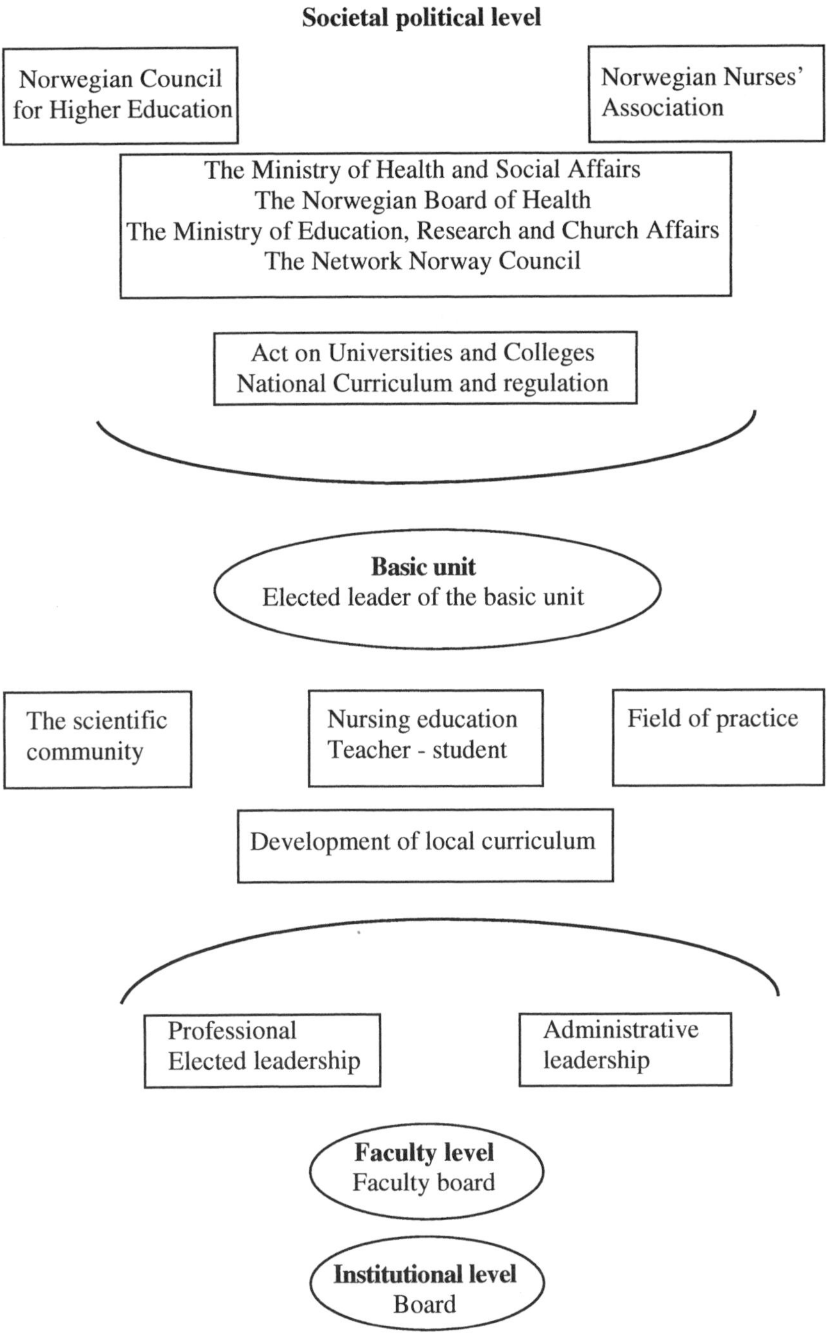

Societal political level

Norwegian Council for Higher Education	Norwegian Nurses' Association

The Ministry of Health and Social Affairs
The Norwegian Board of Health
The Ministry of Education, Research and Church Affairs
The Network Norway Council

Act on Universities and Colleges
National Curriculum and regulation

Basic unit
Elected leader of the basic unit

The scientific community	Nursing education Teacher - student	Field of practice

Development of local curriculum

Professional Elected leadership	Administrative leadership

Faculty level
Faculty board

Institutional level
Board

Figure 1

In other words, there are two ministries who have quite different perspectives and these perspectives correspond to the two major positions concerning the aim of nursing education. Generally speaking, one can argue that for the SHD the aim of nursing education is to train students to become well-skilled practicing professionals. For the KUF, the objective of these programmes should be broader than to educate well-qualified nurses. Nursing education should also provide students with a general education, which qualifies them for graduate studies. Both perspectives are represented in the national curriculum, and, at the local level, debate and negotiation over these conflicting views of nursing education take place within the college and between teachers.

The establishment of the Network Norway Council, which represents an incorporation of the various professional councils into one, has also had an influence on the position of nursing education. In addition, The Norwegian Council for Higher Education was founded 8th May 2000 as a merger of the Norwegian Council of State Colleges and the Norwegian Council of Universities. Established in 1977, the Norwegian Council of Universities was created by the member institutions by expanding the former Norwegian University Rectors' Conference (1960 – 1977) into an association of higher education institutions. When the state colleges came under the same law as the universities in 1995, the Norwegian Council of State Colleges was created to operate in parallel to the university council. The Norwegian Council for Higher Education is a co-operative body for Norwegian universities and state colleges.   The Council has established four national councils for professional education:

- National Council for Teacher Education
- National Council for Engineering Education
- National Council for Economics and Administrative Education
- National Council for Health and Social Work Education

The power and position of the Norwegian Council for Higher Education is not yet clear. The differences in interests and values among its members, however, seem enormous.

6.2. The role of the professional body

Another actor which has played a major role in the history of curriculum development in nursing is the professional body, the Norwegian Nurses' Association. There is no doubt that the restructuring of the college sector has moved the Association to a less powerful position compared with its former role. However, more than 90 percent of the faculty members in nursing education are currently members of the Association.

This means that the Association has considerable influence at the institutional level, where it can work together with other unions, such as the Norwegian Association of Research Workers and the 'Lærerforbundet' (a trade union for pedagogical and administrative personnel at all levels of the Norwegian educational system, from nursery school to college).

The new educational context challenges the position of the professional body within the field. Formerly a powerful actor at the national level in the decision-making process on educational questions, the professional bodies seem to have been shifted to a more peripheral position under the new governance structure. For instance, before the establishment of the Norway Network and the Network Norway Council, there were individual councils for the main fields of professional education (health and social work, engineering and teaching). These councils were closely linked to the professional groups. A more interdisciplinary and inter-professional structure has created a new environment where a new group of actors are coming to the forefront: the educational bureaucrats whose professional identity is not necessarily related to a specific field or profession.

6.3. The division of power between the central authorities and the institution

The college reforms constructed a new governance structure. The structure followed a model used in the university sector, with a division between the administrative and the professional leadership at all levels. From an institutional   (college level) perspective, we can argue that this change has shifted responsibility from the system level to the institutional level, and therefore increased institutional autonomy when it comes to academic, financial and organisational issues.

There has been an international trend in higher education towards an increased emphasis on institutional autonomy (De Boer, Goedegebuure and Van Vught 1996), and in many there has been a change in the traditional relationship between national governments and institutions of higher education. This change has been characterized as a transition from stringent government planning and control towards self-regulatory systems. There is, however, no easy way to measure whether institutional autonomy has actually increased, though these changes have led to a strengthening of institutional administration (Geurts and Maassen 1996: 69). Another trend has been for governments to emphasise a market-oriented approach to the steering of higher education (ibid).

In the evaluation of the college reforms, one of the main conclusions drawn was that the responses to issues of governing and steering were ambiguous and diffuse (Kyvik 1999). Although each college is in a position to make autonomous decisions within the framework of the budget, the experience of study participants at the time of the evaluation was that this freedom was limited by strong governing steering, especially through specifying how the colleges must present their financial reports to the government. In addition, in some areas, such as the establishment of new educational programmes and student enrolment, the autonomy of the colleges was seen as restricted.

National curricula and regulation also limit the degree of autonomy, a point that was made by the leaders of some colleges. They argued that national curricula limits institutional autonomy, and, consequently, suppresses institutional creativity and initiative. They also noted that national curricula can be an obstacle to collaborative teaching activities between faculties. Finally, they suggested that another limitation of national curricula relates to costs (Kyvik 1999). While national curricula limit local autonomy, it is important to recognize that it is not just national governments that regulate professional education. For instance, the European commission requires that nursing education programmes include at least 1.5 years of practical training (Karseth 2000).

6.4. The distribution of power within the institution

In analysing the internal life of the institution we are getting closer to the real practice of higher education. It is important to keep in mind, however, that changes in the relationship between governments and institutions have an impact on the internal governing structures within institutions.

In the preface of the second edition of the book *Process and Structure in Higher Education* (1992) Becher and Kogan point to a major shift in the higher education system in Britain:

> The subsequent extent of external intervention in both the structures and the processes of British higher education makes it impossible to sustain the earlier claims for an independent, self determining network of institutions in which the basic unit reigns supreme (viii)

External intervention can change the position of the basic unit. In addition, the increasing importance of the central institutional administration has also had an impact on academic units (De Boer, Goedegebuure and Van Vught 1996: 111).

Nursing education, as a basic unit, has been placed in a new governing structure that challenges its autonomy. Data from the interviews indicates that the new governing structure is problematic. Teachers in nursing education programmes are now part of a much bigger and complex organisation. Some of the informants described these changes in terms of autonomy. One teacher suggested that:

> The autonomy that the single school had [before the reform] has almost disappeared. Today information is coming from a higher level, and it goes only one way. It happens above the heads of the teachers. In previous days we where much more engaged in the processes. This is a striking change (Karseth 2000: 54).

Another stated:

> Alienation and an increased bureaucratisation is the most critical consequences of the college reform. Most of the teachers feel that they have been removed from influence. The single teacher feels that there is a distance to the decisions... and that's not so strange. There has been a democracy at our school (ibid.)

It is important to note that the experience of nursing education is similar to most of the other undergraduate professional programmes operating under national curricula. All are having to deal with a situation where state authorities want to directly govern the content of professional education. The last curriculum reform in nursing education illustrates this point.

From the perspective of the teacher or the basic unit, a national curriculum may be viewed as an important buffer between the basic unit and the institutional level. In the competition for resources, the existence of a national curriculum can protect the basic unit since the college must pay the costs associated with programme standards; they are not negotiable. Not one of the 35 informants I interviewed voiced the wish to throw away the national curriculum. However, they had some critical comments. Some argued that, compared to the 1987 plan, the 1996 curriculum proposal was too controlling. Another concern was that the language of the plan placed little emphasis on the main field of knowledge: nursing.

The new educational context has placed nursing education, as a basic unit, in a more hierarchical organisational structure. From the point of view of the basic unit, the changes in the governing structure do not represent a form of deregulation. Instead, the new institutional arrangement has placed nursing education within a more centrally regulated framework where one additional level has been added to the old structure.

6.5. Different interests – different strategies within the basic unit

Faculty within the university sector frequently view themselves as members of academic communities outside their own institution. They may be characterized as being cosmopolitans (Gouldner 1958). The teachers in nursing education, however, have had a strong orientation and commitment towards their own local institution and to the local community of practice. Several of the faculty members I interviewed characterized the institutional culture as collectivistic. However, this culture, they argued, is being challenged by the reforms and changes in the reward structure.

One faculty member described it in this way:

> We can see a tendency towards a much more individual working milieu. The single faculty member is in a stronger sense than before occupied by their research activities and teaching tasks. We can see that what was the strength in the nurse education earlier – that we were very good at working together towards a common product and everybody did his or her share – suffer under the way we organize our work (Karseth 2000: 59)

Another argued:

> Solidarity and to stand together, were strong values in our culture before. Many of my colleagues complain that these values are disappearing. And it seems correct that we are becoming more individualistic, people care more for their own individual career. For some it is of course an advantage if you want to make a career, however others fees that something valuable has gone lost (ibid).

One can conclude that the traditional culture of nursing education is been challenged, and that the new structure and regulations may give the individual faculty member greater autonomy in order to plan her own career. Hence, reduced autonomy at the basic unit level does not necessarily mean less autonomy for individual faculty members. The new organisational context also encourages an orientation toward scientific work, an orientation that had not been highly valued within the traditional culture of nursing education.

One important curriculum discussion is related to teaching. As I have already noted, one aim of the college reform was to create a common teaching culture. The data shows important differences in the culture of teaching between the programmes (Karseth og Kyvik 1999). For example, teachers in nursing education spend four hours each week supervising students practicing in the field. These teachers devote more time to supervising field-based practice than teachers in any other programme. In contrast, teachers in teacher education spend less than one hour each week on this activity, since the responsibility for supervising student practice is given to the teachers in the schools. Data from the survey shows that the amount of teaching has decreased after the reforms, however, only a third of the faculty members in nursing education want to increase this amount. At the same time, two-thirds of the faculty members responded that that the intended amount of independent study time for students has increased, and half of the faculty members want it to increase further. The data on teaching then, indicates that there have been changes in teaching practices, which at the moment, appear to moving nursing education in the direction of a more academic culture of teaching.

While data were not collected from students, a number of the interview subjects provided interesting comments on important changes in the role of the students. One faculty member stated:

> It is not sure that they, the students, are going to become nurses in practice. They want to work in different places, travel and experience something exiting and maybe study something else. Some times I tell them that this or that at the moment is probably a little bit difficult to understand, but after having some experience from work they will catch it. Then the students laugh because they do not see them self as working one place for five years. They are young students. They are focused on themselves, while traditionally [in nurse education] we have been focused on the other; the patient. (Karseth 2000: 96)

This indicates that students should not be overlooked when analysing the construction of the curriculum. They play a major role in these negotiations . In order to fully understand the making of curriculum in nursing education, we therefore need to shift our attention to the classroom, the training hall, and the students' reading and coffee rooms, and analyse the operational or interactive curriculum (Goodlad 1988; Goodson 1997). It is only at this level where we can see how the different decisions concerning the content, structure and aims of an educational programme are being dealt with and staged by the main actors: the students and the teachers. Curriculum is a part of cultural life (Gumport 1988).

I am currently involved in a research project where we are studying how nursing students, and others, perceive and understand the moral and normative aspects of education and professional life (Jensen 2000). In this project we are interviewing students at different times in their educational process. This interview data will increase our understanding of what these nursing students view as important in terms of their education and future professional work. These perspectives obviously influence how students act in the classroom, which, in turn, influence teaching practices.

7. DISCUSSION

In this article I have outlined some important changes in the educational context that have consequences for the curriculum making process in nursing education. Curriculum making has been viewed as an ongoing project involving the participation of different actors working at different levels. One important objective of this paper was been to examine changes in the power relations underscoring curricular decisions. I will conclude by discussing two questions.

- Is the power of the professional body on the decline?
- Did the reforms in the college sector lead to a situation where individual faculty member have greater freedom from the norms and values of the profession?

The answer to the first question is that at the societal or system level, the power of the professional body has been reduced. There is, however, reason to believe, as I stated earlier, that the professional body may play an important role at the institutional level.

If the 1990s were associated with a decline in the power of the Norwegian Nurses' Association in terms of its influence on educational questions, the 1980s might be described as 'the golden age'. In 1985, after struggling for more than 20 years, the Institute for Nursing Science (ISV) was established at the University of Oslo. From that moment, nursing formally became a part of the scientific community (Karseth 1994 and 1997). This made it possible for teachers of nursing education to take doctoral degrees in nursing science in Norway. In the years that followed, journals were established, books about concepts and theories in nursing science were written and conferences were organised.

However, the new position of nursing within the university was not easy. Nursing science had to struggle for acceptance. As a 'newcomer', the Institute had to convince the University that it was engaged in a legitimate academic field. The university was very sceptical, and there were doubts about the scientific competence and the scientific relevance of the subject. In trying to convince the University, the Institute developed a strategy, which stressed the potential of the subject as an academic discipline and defended its academic standards. In order words to get access to the University, the faculty members had to play by accepted rules and expectations. There were no alternative approaches to research presented (Karseth 1997).

In addition, there was an increased interest in interdisciplinary perspectives in the fields of health and social work. At the University of Oslo, for example, a section for interdisciplinary studies in health sciences was established in the mid 1990s. Interdisciplinary undergraduate programmes for further education were also established in the college sector in the same period. The Ministry of Education developed curriculum guidelines for interdisciplinary programmes and students from different professions could apply for admission to these programmes.

In short, the reforms and the new interdisciplinary approach placed the Norwegian Nurses' Association and nursing education in a new situation involving new actors with different interests and strategies. The new organisational context challenges the fragile, newly established field of nursing science (see Abbott 1988). A central question is whether the behaviours, types of knowledge, beliefs systems and sense of community traditionally associated with faculty members in nursing education and the leadership of the Norwegian Nurses' Association are valued within the new organisational context. Using Bourdieu's theoretical framework as an analytical tool, we should examine the relationship between the habitus of the actors, the forms of capital that have greatest value and the social condition of the field. If academic capital has high value in the field of higher education, one might conclude that nursing education is in a rather bad position. The professional identity of most of the teachers in nursing education is not primarily based on nursing as an academic discipline, but rather on nursing as a field of practice. The main role conflict for teachers in nursing education is between the expectations of the academic community (the higher education institutions) and the expectations of stakeholders within the labour market. This conflict creates a constant struggle for recognition within the college and recognition from the field of practice.

To answer the second question, more data are needed in order to analyse individual strategies and behaviour. However, although the basic unit, as a collective entity, has lost autonomy, each individual teacher has been given greater freedom from the norms and values of the profession. They have gained more personal autonomy.

The changes in power relations described in this article effect the curriculum making process when it comes to questions like: who will be included in the decision–making process, and which arguments are considered valued in discussions about knowledge, as well as in discourses on the student as learner. Lastly they have influenced the overall aims of the education and disrupted the balance between theory and practice. However, the process is neither linear nor fixed. There is no universal narrative on how reforms in higher education institutions will effect an educational programme and its curriculum. The case of nursing education, however, provides a very interesting example, and shows that in order to understand changes in the curriculum we must analyse the social and the historical context of a particular programme and examine how the curriculum is related to the structure of power in the field of higher education and in society at large.

In summary, this study indicates that changes at one level have consequences for other levels, and that the impact of reform may be greater than what was intended. This suggests a need for greater sensitivity when it comes to studying issues related to governance and change. The view of the curriculum as a cultural and social construction serves as a reminder "that people often know what they do and why they do it. But ", as stated by Foucault, "what they don't know is what they do does"(Foucault sited in Jones 1990: 93).

REFERENCES

Abbott, A. *The System of Professions.* Chicago: The University of Chicago Press, 1988.
Aktuell utdanningsstatistikk Universiteter og høgskoler – Nøkkeltall 2000. Statistisk sentralbyrå. 2000.
Alvsvåg, H. "Velferdsstat versus velferdssamfunn." in H. Alsvåg , N. Anderssen,, E. Gjengedal and M. Råheim (eds). *Kunnskap, kropp og kultur.* Oslo: Ad Notam Gyldendal, 1997, 269-301.
Becher, T. *Academic Tribes and Territories.* Milton Keynes: SRHE and Open University Press, 1989.
Becher, T. and M. Kogan. *Process and Structure in Higher Education.* London: Routledge, 1992.
Bourdieu, P. *Outline of a theory of practice.* New York: Cambridge University Press, 1977.
Bourdieu, P. "The Specificity of the Scientific Field." in Charles, C. (ed). *French Sociology.* New York: Columbia University Press, 1981, 257-292.

Bourdieu, P. *Homo Academicus.* Cambridge: Polity Press, 1988.
De Boer, H., L. Goedegebuure and F. van Vught. "Governance and Management of Higher Education Institution." in Maassen, P. and F. van Vught (eds). *Inside Academia. New challenges for the academic profession.* Utrecht: CHEPS, 1996, 97-111.
Geurts, P. and P. Maassen. "Academic and Institutional Governance." in Maassen, P. and F. van Vught (eds). *Inside Academia. New challenges for the academic profession.* Utrecht: CHEPS, 1996, 69-82.
Goodlad, J. I. "What Some Schools and Classrooms Teach." In J.R. Gress (ed). *Curriculum. An Introduction to the Field.* California: McCutchan Publishing Corporation, 1988, 337-356.
Goodson, I. *The Changing Curriculum.* New York: Peter Lang, 1997.
Gouldner, A. "Cosmopolitans and Locals: Toward an analyses of latent social roles – II." *Administrative Science Quarterly,* 2.4 (1958) 444-480.
Gumport, P. "Curricula as Signposts of Cultural Change" *Review of Higher Education,* 12.1 (1988): 49 – 61.
Heggen, K. *Sykehuset som «klasserom».* Oslo: Universitetsforlaget, 1995.
Jensen, K. "The desire to do good - A study of moral motivation among students within the field of health and social care". Oslo: Oslo University College, 2001.
College: Centre for Studies of Professions. Unpublished. 2000.
Jones, R. "Educational Practices and Scientific Knowledge." in S. Ball (ed). *Foucault and Education. Disciplines and Knowledge.* London: Routledge, 1990, 78-104.
Karseth, B. *Fagutvikling i høyere utdanning. Mellom kunnskapstradisjoner og kunnskapspolitikk.* Dr.polit. avhandling. Universitetet i Oslo: Pedagogisk forskningsinsitutt, 1994.
Karseth, B. "How to Become a Proper University Discipline: The Conflict of Knowledge in Nursing Science". Paper presented at an international conference What kind of University, London: Park Lane Hotel, June 18-12, 1997.
Karseth, B. *Sykepleierutdanning I en reformtid.* Oslo: NIFU rapport 9/2000.
Karseth, B. and S. Kyvik. *Undervisningsvirksomheten ved de statlige høgskolene.* Delrapport no.1 Evaluering av høgskolereformen. Norges forskningsråd, 1999.
Kyvik, S. *Evaluering av høgskolereformen. Sluttrapport.* Norges forskningsråd, 1999.
Larsen, J. *"Hver dag en sjelden gave..."* Festskrift i anledning 90-årsjubileet for sykepleierutdanningen ved Høgskolen i Bergen. Høgskolen i Bergen, 1998.
Martinsen, K. "Men hvem skal pleie de syke?" *Intervju i KvarTano,* 2 (June 1993): 4-5.
Melby, K. *Kall og kamp.* Oslo: Cappelen, 1990.
OECD. *Redefining Tertiary Education.* Paris: OECD, 1998.
Rammeplan 1987. *Rammeplan for 3-årig grunnutdanning i sykepleie, revidert i 1992.* Rådet for høgskoleutdanning i helse- og sosialfag.
Rammeplan 2000 *Rammeplan og forskrift for 3-årig sykepleierutdanning.* Kirke-,utdannings- og forskningsdepartementet.
RHHS 1996. Forslag til revidert rammeplan for sykepleierutdanning. Rådet for høgskoleutdanning i helse og sosialfag.
RHHS 1998 *Sluttrapport.* Rådet for høgskoleutdanning i helse- og sosialfag.
SHD 1997. Rett person på rett plass. Handlingsplan for helse- og omsorgspersonell1998-2001. *Sosial - og helsedepartementet*
Scott, P. and D. Watson. "Managing the Curriculum. Roles and Responsibilities." in Bocock, J. and D. Watson (eds). *Managing the University Curriculum. Making a Common Cause.* Buckingham: SRHE and Open University Press, 1994, 33-47.
Scott, P. *The Meanings of Mass Higher Education.* Buckingham: SRHE Open University Press, 1995.
Slaughter, S. "The Political Economy of Curriculum-making in American Colleges and Universities". Paper presented at a doctoral Seminar: Tensions in Higher Education. The Role of the Academic Institutions and its Members. University of Oslo: Institute for Educational Research, January 30. – February 1
Slaughter, S. "Class, race and gender and the construction of postsecondary curricula in the United States: Social movement, professionlization and political economic theories of curricular change." *Journal of Curriculum Studies,* 29.1 (1997): 1-30.
Stark J. and R.L. Lattuca. *Shaping the College Curriculum. Academic Plans in Action.* Boston: Allyn and Bacon, 1997.
Wacquant, L. J. D. "From Ruling Class to Field of Power: An interview with Pierre Bourdieu on "La noblesse d'Etat"." *Theory, Culture and Society,* 10 (1993): 19-44.

Young, M. F. D. *The Curriculum of the Future: From the "New Sociology of Education" to a Critical Theory of Learning*. London: Falmer Press, 1998.

JEF C. VERHOEVEN AND GEERT DEVOS

INTERDEPARTMENTAL FUNCTIONAL INTEGRATION AND DECENTRALISATION OF DECISION MAKING IN THE MERGED COLLEGES OF HIGHER EDUCATION IN FLANDERS, BELGIUM [1]

1. PROBLEMS AND QUESTIONS

When the Flemish Parliament passed the Law of 13 July 1994 on the colleges of higher education it continued a policy, established in 1989, of decentralisation, deregulation, and increased autonomy of the colleges. This law also assigned the colleges a new mission:

> Colleges should, in the interests of society, be simultaneously active in the field of college education, social service provision and, where appropriate, project-based scientific research in collaboration with a university or other body in this country or abroad. The development and practice of the arts will also be the task of the colleges, which will organise courses in the fields of audio-visual and plastic art, music and drama. The provision of college education will be the primary task of the college (Art. 3 of the Law of 13 July 1994).

Before this law was approved, colleges generally did not conduct scientific research. By decentralising the decision-making structure, the Flemish government granted colleges the right to determine their own policy in a way that had not previously been the case. Under the new arrangement, colleges were to determine their own policy in response to the local challenges. The new law abandoned most of the old regulations of the Belgian centralised system that existed prior to 1989. Deregulation was seen as an instrument to give colleges more freedom to determine their own policy. Nevertheless, the state did not leave all policy decisions in the hands of the colleges, although it did relax the rules in many respects, providing only the framework within which the colleges should act. The government still determines the boundaries within which colleges have to provide education. This law protects the rights of college policy makers, the staff, and the students of the colleges, by, for example, specifying the decision-making and participatory structure of the state colleges and some essential requirements for the non-state colleges, the status of the personnel, the minimum rules to be followed for quality assurance, and a system of control by government commissioners who to determine whether the colleges act according to the law. It also created a lump-sum funding system to be used by the boards of the colleges to attain their objectives. Thus, the colleges acquired more autonomy. In this respect it was very important for state colleges that the organising authority was no longer the Minister of Education, but the board of

Alberto Amaral, Glen A. Jones and Berit Karseth (eds.), Governing Higher Education: National Perspectives on Institutional Governance, 141—162.
© 2002 *Kluwer Academic Publishers. Printed in the Netherlands.*

directors of the college. The state colleges became autonomous, a label that is still being used in their names (Van Heffen et al., 1999: 106 – 108).

The increase in autonomy was a tremendous innovation, for the colleges – more than universities – had always been subject to central regulation. Indeed, many of the colleges started in the beginning of the 20th century as secondary schools and thus were used to the very centralized Belgian education policy system.

Greater autonomy was not the only innovation though. The Flemish government realised that it was impossible for the 163 mostly small colleges that existed at that time to assume greater policy autonomy and included in the law funding principles that made it hard for colleges with less than 2000 students[2] to survive. This law was passed in the Flemish parliament in July 1994, and the colleges were given one year to look for partners. They were free to choose their partner institutions. By the start of the 1995 – 1996 academic year, 29 new colleges has been established, and each was given the right to provide education in one or more of the eleven fields of study determined by the government. The fields of study provided by the new colleges were the same fields offered by the old pre-merger colleges. Typical for this process was that most of the colleges merged with colleges of the same network, that is, state colleges merged with state colleges, provincial colleges with other provincial colleges, and independent colleges with other independent colleges (see Section 2). This was a consequence of the old 'pillarised' educational structure, which was, and still is, characteristic of the Flemish educational structure. Some of the older colleges were large enough to continue and maintain their old structure. However, not all of the colleges could or even wanted to merge into new colleges of at least 2000 students. They waited for new opportunities because the law gave them time to look for other partners. In 1999 – the year we collected the data for this study – most of the colleges had more than 2000 students, but there were still seven colleges with fewer. The merging process is not yet complete. At present (2001), there are 25 colleges, of which five have fewer than 2000 students, but in the near future the number of colleges will probably decrease (MVG 2001: 45 – 46). The merging process was not easy and it created many problems: some old colleges disappeared to become departments in a college; old colleges often had to merge with other old colleges that offered the same programmes of study and became new departments in a new college; directors lost their positions and were not sure if they could become department heads of the new departments in the new colleges. Another problem was that the departments in the larger colleges did not share the same physical campus but were spread over several locations in the town and in some cases over several towns. One consequence of this new arrangement is that students in the same department of the same college sometimes attend classes on different campuses[3]. One might expect that these changes would not be enthusiastically received by the staff, and rightly so when we look at the data of a recent survey (February 2001; N = 773 teachers in 12 merged colleges). Verhoeven, Devos, Smolders et al. (2001: 109) found that 45.7% of the teachers were very dissatisfied with the merger, 23.8% dissatisfied; 18.1% claimed no positive or negative attitude towards the merging, 10.5% were satisfied, and only 1.9% were very satisfied.

The new colleges faced tremendous challenges. First, they had to learn to live with a new policy structure, a new participatory decision-making structure, and a new mission. Second, they had to learn to collaborate with new partners that had once been competitors, and most of the merged colleges had no experience with the process of merging. State colleges could rely on the forms of administration and participation determined by law, but the non-state colleges had to invent their own new forms of administration. The mergers created integration problems for the new administrative structures in each college. If they wanted to create some degree of cohesion, steps had to be taken to integrate the different new parts of the college and at least attain a certain level of interdepartmental functional integration. At the same time, they had to adapt to a new administrative structure in which staff and students could participate in the decision making process, i.e. a level of decentralisation of decision making prescribed by law.

In order to learn more about these processes, we conducted case studies of six new colleges and a survey (January – March 1999) of 808 members of the decision-making and participatory bodies of 16 other new colleges. Our objective in this chapter is not to describe the processes the colleges went through during the merging process, but to analyse the interdepartmental functional integration and decentralisation of decision making in these colleges of higher education as perceived by three important groups: the general managers, the heads of the departments, and the representatives of the teachers on the main decision making and advisory boards. This leads us to three questions: Given the mergers,

1) To what extent do general managers, heads of departments, and staff (all members of decision making and participatory bodies) experience the functional integration of the different departments in the college?
2) Do these policy makers experience decentralisation or centralisation of the administration of the college?
3) Is there a relationship between the interdepartmental functional integration of the colleges and the decentralisation of decision-making in the colleges?

Since the administrative structure and the rights of the actors in state, independent, and provincial colleges differ (see Section 2), we will also consider whether the perception of functional integration and decentralisation is different in each type of college.

Before presenting the theoretical considerations that guided our research and methods, we will briefly review the legal decision-making structure of the colleges.

2. THE LEGAL DECISION-MAKING STRUCTURE IN COLLEGES

To understand the Belgian educational system, it is important to realize the difference between *state colleges* and *non-state* colleges (i.e. independent and provincial colleges). Independent colleges are founded by private individuals, while provincial colleges are established by provincial administrations. Since the Belgian constitution guarantees freedom of education, the state is not allowed to prescribe the administrative structure of non-state colleges except to guarantee a certain level of participation in policy making. This participation, however, is limited to consultation.

The policy-making structure of *state colleges* is specified in the law. A state college is governed by a board of directors, consisting of representatives of the different categories of personnel (elected for 4 year terms by their peers), representatives of the students (elected for 2 year terms by the students, and representatives of the organising body and/or of the socio-economic and cultural sectors (also for a term of 4 years) (Verhoeven and Dom 2001: 34 – 36). The general manager, the head of a college of higher education, plays an advisory role on this council. The board of directors determines the regulations concerning administration, examinations, and discipline, establishes the budget, appoints the personnel, establishes the framework for the organisation and the co-ordination of tasks, and so on. The general manager is appointed (and may be dismissed) by the board of directors and is responsible for the administration of the institute. He or she directs the administrative and other (e.g. international relations officer) staff. The general manager is responsible for the registration of students and their administrative records, as well as the records of each member of the staff. By delegation, the general manager shares responsibility for decisions on the use of funds. Regularly, at least once a year, he or she informs the organising body (the board of directors) of the school's financial situation and prepares the budget for the coming year. This individual is also responsible for the school's physical plant, for maintenance and repairs, and for the purchase of furnishing and equipment. The general manager plays a central role in selecting new teachers and other staff members to be appointed by the organising body. He or she is responsible for all external contacts (with the pedagogical support services, the local community, guidance centre, labour market, etc.) and the public relations of the school in general. Although the law does not prescribe the administrative structure of the non-state colleges, they have a rather similar structure including a board of directors that makes the final decisions and a general manager who is responsible for the everyday affairs of the college.

Each college of higher education, both state and non-state, is divided into departments. For each department in a state college, there is a departmental council composed of representatives much like the board of directors (with the same terms-of-office but with a different balance of representation). This council elects the head of the department, who serves as chair of the council for a 4-year term. The departmental council is responsible for the establishment of the educational programmes and examinations, the establishment of the research programmes, the use of the funds and personnel, the recruitment of temporary personnel, the nomination of personnel for permanent appointments, the internal organisation of the department, the annual budget proposals, and other matters. In state colleges, the departmental council can make decisions that are binding on the board of directors. This is not the case in non-state colleges.

Also at non-state colleges, a departmental council has to be established for each department consisting of the head of the department (who is appointed by the board of directors) as the chair of the council and elected representatives of the teaching staff, the students, and the socio-economic and cultural sectors. This council has the right to obtain and review information on all matters concerning the department and may advise the board of directors on a wide range of department issues when asked by the board or on its own initiative.

While all of these councils and actors have decision-making power, except for the departmental council of non-state-colleges, the councils described below have only an advisory function and will not be included in the analysis presented in Section 5 of this chapter.

For the non-state colleges of higher education, the law provides for a number of administrative bodies that fulfil mainly advisory tasks in relation to the board of directors of the college, such as the academic council. The board of directors of the college must inform the academic council about all matters concerning the educational work of institution. The academic council consists of elected representatives of the board of directors of the college (4 years), the personnel (4 years), and the students (2 years). This council is entitled to receive information and to advise, at the very least, on the educational aspects of certain issues (such as research policy). The academic council also has the 'competence of consultation' for the educational aspects of certain matters, such as the financial policy, the education and examinations policies, and the organisation of study guidance. If there is no consensus, the board of directors of the college makes the final decision.

In addition to these bodies, each college of higher education must establish a council of students consisting of at least 8, and at most 16, elected students. The board of directors (at both state and non-state colleges must consult the council of students beforehand on all matters that are directly relevant to the students (e.g. regulations concerning education and examinations, and the evaluation of the teaching staff). The council of students may also decide to provide the board of directors with advice on other issues.

Concerning the conditions of employment, each college of higher education and each department of that institute has a negotiation committee to regulate the relations between the employer and the unions. The negotiation committee of the college consists of representatives of the board of directors and of the employees. At state colleges of higher education, the departmental negotiation committee consists of representatives of the department council and of the employees. At non-state colleges of higher education, it consists of representatives of the board of directors of the department and of the employees.

3. CHANGING ORGANISATIONS IN A CHANGING SOCIETY

The process of merging and enlarging the colleges in Flanders can be analysed in the context of a process of change from an industrial society to a service society. In this society, more attention is paid to consumption than to production. Instead of producing many similar products, production units want to offer a greater diversity of products to meet the demands of the consumers. Knowledge about the expectations of the consumers comes first, and production is adapted to these changing markets. More than ever, we are living in a knowledge and information society. This development has rendered the old bureaucracies obsolete, and organisation has to be approached differently. Theories on the development of the organisational culture, the learning organisation, the network organisation, knowledge management, third-generation management and post-modernism (Deal and Kennedy 1982; Schein 1992; Senge 1990; Clegg 1990; Whitaker 1992; Gergen 1992; Turner 1992; Reed and Hughes 1992; Bartlett and Goshal 1994; Hamel and Prahalad 1994; Miles and Snow 1994) stress the importance of strong involvement of employees who take initiatives in the organisation in order to deal with the problems of a rapidly changing society. Burns and Stalker (1961) saw the answer to these problems in an organic type of organisation that relies more on common values and goals than on hierarchy. Tasks are divided-up and undertaken throughout the organisation and linked with the overall objectives or tasks of the organisation. On the basis of frequent and regular communication between management and collaborators, these tasks can be adapted to the needs of the moment. This type of management should match the needs of organisations working under conditions of change (Burns and Stalker 1961: 121). Burns and Stalker (1961: 119) also describe the mechanical type of organisation (with the opposite characteristics of the organic type), a type that is more appropriate for organisations working under relatively stable conditions. Contingency theory stresses the same need to match management approach with organisational conditions, and Lawrence and Lorsch (1967: 156 – 158, 187 – 189) note that they arrive at the same conclusions as Burns and Stalker. Effective organisations have to pay attention to the level of diversity and uncertainty in the organisational environment. Bureaucratic and mechanical approaches to organisation cannot adapt to the rapid changes taking place in different parts of our society. To understand the development of an organisation, researchers should pay attention to those factors that influence the organisation and its environment. The challenge for large organisations is that, on the one hand, they have to adapt to a changing society by increasing their reliance on responsible and competent employees. This is the basis for the creation of smaller, rather autonomous units. On the other hand, the scaling-up of the organisation demands rational planned change in order to control the organisation and keep it manageable. In other words, some developments push organisations towards a more flexible or organic structure, while others favour a more bureaucratic or mechanical structure.

Both types of organisational development have emerged in the colleges in response to broader societal pressures. Hanson (1978) refers to two domains in schools: a management domain and a teaching domain. The management domain is mainly bureaucratically organised, while the teaching domain has an organic structure. This type of mixed structure is typical of what Mintzberg (1979: 366 – 371) has called a professional bureaucracy. A professional bureaucracy survives more easily in a relatively stable environment. Colleges exhibit the same characteristics, which would imply that they would find it difficult to respond to the needs of a rapidly changing society. The increase of autonomy and deregulation for colleges could mean that they have to move to an organic structure with less centralisation of decision-making. The growth in importance of consumers (parents and students) also demands more flexibility in terms of decision making and in the participation of the stakeholders. In contrast to this development, the scaling-up of the colleges tends to separate management and implementation (Giesbers 1993: 13 –

16; Hofman 1991: 12 – 15). Scaling-up implies more centralisation. Colleges that merge and became larger are likely to create structures to realise institute-wide college policy, that may, in turn, contribute to centralisation and formalization. Taken together, these contrasting trends seem to indicate that the newly merged colleges would have to look for a road between centralisation and decentralisation to attain their goals. Mary Henkel (2000) and Burton Clark (1998), following P. Hoggett call this development 'centralised decentralisation', and Barbara Sporn (1999) speaks of shared governance.

In addition to centralisation of the decision-making, Miller and Dröge (1986: 543, 559 – 560) consider functional integration (that is, the use of committees, consultation, and relations between 'integrative personnel') as an important structural factor for an organisation. Since the environment of organisations is more uncertain, one might assume that the administrative tasks will become 'more complex and non-routine'. In order to solve this problem, organisations need "more intensive face-to-face liaison devices to promote collaboration and resolve differences... and more power delegated to lower-level managers" (Miller and Dröge 1986: 545). The merged colleges have to find their place in a changing and more competitive society and each must somehow construct a new, large college out of several old, small colleges. Given these observations, functional integration in this chapter will be operationally defined in terms of the steps taken by the college and the departments to promote collaboration between the departments (see Section 4).

In order to study the degree of centralisation, we examined the process of decision-making and the delegation of decision-making in the colleges. This means that we not only considered the level at which a decision was made, but also the steps that led to the decision (Bazerman 1994: 4; Drummond 1991: 20). Theoretically, five steps are important in this process: the collection of information, the preparatory phase, the decision, the implementation of the decision, and the evaluation of the implementation. This is a continuing process that creates new problems and, in turn, pushes the policy makers towards new decisions. This theoretical model is often criticised because of its ideal, rational character. Indeed, the real world is not particularly rational. Individual opinions and interests thwart this rational model. Nevertheless, we used it as a heuristic device to construct an instrument for collecting data on these decision-making processes. Given the limits of a written questionnaire, we confined the analysis to three steps: the decisions made by the different councils and actors, the influence of different councils and actors on these decisions, and the evaluation of the implementation by the different actors.

4. RESEARCH METHOD

Our objective was to analyse the policy-making function and the work of the participatory bodies of the colleges three to four years after the college mergers. Two methods of data collection were utilized. Since the process of organisational change is, to at least some extent, unique to each organisation, we conducted case studies of six colleges: one state, and five non-state colleges (four independent, and one provincial). In each college, ten individuals who were directly associated with policy development and the work of the participatory councils were interviewed in-depth (May – November 1998), and publications of each college were used to obtain a picture of the results of the merging process in terms of the administration and participation in decision-making. We will refer very briefly to some of the findings from this research in this study.

We also wanted to construct a broader picture of the merging process as far as the administration of colleges and the functioning of the participatory councils were concerned. We therefore created a sample of 1,282 members of the different councils in 16 colleges (other than the six mentioned above). To consider the diversity of the departments in the different colleges, we randomly selected 28 departments from 10 (of the 20) independent colleges, 20 departments from 4 (of the 5) state colleges, and 5 departments from 2 (of the 3) provincial colleges. In each department, members (head, staff, students) of the different councils were selected, together with all members of the board of directors, the general manager, and some members of the councils at the college level. We mailed each of these individuals a questionnaire, and sent follow-up questionnaires to non-respondents two additional times. A total of 63% of the individuals responded, but there was considerable variation in the response rate by college (between 47% and 73%). Since one person could be a member of more than one council, the information obtained could concern more than just one council.

The main themes addressed in the questionnaire were the interdepartmental functional integration, and the decentralisation of financial, educational and human-resource policy. The questionnaire also included questions on other important issues, such as the function of the policy making and participatory councils (including the informal councils), participation in the councils, the standardisation of administrative and policy procedures, the style of leadership of the general manager and the head of the department, communication with colleagues, and communication between the negotiation committee of the college and the departmental negotiation committee. For this chapter, we focus primarily on the questions related to interdepartmental functional integration and centralisation.

We defined interdepartmental functional integration as the degree to which departments of the same college have frequent and regular contact and work together to achieve common goals. Interdepartmental functional integration is defined as "integration through the use of liaison devices such as task forces, committees, and integrative personnel" (Miller and Dröge 1986: 543) that build bridges between the different departments of the same (merged) college. The respondents could describe this phenomenon by answering 12 items (see Appendix 1) using a five-point likert-like scale (I strongly disagree, I disagree, neutral, I agree, I strongly agree) (Cronbach's $\alpha = .89$).

Centralisation in colleges was defined as the degree to which decisions in colleges are made at the top (the level of the general manager). Decentralisation, then, is the degree to which decisions are made by heads of the departments and/or the departmental councils.

The decision-making processes were analysed in three phases: 1) the phase of preparing decisions; 2) the phase of influencing the decision-making processes; and 3) the phase of monitoring the decisions.

We focused on three domains of decision-making: 1) finance and equipment; 2) educational policy; and 3) human-resource management. For each domain we provided different fields of decision-making, and we asked the respondents to indicate whether the general manager, the heads of the departments, the departmental councils or other councils or actors were the most important decision makers.

We included a number of policy items for each domain. For the finance and equipment domain we included 4 items: decisions about the annual budget of the college, the distribution of the budget between the departments of the college, the annual departmental budget, and investment in infrastructure (max. score = 4). The items concerning educational policy were the following: general regulation of education of the college, departmental regulation of education, regulation of the examinations, course offerings of the college, course offerings of the department, curriculum innovation, and quality assurance (max. score = 7). Human resource management was indexed on the basis of decisions concerning personnel planning, vacancies, career planning, staff assessment, staff recruitment, and workload (max. score = 6). Cronbach's α's for the different domains are between .67 and .92.

Because we were interested in the general perception of interdepartmental functional integration and centralisation by the most important role players in the colleges, we confined our analysis to the opinion of the general manager, the heads of the departments, and the staff (N = 401 of 14 merged colleges). Two colleges were not included in the analysis because these colleges had not merged. Moreover, it should be noted that some respondents did not answer all the questions.

5. ANALYSIS

In this section we will address the three questions raised at the beginning of this chapter. First, we will describe the interdepartmental functional integration of the merged colleges as experienced by general managers, heads of departments and staff. Second, we will review the different levels of centralisation attained for each domain of decision making as perceived by the same three categories of actors. Third, we will consider the relationship between the perceived level of interdepartmental functional integration and the perceived level of centralisation.

Before answering these questions, we want to stress that, overall, the respondents reported moderately positive perceptions of the functioning of the different councils. Most of the councils (board of directors, the academic council, the departmental council, the council of students, and the departmental council of students) received a score of between 3.11 and 3.68 (max. score 5). This was different for the negotiation committees: the negotiation committee of the college and the departmental negotiation committee scored respectively 2.99 and 2.85, which is less than the theoretical mean of 3. More than 40% of the participants of these negotiation committees were disappointed about the functioning of these committees.

5.1. Interdepartmental functional integration

Since the colleges merged only four years ago, and since the process was not complete at the time the data were collected, it could be expected that the reported level of interdepartmental functional integration would not be very high[4]. The mean score of interdepartmental functional integration was 34.16 (standard deviation: 9.24) on a scale of 60. A little less than 35% of the respondents answered these questions by assigning a score of 30 or less, 39% assigned a score of 31 – 40, and the rest assigned a score higher than 40 (but not higher than 54). The first group (score 30 or less) viewed their college as low in terms functional integration, the second (score 31 – 40) could be called the 'middle' category, and the third group (score > 40) reported that the interdepartmental functional integration was high.

A very common phenomenon is that the leaders of organisations have a more positive opinion about the level of co-operation in organisations than do the other members of the organisation. This was true in this case; general managers and heads of departments saw the colleges as more functionally integrated than did the staff (χ = 54.93; df = 4; p < .0001), although all of the latter were members of decision-making or participatory bodies and should consequently have a good overview of college policy. The mean scores associated with the general managers (44.09 on a scale of 60) and with department heads (42.56) for interdepartmental functional integration do not differ significantly from each other but both do differ significantly from the mean scores reported by the staff (32.86) (F (2,398) = 30,77; p = < .0001). In spite of these differences, we decided to combine the answers of the general managers, the department heads, and the staff to create a common, overall indicator of interdepartmental functional integration.

Table 1. Level of Interdepartmental functional integration of the colleges by respondent category

Integration	General manager		Head of department		Staff		
	N	%	N	%	N	%	Total
Low	0	0	2	4.9	137	39.3	139
Middle	6	54.5	16	39.0	163	46.7	185
High	5	45.5	23	56.1	49	14.0	77
Total	11	100	41	100	349	100	401

Since the legal structure of independent, state, and provincial colleges differs, one might expect that the reported level of interdepartmental functional integration would vary by college type. Independent and provincial colleges had to determine their own organisational structure, whereas the structure of the state colleges was prescribed by law. Members of provincial (mean score of 37.43 out of 60) and independent (34.63) colleges consider their colleges more functionally integrated than members of state colleges (32.19), and the members of the provincial colleges reported a little more interdepartmental functional integration than was reported by respondents from independent colleges (F (2, 398) = 6.27; p = .002).

Also, there was apparently a relationship between the number of students in a college and the perceived level of interdepartmental functional integration ($F(2,398)$ = 6.29; p = .002): the smaller the college, the higher the reported level of functional integration of the college. Colleges with many campuses in several towns are perceived as being less integrated than colleges with only a few campuses in a few towns ($F(3,397) = 6.28$; p = .004). Colleges that offered fewer than 5 fields of study received a higher score on functional integration than those that offered 6 or more fields of study ($F(1,399) = 13.65$; p = .0003). Finally, there was a significant difference between the level of interdepartmental functional integration reported by individual colleges (scores between 2.34 and 3.31). All these relationships remain significant regardless of the category of respondent. We can conclude that the complexity[5] of the structure of a college contributes to less interdepartmental functional integration.

5.2. Centralisation

Instead of employing only one general indicator of centralisation, we used nine: one for each level of decision making (making proposals, influence, and follow up on the decisions) combined with each of the three domains of decision-making (finance and equipment, educational policy, and human-resource management). In the following tables, we present the levels of centralisation for these three domains. As noted above, we define centralisation in terms of the degree to which decisions in colleges are made at the level of the general manager. Decentralisation means that decisions are made by heads of the departments or the departmental councils.

Table 2 shows that the decisions concerning finance and equipment in colleges are more in the hands of the general managers of the college than of the two other parties. General managers make significantly more proposals, have a stronger influence, and monitor more of these decisions than do the other actors. They are more involved in finance and equipment policy than the heads of the departments or the department councils, while the heads of the departments, in turn, are more involved than the department councils.

Decision-making concerning finance and equipment in colleges seems to be rather centralized, although the large standard deviations suggest than this opinion is not shared by all the respondents. Moreover, the rather low scores associated with the general manager for preparing, influencing, and monitoring financial policy indicate that he or she is not seen as the main decision-maker. Indeed, in state colleges the main role players in decision-making and influence in the area of financial policy are the boards of directors and the directorates[6]. On the other hand, the follow-up of these decisions is mainly seen as the task of the general manager (although a score of 1.73 out of 4 is still low; this score is higher than 1.22 reported for the department heads and 1.13 of the departmental councils). But since the department heads and the departmental council also play a role in this field of policy, the decision-making structure is partly centralized and partly decentralized. It is important to note that the departmental council in state schools plays a more prominent role in financial policy than it does in independent and provincial colleges. Indeed, according to the law, departmental councils in state colleges have the right to make certain decisions, which is not the case in the two other types of colleges.

In the independent colleges we see that the same main role is played by the board of directors, and, to a lesser degree than the general manager, by the representative administrator[7]. In these colleges, the influence of the department heads (between a score of 1.91 and 2.49 out of 4 for the three decision-making levels) is reported to be almost as high as that of the general manager (between a score of 2.17 and 2.76 out of 4). Therefore, the findings also suggest a balance between centralisation and decentralisation in the independent colleges, but there is a different reason for this than in the state colleges. The fact that heads of the department have such an important position in relation to decision making in independent colleges is a relic of the old structure. Many former directors of the small, old colleges were appointed to positions as heads of department in the new merged colleges.

In the provincial colleges, respondents indicated that the main responsibility for decisions is shared by the general manager (a score of between 1.86 and 2.25 out of 4) and the official of the provincial government responsible for education[8]. The provincial government does not involve itself very much in college policy. Since departmental councils (a score of between 0.22 and 0.51 out of 4) and the department heads (a score of between 0.78 and 1.29 out of 4) have little influence, the findings clearly indicate that the decision-making structure of the provincial colleges is centralized in terms of financial policy. In both the independent and the provincial colleges, the influence of the departmental council on financial matters is very weak (Devos et al., 2001: 220 – 224).

Table 2. Decision-making about finances and equipment by the general manager, the head of department, and departmental council (means and std) (max. score = 4)

Phase of decision making	Average value	Significant differences(1)	Standard deviation
General manager prepares	1.86	A	1.58
Dep. head prepares	1.56	B	1.37
Departmental council prepares	0.59	C	0.99
General manager influences	2.32	A'	1.55
Dep. head influences	1.85	B'	1.52
Departmental council influences	0.45	C'	0.83
General manager monitors	2.18	A"	1.62
Dep. head monitors	1.78	B"	1.53
Dep. council monitors	0.62	C"	1.06

(1) two sample paired t-test for means (p<.01). Different symbols in the same level of decision-making indicate significant differences.

In comparison with financial policy, decision-making concerning educational policy is more decentralized. Although educational policy needs the approval of the board of directors, and the general manager is supposed to monitor these decisions, the departments have maintained their responsibility for educational matters even after the mergers. Mainly, respondents report that it is the heads of the departments who take initiatives, influence the decisions, and control the execution of the decisions. Although less powerful in the three phases (proposal of policy, influence, and monitoring) of educational policy, departmental councils act the same way as the department heads, and clearly have a more important role than the general managers, except as far as the monitoring of educational policy is concerned (p = .52). However, the large standard deviations suggest that opinions are very diverse, and the reason for this lies in the differences between the legal structures of the colleges.

The state colleges are the most decentralized. For the three phases of decision making, the departmental councils received the highest scores (between 3.46 and 4.02 out of 7) though some scores barely reached the mean score. Department heads have almost the same influence in this field as the councils (between 3.58 and 4.01 out of 7 for the three phases of decision making). The general manager plays a minor role (a score of between 1.33 and 1.61 out of 7).

In the independent colleges, the main actor is the head of the department (between 4.83 and 5.31 out of 7 for the three decision-making phases). This suggests that the former directors of the old colleges maintained the same level of authority they held before the mergers as far as educational policy is concerned. The departmental council and the general manager have a minor position in this respect. Councils are perceived as having a weak role (between 2.25 and 2.86 out of 7) and so are the general managers (between 2.24 and 2.88 out of 7). In these colleges, the department heads have the same role as before the mergers.

Table 3. Decision making about educational policy by general manager, head of department, and departmental council (means and std) (max. score = 7)

Phases of decision making	Average value	Significant differences (1)	Standard deviation
General manager prepares	2.06	A	2.04
Dep. head prepares	4.41	B	2.22
Dep. council prepares	3.25	C	2.25
General manager influences	2.50	A'	2.22
Dep. Head influences	4.61	B'	2.47
Dep. council influences	3.11	C'	2.36
General manager monitors	2.53	A"	2.32
Dep. Head monitors	4.74	B"	2.43
Dep. council monitors	2.70	A"	2.46

(1) two sample paired t-test for means (p<.01). Different symbols in the same level of decision making indicate significant differences.

Respondents from the provincial colleges rated the three parties almost equally. Department heads score higher than the others (between 3.71 and 4.6 out of 7 for the three decision-making phases), but the general manager (between 3.07 and 3.91 out 7) and the council (between 2.71 and 3.66 out 7) are obviously viewed as playing a role in determining educational policy.

Nonetheless, we should not forget that the board of directors in state and independent colleges has an important influence in matters of educational programs, because it is the board of directors that approves programs. According to respondents, the board of directors does not play the lead role, but it can decide to approve or not approve new proposals within the framework established by the law (a college may only offer authorized courses). In spite of this, the evidence indicates that educational policy is decentralized in state and independent colleges, albeit for different reasons. In the state colleges, the departmental councils are seen as having the most influence, while in the independent colleges, the department heads have the most influence. In the provincial colleges, educational policy is not clearly centralized or decentralized. Indeed, the main actors in this policy area in these institutions are the head of the department and the general manager. The representative of the provincial government plays a minor role in educational policy (Devos et al., 2001: 224 – 227).

Human-resource management decisions are also more decentralized than financial management. In spite of the rather low scores, the department heads are seen as the most important decision makers in human-resource management, more than the departmental councils or the general managers. The departmental councils seem to have a minor position in this respect, and are viewed as playing less of a role than the general managers. The large standard deviations show a great range of opinion.

Table 4. Decision-making about human resources by the general manager, the head of department, and the departmental council (means and std) (max. score = 6)

Phases of decision making	Average value	Significant differences (1)	Standard deviation
General manager prepares	2.74	A	2.38
Dep. head prepares	3.85	B	2.21
Dep. council prepares	1.38	C	2.05
General manager influences	2.73	A'	2.42
Dep. head influences	4.30	B'	2.25
Dep. council influences	1.22	C'	2.00
General manager monitors	2.62	A"	2.50
Dep. head monitors	4.21	B"	2.35
Dep. council monitors	1.21	C"	2.05

(1) two sample paired t-test for means (p<.01). Different symbols in the same level of decision-making indicates significant differences.

The reason for this diversity can be found when we analyse the decision-making structure of the state, independent, and provincial colleges separately. In the state colleges, the departmental council has decision-making power, which means that this council (score = 3.19 out of a possible 6) plays almost the same important role in developing human-resource policy as the department heads (score = 3.36). The influence and the monitoring of human-resource policy are viewed more as the responsibility of the department heads (score of 3.60 and 3.85 respectively) than of the departmental councils (score of 2.75 and 2.69 respectively). The data indicate that decisions in this policy domain are decentralized.

This is not the case in the independent colleges. Here the main actor is the department head (preparing score = 4.37; influence score = 4.88; follow-up score = 4.49), who is strongly supported (or guided) by the general manager (preparing score = 3.12; influence score = 3.1; follow-up score = 3.02). The departmental council (only advisory authority) plays a very minor role or no role at all (preparing score = 0.54; influence score = 0.59; follow-up score = 0.55). In the independent colleges, the department heads (often the former directors of the old colleges) have maintained their power in this decision domain. This is a form of decentralisation that leaves the power in the hands of two individuals: the department head and the general manager.

The provincial colleges occupy a middle position. The respondents indicate that the general manager takes the lead in human-resource policy and is supported in this by the department head, but, while the general manager takes the lead in human-resource policy (preparing score = 4.48; influence score = 4.37; follow-up score = 3.96), he seems to rely on the heads of the departments (preparing score = 2.32; influence score = 2.37; follow-up score = 3.7) in many respects. Again we can speak here of a partly centralized and a partly decentralized decision making structure (Devos et al., 2001: 233 – 236).

5.3. Interdepartmental functional integration and decentralisation

The founding of new colleges has different consequences as far as interdepartmental functional integration and decentralisation are concerned. Because each general manager is faced with the challenge of bringing the college together to form a new cohesive institution, there may be a tendency to centralise decision-making power in the central administration. However, in facilitating the interdepartmental functional integration process, they might offer more opportunities for a decentralized decision-making structure. Therefore, we hypothesized that a higher level of decentralisation would be related to a higher level of interdepartmental functional integration. According to the theory of Burns and Stalker, a modern organisation will function better as an organic type if the organisation is working under conditions of change. As noted at the beginning of this chapter, the merging of the colleges represented a tremendous change for these institutions, at a time when important changes were also occurring in the broader society (e.g. law, economy). Therefore, an organic type of organisation in the colleges could be expected, with interdepartmental functional integration and decentralisation being linked to each other.

Since the level of perceived decentralisation varied depending on the domain of decision making, we tested this hypothesis for each level and domain of decision making. Given that the legal rights of the department heads and the departmental councils (see above) differ between state, independent, and provincial colleges, we controlled for the function of the respondents and the legal position of the colleges.

Table 5. Correlations (Spearman) between the different phases and domains of centralisation and interdepartmental functional integration

	Finance	Education	Human resources
General manager prepares	.133**	.105	.194**
Dep. head prepares	.146*	.094	-.009
Dep. council prepares	-.051	.117*	-.093
General manager influences	.077	.190**	.232***
Dep. head influences	.106	.063	.027
Dep. council influences	.041	.165**	.088
General manager monitors	.133*	.193*	.230***
Dep. head monitors	.160**	.110	-.008
Dep. council monitors	-.003	.017	-.089

*p<.05   **p<.01   ***p<.001

5.3.1. Decentralisation of finance policy and interdepartmental functional integration

The hypothesis that decentralisation in decision making about financial matters is linked to an increase in interdepartmental functional integration is not supported. This could be expected on the basis of the data on centralisation, because we can only speak about decentralisation in provincial colleges. In the state and independent colleges there is a balance of centralisation and decentralisation.

Using correlation analysis (Spearman), we found a positive significant relationship only between interdepartmental functional integration and the act of making proposals in financial matters by the department head (r = .146) and the general manager (r = .133), and the monitoring of the decisions by the department head (r = .16) and the general manager (r = .133). As we have already noted, the general manager and the department head are the most important decision-makers in this domain (see Table 2). Although these relationships are not strong, they do show that the perceptions of interdepartmental functional integration is linked to the perceptions of the behaviour of two important actors in financial policy: the general manager who tends more to centralisation; and the department heads who tend more to decentralisation.

We analysed these relationships for each type of college. For responses from the independent colleges, we found a positive relation between interdepartmental functional integration and centralisation; interdepartmental functional integration increases together with the increase in the frequency of reporting the general manager as the main actor in preparing (r = .168) and monitoring (r = .166) financial policy. Interdepartmental functional integration in independent colleges was not linked with the perception of the head of the department as an important actor in preparing and monitoring the financial policy. The opposite was true for the state colleges; interdepartmental functional integration increases when the heads of departments play an important role in preparing (r = .211) and monitoring (r = .272) financial policy but not when the respondents mention the general manager as an important actor. In the provincial colleges, there does not appear to be a relationship between interdepartmental functional integration and centralisation.

It is also important to note that the assessment of the influence of the general manager, the department head, and the departmental council on financial policy is not linked to the perceptions of interdepartmental functional integration of the members of the merged colleges.

5.3.2. Decentralisation of educational policy and interdepartmental functional integration

Financial policy is more centralized than educational policy. This means that the responsibility for educational policy is more in the hands of the department heads and/or the departmental councils. This is not the case in all the three types of colleges since the provincial colleges appear to have balance of centralisation and decentralisation (see Table 3). Since respondents saw more educational policy initiatives coming from the department heads and the departmental councils, we expected that they also would experience a higher degree of interdepartmental functional integration. Here again, the data do not confirm this hypothesis (see Table 5).

When heads of departments are perceived to prepare, influence and monitor educational policy the level of perceived interdepartmental functional integration of the college is no higher than when this is not the case. A higher activity level of the departmental councils could also contribute to a greater feeling of interdepartmental functional integration. Two positive relations confirm this hypothesis: if the council is active in preparing (r = .117) and influencing (r = .165) educational policy, the perception of interdepartmental functional integration of the college is higher. Nevertheless, variance analysis refutes these relationships (F(2,307) = 2.12, p = .122; F(2,284) = 2.80, p = .063). Controlling for the type of college, it becomes clear that only in independent colleges is the relationship between preparing the educational policy by the departmental council and interdepartmental functional integration significant (r = .158).

Interdepartmental functional integration of the college seems to be supported by the centralisation of decisions on educational policy (see Table 5). If respondents perceive that the general manager influences (r =.189) and monitors (r =.193) educational policy, they also tend to assess the level of interdepartmental functional integration as higher. This is not the case if the general manager is perceived as being very active in preparing educational policy. Variance analysis shows that this relationship is still present when we control for the type of college: when the general manager influences the educational policy (F(2,282) = 8.58; p =.0002) and when he monitors it (F(2,274) = 3.33; p = .037).

5.3.3. Decentralisation and human resource policy

Once again, our data do not support the relationship between decentralisation of human-resource policy and the level of interdepartmental functional integration of the colleges (Table 5). When the respondents report that the department head and the departmental council play a role in human-resource management, they do not report more interdepartmental functional integration. On the contrary, when they report that the general manager prepares the policy ($r = .19$), influences the policy ($r = .23$), or monitors the policy ($r = .23$), they see more interdepartmental functional integration of the college. Variance analysis shows that, after controlling for the type of college, these statements stand for preparing the human-resource policy by the general manager ($F(2,240) = 3.86$; $p = .022$) and for monitoring this policy ($F(2,221) = 7.42$; $p =.0009$). The more centralized the human-resource policy, the more the college is viewed as functionally integrated.

6. DISCUSSION AND CONCLUSIONS

The merging of 163 colleges into 29 colleges was a tremendous challenge for the new general managers and the board of directors, but also for policy makers at lower levels of these new institutions and the members of other college councils. Most of these colleges were totally new organisations. The general managers and boards of directors were assigned new roles that did not exist under the old college structure, and the directors of old colleges lost their jobs. Some of the former directors were appointed as department heads in the new colleges, others were elected to department head positions or left the colleges entirely, depending on the legal character of the college. In the state colleges, department heads are elected, while in the independent colleges they are appointed by the board of directors. Very often, a director of a former independent college became the head of a department in a new independent college.

Although the colleges were a new organisational form, they did not have to start from scratch. The government had determined the decision-making line authority and the role of participatory councils for the state colleges. The other colleges had more freedom to establish their own decision-making structure, albeit one that was bound by official regulations. For example, the independent and provincial colleges have had to establish department councils and provide the staff and students with an opportunity to participate in deliberations, although the college administration does not have to accept their advice. Thus, a departmental council in the state colleges can determine specific types of policy, but the same council in the independent and the provincial colleges is assigned only an advisory function.

In general, one can argue that the new decision-making structure of both the state and the non-state colleges allows for the possibility of developing a decentralised organisation. This means that they have a basic structure for deliberation among the different members (general manager, department head, staff, students, members of the board, etc.) of the organisation, which can contribute to the establishment of common values and goals by the members beyond the level that might be associated with a traditional hierarchical structure (Burns and Stalker 1961). On the other hand, the fact that these were new organisations meant that they had to be forged into units to fulfil their mission as a college. Given this situation, the role of the general manager and of the department heads can be viewed as difficult and challenging. If the general manager gives more freedom to the subdivisions (departments), it is possible that he or she will have more difficulty in bringing the college together to form a unified organisation. However, if the departments believe that their advice is taken seriously, this might contribute to the interdepartmental functional integration of the college as well. This was the problem that general managers and boards had to face. How did they deal with this dilemma?

Obviously, policy makers have to follow the rules laid down by law or regulations. This means that all official decisions of the colleges are made by the general manager and/or the board of directors. However, other members of the colleges can contribute to the process of decision-making. What Coffman (1996: 131) saw as an advantage of the merging process in his case study could also be expected in Flemish colleges. However, our data show that the answer is more complex. Decentralisation did not occur in all domains of decision-making. Finance and equipment policy is seen to be mainly the domain of the college leadership and partly of the department heads. The departmental councils play only a minor role in this policy domain. The trend to centralise decisions on finance and equipment policy was also found in six of the ten case studies. However, there were two cases where this policy domain was highly decentralized. The educational policy domain, however, is different. For these decisions, decentralisation is the main trend in the state and the independent colleges. In the provincial colleges, the respondents' perceive a mixed form of centralisation and decentralisation. The case study data confirm this pattern. Educational policy seems to be the prerogative of the departments. What is interesting here is that the departmental councils also play a role, albeit a lesser role than the department heads. Human-resource policy is also perceived as decentralised in the state and the independent colleges, while in the provincial colleges it is mixed. However, this decentralisation differs from the decentralisation of educational policy. Human-resource policy is mainly the domain of the department head with the departmental councils playing only a minor role. The colleges have reached a certain level of what P. Hoggett called a "centralised decentralisation" (Henkel 2000: 57), but not to the same extent for all domains of decision making.

Our hypothesis was that, given the trend towards the development of learning or network organisations in our society, which implies a more organic pattern of organisation, interdepartmental functional integration of the colleges could be related to a decentralisation of the decision-making process. When a greater level of participation in governance is granted to all members of the college, one could expect that a new, more integrated college would emerge. Before discussing this relationship, it is important to recall that the interdepartmental functional integration of the colleges reported by our respondents was not very high (score 34.16 out of 60), although the general managers and the department heads viewed the level of integration as much higher than the other respondent groups. Even with a rather low interdepartmental functional integration score, it was still reasonable to expect that interdepartmental functional integration would be supported by decentralisation (Clark 1998: 137; Henkel 2000: 57; Sporn 1999: 284). The assumption is that a college, as required under the new law, is indeed a democratic organisation with the right of representative participation in the decision making for all staff and students. In spite of this, our hypothesis was not supported by the data. When we analyse the statistical relationships presented in Table 5, we note that 7 out of 9 possible relationships support the thesis that interdepartmental functional integration of the college is perceived to be related to centralisation; the more the general manager is involved in decision making, the more the colleges are perceived to be functionally integrated. The department head and the departmental council do not seem to have the same relationship to perceptions of integration. If the department head is seen as the main decision maker only two relationships are significantly linked with the interdepartmental functional integration of the college (Table 5). The latter was also the case when the departmental council is seen as the main actor (decentralisation). Only 4 out of 18 possible relationships support the hypothesis that interdepartmental functional integration of the colleges is linked with decentralisation. Decentralisation seems to contribute less to interdepartmental functional integration than centralisation. This could be a consequence of the responses from the general managers and the department heads who may want to attribute more influence to themselves than they actually have. We checked this hypothesis, but it was not supported by the data.

How can this relationship be explained? We believe that we have to place these statements within the context of the innovation process. General managers and boards of directors were facing the amalgamation of departments that were used to functioning independently. The challenge was to find a way to create some sense of cohesion among what had previously been separate, independent units. It is obvious that this could be a reason for managers to play an explicit, integrative role. This phenomenon will obviously have an impact on how decision-making processes are perceived by the members of the colleges. Because of this, centralisation is assigned a more prominent place in the opinion of the actors. At the same time, department heads and departmental councils do play a role in the decision-making process in the colleges, and thus support decentralisation, but these activities are not linked to interdepartmental functional integration. This does not mean that decentralisation hindered interdepartmental functional integration, but that decentralisation did not operate in parallel with interdepartmental functional integration. Given the formal decision-making structure of the colleges, we expect that, over time, these colleges will move towards greater decentralisation in decision-making as they become more functionally integrated.

NOTES

[1] This chapter is based on data collected within the framework of a research project financed by OBPWO (Fund for Educational Policy and Practice-oriented Scientific Research, Brussels) as Contract 97.01.
[2] The process of merging in Flanders shows a lot of similarities with the merging of colleges in the Netherlands and Australia, with the exception of the abolition of the binary system in Australia (Goedegebuure and Meek 1991; Goedegebuure 1992; Van Heffen et al., 1999: 23 – 24; Gamage 1993).
[3] For a long list of the problems that can emerge during a process of merging, see Coffman, 1996.
[4] Goedegebuure (1992: 75) states "...it takes some ten years for the wounds to heal and the new organization to operate in a more or less normalized way".
[5] The structure of a college is considered complex when the college has many campuses and provides many fields of study. The more campuses, and the more fields of study a college has, the more complex is the structure.
[6] The Directorate consists of the chairman of the board of directors, the general manager, and 3 representatives of the personnel.

[7] This function exists only in independent colleges.
[8] This function exists only in provincial colleges.

REFERENCES

Bartlett, C.I. and S. Goshal. "Beyond Strategy, Structure, Systems to Purpose, Process, People: Reflections on a Voyage of Discovery." In Duffy, P.B. (ed). *The Relevance of a Decade*. Boston: Harvard Business School Press, 1994, 323 – 345.

Bazerman, M. H. *Judgment in Managerial Decision Making*. New York: John Wiley & Sons, 1994.

Burns, T. and G.M. Stalker. *The Management of Innovation*. London: Tavistock, 1961.

Clark, B. R. *Creating Entrepreneurial Universities. Organizational Pathways of Transformation*. Oxford: Pergamon, 1998.

Clegg, S. *Modern Organizations. Organization Studies in the Postmodern World*. London: Sage, 1990.

Coffman, S.L. "A Description of Merger Applied to the Montana State University Context." *Journal of the Association for Communication Administration* 2 (May 1996): 124 – 136.

Deal, T.E. and A. Kennedy. *Corporate Cultures: The Rites and Rituals of Corporate Life*. Reading, (MA): Addison-Wesley, 1982.

Devos, G., J.C. Verhoeven, S. Maes and K. Vanpée. *Bestuur en Medezeggenschap in Vlaamse Hogescholen*. Leuven/Gent: Departement Sociologie/Vlerick Leuven Gent managementschool, 2001.

Drummond, H. *Effective Decision Making. A Practical Guide for Management*. London: Kogan Page Limited, 1991.

Gamage, D.T. "The Reorganisation of the Australian Higher Educational Institutions towards a Unified National System." *Studies in Higher Education* 18.1 (1993): 81 – 95.

Gergen, K.G. "Organization Theory in the Postmodern Era.", in Reed, M. and M. Hughes (eds). *Rethinking Organization. New Directions in Organization Theory and Analysis*. London: Sage Publications, 1992, 207 – 226.

Giesbers, J.H. "Schoolbestuur en schoolleiding." In Creemers, B.P.M., J.H.G.I. Giesbers, M.L. Krüger and C.A. van Vilsteren (eds). *Handboek Schoolorganisatie en Onderwijsmanagement*. Alphen aan den Rijn/Diegem: Samsom, 1993, A1430, 1 – 29.

Goedegebuure, L. *Mergers in Higher Education. A Comparative Analysis*. Enschede: CHEPS, 1992.

Goedegebuure, L. and L. Meek. "Restructuring Higher Education. A Comparative Analysis between Australia and the Netherlands." *Comparative Education* 27.1 (1991): 7 – 22.

Hamel, G. and C.K. Prahalad. *Competing for the Future*. Boston: Harvard Business School Press, 1994.

Hanson, E.M. *Educational Administration and Organizational Behavior*. Boston: Allyn & Bacon, 1979.

Henkel, M. *Academic Identities and Policy Change in Higher Education*. London and Philadelphia: Jessica Kingsley Publishers, 2000.

Hofman, R.H. "De Bijdrage van Schoolbesturen aan Kwaliteit van Scholen." In Creemers, B.P.M., J.H.G.I. Giesbers, M.L. Krüger and C.A. van Vilsteren (eds). *Handboek Schoolorganisatie en Onderwijs-management*. Alphen a/d Rijn/Diegem: Samsom, 1991, A1300, 1 – 22.

Lawrence, P.R. and J.W. Lorsch. *Organisation and Environment. Managing Differentiation and Integration*. Boston: Division of research, Graduate School of Business Administration, Harvard University, 1967.

Miles, R.E. and C.C. Snow. *Fit, Failure and the Hall of Fame: How Companies Succeed or Fail*. New York: The Free Press, 1994.

Miller, D. and C. Dröge. "Psychological and Traditional Determinants of Structure." *Administrative Science Quarterly* 31 (December, 1986): 539 – 560.

Mintzberg, H. *The Structuring of Organizations: a Synthesis of the Research*. Englewood Cliffs (NJ): Prentice Hall, 1979.

Ministerie van de Vlaamse Gemeenschap, Departement Onderwijs (MVG) *Vlaams Onderwijs in Cijfers 2000-2001*. Brussels: Ministerie van de Vlaamse Gemeenschap, 2001.

Reed, M. and M. Hughes. *Rethinking Organization. New Directions in Organization Theory and Analysis*. London: Sage Publications, 1992.

Schein, E. *Organizational Culture and Leadership*. San Francisco: Jossey-Bass, 1992.

Senge, P. *The Fifth Discipline. The Art and Practice of Learning Organization*. Garden City: Doubleday, 1990.

Sporn, B. *Adaptive University Structures. An Analysis of Adaptation to Socioeconomic Environments of US and European Universities.* London and Philadelphia: Jessica Kingsley Publishers, 1999.

Turner, B.A. "The Symbolic Understanding of Organizations." In M. Reed and M. Hughes (eds). *Rethinking Organization. New Directions in Organization Theory and Analysis.* London: Sage Publications, 1992, 46 – 66.

Van Heffen, O., P. Maassen, J.C. Verhoeven, F. de Vijlder and K. de Wit. *Overheid, Hoger Onderwijs en Economie. Ontwikkelingen in Nederland en Vlaanderen.* Utrecht: Uitgeverij LEMMA, B.V., 1999.

Verhoeven, J.C. and L. Dom. *Flemish Eurydice Report 2000: Education Policy and Education Organisation in Flanders.* Brussels: Ministry of the Flemish Community, Department of Education, Policy Coordination Division, 2001.

Verhoeven, J.C., G. Devos, C. Smolders, W. Cools and J. Velghe. *Hogescholen enkele jaren na de fusie.* Leuven: Departement Sociologie, 2001.

Whitaker, A. "The Transformation in Work: Post-Fordism Revisited." in M. Reed and M. Hughes (eds). *Rethinking Organization. New Directions in Organization Theory and Analysis.* London: Sage Publications, 1992, 184 – 206.

APPENDIX

Scale of interdepartmental functional integration

- in the college the members of the different departmental councils deliberate informally;
- the different departments are on good terms with each other;
- in the college, some people take care of the co-ordination of the quality assurance between different departments;
- before deciding, the department heads of the different departments deliberate together;
- the central administration is on good terms with the departments;
- in this college, departments exchange staff;
- each department decides more or less independently;
- the decision making at the top of the college is influenced by engagements on the interdepartmental level;
- the college organises meetings (e.g. the beginning of the academic year, receptions) for all the staff of the different departments;
- when the departments have to plan the staff for the coming academic year, they consult each other;
- departments collaborate (informally) to reach a collective decision for the whole college;
- the college organises information meetings for all the employees of all the departments.

MICHAEL I. REED

NEW MANAGERIALISM, PROFESSIONAL POWER AND ORGANISATIONAL GOVERNANCE IN UK UNIVERSITIES: A REVIEW AND ASSESSMENT

"Governing is about managing the gap between expectations and reality."[1]

1. INTRODUCTION

The impact of the ideas and practices associated with 'new managerialism' or 'new public management' on the organisation, management and delivery of public sector services in Anglo-American and European welfare states has been extensively researched, discussed and evaluated in recent years (Ferlie et al., 1996; Exworthy and Halford 1999; Politt and Bouckaert 2000). However, higher education has been, and remains, a relatively neglected institutional sector (Trowler 2001) in which the trajectories of institutional and organisational restructuring typical of new managerialism/new public management continue to be poorly understood. This chapter synoptically reports on and interprets a recently conducted research project on the extent to which the ideological, institutional and organisational reforms associated with the latter have impacted on UK universities. The project was undertaken with particular regard to the selection, roles and practices of manager-academics and their implications for the longer-term position of professional academics.

This multi-disciplinary project, entitled, 'New Managerialism and the Management of UK Universities' was conducted by a team of researchers based at Lancaster University between October 1998 and November 2000. The study was funded by the Economic and Social Research Council (grant no R000237661). The remit of the project was to examine the extent to which New Managerialism/New Public Management, a set of reforms of the management of publicly-funded services popular with many western governments during the 1990's, was seen to have permeated the management and governance of UK universities. The study also explored the roles, practices, selection, learning and support of manager/manager-academics such as heads of departments, deans, pro-vice-chancellors and vice-chancellors. The first phase of the study comprised focus group discussions with learned societies from several disciplines where respondents considered what was changing to the activities and management of their disciplinary specialisms within UK universities. The second phase involved interviews with 135 manager-academics (from Head of Department to Vice-Chancellor) and 29 senior administrators in 12 pre-1992 and post-universities. The interviews explored the

Alberto Amaral, Glen A. Jones and Berit Karseth (eds.), Governing Higher Education:
National Perspectives on Institutional Governance, 163—185.
© 2002 *Kluwer Academic Publishers. Printed in the Netherlands.*

backgrounds, current management practices and perceptions of respondents. In phase 3, in-depth case studies of the cultures and management of 4 universities enabled comparisons of the views of manager-academics with those of academics and support staff.

The strategic intellectual objective of the research project was to identify and explore the diverse range of 'narratives of change' that emerged from the focus groups, interviews and case studies and to link these to wider movements within the political economy and institutional domains of UK universities. The chapter opens with a theoretical discussion of the concept of new managerialism/new public management and its broader implications for the institutional and organisational restructuring of UK higher education as a component part of the UK 'public sector'. Subsequently, it moves on to consider the impact of the changes associated with the former on the autonomy and power/control of the academic profession within the UK. It attempts this in relation to broader theoretical interpretations of new forms of professional work and organisation within Anglo-American political economies (Freidson 2001; Leicht and Fennel 2001). Finally, the chapter reflects on the intensifying tensions and contradictions that continue to characterise UK higher education and their longer-term implications for the distribution and ordering of resources, routines and relations within British universities.

The conception of 'university governance' employed in this chapter is relatively broad and inclusive. It is taken to refer to the general *organisational technologies and practices* through which higher education institutions attempt to regulate and control what happens within their, increasingly porous and contested, boundaries. In this respect, this chapter focuses on university governance as referring to a range of organisational forms, modes of control and regulatory practices through which individual and collective behaviour is routinely monitored, evaluated and modified. This is a significantly wider, even 'looser', conception of university governance than that conventionally adopted in studies and analyses primarily concerned with formal institutional machinery and structures. Nevertheless, it has the distinct advantage of focusing upon the actual 'coal-face' organisational programmes and managerial practices through which recent UK university reform has been attempted, within the wider institutional context set by changing government policy on HE and the global political economy in which it is embedded. In this sense, it is in keeping with contemporary research concerned with the longer-term impact of new managerialist discourses and practices on the changing forms of academic life and identity typical of UK universities at the present time (Trowler 1998, 2001; Taylor 1999; Henkel 2000; Prichard 2000).

2. NEW MANAGERIALISM AS A THEORY OF INSTITUTIONAL AND ORGANISATIONAL CHANGE

The conception of 'new managerialism' that has informed our research project can be defined in relation to three loosely coupled or overlapping structural elements. First, as a generic *narrative of strategic change* which is constructed and promulgated in order "to persuade others towards certain understandings and actions" (Barry and Elmes 1997: 433) in relation to the established governance and management of universities. Second, as an emergent but *distinctive organisational form* that provides the administrative mechanisms and managerial processes through which this theory of change will be realised. Third, as a *practical control technology* through which strategic policies and their organisational instrumentation can be potentially transformed into viable practices, techniques and devices that challenge, or at the very least substantially modify, established systems of 'bureau-professionalism' (Clarke and Newman 1997: 68 – 70). Taken as a package of cultural, organisational and managerial interventions, 'new managerialism' constitutes an alternative model of governmental and institutional order for higher education within the UK to that which has existed under the traditional compromise between corporate bureaucracy and professional association from the mid-1940's onwards (Jary and Parker 1998; Smith and Webster 1997). The latter shaped the post-Second World War development of British higher education to the extent that it facilitated a viable trade-off between managerial control and professional autonomy as exemplified in the organisational logic and practice of 'professional bureaucracy' (Mintzberg 1979). 'New managerialism', however, radically questions, indeed undermines, the terms on which that political trade-off and organisational compromise was originally struck and subsequently maintained. This is so to the extent that it is grounded in an ideological, cultural and political critique of existing institutional structures and organisational forms within higher education that articulates their *endemic* lack of external accountability, internal managerial discipline and routine operational efficiency (Ackroyd, Hughes and Soothill 1989). In turn, this critique, and the alternative logic of organising and managing that it generates, draws on a large body of organisational and managerial theorising in order to sustain and *legitimate* the narrative of institutional transformation that it promulgates.

As a generic narrative or theory of macro-level change in institutional forms and their underlying cultural rationale, 'new managerialism' draws on an eclectic body of literature that legitimates the, largely untrammelled, exercise of managerial prerogative within the modern private and public sector corporation (Child 1969; Anthony 1986; Enteman 1993). The justification for this unqualified assertion of managerial authority within modern society and organisations is based on a potpourri of ideological claims relating to the universal specialist expertise assumed to reside in 'management' as a general capacity overriding specific (e.g. 'craft' and/or 'professional') knowledge and skill (Locke 1989, 1996; Glover and Tracey 1997). However, 'new managerialism' rests on a more inclusive, not to say totalising, ideological foundation. It locates itself within a mythology of 'market populism' that can explain and legitimate any social and organisational change in terms of the presumed infallibility of *'the'* market mechanism as a universal solution to all social problems – irrespective of their historical and institutional provenance (Frank 2001). Thus, 'new managerialism' – as a meta-narrative of social and organisational transformation – can be contextualised within an ideology of *market-based managerialism* that would be mobilised right across the public sector as an institutional logic that would simultaneously break the power of professional 'producer cartels' (Ackroyd et al., 1989; Exworthy and Halford 1999) and the ingrained organisational inertia characteristic of corporate bureaucracy (Pollitt 1993; Pollitt and Bouckaert 2000). The introduction of the market mechanism into the delivery and management of a wide-range of social and public services, the advocates of 'new managerialism' contended, would provide that imperative drive towards operational efficiency and strategic effectiveness so conspicuously lacking in the sclerotic professional monopolies and corporate bureaucracies that continued to dominate public life (Osborne and Gaebler 1992; DuGay 1994, 2000; Maddock and Morgan 1998). In local government (Farnham and Horton 1993; Walsh 1995; Keen and Scase 1998), health and social care (Pettigrew, Ferlie and McKee 1992; Ferlie, Ashburner, Fitzgerald and Pettigrew 1996; Dent, O'Neill and Bagley 1999; Mark and Dopson 1999; Flynn 1992, 1999; Maddock and Morgan 1998; Ham 1999) and education (Rustin 1994; Cowen 1996; Dearlove 1997, 1998 a and b; Henkel 1997) the legitimatory discourse driving organisational restructuring identified the introduction of market, or at least quasi-market, mechanisms as the solvent to bureaucratic rigidity and professional intransigence. By imposing market competition through political dictate and administrative fiat, the ideology of 'new managerialism' attempted to destroy, or at least weaken, the regulatory structures that had protected unaccountable professional elites and their monopolistic labour market and work practices across the full range of public sector service provision throughout the 1980's and 1990's.

At the middle-range level of organisational forms and practices, 'new managerialism' entailed a number of interrelated changes in structural design and operating systems. These seemed to clear the ground for a more tightly integrated regime of managerial discipline and control which departed radically from the untidy but stabilising compromises of bureau-professionalism (Harrison and Pollitt 1994; Clarke and Newman 1997; Hood 1995; Webb 1999). At the same time, this programme of intra-organisational reforms dovetailed with changes to the regulatory environment in which public sector agencies and professionals operated. The latter were to become subjected to a much more rigorous regime of external accountability in which continuous monitoring and audit would be the dominant realities (Kirkpatrick and Lucio 1995; Power 1997; Morgan and Engwall 1999). In relation to organisational structure, the major initiative that 'new managerialism' facilitated was the deconstruction of integrated bureaucratic hierarchies into dispersed networks of 'purchasers' and 'providers'. Within the latter, services were bought and sold on a contractual basis where regulated market exchange was the prevailing norm (Tilley 1993; Walsh 1995; Kitchener 1999). However, a strategic infrastructure of indicative planning and control was retained at the centre so that it continued to set the overall resource and policy constraints within which service providers must operate. Eventually, this would be combined with an extremely detailed framework of devolved performance criteria against which operational efficiency and effectiveness at the unit level would be monitored and assessed. Considered in these terms, this, *simultaneously strategically centralised and operationally devolved*, new surveillance and control regime provided some of the organisational scaffolding on which the 'entrepreneurial' (Clark 1998) or 'postmodern' (Scott 1999) university could possibly be constructed.

Consequently, the most significant change to internal operating systems lay in the increasing emphasis given to performance target-setting and management against predetermined operational efficiency norms and strategic effectiveness outcomes (Smith 1993). Within the context of much more intrusive and pervasive performance management, a consistent emphasis on the detailed monitoring and evaluation of 'quality' standards in service delivery and outcomes emerged as the overriding priority. This was embedded within a public sector management ideology and practice remodelled on private sector commercial enterprise and its putative obsession with 'total quality management' (Kirkpatrick and Lucio 1995). The programme of structural and operational reforms entailed in the ideology of 'new managerialism' were intended to coerce public sector managers and professional service providers into a more meaningful and direct engagement with their relative competitive position within an increasingly fragmented and uncertain market environment. Here, the needs and demands of the 'customer', rather than the 'provider', were to be regarded as paramount (DuGay and Salaman 1992; DuGay 1996; Whittington, McNulty and Whipp 1994). In turn, there was a clear expectation that this would encourage, if not force, public sector managers and professionals into a more realistic appreciation of the austere political and financial constraints that their organisations now faced and their stark implications for budget control and management. The halcyon days of the public sector 'free lunch' were over. A new age of financial rectitude and draconian resource management would necessarily flow from the dismantling of professional bureaucracy in all its profligate and monopolistic ways. The operational autonomy and political power of unaccountable professional interest groups would be severely restricted and eventually broken by restructured organisational forms and performance review systems that had traditionally protected them within the labour market and the workplace. Neo-liberalism or market populism provided the wider ideological legitimation for this programme of organisational reform; the latter initially fabricated and then maintained the instrumentation through which this programme would be achieved.

The programme of organisational reforms with which 'new managerialism' is associated also facilitated the development of a micro-level political technology through which strategic policy objectives and structural redesigns would have a realistic chance of being implemented. The ideology of market-based, technocratic managerialism and the programme of organisational reform that it legitimates and instigates both require a practical configuration of techniques, devices and tools if they are to be operationalised 'on the ground' (Mitchell 1999; Rose 1999). If one is to reform individual and institutional conduct in a direction that makes it more competitive, entrepreneurial and efficient, then one needs a technology of discipline and control through which that 'enterprising culture' can be practically accomplished (Keat and Abercrombie 1991). Recalcitrant public sector professionals and managers do not become innovative, market-driven and self-motivated entrepreneurs overnight! Their occupational ideologies and organisational identities have to be captured or 'colonised' by new discourses and practices that attempt to enrol them within a transformed understanding of their innate entrepreneurial potentialities and 'powers' that remain repressed by the dead weight of professional mendacity and bureaucratic mediocrity. In this respect, the new technology of micro-level surveillance, discipline and control that 'new managerialism' generates has radical implications for established regimes of professional ethics and organisational conduct. The 'cultural revolution' that 'new managerialism' sets in motion requires a technology of workplace control, within a restructured governance and management structure, in order to make it a viable as a coherent strategy and programme of change. To have any chance of realising its ideological aspirations and transformative intent, 'new managerialism' must foster the design and implementation of an operational control technology that will penetrate the patina of producer-driven regulatory protections in which public sector professionals and managers have been indulgently cocooned.

This micro-level control technology is grounded in a set of practices and devices that are focussed upon the highly complex and inherently risky task of re-engineering the labour process within and through which public sector professionals and managers do their work (Reed 1995, 1999). It also strives to transform the organisational culture within which this, appropriately re-engineered, professional/managerial labour process is embedded. Re-engineering the professional labour process is attempted through a number of relatively mundane, and also rather more sophisticated, devices such as financial monitoring, quality audit, performance measurement and work rationalisation. Overall, these incremental re-engineering changes can be seen to be driven by the need to make the professional labour process more visible, transparent, measurable and hence accountable – to both external and internal managerial hierarchies now relocated in more streamlined strategic control centres (Deem 1998).

Cultural re-engineering is pursued through the construction and dissemination, often in very indirect and subtle ways, of a new matrix of symbols and values and a new lexicon of terminology. In the fullness of time, it is anticipated that these mechanisms of cultural re-identification and transmission will provide the means through which innovative institutional procedures and linguistic practices can become accepted as 'the norm' (Shore and Roberts 1995; Shore and Wright 1998). Professional and managerial personnel are encouraged, indeed expected, to internalise and accept these new value systems and languages as an explicit recognition and indication of their duly reconstructed occupational and organisational identities. New bodies of expert knowledge and skill linked to 'quality', 'development' and 'empowerment' are developed and transmitted to professionals and managers who can no longer afford to define themselves through tried and trusted cultural stereotypes of 'professionalism' (Gane and Johnson 1993). They must now both work with the new tools and instrumentation that their redesigned work tasks demand, as well as internalising the new values and languages that their contemporary work relationships embody. Obsolete cultural stereotypes associated with professional 'craft skills', individual judgement and collegiality are to be superseded by a culture of self-managing teams, project groups and technical experts. The latter would now exercise continuous surveillance and policing over each other within a never-ending competitive struggle to survive (Parker and Jary 1994; Ozga 1995; Prichard and Willmott 1997).

In this way, the programme of organisational reform that 'new managerialism' advocated drew on forms of management theory and technique that seemed to provide a justification for the move towards more streamlined and decentralised organisation structures and 'empowering' organisation cultures. The literatures on 'business process re-engineering' (Hamer and Champey 1993; Knights and Willmott 2000) and on 'total quality management' (Wilkinson and Willmott 1995; Keleman, Forrester and Hassard 2000) provided recipes for 'root and branch' organisational restructuring that seemed to eradicate the confusion, waste and redundancy characteristic of professional bureaucracy. 'New managerialism' also drew on a growing body of literature focussed on *cultural*, rather than structural, re-engineering in which the motivational and social preconditions deemed necessary for the radical transformation of established occupational and organisational identities could be realised. In this context, contemporary management theories of 'transformational leadership' (Hechscher, Eisenstat and Rice 1994; Sjostrand 1997), 'self-managing teams' (Tjosvold 1991; Jenkins 1994) and 'high trust work cultures' (Fox 1974; Misztal 1996; Lane and Bachmann 1998), putatively facilitating both individual and collective empowerment, were very prominent. In turn, the strategies of structural and cultural re-engineering promoted by 'new managerialism' were brought together in theories of the 'post-bureaucratic' or 'network' organisation (Hechscher and Donnellon 1994). The latter predicted that the endemic failings of professional bureaucracy were to be overcome by a complex conjuncture of technological, structural and cultural changes that would inevitably entail the demise of hierarchical authority, functional specialisation and rule-based control. In their place, the theorists of the 'network' or 'virtual' organisation (Castells 1996; Van Dijk 1999) anticipate a future in which management will be forced to re-organise their conventional strategic forms and operational practices in a highly radical and often dislocating manner.

This process of radical reform, advocates of 'new managerialsm' insist, will be necessarily framed within a new logic of competition in which entrepreneurial dynamism and collaborative innovation emerge as the dominant features (Best 1990). These new realities can only become institutionalised in the form of the 'entrepreneurial firm' once the structural and cultural restraints embedded in Fordist/Taylorist bureaucracy have been swept away by the global competitive pressures and cultural demands generated by the inexorable movement towards the 'new economy'. Thus, a putative 'paradigm shift' in the international economy, corporate structures and organisational cultures (Korten 1995; Clarke and Clegg 1998; Clegg, Ibarra-Colado and Bueno-Rodriquez 1999) provides the wider context in which the reforms associated with 'new managerialism' can be located. Professional bureaucracy cannot be saved; its irreparably damaged by its inherent limitation and its inability to move with the times. 'New managerialism' is its nemesis. It's also the genesis of a new moral and organisational order in which traditional conceptions of professional specialisation and demarcation are superseded by new corporate cultures and structures. Within the latter, a revitalised corporate paternalism and collectivism promotes unitary notions of 'family' and 'team' rather than the fragmentary and often conflictual identities associated with occupationally and functionally-based professionalism (Casey 1995).

As previous discussion has indicated, 'new managerialism' aspires to define and integrate a meta-narrative of strategic change, a programme of organisational reform and a political technology of workplace control. Insofar as it succeeds in this quest, then it can be seen to provide the foundations for the development of core strategies and structures associated with 'centralised decentralisation' or 'regulated autonomy' (Hoggett 1991, 1996) and the new form of innovating organisation that it sustains (Pettigrew and Fenton 2000). However, a great deal of the recent research on the *implementation* of the change strategy, programme of organisational restructuring and control technology redesign associated with 'new managerialism' suggests that, to date, practical outcomes are rather more ambiguous and contradictory than its *emergent theory of change* anticipated or indeed promised (Reed and Deem, forthcoming). As such, the research literature on implementation indicates that the emerging leitmotiv is *'hybridisation'* – of institutional structures, organisational forms, control technologies and occupational cultures and work identities and relations (Ferlie et al., 1996; Kean and Scase 1998; Exworthy and Halford 1999; Brock, Powell and Hinings 1999; Pollitt and Bouckaert 2000). It is the combination and recombination of 'the old' and 'the new' within what we might call 'soft bureaucracy' that seems to define the contemporary trajectory of institutional and organisational restructuring within the public sector (Reed 1999; Flynn 1999, 2000; Courpasson 2000). In part, this might be interpreted as the, necessarily, piecemeal and long-term nature of public sector change. In might also be viewed as the outcome of an inevitable confrontation between the ideology of 'new managerialism' and the reality of its operational translation into organisational and professional practice. This confrontation unavoidably produces all sorts of endemic contradictions and tensions – between intensified market competition and institutional stability, between more detailed and intrusive managerial control and effective professional practice, etc., – that have to be coped with in some way or another on a localised, everyday basis. While public sector institutions and organisations have always been hybridised combinations of 'markets', 'bureaucracies' and 'networks', the dissemination and implementation of the package of reforms associated with 'new managerialism' has drastically exacerbated the endemic contradictions and tensions that they contained. This has generated an organisational response in which new managerial cultures and control technologies have been selectively 'grafted on', in an adaptive and piecemeal fashion, to pre-existing structures and cultures of bureaucratic and professional power. As a result, the latter are being incrementally diluted, dispersed and displaced by the ideological, institutional and organisational reforms that 'new managerialism' has initiated.

Yet, the longer-term impact of this process of 'dilution, dispersal and displacement' on occupational identities, organisational cultures and work behaviour should not be underestimated. Public sector professionals and managers are finding themselves increasingly caught within a revitalised and refurbished matrix of controls that are significantly changing the institutional fields and organisational settings in which they function. This is also changing the ways in which they see themselves, as they are viewed through the ideological, organisational and political prisms through which occupational identities and work behaviour are inevitably refracted. Many of these changes are still subject to complex negotiation and mediation (Kitchener 2000; Kitchener, Kirpatrick and Whipp 2000). But the cumulative weight of evidence indicates that a substantial restructuring of power and control is underway in which established professional groups are struggling to maintain their positions (Brooks 1999).

By deftly combining decentralised functional responsibilities with the recentralisation of strategic control, and overlaying both with a quasi-entrepreneurial culture, 'soft bureaucracy' is a peculiar hybrid of governmental rationalities and organisational practices. It will ensure that 'new managerialism' leaves a distinctive and durable imprint on the public sector for many years to come. As Webb (1999: 757) has recently argued, 'new managerialism' has let loose a series of interconnected strategies and practices for restructuring public services focussed on work intensification, service commodification and 'remote control' or 'control at a distance'. In theory, this puts the state, if not its subordinate agencies, in an ideal position of selectively choosing when, where and how it might intervene in relation to a particular policy field or issue, while absolving itself of any responsibility should things go wrong. However, this is also likely to lead to "the emergence of schisms within the public service class between 'old-style' professionals who use the language of welfare and care and 'new style' senior managers and professionals who use the language of markets and efficiency" (Webb 1999: 757). In these terms, Webb is developing a more specific articulation of Sennett's (1998: 59) overarching evaluation that in "the revolt against routine, the appearance of a new freedom is deceptive. Time in institutions and for individuals has been unchained from the iron cage of the past, but subjected to new, top-down controls and surveillance. The time of flexibility is the time of a new power. Flexibility begets disorder but not freedom from restraint".

3. NEW MANAGERIALISM AND MANAGER-ACADEMICS IN UK UNIVERSITIES

Within a UK university context, the potential impact of new managerialist philosophies and practices on HE might be characterised in relation to four major changes from the position that prevailed for much of the 1945 to early 1980's period:

(1) the, relatively aggressive, assertion of managerial prerogative as a necessary precondition for the implementation of market/private-sector discipline as a generalised solution to the resource problems of HE and a new regulative mode within which all types and grades of staff, but particularly academic staff, have to operate;

(2) the direct and indirect regulation of the professional academic labour process and practice through the design, implementation and monitoring of various control mechanisms geared to the detailed and relatively intrusive auditing and continuing evaluation of professional academic work in relation to various, externally-determined, performance measures;

(3) the redefinition and legitimating of higher education as a commodity providing service in which educational needs and priorities are reduced to codifiable and measurable performance outcomes and indicators that become

institutionalised benchmarks against which individual institutional operations and outcomes can be assessed and continually re-assessed;

(4) the re-engineering and re-organisation of the institutional forms, disciplinary matrices and occupational cultures on which UK higher education has conventionally been founded to ensure, as far as is possible, that they will be revitalised to release and redirect the innate creative, innovative and entrepreneurial talents and capacities of academic staff from the stultifying and suffocating embrace of corporate bureaucracy and academic collegiality.

Broadly speaking, our research project set out to describe and assess the impact of this, loosely-coupled, package of strategic discursive change and the associated redesign of supporting institutional structures, organisational mechanisms and implementation technologies on the thinking and practices of manager academics and academic staff. If manager-academics were to be the 'shock-troops' of the 'managerial revolution' in higher education that new managerialism demanded, were they anywhere near ready, able and willing to fulfil their historic destiny of transforming HE from a moribund, inward-looking and provider-dominated service into a dynamo of technological and economic transformation? What kind of stories would our manager-academics tell us about the past achievements, current predicaments and dilemmas, and future prospects of their disciplines, profession and institutions? What would this tell us about the putative shift from professional bureaucracy or 'bureau professionalism' (Clarke and Newman 1997) to 'entrepreneurial governance' (Osborne and Gaebler 1992) or 'the neo-entrepreneurial workplace' (Leicht and Fennell 2001) heralded by new managerialism and its supporting cast of organisational reformers and reforms? How would these changes be seen and interpreted by our informants as they struggled, as manager-academics operating in a diverse range of institutional contexts, organisational locales and disciplinary communities, to cope with the tensions, conflicts and contradictions that new managerialist ideology and practice inevitably generated?

What was supposed to be 'new' about new managerialism is that it seemed to signal and represent a radical break with older managerialist ideologies and control strategies that had been primarily focused on the restructuring of organisational forms and practices through bureaucratic rationalisation. Thus, the 'corporatist managerialism' of the 1960's and 1970's was largely geared, in cultural and organisational terms, to the implementation of neo-Taylorist/Fordist control systems and managerial structures in which cost-reductions, work rationalisation and operational integration were the dominant themes. In general terms, these reforms did not threaten professional or producer power and autonomy in any direct way, but they did indicate a shift towards much tighter regulative regimes in which the financial, political and organisational constraints within which professional academic practice was embedded became more transparent, limiting and pressing. The new managerialism of the 1980's and 1990's, however, did, potentially at least, entail a much more direct ideological and political attack on institutional and professional autonomy that could not be smoothed over by emollient political rhetoric or ritual genuflection in the direction of academic collegiality. Dominant political elites seemed to be turning away from the rather 'cosy' collaborative networks of the UGC and quinquennial reviews towards a much harsher and competitive regime of direct centralised management and control (Halsey 1992; Trow 1974). The latter rejected the informal, tacit agreements and understandings on which a negotiated balance of power and influence between state agencies, institutional actors and professional/provider interest groups had historically and politically depended. It also entailed the legitimation and implementation of much more intrusive and intensive modes of governance and regulation in which market mechanisms, performance measurement and consumer-led, rather than producer-led, strategies of organisational restructuring were to become the dominant themes. Thus, the dead-hand of bureaucratic regulation and producer-dominated service monopolies, in which professional 'restrictive practices' were assumed to be rife, were to be swept away by the invigorating ideological force of neo-liberalism and the micro-level control technologies through which the latter was to be implemented (Barry, Osborne and Rose 1996).

How would our manager-academics manage to cope in this 'brave new world' of new managerialism? How would they see the radically-changed contemporary sectoral conditions, institutional contexts and organisational worlds in which they were located and how would they respond to the challenges that the changes associated with new managerialist ideology and technology presented? Did the notion of the 'entrepreneurial university' (Clark 1998) mean anything to them as they struggled to come to terms with the much more competitive, differentiated and fragmented HE environment that the former reflected and reinforced (Trolwer 1998)?

As one might have expected, our research findings suggest that the implementation of the reforms associated with new managerialism have been rather more ambiguous, contested and contradictory than the latter's advocates or theorists anticipated. Nevertheless, they also indicate that some very significant changes may have occurred 'on the organisational ground' within British universities and in relation to the wider institutional and ideological contexts within which the academic labour process and the professional 'jurisdictional domains' (Abbott 1988) that it generates and supports are embedded.

Overall, our research data indicated a generalised perception of increasing managerial *and bureaucratic* control with declining levels of trust in and discretion afforded to professional academic mores and practices. While this generalised perception of 'advancing managerialism' was expressed more strongly by non-managerial academic staff, even amongst our manager-academics there was a very clear view that new managerialism – as a 'theory of practice' – had deeply and extensively permeated UK universities' organisational cultures and practices over the last decade or so. The picture revealed by our research data is, in many respects, quite complex and often contradictory. The narrative accounts of change articulated through our focus group interviews, institutional-based interviews and more intensive organisational case studies articulate a recurring theme of the combination and recombination of traditional forms of university management with newer elements (e.g. performance measurement technologies) in which new managerialist theory and practice is more evident. Certain crucial components of traditional self-governmentality and management, such as academic peer review in selection and promotion procedures, were seen as retaining a significant and continuing role in university management and the organisation of the academic labour process. But these were seen to be increasingly overlain and undermined by new managerial control structures and practices – such as target-setting, performance monitoring, direct supervision, work rationalisation and employment casualisation – that, cumulatively, were substantially eroding what was left of academic self-government and management.

One widely-held perception that emerged in both focus group sessions and individual interviews was that the continuous pressures for greatly enhanced visibility, transparency and accountability in the use of scarce and vital resources within the academic labour process had led to a much greater emphasis on academic and institutional team-working. However, this was interpreted – both by manager academics and non-managerial academic staff/students – as very much a 'double-edged sword'. Positive elements of improved collaboration, support and understanding were seen to be combined with negative features of self-imposed discipline, closure and control that ran directly counter to more traditional forms of academic collegiality – no matter how attenuated these may have become in practice. Indeed, these new and more encompassing forms of academic team-working were often seen to be dominated by competitive, defensive and/or exclusionary political interests and tactics typical of an organisational regime and technology of 'concertive control' (Barker 1993, 1999; Reed 1999). Within the latter, academics collaborate to develop the collective means of their own *self-discipline, surveillance and control* rather than having the latter externally imposed upon them. As one of our focus group respondents (a head of department) argued:

> managerialism is very much control without the admission by the centre that it's actually doing any controlling, with the protestations of democracy, grass roots, and the need to exercise flexibility. But you make one flexible decision that lies outside the set of guidelines that have already been set, then you are called up to the Dean and asked to explain it....What I worry about with new managerialism is a lack of critical debate, of critical scrutiny of the very policies and practices of management...there are deep problems there, deep problems in terms of democratic accountability and actually being able to speak...I can't really speak like this in my own institution because one is fingered.

Thus, the shift from a traditional academic ideology and organisation, consisting of cultural and structural elements of both collegiality and hierarchy that often sit rather uneasily with each other, to one supposedly based on a more egalitarian, meritocratic and technocratic value-system/organisational structure may not be as straightforward as many suppose. Indeed, our research data suggests that both manager and non-manager academics across the universities included in our study collectively perceive the institutional reforms and organisational changes pushing towards a more 'transparent' academic labour process as potentially threatening to their established professional identity, status and authority. The ideology and technology of 'transparency' is conventionally legitimated in terms of enhanced openness, participation, accountability and trust. But our informants' interpretations of these developments resonate much more strongly with a complex mixture of resigned fatalistic acceptance of the inevitability of 'creeping managerialism' and a much more positive perception of improved institutional governance and organisational management. However, this is often paralleled by a relatively hostile resistance to the radical encroachment on professional autonomy and power that internalised norms of work performance and technologies of evaluation, consequent upon the shift towards more 'transparent' forms of self-management and governance, necessarily entail. As one head of department articulated this paradox:

> I think this whole more intrusive culture means that people aren't left to just get on with it in the way that they were…certainly in the past there wasn't enough accountability. But I now feel that we have now perhaps swung too far in the other direction…perhaps there is too much monitoring and too much written reporting and so that is a bit of a dilemma, being asked to implement that on the one hand whilst having misgivings about it.

Our manager-academics, by-in-large, are very 'reluctant managers' who seem rather unwilling to fulfil the historical destiny that the ideology and practice of new managerialism has scripted for them. Rather than constituting the 'storm troopers' of a managerial revolution that will sweep away outmoded and inefficient organisational practices and recalcitrant professional producer-monopolies, they find themselves in the somewhat unenviable position of trying to hold together fundamentally incompatible imperatives of an 'ancient regime' that is badly damaged but will not die and a modernising ideology that is still only half-formed.

Thus, the dominant theme in the implementation of new managerialist discourse and strategy within UK universities, as of the UK public sector as a whole, is one of 'hybridisation' – of institutional structures, organisational forms, occupational cultures and control technologies. But the, often indiscriminate, mixing and matching of seemingly contradictory principles and practices of institutional governance, organisational management and professional forms – in which selected core elements of the 'market', 'organisation' and 'profession' have somehow to be linked together in a viable modus vivendi – within HE has been significantly different from, say, the NHS (Ferlie et al., 1996), local government (Kean and Scase 1998) and social services (Jones 1999). Unlike within the NHS, where early reforms introduced radical cultural and structural surgery alongside a new cadre of general managers from outside the health service (Reed and Anthony 1993), new managerialism within the university sector has developed within existing institutional structures and without significant 'managerial entryism' from sectors outside HE. Again, unlike other sectors, the control strategies and mechanisms deployed by HE manager-academics to try to secure required levels of individual and organisational performance, seem, in relative terms at least, rather muted and less crudely coercive than elsewhere within the public sector system as a whole. But the longer-term impact and significance of these, more incremental, subtle and supposedly continuity-facilitating reforms should not be underestimated. The inherent contradictions, tensions and stresses remain; in many respects they seem to be intensifying. As usual, much depends on where you stand within a public sector system in a permanent state of flux and uncertainty where today's 'change masters' are tomorrow's 'change-casualties or victims'.

4. NEW MANAGERIALISM AND MANAGING ACADEMICS IN UK UNIVERSITIES

As previous discussion has already indicated, our manager-academics relied on a broad range of techniques and mechanisms to try and 'manage', at all institutional levels, within an increasingly complex and unstable HE environment. This included enhanced reliance on methods of self-regulation of research and teaching quality (in relation to more explicit, internally and externally generated, financial and performance criteria), more intrusive work performance and allocation systems that require staff to self-assess individual action and outputs across a range of measures, and more formalised peer-review scrutiny of individual and collective performance. The generalised perception of increasingly finance-driven, or at least finance-led, institutional decision-making and managerial control was widespread throughout all types of research data generated by our project. A 'long hours' or 'presentist' work culture was also identified by a large number of our informants, so that a 50 to 60 hour working week was seen to be fast becoming 'the norm' amongst manager and non-manager academics alike. Academic autonomy was still seen as a significant feature and attraction of professional work culture and patterns within UK universities. But it was also perceived to be under increasing and direct pressure, indeed threat, from both externally-imposed and self-imposed systems of surveillance and discipline that incrementally erode the jurisdictional 'task domains' on which academic professionalism was operationally based and culturally legitimated. The implementation and legitimation of the organisational practices associated with new managerialism within UK universities was seen (especially in pre-1992 universities) to require a considerable degree of compromise with and retention of some long established cultural and structural elements. But, as Deem (1998:8,italics added) has argued, "the extent to which *visible performativity* is now significant in the management of academic labour in universities" should not be underestimated.

Consequently, our research project reinforces the findings of other studies (Parker and Jary 1994; Rustin 1994; Willmott 1995; Prichard and Willmott 1997; Edwards 1998) that identify a trajectory of intensified manageralist focus on visibility, transparency and measurability within the academic labour process. These have become the structural and operational prerequisites for the achievement of continuous internal and external monitoring of and accountability for professional academic performance and the resources it consumes. In Smith and Webster's (1997: 100, italics added) terms,

> these and other changes have placed enormous pressures on the university system. They have certainly resulted in a noticeable shift in the 'feel' of university life. For many academics *this has been experienced as an appreciable loss of control* over what they do, initiatives coming from the central management teams that drive the organisation and from politicians from without the university. A result is that *institutions are experienced more as places of 'work'* than the community of scholars that motivated many academics to chose their vocation.

If the concept of the 'postmodern university' (Scott 1997) has any empirical validity, then its operationalisation seems to rely on highly modernist organisational control strategies and practices. These unavoidably increase organisational uncertainty and job insecurity for the majority of academic staff by exposing them much more to the vagaries of external market pressures – however much these may be mediated and moderated in practice – and direct managerial regulation of professional task performance. Yet, at the same time, the effective realisation of the latter is fraught, for manger-academics and non-academics alike, with all sorts of complexities and contradictions. This requires an in-built institutional capacity to cope with relatively high levels of paradox and ambiguity that are likely to stretch material and cultural resources close to breaking point (Dearlove 1998a, 1998b; Cowen 1996). This is particularly the case when we take into account that a form of 'double surveillance' (Edwards 1998) is evident within HE. Both internal and external regulatory/accountability mechanisms have to be simultaneously placated, in some way or another, before the operation and outcomes of the academic labour process can hope to achieve any kind of, often grudging, recognition from powerful managerial/political hierarchies within and without the academy. However, they often push and pull in opposing directions; external pressures towards a much stronger sense and practice of corporate integration, while intensified internal surveillance and control generates enhanced intra-organisational competition and fragmentation. As Henkel (1998: 179) has suggested, this may be interpreted as the organisational articulation of "a deep contradiction at the heart of new public management between the drive towards powerful vertical and bounded systems of accountability and that towards the more diffuse, horizontal influences of multiple markets".

5. CONTESTED ACADEMIC FUTURES

The analysis offered above raises some pertinent, and potentially vital, questions about the longer-term position and influence of the academic profession within UK higher education at a time when the latter is still undergoing some profound changes in its institutional form and intellectual rationale.

Much of the previous discussion and analysis suggests that a radical transformation is occurring in the HE environment in which UK manager-academics and academics are located. A series of cumulatively intersecting environmental shifts have occurred that push in the direction of massification, rationalisation, commodification and managerialisation. As already indicated, these macro-level shifts or trends inevitably become diluted or attenuated at the micro-level of individual institutions and their complex internal operational dynamics. Yet, they have major strategic or 'generative' implications for changes to the governance, organisation, management and delivery of higher education in the UK and beyond (Slaughter and Leslie 1997; Jary and Parker 1998; Trowler 1998; Calas and Smircich 2001). In particular they raise fundamental questions about the characteristic occupational culture, identity and form of the academic profession as it struggles to come to terms with the 'brave new world' of globalisation, flexibilisation, intensification and casualisation. No longer seen as the disinterested guardians of esoteric disciplinary knowledge guaranteeing expert status as recognised 'professionals' but as 'knowledge producers or workers' routinely engaged in generating and communicating socially relevant and economically useful skills or techniques, academics seem adrift on a 'sea of utilitarian pragmatism'. For many researchers/commentators, "they [academics] will have to adjust from being adept *producers* of (mainly disciplinary knowledge) to being creative *reconfigurers* of knowledge in solving increasingly complex problems" (Muller and Subotzky 2001: 168 – 169). This does not, necessarily, imply an inexorable process of academic deskilling or deprofessionalisation or, even worse, proletarianisation (Reed 2000). But it does indicate that a continuing commitment to core disciplinary values and identity may be overlain by a set of structural and cultural changes, encapsulated in the theory and practice of new managerialism, that further fragments and polarises the academic profession (Fulton 2001).

This scenario is consistent with Freidson's (1994: 2001) recent work and prognostications on the contemporary condition of and future prospects for professionalism in general and academic professionalism in particular. Freidson argues that professionalism is the 'third logic' of occupational and work organisation that parallels the market and bureaucracy as the dominant ideal types of institutional regulation and management in modern industrial society. It is based on a set of axiomatic assumptions and principles that differentiate it from the other two ideal types. This is so to the extent that it depends on an organisational mode of delivering and controlling specialised work performance based on accredited and legitimated expertise – that is, formalised expert knowledge – which is accorded the privileged status of monopoly supplier and evaluator of the services that it provides. This right of expert autonomy and discretion "implies being trusted, being committed, even being morally involved in one's work" (Freidson 2001: 34).

Freidson argues that this institutionalised right to monopoly supply, accreditation and evaluation of expert services and the specialised knowledge/skill base on which it rests has been, and will continue to be, under attack from various directions (Reed 2000). One of the, if not the, most important of these threats is that posed by managerialism. This is the case insofar as it entails an incremental, but pervasive, assault on the technical effectiveness and ethical legitimacy of a mode of occupational organisation and control that has outlived its social relevance and usefulness in a modern, globalised economy. Managerialism poses a serious threat to professionalism in that it maintains that not only have contemporary, and foreseeable, socio-economic trends made monopoly organisation and control of expert services redundant but also that the ethically retrograde implications of the latter are now so strong as to make it morally obsolete. Economic efficiency and moral rectitude come together in a managerialist critique of the 'professional state' that berates its inherent wastefulness and corruption.

This critique is reinforced by material developments at the workplace level where ongoing technological, organisational and cultural change generates a 'neo-entrepreneurial' organisation of professional and managerial work in which the latter literally 'change places' with the former (Leicht and Fennell 2001). This thesis suggests that managers and professionals are changing structural and ideological places in an increasingly unified elite division of expert labour that virtually excludes the middle and lower tiers of managerial/professional workers from effective participation in strategic corporate decision-making. A melding of elite managerial and professional work worlds produces a situation in which "elite managers are becoming the 'new professionals', while professionals are being captured by organisational stakeholders that consume and pay for professional services" (Leicht and Fennell 2001: 2). The typical professional is reduced to the status of a subcontractor at the mercy of elite groups of financial and managerial stakeholders that are driven by short-term pressures and demands inimical to the archetypal professional focus on long-term service objectives and priorities uncontaminated by considerations of costs and profitability. Freidson's (2001: 210 – 212) prognosis for the future of academic professionalism is worth quoting at some length in this context:

> Employing organisations are likely to intensify efforts to standardise the work of rank-and-file professionals in order to reduce their cost and better control and supervise them. Standardisation of work in universities, for example, can occur by mandating standard syllabi and examinations for courses taught by part-time instructors, or in health care organisations by establishing standard protocols for primary care examination, treatment and referral...I have no doubt that the faculty will remain composed primarily of credentialled professionals, but the curricula they create and administer will have to respond more than previously to the demand for practical training, equipping students to perform the particular tasks required by employers after matriculation....Some of the humanistic disciplines which have no clear vocational value may not survive at all, and those that do will be pressed by students to be entertaining. Neither "pure" nor "disinterested" research and scholarship which follows out the logic of abstract questions raised by theory nor idle curiosity will be forbidden in principle, but in the scientific disciplines their prominence is likely to be discouraged by shrinking support and respect...The educational climate created by strong emphasis on practical service to profitable private investment or the state or on relevance to mass popular culture will probably make universities and professional schools less hospitable to faculty members who devote themselves to clarifying and extending the traditional intellectual problems of their disciplines, and to debating moral and intellectual goals... [academic] professionals will indeed become merely technical experts in the service of the political and cultural economy.

Freidson's bleak prognosis clearly suggests that academic professionalism is almost certain to be considerably weakened in its occupational legitimacy, organisational power and cognitive coherence by the combined effects of the interacting set of changes outlined in this chapter and encapsulated in the theory and practice of new managerialism. Our research data indicates that the current trend towards further standardisation, regulation and control of academic work, from a variety of external and internal sources, is unlikely to moderate. It also implies that a further dilution and weakening of academic professionalism consequent upon fragmentation, rationalisation and casualisation is a distinct possibility. However, as earlier sections of this paper have argued, the overall trajectory of change and its longer-term consequences are not easy to predict. Hybridisation of organisational forms and occupational cultures within UK universities is likely to have all sorts of unforeseen and unintended consequences that are likely to generate more complex and diverse outcomes than those envisaged in a mono-causal or linear 'de-professionalisation' thesis. More specifically, our research suggests that the package of organisational reforms engendered by new managerialism does present a very substantial threat to the concept and practice of an integrated academic profession unified around core occupational values and routines that continue to reflect and reinforce a culture of 'academic collegiality'. In addition, it also signals the reality of manager academics being increasingly drawn further into pro-active performance management, and hence control, of academic staff through a variety of organisational mechanisms. But most of our informants, including the majority of manager academics, also continued to exhibit strong personal commitment to traditional academic values and saw themselves as trying to defend, if not expand, the practical significance and impact of those values within their institutions and beyond to the wider HE system. This also led them into situations where new monitoring and control mechanisms were 'adapted' to purposes for which they were not originally intended. They were 'turned' to defend and expand localised domains of academic autonomy and discretion by appropriating new performance measurement and management systems in such a way that centralised organisational surveillance and control become more, rather than less, problematic. Nevertheless, this type of behaviour could also have the perverse effect of reinforcing the powerful competitive drive and fragmenting dynamic set in motion by the ideological and operational momentum inherent in new managerialist philosophies and practices.

6. CONCLUSION

The quotation which heads this paper maintains that the core of governing is a highly sophisticated form of political cum impression management that closes the gap, if not chasm, between public expectations and actual outcomes. The argument developed within the paper suggests that new managerialism within UK universities is a discourse of strategic change and a cluster of related organisational reforms that attempt to *redefine the reality* of higher education for all of those who participate in its design, delivery and consumption. New managerialism strives to close the inevitable 'reality gap' between expectations and delivery by denying its existence or relevance. However, the grounded experience of the changes associated with new managerialism, for its creators, agents and consumers, has been much more ambiguous, not to say tendentious, for all concerned. In the very act of its organisational consummation, new managerialism seems to create even bigger gaps or fissures within the institutional order and moral foundations of higher education that then have to be bridged or repaired in some way or another.

Of course, one needs to retain a proper historical perspective in any assessment of new managerialism's longer-term impact on UK universities in general and academic professionalism and management in particular. It can be persuasively argued that the orthodox model of academic professionalism and university governance/administration began to unravel from the late 1960's onwards. The political compromises and organisational trade-offs between corporate bureaucracy and professional power that had dominated university governance up until this time began to look increasingly tarnished and unattractive as values and movements associated with democratic participation and managerial effectiveness gathered momentum. In turn, these developments began to erode the cultural and moral foundations of an elitist system of higher education. The latter had clothed itself in the ideological garb of collegiality, community and exclusivity but was relatively powerless in the face of a radicalising, egalitarian critique that anticipated the meritocracy and technocracy of the 1980's and 1990's. Thus, the virulent hybridising dynamic of the 1980's and 1990's can be seen to have its political and organisational roots in a cultural critique of university elitism and hierarchy that became increasingly influential in the 1960's. In this respect, the new managerialism of the 1990's may be seen as an ideological and organisational offspring of a much earlier phase of critical scrutiny and evaluation that simply could not anticipate the triumph of a managerialist discourse and practice thirty years later.

However, this leaves 'our' contemporary middle-level manager-academics in a key position and role as mediators of the unavoidable tensions and conflicts that hybridisation has unleashed. It is they who have to find ways of coping with the uncertainties and instabilities generated by the deep contradictions discovered in the heart of new managerialism (Henkel 1998). If the core contradiction between vertical command and control and horizontal autonomy and self-regulation defines the ideological and structural essence of new managerialism, then it is the manager-academics who have to deal with the, incredibly messy, political 'fallout' that the former releases. They have to find the words, actions and relationships that mediate between the imposition of more intrusive, detailed, even 'alien', managerial controls and the continued demand, indeed practical need, for localised professional academic discretion and diversity. Of course, this mediating process and practice is necessarily partial, incomplete and contested. Universities are always "a mix of organising practices, which are historically resilient to being wholeheartedly overthrown by the 'new managers'" (Prichard and Willmott 1997: 289). The sedimentation and layering of new discourses, practices and structures in universities, as in other organisations, is a highly complex process characterised by overlapping circuits of regulation and control that incrementally change dominant forms and patterns. Elements of conflict, discontinuity, displacement and replacement co-exist with elements of collaboration, continuity and stability (Taylor 1999). Nevertheless, the general structural features and political effects of new managerialism are, by now, somewhat clearer. This is so to the extent that the latter has generated a series of 'power re-distributions and re-allocations' between constituent 'power blocks' and interest groups which has left professional academics in a much weaker position relative to manager-academics and administrators.

Yet, 'our' manager-academics remain in a position and place where the tensions and conflict released, or at least exacerbated, by new managerialism remain as real and, seemingly, intractable as ever. As one of them – a head of department – remarked in an interview,

> you have to trust your colleagues to deliver what they are supposed to deliver. There is a considerable amount of autonomy, however much managerialism you try to inject into the system. Part of the managerial role involves a considerable amount of trust in managing academic staff. You can't actually make them do it.

But the extent to which the control ideology and practice that defines new managerialism as a strategic discourse and programme for transforming university life can facilitate, *indeed permit,* the necessary levels of trust-based autonomy for 'delivering the goods' may be the underlying conundrum that our manager-academics remain fated to confront?

NOTES

[1] Quoted in Rawnsley, A. *Servants of the People*, Revised Edition, Penguin 2001.

REFERENCES

Abbott, A. *The System of Professions: An essay on the Expert Division of Labour*. Chicago: University of Chicago Press, 1998.

Ackroyd, S., J. Hughes and K. Soothill. "Public Sector Services and their Management." *Journal of Management Studies* 26.6 (1989): 603 – 619.

Anthony, P. *The Foundation of Management*. London: Tavistock, 1986.

Barker, J.R. "Tightening the Bureaucratic Cage: Concertive Control in Self-Managing Teams." *Administrative Science Quarterly* 38 (1993): 408 – 437.

Barker, J. R. *The Discipline of Teamwork: Participation and Concertive Control*. California: Sage, 1999.

Barry, A., T. Osborne and N. Rose. *Foucault and Political Reason*. London: UCL Press, 1996.

Barry, D. and M. Elmes. "Strategy Retold: A Narrative View of Strategic Discourse." *Academy of Management Review* 22.2 (1997): 429 – 52.

Best, M. H. *The New Competition: Institutions of Industrial Restructuring*. Oxford: Polity, 1990.

Brock, D., M. Powell and C.R. Hinings (eds). *Restructuring the Professional Organisation*. London: Routledge, 1999.

Brooks, I. "Managerialist Professionalism: the Destruction of a Non-Conforming Subculture." *British Journal of Management* 10.1 (1999): 41 – 52.

Calas, M. and L. Smircich (eds). "Special Issue on re-Organising Knowledge, Transforming Institutions: Knowing, Knowledge, and the University in the 21st Century." *Organization* 8.2 (2001): 147 – 454.

Casey, C. *Work, Self and Society: After Industrialism*. London: Routledge, 1995.

Castells, M. *The Rise of the Network Society*. Oxford: Blackwell, 1996.

Child, J. *British Management Thought*. London: Allen and Unwin, 1969.

Clark, B. R. *Creating Entrepreneurial Universities: Organisational Pathways to Transformation*. Oxford: IAU/Pergammon, 1998.

Clarke, J. and J. Newman. *The Managerial State*. London: Sage, 1997.

Clarke T. and S. Clegg. *Changing Paradigms: The Transformation of Management Knowledge for the 21st Century*. London: Harper Collins, 1998.

Clegg, S., E. Ibarra-Colado and L. Bueno-Rodriquez. *Global Management: Universal Theories and Local Realities*. London: Sage, 1999.

Courpasson, D. "Managerial Strategies of Domination: Power in Soft Bureaucracies." *Organisation Studies* 21.1 (2000): 141 – 62.

Cowen, R. "Performativity, Post-Modernity and the University." *Comparative Education* 32 (1996): 245 – 258.

Dearlove, J. "The Academic Labour Process: From Collegiality and Professionalism to Managerialism and Proletarianisation?" *Higher Education Review* 30.1 (1997): 56 – 75.

Dearlove, J. "The Deadly Dull Issue of University Administration: Good Governance, Managerialism and Organising Academic Work." *Higher Education Policy* 11 (1998a): 59 – 79.

Dearlove, J. "Fundamental Changes in Institutional Governance Structures: The United Kingdom." *Higher Education Policy* 11 (1998b): 110 – 120.

Deem, R. "New Managerialism in Higher Education: The Management of Performances and Cultures in Universities." *International Studies in the Sociology of Education* 8.1 (1998): 56 – 75.

Dent, M., M. O'Neil and C. Bagley. *Professions, New Public Management and the European Welfare State*. Staffordshire: Staffordshire University Press, 1989.

DuGay, P. "Colossal Immodesties and Hopeful Monsters: Pluralism and Occupational Conduct." *Organization* 1.1 (1994): 125 – 48.

DuGay, P. *Consumption and Identity at Work*. London: Sage, 1996.

DuGay, P. *In Praise of Bureaucracy*. London: Sage, 2000.

DuGay, P. and G. Salaman "The Cult(ure) of the Customer." *Journal of Management Studies* 29.4 (1992): 616 – 633.

Edwards, M. "Commodification and Control in Mass Higher Education: A Double-Edged Sword." In Jary, D. and M. Parker (eds). *The New Higher Education: Issues and Directions for the Post-Dearing University.* Stafford: Staffordshire University Press, 1998, 253 – 73.

Enteman, W. *Managerialism: The Emergence of a New Ideology* Wisconsin: University of Wisconsin Press, 1993.

Exworthy, M. and S. Halford (eds). *Professionals and the New Managerialism in the Public Sector.* Buckingham: Open University Press, 1999.

Farnham, D. and S. Horton (eds). *Managing the New Public Services.* London: Macmillan, 1993.

Ferlie, E., L. Ashburner, L. Fitzgeral and A. Pettigrew. *The New Public Management in Action.* London: Sage, 1996.

Flynn, R. (1972), *Structures of Control in Health Management.* London: Routledge

Flynn, R. (1999), "Managerialism, Professionalism and Quasi-Markets." In Exworthy, M. and S. Halford (eds). *Professionals and the New Managerialism in the Public Sector.* Buckingham: Open University Press, 1999, 18-36.

Flynn R. "Soft Bureaucracy, Govenmentality and Clinical Governance: Theoretical Approaches to Emergent Policy." Unpublished Paper, ESRC Seminar Series on Governing Medicine, November, 2000

Fox, A. *Beyond Contract: Work, Power and Trust Relations.* London: Faber & Faber, 1974.

Frank, T. *One Market Under God: Extreme Capitalism, Market Populism and the End of Economic Democracy.* New York: Secker and Warburg, 2000.

Freidson, E. *Professionalism Reborn: Theory, Prophecy and Policy.* Cambridge: Polity Press, 1994.

Freidson, E. *Professionalism: The Third Logic.* Cambridge: Polity Press, 2001.

Fulton, O. "Managerialism and the Academic Profession." Unpublished Paper, 2001.

Gane, M. and T. Johnson (eds). *Foucault's New Domains.* London: Rouledge, 1993.

Glover, I. and P. Tracey. "In search of Technik: Will Engineering Outgrow Management?." *Work, Employment and Society* 11.4 (1997):759 – 776

Halsey, A. H. *Decline of Donnish Dominion: The British Academic Professions in the Twentieth Century.* Oxford: Claredon Press, 1992.

Ham, C. *Health Policy in Britain.* 4th edition, London: Macmillan, 1999.

Hammer, M. and J. Champey. *Re-engineering the Corporation: A Manifesto for a Business Revolution.* New York: Harper Collins, 1993.

Harrison, C. and C. Pollitt. *Controlling Health Professionals: The Future of Work and Organisation in the NHS.* Buckingham: Open University Press, 1994.

Heckscher, C., R. Eisenstat and T. Rice "Transformational Processes." In C. Heckscher and A. Donnellon (eds). *The Post-Bureaucratic Organisation: New Perspectives on Organisational Change.* California: Sage, 1994, 129 – 177.

Heckscher, C. and A. Donnellon (eds). *The Post-Bureaucratic Organisation.* California: Sage, 1994.

Henkel, M. (1998), "Higher Education." In M. Laffin (ed). *Beyond Bureaucracy: The Professionals in the Contemporary Public Sector.* Aldershot: Ashgate, 1998, 183 – 200.

Hoggett, P. "A New Management in the Public Sector?" *Policy and Politics* 19.4 (1991): 243 – 256

Hoggett, P. "New Modes of Control in the Public Service." *Public Administration* 74 (1996): 9 – 32.

Hood, C. "Contemporary Public Management: A New Global Paradigm?" *Public Policy and Administration* 10.2 (1995): 104 – 117.

Jary, D. and M. Parker (eds). *The New Higher Education: Issues and Directions for the Post-Dearing University.* Staffordshire: Staffordshire University Press, 1998.

Jenkins, A. "Teams: From Ideology to Analysis." *Organisation Studies* 15.4 (1994): 849 – 860.

Jones, C. "Social Work: Regulation and Managerialism." In Exworthy, M. and S. Halford (eds). *Professionals and the New Managerialism in the Public Sector.* Buckingham: Open University Press, 1999, 37 – 49

Keat, R. and N. Abercrombie (eds). *Enterprise Culture.* London: Routledge, 1991.

Kean, L. and R. Scase. *Local Government Management: The Rhetoric and Reality of Change.* Buckingham: Open University Press, 1998.

Keleman, M., P. Forrester and J. Hassard "BPR and TQM: Divergence or Convergence?" In Knights, D. and H. Willmott (eds). *The Re-Engineering Revolution.* London: Sage, 2000, 154 – 173.

Kirkpatrick, I. and M. Lucio. *The Politics of Quality in the Public Sector: The Management of Change.* London: Routledge, 1995.

Kitchener, M. "All Fur Coats and No Nickers: Contemporary Organisational Change in UK Hospitals." In Brock, D., M. Powell and C.R. Hinings (eds). *Restructuring the Professional Organisation.* London: Routledge, 1999, 183 – 199.

Kitchener, M. "The Bureaucratisation of Professional Roles: The Case of Clinical Directors in UK Hospitals." *Organization* 7.1 (2000): 129 – 154.

Kitchener, M., I. Kirpatrick and R. Whipp. "Supervising Professional Work under New Public Management: Evidence from an 'Invisible Trade'." *British Journal of Management* 11.3 (2000): 213 – 226.

Knights, D. and H. Willmott. *The Re-engineering Revolution: Critical Studies in Corporate Change.* London: Sage, 2000.

Korten, D. *When Corporations Rule the World.* London: Earthscan Publications, 1995.

Lane, C. and Bachmann, R. *Trust Within and Between Organisations.* Oxford: Oxford University Press, 1998.

Leicht, K. and M. Fennell. *Professional Work: A Sociological Approach.* London: Blackwell, 2001.

Locke, R. *Management and Higher Education since 1940.* Cambridge: Cambridge University Press, 1989.

Locke, R. *The Collapse of the American Management Mystique.* Oxford: Oxford University Press, 1996.

Maddock, S. and G. Morgan "Barriers to Transformation Beyond Bureaucracy and the Market Conditions for Collaboration in Health and Social care." *International Journal of Public Sector Management* 11.4 (1998): 234 – 251.

Mark, A and S. Dopson (eds). *Organisational Behaviour in Health Care: The Research Agenda.* London: Macmillan, 1999.

Mintzberg, H. *The Structuring of Organisations.* Englewood Cliffs, NJ: Prentice Hall, 1979.

Misztal, B. *Trust in Modern Societies.* Cambridge: Cambridge University Press, 1996.

Mitchell, D. *Governmentality: Power and Rule in Modern Society.* London: Sage, 1999.

Morgan, G. and L. Engwall (eds). *Regulation and Organisations: International Perspectives.* London: Routledge, 1999.

Osborne, D. and T. Gaebler. *Re-inventing Government: How the Entrepreneurial Spirit is Transforming the Government.* Reading MA: Addison-Wesley, 1992.

Ozga, J. "Deskilling a Profession: Professionalism, Deprofessionalism and the New Managerialism." In H. Busher and R. Saran (eds). *Managing Teachers as Professionals in Schools.* London: Kogan Page, 1995, 42 – 57.

Parker, M. and D. Jary "The McUniversity: Organisations, Management and Academic Subjectivity." *Organisation Studies* 2.2 (1995): 319 – 338.

Pettigrew, A., E. Ferlie and L. McKee. *Shaping Strategic Change: making Change in Large Organisations.* London: Sage, 1996.

Pettigrew, A. and E. Fenton (eds). *The Innovating Organisation.* London: Sage, 2000.

Pollitt, C. *Managerialism and the Public Services.* Second Edition. Oxford: Blackwell, 1993.

Pollitt, A. and G. Bouckaert. *Public Management Reform: A Comparative Analysis.* Oxford: Oxford University Press, 2000.

Power, M. *The Audit Society.* Oxford: Oxford University Press, 1997.

Prichard, C. and H. Willmott. "Just how Managed is the McUniversity?" *Organisation Studies* 18.2 (1997): 287 – 316.

Reed, M. "Managing Quality and Organisational Politics: TQM as a Governmental Technology." In Kirkpatrick, I. and M. Lucio (eds). *The Politics of Quality in the Public Sector: The Management of Change.* London: Routledge, 1995, 44 – 64.

Reed, M. "From the cage to the Gaze?: The Dynamics of Organisational Control in Late Modernity." In Morgan, G. and L. Engwall (eds). *Regulation and Organisations: International Perspectives.* London: Routledge, 1999, 17 – 49.

Reed, M. "Alternative Professional Futures", Unpublished Conference Paper, Europen Group for Organization Studies Conference, Helsinki, 2000.

Reed, M. and P. Anthony. "Between an Ideological Rock and an Organisational Hard Place: NHS Management in the 1980's and 1990's." In Clarke, T. and C. Pitelis (eds). *The Political Economy of Privatisation.* London: Routledge, 1993, 185 – 204.

Reed, M. and R. Deem. "New Managerialism: The Manager-Academic and Technologies of Management in Universities-Looking Forward to Virtuality?" In Robins, K. and F. Webster (eds). *The Virtual University: Information, Markets and Managements.* Oxford: Oxford University Press, forthcoming.

Rose, N. *Powers of Freedom: Reframing Political Thought.* Cambridge: Cambridge University Press, 1999.

Rustin, M. "Flexibility in Higher Education?" In Burrows, R. and B. Loader (eds). *Towards a Post-Fordist Welfare State?* London: Routledge, 1994, 177 – 203.

Sennett, R. *The Corrosion of Character: The Personal Consequences of Work in the New Capitalism.* London: Norton and Company, 1998.

Scott, P. "The Postmodern University?" In Smith, A. and F. Webster (eds). *The Postmodern University?: Contested Visions of Higher Education in Society.* Buckingham: Open University Press, 1999, 36 – 47.

Shore, C. and S. Roberts. "Higher Education and the Panopticon Paradigm: Quality Assurance as a Disciplinary Technology." *Higher Education Quarterly* 27.3 (1995): 8 – 17.

Shore, C. and S. Wright "Audit Culture and Anthropology: Neo-Liberalism in British Higher Education", Unpublished Conference Paper, 1998.

Sjostrand, S. *The Two Faces of Management: The Janus Factor.* London: Thompson Business Press, 1997.

Slaughter, S. and L. Leslie. *Academic Capitalism: Politics, Policies and the Entrepreneurial University.* Baltimore: John Hopkins Press, 1997.

Smith, P. "Outcome-Related Performance Indicators and Organisational Control in the Public Sector." *British Journal of Management* 4.3 (1993): 135 – 152.

Smith, A. and F. Webster (eds). *The Postmodern University?* Buckingham: Open University Press, 1997.

Taylor, P. *Making Sense of Academic Life: Academics, Universities and Change.* Buckingham: Open University Press, 1999.

Tilley, I. (ed). *Managing the Internal Market.* London: Paul Chapman, 1993.

Tjosvold, D. *Team Organisation: An Enduring Competitive Advantage.* London: Wiley, 1991.

Trowler, P. *Academics Responding to Change: new Higher Education Frameworks and Academic Cultures.* Buckingham: Open University Press, 1998.

Trowler, P. "Captured by the Discourse?: The Socially Constitutive Power of New Higher Education Discourse in the UK." In Calas, M. and L. Smircich (eds). "Special Issue on re-Organising Knowledge, Transforming Institutions: Knowing, Knowledge, and the University in the 21st Century." *Organization* 8.2 (2001): 183 – 201.

Van Dijk, J. *The Network Society: Social Aspects of New Media.* London: Sage, 1999.

Walsh, K. *Public Services and Market Mechanisms: Competition, Contracting and the New Public Management.* London: Macmillan, 1995.

Webb, J. "Work and the New Public Service Class?" *Sociology* 33.4 (1999): 747 – 766.

Whittington, R., T. McNulty and R. Whipp. "Market-Driven Change in Professional Services: Problems and Processes." *Journal of Management Studies* 31 (1994): 829 – 45.

Wilkinson, A. and H. Willmott (eds). *Making Quality Critical: New Perspectives on Organisational Change.* London: Routledge, 1995.

Willmott, H. "Managing the Academics: Commodification and Control in the Development of University Education in the UK." *Human Relations* 48.9 (1995): 993 – 1027.

OLIVER FULTON

HIGHER EDUCATION GOVERNANCE IN THE UK: CHANGE AND CONTINUITY[1]

1. INTRODUCTION

The tensions at the heart of academic governance can be said to exist at two levels. The first level concerns universities' place in their wider environment. Here the key tension concerns the balance of power, authority and accountability to be exerted over the system of higher education as a whole, as between: academics (as, in the traditional formulation, the owners of expert knowledge); the state (as the licenser of universities and in public systems their funder); and a range of stakeholders potentially including students, graduates, the employers of graduates and the range of other potential clients for university services. At the second, intra-institutional level, there are further tensions around the balance between working academics, 'managers', 'governors' and other stakeholders (notably students but in principle all other 'clients'): tensions exemplified in the case of managers and governors not only in the balance of their roles and responsibilities, but also in questions of who should constitute each of these groups and how responsive they are, or should be, to external and internal influences.

And of course the two levels are connected. As the ultimate authority which licenses (and could prohibit) universities to award degrees, the state can always, in principle, alter the balances at system level, whether by intervening or 'stepping back', for example (as recently in the UK) by drawing external stakeholders into formal decision processes or by allowing the market to substitute for its own 'steering' role. It can act directly on the publicly-funded system and it has the power to intervene in the conditions under which private institutions may be permitted to operate. At the institutional level too, there is in the UK no formal constitutional protection to prevent the state from similarly redrawing the internal balance sheet or requiring it to be redrawn.

This paper addresses these balances in two main sections. In Section 2, I describe the changing UK context of governance, analyse recent changes and discuss current tensions. Here a convenient peg for the discussion is the changing conceptualisation and implementation of the idea of institutional autonomy, but the basic purpose is to analyse when and why the state has either taken an explicit position, or changed previous working assumptions, on issues of governance, whether institutional or at system level. The starting point for Section 3, which picks up intra-institutional issues, is the, arguably ideal-typical, dual governance structure of British universities, established in the 19th century, consisting of 'Senate' and 'Council'.

Alberto Amaral, Glen A. Jones and Berit Karseth (eds.), Governing Higher Education: National Perspectives on Institutional Governance, 187—211.
© 2002 *Kluwer Academic Publishers. Printed in the Netherlands.*

(University Senates have academic membership and a supposedly irreducible primary responsibility for academic concerns; Councils include 'lay' (i.e. external) members and generally have the final say on broad strategic issues and particularly on financial matters: see note 5, below). Here I show, first, how the representation and the powers of academic staff of various grades first increased and then waned over the 20th century and, second, briefly summarise the more indirect threats to their autonomy and professional status. In the final section of the paper I outline a range of theoretical positions that might help to explain the changes which appear to be taking place.

2. THE CONTEXT OF GOVERNANCE. THE STATE AND THE 'AUTONOMOUS' UNIVERSITY – THE LIMITS OF AUTONOMY IN THE UK

2.1. University charters: a provisional licence from the state

It is often assumed that, compared with the centralised systems of many European countries and even with many public institutions in the USA, the 'Royal Charter' of the longstanding UK universities[2] has given them a quasi-private status, with a high degree of self-government, and constitutional protection from external regulation or direction. Notably, the colleges of Oxford and Cambridge Universities at the turn of the 19th century are frequently taken to constitute as clear an example as can be found of the pure 'guild' model of the fully autonomous institution, governed and owned by its academic staff. Here were corporations, chartered or otherwise licensed by the State, and fully endowed by public or private donors some centuries earlier: institutions fully and solely owned and governed by their members, and thus protected from the market (and hence subject to Adam Smith's and others' withering critique) by their wealth. Admittedly, as colleges they did not possess the power to award degrees (equally, however, many of their students were not much concerned with qualifications). But the two universities, which performed examining and degree-awarding functions, did so effectively on the basis of pooled sovereignty: the universities were little more than the sum of the colleges.

However, there are some important caveats which suggest that this is something closer to an ideal-type conceptualisation than a historically accurate description. The first concerns the definition of 'members': Moodie and Eustace (1974) point out that the governing councils of both the universities and of most of their colleges included among their members all of their graduates, and a sometimes large number of non-resident, and non-teaching, 'fellows': contrary to the general impression, therefore (and indeed to Adam Smith's strictures) they were certainly not institutions governed solely by their teaching staff. Moodie and Eustace suggest (1974: 27) that in practice "the rationale of staff self-government was based as much on the rights of property as on the needs of scholarship": this may be an understatement.

But second, and much more important in the long term, in the British constitutional context of absolute Parliamentary sovereignty not even the Oxbridge colleges (nor yet the universities) were immune from external intervention. Not only did the Crown retain (and does so to the present day) the right of appointment to certain posts, including the prestigious so-called Regius Professorships. But, more significantly, the state has repeatedly chosen to intervene in matters of supposedly private governance, in response to changing interpretations of the public good. It has done so through legislation, regulation and financial leverage which have been designed to direct or steer universities in state-approved directions, and even – and perhaps more surprisingly – by taking a strong interest in not only prescribing but revising the conditions inscribed in universities' charters, supposedly their guarantee of autonomy[3].

During the 19th century, for example, there was growing public outrage at Oxford's and Cambridge's refusal to admit anyone as either a 'junior' or 'senior' member (i.e., as student or staff) who was not prepared to declare allegiance to the Church of England and its beliefs. In due course – and admittedly after considerable controversy about the legitimacy of intervention in what legal conservatives regarded as the private affairs of the colleges – parliamentary legislation was passed to require changes in the colleges' charters and so remove religious barriers to membership, first from students and, some years later, from staff[4]. The late 20th century saw further waves of imposed charter revisions, as I describe below.

Moreover, although Oxford and Cambridge may be viewed, however inaccurately, as the ideal-typical model of the autonomous institution, those UK universities founded in the 19th and 20th century never enjoyed the same degree of autonomy from the state, nor yet the same level of insulation from external interests. As far as external representation is concerned, these institutions were almost all founded – as 'colleges' in the first instance – as a result of local initiative, and especially in their early days they were almost entirely governed by 'lay' members, whom Moodie and Eustace (1974) describe as predominantly "local notabilities". It is true that certain academic functions, notably examining, were performed by over-arching universities such as the University of London, or the Victoria University which for a time awarded degrees to students of the future autonomous universities of Leeds, Liverpool and Manchester, and that these bodies were less subject to lay control. But in due course many of the 'civic' colleges acquired their own charters and achieved degree-granting autonomy as independent universities. Even at that point their constitutions, in order to be approved by the state, were required to give lay members the majority in the university 'Council'[5] which constituted their supreme governing body. (I pick up the issue of lay participation in section 3.1.)

The state's authority over the new universities of the 19th and 20th century was asserted in a number of ways, of which the granting of a formal charter of (evidently provisional) autonomy was only the beginning. The decision to award a charter was itself subject to a series of conditions of varying degrees of explicitness. The aspiring university was, not surprisingly, expected to demonstrate its academic worthiness: right through to the 1960s, would-be new universities did so through a process of, effectively, apprenticeship to an existing chartered university, followed by scrutiny of their academic acceptability by senior academic 'advisers' drawn from a range of institutions[6].

The effects of this 'apprenticeship' on academic innovation and diversity are a matter for debate. But it would not be surprising if the parallel process of applying for a charter of governance from the Privy Council led to a degree of imposed structural isomorphism, although it was not until 1963 that the Council issued a 'Model Charter' to guide new aspirants to university status (Moodie and Eustace 1974: 35). Despite this, Moodie and Eustace demonstrate that there were in practice real differences between contemporaneous charters, notably in the range of powers allocated respectively to Council and Senate. In an extreme example, one Council was given "over-riding" powers to "review and control or disallow any act of the Senate and give directions to be obeyed by the Senate" (Birmingham University 1900, quoted in Moodie and Eustace 1974: 34) – powers which continued to appear in slightly diluted form in most, but by no means all, charters over the next 70 years. But these powers were frequently balanced by a declaration such as that the Senate was the "supreme academic body"; must be consulted on any, even financial, decision which "directly affects the educational policy of the University"; or even must "advise the council on the allocation of resources for teaching and research" (Moodie and Eustace 1974: 35).

Other areas of interest – and of variability – covered by the charters include: the rights of Senate and Council to participate in appointments, both of the Vice Chancellor and of senior and junior academic staff; the representation of academic staff on Council; and the representation of non-professorial staff, non-academic staff and students on Senate. In each of these areas, Moodie and Eustace (1974) claimed to be able to detect a central tendency, more or less fully embodied in the 1963 Model Charter, and also a gradual trend towards giving greater power and authority to the academics (see section 3.1). But here too they give examples of what appear to be far from trivial degrees of variation between one institution and another[7]. Given the relative uniformity of approach of the Privy Council as the national authority, there is the clear implication that variations must have stemmed from perceptions of local appropriateness and/or from institutional requests.

As has already been made clear, in the British context the award of a charter does not represent a permanent and unconditional grant of autonomy. Since the 1970s, when the last of the pre-92 universities were founded, there have not only been charter revisions initiated mainly for technical reasons by universities themselves, but two systematic interventions by the state. The first of these took place in 1987, when the then government decided that academic tenure, in the strict sense defined in most institutions' charters, was a barrier to the kind of flexible employment policies which it wished to see applied across the public services[8]. It was simply announced that the forthcoming (1988) Education Reform Act would require all university charters and statutes to be amended to remove references to exceptional tenure rights (i.e. any rights to security of employment beyond those guaranteed by national employment law), and that until the Act had become law, universities should immediately cease to include the right of tenure in all future employment contracts. More recently, the Dearing Committee, a national enquiry into current issues of higher education policy which reported in 1997, declared that most chartered universities' Councils and Senates were inefficiently large and should be reduced in size. Pressure has been and is still being applied to universities to redraft their charters accordingly[9].

However, while the granting and amendment of charters constitutes clear and visible evidence of direct intervention by the state in regulating governance, this is really only the tip of the iceberg. The nature of governance is mediated through a whole range of mechanisms by which academic functions are steered or influenced by external actors, and there have been other policy changes by the state which have had a direct impact on the powers and autonomy of the university and its stakeholders. I turn next, therefore, to a brief account of such changes in the period up to 1992, when the chartered universities were joined, and the terms of engagement were radically changed, by the creation of new universities with a quite different institutional history.

2.2. The chartered universities: autonomy and state control, 1918 – 1992

Aside from the reserve powers embodied in charter revision, up to 1988 central government's control of the universities was exercised through the University Grants Committee [UGC]. This body was appointed by government in conditions of some secrecy, but was predominantly composed of academic staff drawn from across the universities with a minority of lay membership drawn from other stakeholders such as secondary schools and industry. In its classic formulation as a "buffer" (Moodie 1983; Shattock 1994) between state and universities it served a dual purpose. On one hand it had the task of interpreting and implementing broad government policy (e.g. for the size of the higher education system or for the balance of science and 'non-science' student places) in the light of expert knowledge: in effect (or so the constitutional theory declared), while policy goals were nationally determined, the means of achieving them were devised for the universities by internal rather than external authority. On the other hand, in its heyday the UGC was also entrusted with the job of assessing both the feasibility and the cost of universities' own ambitions and plans in the light of government's broad policy aims: in effect, the UGC totalled up these costs and presented the government with an estimate of the 'deficiency' which would need to be funded. This method of funding, with its heavy reliance on trust and on effectively unaccountable expertise, gradually became unsustainable after the oil crisis of the 1970s led to more direct resource allocation through shorter-term and firmly capped budgets.

However, the UGC is generally seen as having suffered its fatal loss of credibility in 1981, when it was required by government to implement unexpected and suddenly imposed sharp cutbacks in resources: it chose to do so by reducing the number of students to be admitted at very short notice (thus infuriating government which had to bear the political backlash) and by distributing the cuts across the system not only selectively (which might have been defensible) but using undeclared criteria which were immediately strongly attacked by the numerous losers (Kogan and Hanney 2000)[10]. The consequence was a determination by the Thatcher government to end (or modify out of all recognition) a system of planning and control that was now declared to have been unacceptably 'producer-dominated' – very much in line with more widespread attacks on the professions by that government.

But the 1980s also saw the discovery of some serious ambiguities in the concept of university autonomy, which also helped to prompt legislative change. The most notorious of these concerned the University College of Wales, Cardiff, whose then Principal, according to the generally received account, persisted in certain actions which resulted in the university's becoming technically bankrupt. The subsequent enquiry revealed, first, that whether through lack of information or a failure to intervene decisively, the Council had not performed the duty of ensuring sound financial management which the College's Charter required it to carry out; second, that the UGC (officially the planning body which was responsible for monitoring the performance of the institutions in its care) had not been fully informed of the position and, worse, that even if it had had more reliable information, its powers of intervention were unclear; and third, that despite the appearance of autonomy, ultimate legal responsibility for its failure lay not with the College itself nor yet with the UGC but with the central government ministry, the Department of Education and Science [DES] (Shattock 1994: 113 – 127). At the height of its crisis, Cardiff had been under severe pressure from its bankers (Shattock 1994) and was expected by government and UGC to resolve its own difficulties: but if its bankers had refused to extend its credit, it appeared that it was not Cardiff that would have paid the bills. As a consequence (see Kogan and Hanney 2000: 153 – 4; Shattock 1994) the Education Reform Act of 1988 declared for the first time that universities were now financially autonomous: it was henceforth the full legal responsibility of their governing body alone should they become financially unviable. Under the same Act, the UGC was replaced by the Universities Funding Council – with increased lay membership – which was expected to be more responsive to central government direction, while also moving to funding mechanisms which used 'transparent', and accountable, formulaic methods of resource allocation. In theory, therefore, universities could from then on predict and determine their own financial future. They must 'live within their means' and could be declared bankrupt – in which case there would be no obligation on their Funding Council to bail them out. Indeed, to do so would be inconsistent with formula-based funding, since it would require taking resources away from other institutions which had been more prudent.

In themselves, these moves could be seen (and were proclaimed) as liberating universities from the shackles of an unwieldy and outmoded planning system, and giving them the freedom and autonomy to fully determine their own destiny in the new marketplace (see also below section 2.4.). In this respect, the British government was one of the leaders of the Europe-wide movement for governments (or in the UK case, an intermediary funding body) to "step back" from detailed management (Van Vught 1989; Neave and Van Vught 1991).

However, at the same time as it offered nominally increased autonomy, the UK government was also tightening some of its shackles. Governing bodies, newly empowered to determine their institution's destiny, were also warned that they would henceforth be held fully accountable to the newly created Funding Council to demonstrate that they were undertaking sound financial management practices. Since 1988, the UFC and its successors the Higher Education Funding Councils [HEFCs – for England, Wales and Scotland] have had the power effectively to place universities into administration if their financial situation appears critical. The rationale is obvious enough: although bankruptcy is a theoretical possibility, the political consequences could well be as difficult for the government as before 1988, whatever the change in the formal position. Thus the Funding Councils still find themselves in the position of funder of last resort, and in return they demand increasingly detailed monitoring of the institutions they fund (see 2.4., below).

Also in the mid-1980s, the 'Jarratt Report' (1985) had been commissioned by the universities themselves (under pressure from a defensive UGC) to review their 'efficiency'. It produced a strongly if conventionally managerialist set of recommendations: to strengthen corporate management in universities (including the setting of objectives, use of performance indicators, etc.), to identify the Vice Chancellor as 'Chief Executive', to strengthen lay members' involvement in governance, and perhaps most contentiously, to reduce the veto power of Senates and departments, the effects of which were described as liable to both 'conservatism' and self-interest. Jarratt's recommendations were technically advisory, though they do appear to have provided an agenda for discussion between universities and the UGC; and although greeted with some hostility in non-management circles, the report has been said to have done little more than codify what was already established practice in some institutions (Kogan and Hanney 2000: 185 – 187). (Ironically, as Shattock (1994) points out, the Jarratt prescription of a strong managerialist Vice Chancellor and a Council dominated by lay members was a fair description of the situation at Cardiff, where academic staff had for some years expressed great concern, but with no power to put a stop to actions which were endangering the university's survival). However, a few universities do appear to have implemented its prescriptions with enthusiasm.

2.3. The former polytechnics: an alternative model of external control

Even in the 1970s the chartered universities represented only one segment of the higher education landscape. The range of higher education-providing institutions in the UK today includes not only the chartered, 'pre-92' universities which we have just discussed, but also the powerful group of 'post-92' universities, nearly all of them former polytechnics. The polytechnics acquired university status in three stages: they were created, and designated as higher education institutions, out of smaller, 'mixed economy colleges'[11] in the 1960s; after 20 – 25 years of external management they were 'incorporated' as autonomous bodies under the Education Reform Act of 1988, and then given full university status under the 1992 Further and Higher Education Act. Moodie and Eustace do not discuss governance in the polytechnics – and it would be anachronistic to criticise them for this. Nevertheless, even in the 1970s these institutions offered an alternative and very different model of national control and institutional governance.

There are a number of reasons why this model deserves examination. First, the polytechnics were successful in due course in progressing to acceptance as universities, and as we shall see, some of their governance features ended up becoming the norm for universities as a whole. Second, although the polytechnics as such were created in the late 1960s, virtually all were the result of amalgamation, or of rapid expansion, of pre-existing institutions – institutions whose original character and mission had often been very similar to those of some of the more recently created pre-92 universities[12]. Thus the polytechnics provided a visible example of an alternative means of governing higher education providers. Third, an account of how the polytechnics' national planning and institutional governance structures were transformed, and how the pre-92 universities' situation was in turn aligned with them, may help to reveal more of the government agenda.

The polytechnics were set up in the late 1960s by the then Labour government as a conscious alternative to the universities. Under the 'binary policy' declared in 1965 – and contrary to the Robbins Report of 1963 which had proposed a blueprint for the expansion of higher education in which all higher education providers would in due course become universities – aspiring institutions would henceforth not join what was labelled the "autonomous sector", but constitute a new "public sector" which would remain "under social control" (Pratt 1997: 7 – 18). Thus the polytechnics operated throughout their lifetime as institutions with highly restricted formal and operational autonomy. They did not possess degree-awarding powers: the degrees for which they taught were awarded by the independent national Council for National Academic Awards [CNAA], which was dominated in its early years by members of the pre-92 universities, and which exercised powers of academic inspection and approval which it only gradually began to delegate. In the non-academic sphere, they were tightly controlled and regulated by a combination of primarily local but also national governmental systems. They were fully owned and formally managed by the local education authorities [LEAs] which provided all forms of education apart from universities in their area. The LEAs were naturally preoccupied, primarily, by their responsibilities for schools – but also for 'non-advanced' further education [mainly vocational training for 16 – 18 year olds]: during the 1980s in particular, polytechnic managers frequently complained that they were required to manage their institution as if it were an over-sized primary school, and that they depended on the external LEA bureaucracies and committee structures for even the most basic decisions, including finance (down to the level of minor purchases) and appointments. (Even their governing boards, whose powers were limited, provided no kind of counterweight, since their lay members were almost all representatives or nominees of their local education authority). In addition to CNAA's degree validation, the polytechnics were inspected and advised by the national education inspectorate (Her Majesty's Inspectorate [HMI]) whose origins and central concerns also lay with the compulsory schooling sector; and all curricular innovation was controlled not only for academic purposes by the CNAA, but also in planning terms. During the 1970s national planning was managed by committees of regional advisers to the ministry of education [DES], and in the 1980s by the 'National Advisory Body', composed of local and central government representatives: the consequence was that governmental 'planning permission' was needed for all new course initiatives, and indeed for expansion of existing student numbers on all courses. Thus, compared with the universities, which frequently offered comparable degree courses, in some cases with identical titles[13], the polytechnics' freedom of operation even in what might be regarded as the core academic sphere, was severely constrained. They possessed none of the seven elements of autonomy listed in Frazer's categorisation (Frazer 1997 in Kogan et al., 2000: 99 – 100).

However, during the 1980s the polytechnics persistently argued that this combination of external controls was inappropriate to mature higher education institutions, and should be scrapped[14] – and by 1987 these arguments had largely been accepted. Under the Education Reform Act of 1988, they were removed from local authority control and incorporated as independent (but not chartered) institutions. Four years later, the Further and Higher Education Act of 1992 gave them the title of university – but still no charter. Indeed, whereas the pre-92 universities had been offered a 'model charter' with the potential for negotiation around a proposed norm, the incorporated polytechnics and their successor universities were given a firm legal prescription for the number and sources of members of their governing board: indeed, their first board was appointed by the then Minister (they later became effectively self-perpetuating). The powers and duties of the new governing boards – including not only finance and resources but 'determining the educational mission' of the institution – were also prescribed, and in terms which clearly distinguished them from the powers and duties of the pre-92 universities' Councils as these had been previously understood. (See section 3.1.)

2.4. The new mass university system: autonomy and centralisation post-1992

2.4.1. Massification and markets

The new era for higher education following the major reforms of 1988 – 1992 has been described extensively elsewhere (see for example Scott 1995; Fulton 1996; Kogan and Hanney 2000). A few key points need to be emphasised here which relate directly to the themes of external control and the redefinition of autonomy.

First, the reforms took place – not coincidentally – at a time of spectacular expansion: effectively the participation rate for young people in full-time higher education doubled in less than ten years, and other rates (for older students and part-time higher education) increased virtually in parallel. The two previous systems of control which, though politically suspect, were each just about manageable in the mid-1980s, became unsustainable, simply for technical reasons, once the participation rate had reached 30%. Neither the flawed subjectivism of the UGC nor the precise engineering of the 'public sector' planning of the polytechnics could possibly cope with the scale of the emerging system: as Trow has persuasively pointed out, the logic of mass systems simply outruns the lumbering efforts of traditional governmental management and control.

Second, the Thatcher-Major governments had evolved an over-riding commitment to the marketisation of the public services, with a range of objectives (depending on the policy recipient's perspective): to sharply reduce unit costs – to the state if not to the individual – by introducing competitive bidding, even for government funds; to increase efficiency by incentivising staff; and/or to undermine once and for all the power of bureau-professionals and their institutions (see Reed, this volume). The kinds of market mechanisms that they introduced into higher education were undoubtedly incomplete: most notably, as soon as the full net costs of the high-speed expansion became clear, tight central controls were re-imposed on maximum student enrolments per institution. Nevertheless, the new financial autonomy (and risk exposure) was, and remains, a widely-perceived threat to institutional survival, especially since annual increases in total government funding for the whole system have been relentlessly kept below inflation levels, and student demand has been weaker in relation to supply in the past 2 – 3 years than it has been for many years past.

In this new entrepreneurial context, Shattock points out that government and Funding Council policy since 1992 has been to underline the strategic financial responsibilities of all governing bodies, and not only those of the post-92 universities as defined in the Act of 1992. Since that time, both legislation and 'financial memoranda'[15] have consistently and explicitly laid all new duties on the *governing bodies* of institutions, whether pre-92 or post-92, rather than simply on the institutions as a whole (Shattock 1999: 277).

2.4.2. Levelling up or levelling down?

In this context it is interesting to construct a balance sheet of gains and losses in autonomy after 1992. The 'spin' put on the conversion of the polytechnics to university status was of course one of the liberation of mature institutions from restrictions which were no longer appropriate. In this, government precisely echoed the demands of the polytechnics' senior management during the 1980s. And it is certainly true that (subject to the vagaries of league tables and to the persistence of former perceptions – and underlying realities – of status and quality) both their new university titles, and the elements of formal autonomy (mainly finance-related) which came with incorporation and the removal of LEA management, brought economic and status rewards to a fair number of (mainly senior) employees.

However, viewed on the larger canvas of specific areas of power and authority, the balance sheet is more mixed. It is almost a commonplace now (e.g. Fulton 1996) to argue that in the area of research, the net effect of turning polytechnics into universities was to dilute previous understandings of the core of university activity. The expansion of university status coincided – again not by accident – with the strengthening of the UK's four- or five-yearly Research Assessment Exercise. It would have been unthinkable, economically, politically or indeed academically, to fund all new university (former polytechnic) staff for research time and resources on the same basis as had always been done for staff in the pre-92 universities. But by making the right to research funding contingent on regular national peer-review assessments, the result was that all university staff, including those in the pre-92 institutions, lost the automatic entitlement to funded research time which they had previously held by virtue of their employment in a university[16].

What has perhaps been less obvious outside the UK is that the same logic can be applied to a wide range of other areas where the pre-92 universities had enjoyed considerable powers of self-government, but the polytechnics had not. A conspicuous example is the area of institutional and departmental quality assurance. I referred earlier to the CNAA, which alone held the power to award the degrees for which the polytechnics taught. Although it was wound up in 1992 and the

polytechnics were awarded their own degree awarding powers as an essential part of
their new university status, most of the activities which the CNAA had carried out
were continued under other auspices. Government ministers had let it be known in
the late 1980s that they were concerned about the lack of academic accountability of
the old (pre-92) universities, and indeed might well propose extending the inspection
powers of the national inspectorate (HMI) to cover the old universities, whatever
their charters might suggest. In response, the universities in 1990 set up an
'Academic Audit Unit' (AAU), funded by themselves, to monitor, and report
publicly on, not academic standards as such, but how universities organised
themselves to maintain and enhance standards and quality – a position very similar
to that increasingly adopted by the CNAA in the immediately preceding period. The
concept of 'institutional audit' was then carried forward by two successor bodies to
the AAU, both funded by the higher education institutions themselves, and it forms
a central part of policy to this day: however, ministers have frequently made it clear
that although they are not averse to a system in which the universities own and fund
the auditor, they will intervene with legislation if they regard the audit process as
inadequate. In addition, although the HMI in 1992 lost the right to inspect courses in
the former polytechnics, the 1992 Higher and Further Education Act required the
new Funding Councils to set up ways of assessing quality and standards at
departmental level. The resulting mechanisms, whose history has been particularly
contentious, could hardly be described as less intrusive than the previous HMI
system – and all institutions, including the pre-92 universities, are now subject to
them. Whatever the formal structures of ownership and consultation (and both
exist), government has made very clear that it has largely withdrawn whatever trust
it previously placed in professional norms and standards: here again this constitutes
a major loss of autonomy in a core academic area.

2.4.3. Restricted autonomy in the marketplace
There are a number of other areas in which institutional autonomy has been
remarkably limited, and in some ways reduced – at least if one takes seriously the
rhetoric of a market system. One of these concerns prices and costs.

On the price side, the new Labour government of 1997 took the decision to
introduce (means-tested) tuition fees for full-time undergraduates, largely in an
attempt to shift the balance of payment somewhat towards the beneficiary and away
from the state (another consequence, arguably, of mass participation combined with
downward pressure on public expenditure). However, an essential part of the new
regime, in response to demands from organised students and from lower status
institutions, was that legislation was passed not only to set a national fee rate, but to
prevent any university or college in receipt of state support (in other words, every
significant university and college) from charging more. There are of course some
good policy arguments to be made in favour of this approach, but it is hard to deny
that the financial autonomy of institutions (and disciplines) in high demand has been
considerably reduced by the decision. Although other areas of pricing (such as fees
for postgraduate and part-time courses) are not restricted in the same way, national
concerns with 'value for [public] money' mean that the Funding Councils have set

up regimes of quite intrusive monitoring and even regulation of universities' charges for, or their use of income generated by, other activities as well.

On the cost side, equally, autonomy is far from complete. A key element of university autonomy under the UGC regime was that resources were handed over in a single lump sum; and until the 1980s, universities were not even given any indication of how the sum had been derived, on the grounds that this knowledge might constrain their freedom to spend as they saw fit. Line budgeting would have been entirely unacceptable. Now, however, the Funding Councils allocate their payments to institutions in two main streams, for teaching and research, each of which is further sub-divided into resources 'earned' by specific departments on two bases of, on one hand, research quality ratings and research volume, and on the other, student enrolments. Although there is no attempt to monitor transfers between departments, which are still regarded as an institution's strategic prerogative (but see below), both the Treasury and Parliament have repeatedly expressed concern about the danger that funds allocated for teaching might be diverted to support research (or presumably in theory, the reverse, though that is regarded as much less likely). Enquiries began some years ago with research projects designed to assess the scale of possible 'cross-subsidy', but have now moved close to the point of requiring institutions to provide a full accounting for the use of each stream of funds. Not only does this restrict institutions' strategic freedom, and create a potentially intrusive monitoring regime, but it reifies a distinction between specific 'teaching' and 'research' activities in ways which many academics find absurd.

Academic salaries, the largest cost element in most academic disciplines, are also subject to external influence. Here the position is less clear-cut: until the 1990s government was a full partner in salary negotiations in both universities and polytechnics, and insisted on, and played a direct role in prescribing, national salary scales and conditions. However, government has now withdrawn from direct participation, claiming that it is for institutions themselves to decide how they will spend their resources. Indeed, there is now nothing to prevent institutions from undertaking local salary negotiations and setting their own pay scales and conditions of service. In practice, and for familiar reasons, the universities have set up a joint employers' organisation to negotiate on their behalf, and there appear to be very limited examples of deviation from national agreements. However, this is not a simple switch from external prescription to internal responsibility: while government generally disclaims responsibility for what the unions claim are exceptionally low rates of pay by European or world standards, it is not averse to offering – or hinting at – more money for pay near the time of an election, or to imposing quite onerous conditions for increased funding, such as a requirement to redress gender inequality or to introduce larger elements of performance-related pay.

Finally, in recent years and clearly at the behest of government, the Funding Councils have begun to introduce a wide range of more intrusive monitoring and even control mechanisms. For some years, both central government departments and the Funding Councils have used 'categorical funding' models of competitive bidding against fixed criteria – for curriculum change, for infrastructure support and so on[17]. Following a barrage of complaints from universities and colleges about the excessive demands, including the opportunity costs, of what has been criticised as the 'bidding culture', the Funding Councils have recently begun to move away from competitive bidding and towards formula funding of new initiatives. But the price of this change is to require detailed plans for each initiative, generally demonstrating the 'additionality' which will be provided in return for new funding, and including pre-specified output performance indicators, before the funds are released[18]. The performance indicators are then subject to regular and close monitoring, thus sharply increasing external control in exchange for a reduction in uncertainty and in competition.

In addition, all institutions are now required to produce and regularly update strategic plans for all of their core activities. It is claimed by the Funding Councils that institutions' plans, although prescribed as to the topics they must address, can and should represent each institution's distinctive 'vision' of its future, and that the Councils will not insist on any particular shape for the vision. In practice, however, government policy priorities backed up by frequent exhortation, which the Funding Councils echo, mean that there will inevitably be strong convergence on the major policy themes of the day. Recent examples include strong emphases on widening participation, regional economic development and inter-institutional collaboration. Essentially, any institution which does not have these three areas as high priorities in its strategic plans can expect constant pressure from its Funding Council.

2.4.4. Assimilation to the private sector

Until the late 1980s, and arguably throughout the long Thatcher-Major years of Conservative government, higher education – both the pre-92 universities and the polytechnics/post-92 universities – occupied distinctive niches in government policy, even if with rather fewer accompanying privileges than it might have preferred. But in recent years the UK has seen this distinction gradually eroded through government action. We have seen how the assimilation of the two sectors has led to a common model offering some of the less attractive features of each side. But beyond this, there has been an increasing inclination in government to impose standard expectations on universities in areas in which they were previously given special treatment. One example is an incremental set of requirements to conform to national legislation on equal opportunities – with respect to gender, race and most recently, disability – from which, for better or worse, earlier legislation offered partial exemption. Another new national requirement, following instances of corruption in other public services, is for institutions to create and publicise procedures to protect 'whistle-blowers'[19]. The most striking example, however, is the Funding Councils' requirement, laid down in its memoranda, that all governing bodies must set up independent committees (i.e., committees controlled by or made up of external members) for audit, remuneration (of senior staff) and 'nomination' (of new governors): and the gradual extension of audit committees' recommended powers and responsibilities from financial matters into issues close to the academic core of the institution. This is a model of governance drawn directly from 'good practice' recommended for private sector corporations, with 'non-executive directors' representing shareholder interests and monitoring the activity of 'executives'[20] (Shattock 1999: 277 – 278).

2.4.5. *Qualified and limited autonomy*

This section has revealed how government has always constrained internal governance structures, even for the older universities. Compared with continental Europe, the pre-92 universities once possessed a much higher degree of formal autonomy. On the other hand, this has always been qualified and contingent, rather than a constitutionally protected right. Since 1992, in the changed contexts of mass higher education and marketisation, external agencies have substantially taken over many areas in which universities were previously more or less self-governing (including quality assurance[21], accountability and many aspects of strategic planning), while handing over financial 'independence' to the institutions, but retaining and even enhancing well-established tight controls in other areas such as prices and costs. In other words, compared with many other European systems where the state has visibly 'stepped back' and adopted 'steering at an (increased) distance', the UK provides an example of a state which has certainly strengthened its steering, and in many respects lessened the distance, while arguably doing its best to distance itself from the potential negative consequences. This is the new national governance 'envelope' within which institutions are now expected to exercise such qualified autonomy as they have achieved, or retained, to govern themselves.

3. INTERNAL GOVERNANCE ISSUES

3.1. *Formal structures*

There can be little doubt that previous certainties have been challenged by events over the past quarter century. Moodie and Eustace, writing in the early 1970s, took a clear and basically Whig view of the evolution of what they evidently saw as a mature and relatively stable system of institutional governance. Key elements at the end of the 19th century had been:

> a large (and largely inert) court[22] and a smaller (and executive) council, each with a heavy lay majority. These bodies bore a direct financial responsibility for their colleges and therefore exercised close control over all expenditure. [...] In addition they had control of appointments and new developments, but had little responsibility for other academic matters... [However] the power of the laymen was shared increasingly with academics ... headed by a permanent principal[23] [... who] was a member of both court and council, where he [sic] was joined by a small but steadily increasing number of professors. The principal and all professors were also members of the senate, a purely advisory body concerned mainly with the academic matters which lay within the jurisdication of the colleges. (Moodie and Eustace 1974: 30 – 31).

Shattock (2002) underlines and develops Moodie's and Eustace's point about financial responsibility. In the 19th century it was generally the lay members of Council who had taken the initiative and raised the funds for the establishment of their city's university, and in the absence of substantial government funding their support continued to be necessary. Whatever the letter of charters and statutes, it would have been impossible for the academics to disregard their lay supporters' views on any aspect of university development. However, once regular government funding began to flow, the balance of power was reversed; and Shattock goes so far as to say that by 1945, when 95% of university funds were provided by the UGC, it was inevitable that Councils would be marginalised.

In any event, by the mid-20th century all aspects of university governance were very largely in the hands of the Senate, and in most institutions this was in turn dominated by the professors and the Vice Chancellor. Most of the 19th century civic universities had been founded on the 'chair' principle, whereby a department's single professor was the first and frequently the only university appointment. He (almost always he) was solely responsible for the short-term appointment of his assistants, who thus had no rights of involvement in governance. Despite the growth in university appointments of junior staff, little had changed as far as Senate membership was concerned by the mid-1960s: Halsey and Trow (1971: 107) describe the typical 'Redbrick' university Senate as including "all professors [and] a handful of more junior academic staff". However, Moodie and Eustace (1974: 207 – 216) recount increasingly powerful and eventually effective challenges to the status quo by 'non-professorial staff' from 1945 onwards: challenges which, not surprisingly, took root most quickly in the constitutions of new universities where there was no professorial establishment which had to be persuaded to share its privileges.

Thus the world began to change in the 1960s. The new campus universities founded at the beginning of that decade were constituted on more democratic lines as far as staff were concerned, with fewer professors on Senate, more representatives of junior staff and in some cases student members as well[24]. The events of 1968, and of the late 1960s more generally, had much less impact on university governance in the UK than in other European countries. But student 'militancy', however muted, did gradually achieve considerable success: first by insisting on student representation on bodies directly concerned with student interests (mainly student welfare and discipline) and then building on these successes by demanding representation on the more central organs of academic government, at department, faculty and even Senate level (Moodie and Eustace 1974: 196 – 207).

In summary, Moodie and Eustace identify four "governmental principles" which appeared to have become accepted by the Privy Council by 1970, even if not fully incorporated into its Model Charter. The first three were:

> 1. That general university government may be substantially in the hands of staff and that junior staff should have a significant part in it;
>
> 2. that senate should have a wide area of complete independence, a veto at least on academic and senior administrative appointments and the right of consultation in financial matters; and
>
> 3. that it is proper and perhaps necessary to specify machinery of collective government at the 'subject' level;

and the last, which they saw as an emergent principle for which they had less definitive evidence, was:

> 4. that students should have some share in general university government. (Moodie and Eustace 1974: 42 – 43).

At the same time, Pratt (1997) suggests that for the first time in non-university higher education institutions, academic staff in the polytechnics began to acquire a significant role in governance. 'Governing Bodies' and 'academic boards' were set up for each polytechnic, and their membership and powers were inscribed in 'instruments and articles of government' which were approved by the Minister. Under these provisions, the governing body included a substantial number, albeit a minority, of elected academic members, while the academic board "usually consisted of the senior staff of the polytechnic with elected representation of other staff and students". Thus staff and students were, evidently, rather better represented – staff on the governing body and students on the academic board – than in most universities at that time[25].

The academic board "was responsible for 'planning, co-ordination, development and oversight of academic work'"; but the governing body was responsible for the "general direction of the conduct and curriculum", and the academic board's decisions were "subject to the general approval of the governing body" (Pratt 1997: 277 – 279). This is, as Bargh et al. (1996) note, a rather different balance from the pre-92 universities: polytechnic academic boards were more sharply defined as advisory and subordinate. In practice, however, the main area of contention was between governing bodies and their local education authority, where in Pratt's view (and that of numerous others whom he quotes) the lack of autonomy described in section 2.3., combined with uneasy compromises over the two sides' responsibilities in the articles of governance, created, in the worst cases, a long-running "poisonous" relationship.

In summary, on both sides of the binary line the academic voice was prominent in 'general university [and polytechnic] government' – including even financial issues; and academic members involved in governance now tended to include relatively junior staff and, increasingly frequently, some student representation as well. If this did not constitute complete academic autonomy, it certainly gave academics a relatively commanding position. Much of the detail of Moodie's and Eustace's study, focusing on the exercise of power and authority at different levels within the university, strongly supports this point of view.

However, in Dearlove's words (2002), the powers of Councils had not so much been removed as withered through disuse – and could still be revived. In retrospect, it can quite easily be argued that rather than marking a position of maturity and stability, as Moodie and Eustace imply, the 1970s constituted the high water mark for both the extent and the legitimisation of academic staff – and student – participation in, and even control of, institutional governance. This is true both in the wider sense described in section 2, in that the space for institutions to exercise independent decision making has been much reduced; but also in the stricter sense that at the institutional level too, other interests have reasserted and strengthened their authority.

It needs to be emphasised that although, through the 1992 Further and Higher Education Act, the new and old universities were fully assimilated to a common model of external steering and control, their internal governance was not aligned in the same way. The post-92 universities were not chartered: as described in section 2.3 above, they were set up in 1988 as 'higher education corporations' (or in a few cases as limited companies) with charitable status, and they were required to adopt articles of government approved by the Secretary of State for Education (with model articles provided as guidance), to apply to the minister again for any changes, and also to obtain his approval for the membership of their first governing body. If government wishes to change the balance of membership or its powers, it can do so quickly and simply by issuing an order to that effect. In other words, they were and are much more directly subject to control of their governance structures by the ministry which funds them than are the pre-92 universities, whose charters come from the Privy Council, a body with broader legal responsibilities. In addition, in practice the new model articles were considerably more prescriptive, especially in the area of governing body membership, than even the Privy Council's model charter had ever turned out to be. All the new universities were required to sharply reduce the numbers of local government nominees and representatives[26]. As a consequence, Bargh et al. (1996) claimed that following these reforms, the pre-92 universities, which evolved during the mid-20th century with much weaker formal connections with their locality than did the polytechnics, were far more likely to include an influential group of local representatives in their governing bodies. The new universities were also required to reduce the number of staff representatives on their governing bodies (indeed a few asked, and were permitted, to appoint no staff governors at all). At the same time, the new articles made it clear that the governing bodies were supreme in all areas and that academic boards' role was strictly advisory.

In the pre-92 universities there was no sudden change in internal governance over the years from 1988 – 1992. The Jarratt report and its managerialist assumptions had gradually become part of the discourse, picked up and amplified in due course by the Dearing Committee when it reported in 1997. The Privy Council has followed Jarratt and Dearing in encouraging any universities seeking to revise their charters to reduce the size of their Council and Senate. Intriguingly, however, whereas Dearing proposed a maximum size of 24 for Councils (the same size as was prescribed for post-92 universities' governing boards) the Privy Council has apparently settled in a number of known cases for more modest reductions in Councils and has not insisted on reductions in the size of Senates.

3.2. The new context of governance

Descriptions of the formal representation and powers of the various stakeholders in academic governance cannot tell the whole story. Issues of governance blur into those of management, and the formal into the informal. Formal accounts such as that provided above rely on long-standing categories: Vice-Chancellors and Pro-Vice-Chancellors, senior and junior academic staff, students, 'lay' governors. But the occupants of these categories, the roles they play and the authority they bring to them, are all subject to change.

To begin with academic staff, many of the traditional assumptions on which academic participation in governance was based have become problematic in the last few years. In particular, the nature of academic work itself has changed (Fulton and

Holland 2001). Implicitly if not explicitly, academic participation, whether by professors / heads of department or by academic staff more widely, was predicated on a notion of 'the academic' as a kind of panoptic authority on all of the university's educational activities. But in British universities, as elsewhere, there is now a set of complementary (or competing) 'service providers', each of whom can claim their own area of educational expertise with its own professional competence. Examples include generic teaching and learning specialists, student advice and counselling staff, professional development workers, librarians, communications and information technology specialists, and so on. Most of these posts have existed for many years, but their roles have gradually changed from more or less humbly supporting academic staff to virtually relieving them of whole areas of traditional authority and expertise. Whether this amounts, as some people would argue, to a 'Fordist' division of labour – which may be leading to production-line methods of processing students and a concomitant proletarianisation of the academic profession – is open to debate. But as far as governance is concerned, these developments cast a double shadow: they challenge academic authority both at a symbolic level and because many of the most urgent issues for debate by governance bodies require the contributions of these new 'para-academics' just as much as they need academic input.

As has often been argued (see Reed in this volume) academic authority has been equally seriously challenged by the changing environment and its implications for university management. I have already referred to the external assessment of teaching and research quality, and the disappearance of the state's earlier reluctance to intervene in areas such as equal opportunities. For the institution, the price of failure in any of these challenges has risen inexorably: there is a direct loss of funding in the case of research assessment; in other areas there can be loss of reputation and status, damaging publicity, and a consequential impact on market position. There are also huge risks in areas such as student recruitment and admissions, for which the penalties for missing targets – whether exceeding them or falling short – are now immediate and draconian. These risks need to be managed, and in most institutions senior university managers are under great pressure to take a firm hand. (A significant source of this pressure, of course, is lay governors, since the Funding Councils now instruct governing boards to undertake regular and thorough risk assessments). Thus debates in Senates and academic boards, and recourse to academic rationales in Councils and governing bodies, can now be legitimately cut short by reference to the survival of the institution. Moreover, decisions have to be taken which cannot wait for the next round of the academic committee cycle. So, alongside the new experts referred to above, we find the new managers – no longer administrator-bureaucrats: not only Vice-Chancellors and Pro-Vice-Chancellors, but quality managers, finance directors, fund-raisers, marketing and sales directors. Like the new experts, they all have plausible claims to play a role in governance alongside the academics. What is more, for some of them the traditional academic activities of undergraduate and postgraduate teaching and basic research are visibly of less interest and importance than the new near-market activities: full-cost training, commercial research, intellectual property development and technology transfer. Whether their appointments are permanent or temporary (with the right to revert to a full academic position once their term of office is completed) it can no longer be assumed, as Moodie and Eustace (1974) clearly believed in the 1970s, that senior managers will see themselves, and act, as essentially academic, even if powerful, leaders.

It is also very clear that the renewed emphasis – from committees such as Jarratt and Dearing, from government and Funding Councils – on the powers and duties of lay governors has been motivated by the desire to tilt the balance of power and authority in universities away from academic values and preoccupations, and to introduce 'business' values and perspectives as legitimate alternatives (Bargh et al., 1996: 19 – 23).

Interestingly, however, the evidence is rather mixed. The ESRC "new managerialism" project (see Reed, this volume) suggested that despite all the pressures, universities have not yet seen the kind of polarisation between academic and 'business' imperatives – and their advocates – which this analysis would predict. Nor does the Bargh et al. (1996) study of governors reveal lay members as habitually invading 'academic space' or overruling academic decisions. Change has been more subtle, and Bargh et al. (1996: 177) conclude by suggesting that governance and management practices, far from spearheading change, have "only played a subordinate role in [the] transformation" of higher education. In the final section of this paper I begin to explore how and why that role may have been played out.

4. DISCUSSION AND CONCLUSIONS

So far I have offered a largely descriptive account of changes in governance in the UK, both those which have been prompted or mediated by the state and those which seem to have been more internally generated. Certain causal processes have been suggested, but it may be useful now to gather these together into a more coherent set of alternative theoretical approaches which may help to interpret recent events.

We might start with a number of broadly functionalist and/or rational interpretations. The simplest of these is the purported rational-managerial approach of the Jarratt report and other official or para-official documents such as the Dearing enquiry. Governance structures, they argued, had simply failed to adapt to new realities and needed to be brought up to date. These new realities – increased uncertainty, volatile markets, need for new types of income – imposed the necessity for universities to be more flexible and faster-reacting than had been required in their traditional environment. Both Jarratt and Dearing were clear that the processes of academic decision-making were too slow and ponderous to be allowed to persist unchanged. And of course there is some plausibility to this view, given the pace of demands from external bodies. It is quite true that not only commercial clients but even official agencies such as the Funding Councils have the habit, for example, of demanding tenders and signed contracts at much higher speeds than the standard academic processes of consultation, consensus-building and approval can cope with[27].

But of course these arguments are ideological as well as rational. Jarratt and Dearing were making – and promoting – value judgements: alongside relatively innocent comments about speed there are accusations of inertia ... conservatism ... and even malign self-interest. In the early 1980s the Conservative "discourse of derision", in Stephen Ball's much-quoted phrase, placed universities (along with the whole public sector) on the wrong side of a manichaean divide between the 'wealth creating' and the 'wealth consuming' sectors of the economy. As the absurdity of this attitude to knowledge became more apparent, the critique was slightly modified: but even if some wealth was created, much was unnecessarily consumed by inefficiency and managerial incompetence. Nor was this an accident, since the universities were, in another depressingly common catch-phrase, 'producer-dominated' (and so ripe for the discipline of the market): producers, unlike professionals, are of course by definition self-interested. There is plenty of evidence (see for example interviewees quoted in Kogan and Hanney 2000) of persistent deep impatience in government circles with university management practices and capacities – part of a general impatience with public-sector workers and their practices which the present British government, and particularly the Prime Minister and his office, have taken considerable pains to emphasise around the time of writing. Notable among such practices, it seems, is academics' (and medical practitioners', to take another topical example) perverse insistence on professional self-government.

One only has to contrast all this with the Robbins Committee's (1963) views on academic freedom and the right of academic self-government, as quoted by Salter and Tapper (1994: 11):

> We are convinced also that such freedom is a necessary condition of the highest efficiency ... and that encroachments upon their liberty, in the supposed interests of greater efficiency, would in fact diminish their efficiency and stultify their development (Robbins Report 1963: 228).

Here of course is a counter-ideology, intriguingly also rationalised on grounds of 'efficiency'. How can we best understand this discursive change, which seems to have been so clearly echoed in policy movements, and in a more muted way in governance structures and practices?

I suggested earlier that the 1960s recorded the high water mark of academic autonomy and self-government. The tide seems to have been swollen (to continue the metaphor) by a number of more or less coincident waves. The most obvious of these was that the universities were popular. The Robbins Committee was set up, like all such enquiries, to deal with a crisis – in this case a crisis of excessive demand: applications to British universities were rising too fast to be accommodated without a set of step-changes. Expansion in the UK was part of an OECD-wide phenomenon, which gave confidence and credibility to universities as prime agents of social and economic transformation. High student demand was paralleled by increasing confidence in the strategic role of universities in knowledge creation in the post-Sputnik era (and in the UK, university research was also seen as having 'had a good war' [World War II]).

The implications for governance should have been as Robbins described them. Lay governors, as Shattock pointed out (see 3.1 above) were no longer important as fundraisers; and as national institutions, universities had little need of the political or economic connections which local dignitaries might bring with them[28]. More positively, universities had demonstrated that their senior academic staff had built successful institutions, driven by the development of valuable knowledge and its transmission to highly selected and privileged students. In the classic Mertonian formulation later taken up by Clark (e.g. 1983) among others, universities firmly based on the development of disciplinary specialisms could only be effectively governed by experts in those disciplines. Equally, as had been endorsed in other systems where the issue had been far more problematic, universities' other purpose of social critique could best be protected by drawing sharp defensive lines around the idea of academic self-government.

We have already seen how quickly this ideology crumbled. The consequences of massification (see for example Scott 1995) are the obvious starting point. Much has been made recently in the UK of the likely consequences of the introduction in 1997 of student fees, which have been proclaimed as tilting the balance of authority from academic to student, as a newly-paying consumer. But the crucial shift surely happened much earlier, when the adoption of the policy of mass higher education converted access to higher education from a privilege in the hands of the 'dons' to a rightful expectation of every young person who achieved standard qualifications. And that shift was the chief Robbins legacy. It coincided with the first wave of consumerism in the UK (for example, the setting up of consumer organisations), the 'end of deference' of the 1960s, and student militancy which was fuelled not just by global or national political events but by demands for fair and inclusive regard for student needs. Other elements of massification – notably the dilution of elite status for academics (and for students) – reduced their mystique and their authority. Student militancy was built up by politicians and the press into a significant cause of popular suspicion, if not envy. Rising costs, the persistence of national economic decline (contrary to the apparent promises of Robbins and the OECD), newly-visible graduate unemployment all played their part in weakening the claims of higher education to a distinctive pattern of governance.

At the same time (the early 1960s), Robbins' prescription of university status for all higher education providers was rejected by a Labour minister who introduced the binary system specifically in order to keep a section of higher education 'under social control' (Section 2.3, above). Salter and Tapper (1994) have charted the emergence from that point of an economic and utilitarian ideology, orchestrated by civil servants as much as by politicians, whose adoption made it almost inevitable that higher education would be seen as too important to be left to the academics. The notion (but not the term) of 'stakeholders' in education was first introduced to politics in 1976, by a Labour Prime Minister whose government went on to intervene in traditional patterns of governance for schools in order to increase 'accountability'. And underlying these developments, of course, there are deeper social and economic changes perhaps best understood by Weberian analysis of the competition of social and economic interests (Archer 1979; Perkin 1989).

How some of these interests have targeted the 'welfare state', and post-war arrangements for the public services in general, and how higher education fits into that larger picture, is a long debate for which there is neither time nor space here. But we should not pass over it without commenting on the key role of finance in the transformation of higher education. Cutting the cost (not only the *per capita* cost, which has shrunk by half over the past decade, but even the net cost) of higher education has been an aim in its own right. But it has also been the most successful mechanism yet devised to induce radical change in universities. As we have seen, financial transparency, the devolution of financial autonomy and exposure to market forces have proved to be the most irresistible means so far of shifting authority from academics to managers and governors – and indeed of converting academics into managers. Their effects have been enormously amplified by the shrinking pool of public funds for which universities have been expected to compete. Intriguingly, it does not seem that managers and governors have (yet) fully bought into the kind of technicist, business-oriented approaches to managing universities which might have been expected as a result, and indeed which have been forcefully recommended to them. Whether this is a tribute to the persistence of collegial values, or to the deeper functionality of collegial practices for the survival of the institution, is an interesting question which may be resolved in the next few years.

NOTES

[1] My thanks for their comments and very helpful suggestions on the first draft of this paper to fellow members of the Douro seminar, especially Jef Verhoeven, commentator; Glen Jones and Alberto Amaral, editors – not least for their patience; and Mike Reed, colleague and informal discussant on the journeys from and to Lancaster. Errors and omissions are of course my own.

[2] Those created prior to 1992, sometimes referred to as 'old' or 'chartered' universities but hereafter simply as 'pre-92' universities. (See note 3, below, for an explanation of the 'charter'.)

[3] From the early 19th century until the creation of the 'new' universities (a large group of former polytechnics and colleges [hereafter 'post-92' universities]: see section 2.3. below) under the Further and Higher Education Act of 1992], the licensing and incorporation of a university was marked by the granting of a 'Royal Charter' (see also Jones, this volume). The charter bestows the right to award degrees, and the charter and its associated 'statutes' are effectively the constitution of the university, defining and delimiting its governance structures and procedures, including specifying the representation of internal and external stakeholders and the powers of the governing bodies on which they are represented; and also – but somewhat variably between institutions – establishing the rights and responsibilities of members (e.g. tenure, dismissal procedures, student appeals). The charter is signed by the monarch, and its conditions are set out or negotiated by the Privy Council, an obscure quasi-judicial and quasi-administrative body which is technically advisory to the monarch and hence supposedly somewhat detached from day-to-day government. However, it would be quite wrong to see the Privy Council, whose members include government ministers, as independent of current policy preoccupations.

[4] The case of gender barriers is intriguingly different. New colleges for women were founded at both universities during the late 19th century. Oxford University agreed to confer degrees on women after a modest interval of some 20 years, but Cambridge did not do so until 1948. Whether the absence of state intervention is a symbol of a general reluctance of Parliament to intervene, or of a long-standing lack of concern with women's exclusion, is an interesting question.

[5] British universities (other than Oxford and Cambridge) operate on the familiar bicameral principle. A generalised sketch would be roughly as follows. The Senate ['Academic Board' in some post-92 universities and colleges] is, either *de jure* or *de facto* (see note 7), the body with responsibility for decision-making on all academic issues in relation to teaching, learning and assessment and to

research; the Council [or Corporation Board or Governing Board] is the supreme decision-making body with responsibility for finance and resources, [non-academic] terms and conditions of employment of staff, etc. Issues such as the 'mission' or strategic direction of the institution, although formally the responsibility of the Council, may in practice be largely delegated to, or dictated by, the Senate. The Council contains both external members and academic staff; the Senate, mainly academic staff, normally contains very few external and no strictly non-academic members. Both Senate and Council may include students (see also below Section 3).

6   For the first and only time, the new universities of the 1960s were permitted to speed up the process by simply working under a small scrutiny board for two or three years before applying for their charters.

7   They also rightly point out that charters and statutes provide no more than a formal framework and that institutional practice may well be considerably more variable – even, in some cases, directly in conflict with the charter's prescriptions.

8   In essence, lifetime tenure had generally been awarded (by national agreement with the trade unions) after no more than 3 years' 'probationary' service, and in most universities employment contracts were backed up by definitions of membership in the charter and statutes which gave very strong protection against dismissal – even if a staff member's department proved to be unviable. The language used by ministers to justify the change took two forms. One form was the managerial language of incentives and flexibility, in other words to attempt to 'motivate' staff, in part, by making it possible to close 'unprofitable' sections of a university (and the concept of profit in the university context was still quite unfamiliar at this time), and to make the staff of such sections redundant without incurring the unsustainable liability, implicit in tenure, to compensate dismissed staff for lifetime loss of earnings. The other, more directly menacing form was the allegation that universities were full of incompetent or inefficient academic staff, with the implication that such staff had been protected by their tenure from firm managerial action to dismiss them – which would now be expected to take place. In each case, it is debatable whether tenure had ever provided full protection – but equally, whether its legal abolition has in practice much altered managers' room for manoeuvre.

9   It should be noted, though, that neither of these proposals has been uncontested. In the case of tenure, the House of Lords (which includes a number of powerful national figures who can be relied on to speak for the universities) inserted a clause to make clear that academic freedom must be protected: in other words that dismissal could only take place on the grounds of redundancy or professional failure, and not of the adoption of unpopular views. Less dramatically, the proposed reductions in size of the governing bodies have not (yet) been fully enforced. As in Canada (see Jones, this volume) there seems to be some reluctance in government to demand immediate charter revisions, and a common technique for aligning charters with changing national expectations has been for the Privy Council to wait until a university needs to amend its charter for its own reasons (for example, to take account of internal restructuring), but then demand other amendments, such as streamlining its decision-making bodies, in line with current thinking. As Jones suggests, a wholly predictable consequence has been that universities may make great efforts to avoid making desirable internal changes which are inconsistent with a charter drafted many years earlier; or may decide to live dangerously in breach of their charters (see note 7, above).

10 The UGC had always acted selectively, and had never made public its judgements of individual institutions, but this had been tempered by the overall growth in the system which meant increased funding for virtually all institutions, albeit at different rates.

11 A term now used to describe colleges offering a mixture of higher education and further education (i.e. lower-level) courses.

12 A group of 10 'Colleges of Advanced Technology' which became universities in the early 1960s were, as their name implies, chiefly distinguishable from other 'Colleges of Technology', many of which emerged shortly afterwards as constituents of polytechnics, by the proportion of 'advanced', i.e. degree-level, courses which they offered.

13 The binary policy was designed *inter alia* to encourage the provision, and raise the status, of vocational courses. For a number of reasons, considerable cross-over ensued, with universities offering vocational courses in some fields and polytechnics offering academic courses where there was demand.

14 They were helped in the political argument by a number of factors including Thatcherite hostility to local government (which still owned and managed them); and by their perceived greater responsiveness to national agendas, notably cost efficiency (even though – or because – their apparently lower unit cost per student was primarily due to the fact that they were not research institutions) (Fulton 1991).

[15] Instructions from the Funding Council on the use and reporting of Council-provided funds.

[16] It is clear that the decision to fund research selectively rather than by formula was taken by government (and introduced step by step over the 1980s and early 1990s) with the strong support of leading researchers who were keen to protect their own share of a diminishing national resource (Kogan and Hanney 2000).

[17] In formal terms, categorical funding preserves institutional autonomy, since institutions have a free choice of whether or not to bid – and can submit bids which they have designed to be consistent with their institutional mission. The complaint from institutions during the late 1990s was that funding was so tight that they had little choice but to bid for virtually everything.

[18] Examples of such initiatives include funding for 'widening participation' and for developments in teaching and learning.

[19] This refers to employees who take action against fraud, corruption etc by their superiors – *in extremis* by going to the media – having exhausted routine opportunities for complaint. There have been very few such cases in higher education.

[20] As a member (elected academic representative) of my own university's Council, I have heard lay members referring to themselves quite unselfconsciously as 'non-executives', and challenging the moral right of 'executive' members to participate in the selection of a new Vice-Chancellor – despite this right being clearly defined in the university's charter and statutes.

[21] But this is still hotly contended.

[22] Most pre-92 universities have a 'Court', a large body with representation of a wide range of local interests. Generally, Courts meet once per year to receive the University's Annual Report presented by the Vice-Chancellor; elect some of their Councils' lay members; and have reserve powers (not normally exercised) including in some cases to approve amendments to the university's charter and statutes for recommendation to the Privy Council (see Moodie and Eustace 1974: 94 – 96).

[23] Except in Scotland, the director of a college is normally known as the principal and of a university as the vice-chancellor.

[24] Halsey and Trow (1971) rather oddly describe "the issue of democracy within the academic profession" as "pretty much neglected" by the new universities, despite acknowledging their increased emphasis on non-professorial representation in Senates and in committees. Nor do they mention student membership in this context.

[25] Indeed, the troubles of the Polytechnic of North London, which probably suffered more disruption from student militancy than any other UK institution in the late 1960s and early 1970s, were blamed by right-wing critics on the "domination" (36%) of its academic board by student representatives (Jacka et al., 1975, cited in Pratt 1997: 299).

[26] At least half of their governors were required to be 'independent' [of both the institution and the local education authority].

[27] It is also the case, of course, that most university Senates grew in size, and perhaps therefore in unwieldiness, over the period of expansion between the 1950s and the 1990s: partly as new disciplines and departments were added, partly as new constituencies were incorporated – not usually (unsurprisingly) at the expense of existing members.

[28] The experience of Warwick University, which was disrupted by its students –and heavily criticised by staff – for permitting 'undue influence' to a number of local industrialists co-opted onto its Council, presumably served to underline the risks involved (see Moodie and Eustace 1974: 234 – 241).

REFERENCES

Archer, M.S. *Social Origins of Educational Systems.* London: Sage, 1979.

Bargh, C., P. Scott and D. Smith. *Governing Universities: Changing the Culture?* Buckingham: Society for Research into Higher Education and Open University Press, 1996.

Clark, B.R. *The Higher Education System: Academic Organization in Cross-National Perspective.* Berkeley: University of California Press, 1983.

[Dearing Report] The National Committee of Inquiry into Higher Education. Higher Education in the Learning Society. London: HMSO, 1997.

Dearlove J. "The Role of the Academic Community in University Governance." *Higher Education Quarterly* 56.3 (2002 forthcoming).

Frazer M. "Report on the Modalities of External Evaluation of Higher Education in Europe: 1995-1997." *Higher Education in Europe* 22.3 (1997): 349 – 402.

Fulton O. "Slouching Towards a Mass System: Society, Government and Institutions in the United Kingdom." *Higher Education* 21 (1991): 589 – 605.

Fulton O. "Differentiation and Diversity in a Newly Unitary System: the case of the United Kingdom." In Meek, V.L., L. Goedegebuure, O. Kivinen and R. Rinne (eds). *The Mockers and Mocked: Comparative Perspectives on Differentiation, Convergence and Diversity in Higher Education* Oxford: Pergamon, 1996, 163 – 187.

Fulton O. and C. Holland (2001) "Profession or Proletariat: Academic Staff in the United Kingdom." In Enders, J. (ed). *Academic Staff in Europe: Changing Contexts and Conditions*. Westport, Conn.: Greenwood Press, 2001, 301 – 321.

Halsey A. H. and M. Trow. *The British Academics*. London: Faber & Faber, 1971.

Jacka K., C. Cox and M. Marks. *Rape of Reason: The Corruption of the Polytechnic of North London*. Lancing, Sussex: Churchill Press, 1975 [cited in Pratt (1997): 299].

[Jarratt Report] Committee of Vice-Chancellors and Principals (CVCP). Report of the Steering Committee for Efficiency Studies in Universities. London: CVCP, 1985.

Kogan M. and S. Hanney. *Reforming Higher Education*. London: Jessica Kingsley Publishers, 2000.

Kogan M, M. Bauer, I. Bleiklie and M. Henkel. *Transforming Higher Education*. London: Jessica Kingsley Publishers, 2000.

Moodie G. "Buffer, Coupling and Brake: Reflections on 60 Years of the UGC." *Higher Education* 12 (1983): 331 – 347.

Moodie G. and R. Eustace. *Power and Authority in British Universities*. London: Allen & Unwin, 1974.

Neave G. and F. van Vught. *Prometheus Bound: The Changing Relationship between Government and Higher Education in Western Europe*. Oxford: Pergamon, 1991.

Perkin H. *The Rise of Professional Society: England since 1880*. London: Routledge, 1989.

Pratt J. *The Polytechnic Experiment, 1965-1992*. Buckingham: Society for Research into Higher Education and Open University Press, 1997.

[Robbins Report] Higher Education: Report of the Committee appointed by the Prime Minister under the Chairmanship of Lord Robbins 1961-63. Cmnd. 2154 London: HMSO, 1963.

Salter B. and T. Tapper. *The State and Higher Education*. Ilford: Woburn Press, 1994.

Scott P. *The Meanings of Mass Higher Education*. Buckingham: Society for Research into Higher Education and Open University Press, 1995.

Shattock M. *The UGC and the Management of British Universities*. Buckingham: Society for Research into Higher Education and Open University Press, 1994.

Shattock M. "Governance and Management in Universities: The Way We Live Now." *Journal of Education Policy* 14.3 (1999): 271 – 282.

Shattock, M. "University Governance Reforms Post-Dearing: First Steps Towards or Away from 'Shared Governance.'" *Higher Education Quarterly* 56.3 (2002 forthcoming).

Van Vught, F. (ed). *Governmental Strategies and Innovation in Higher Education*. London: Jessica Kingsley Publishers, 1989.

GLEN A. JONES

THE STRUCTURE OF UNIVERSITY GOVERNANCE IN CANADA: A POLICY NETWORK APPROACH

1. INTRODUCTION

Research on higher education governance in the United States and Canada has tended to emphasize the importance of a number of analytical approaches (Birnbaum 1988; Hardy 1990; Pusser and Ordorika 2001). While these approaches are frequently discussed as 'models' of higher education governance, they are perhaps best understood as different organisational frames or analytical lenses. The bureaucratic frame, for example, applies Weber's characteristics of bureaucracy to the university setting in order to illustrate a rational arrangement of hierarchical authority relationships (Stroup 1966). The collegial frame begins with the assumption that the university can be understood as a community of scholars where decisions are made by consensus (Goodman 1962; Millet 1962), while the political frame described by Baldridge (1971) assumes that the university is a pluralistic entity where the decision making process involves a competition between competing individual and group interests. Other analytical frames have included organised anarchy (Cohen and March 1974), professional bureaucracy (Mintzberg 1991), and 'mixed models' that attempt to combine different frames and/or relate these frames to theories of organisational culture (Hardy 1990; Pusser and Ordorika 2001). While each of these frames contributes to our understanding of different ways of understanding university governance and decision making, the utility of each approach in the empirical analysis of university governance is limited since each begins with a template of normative characteristics. What one sees depends on the lens that one has chosen to look through, and yet many observers have noted that elements of each frame can be found in the same institution.

This study utilizes the concept of policy networks and employs a structural approach to understanding these networks (Coleman and Skogstad 1990). The central assumption is that policy decisions are made by policy networks. At the core of the policy network is the governing body, agency, and/or official that has been assigned formal authority over this area of policy. The approach emphasizes the importance of understanding the formal structure of the governance process and how these arrangements or structures are understood by those who play a formal role in this process. At the same time the approach allows for the possibility that policy networks might include other groups, organisations, and/or individuals who have a particular interest in the policy arena and who play an active role in attempting to influence policy decisions. Rather than begin with normative assumptions on the

Alberto Amaral, Glen A. Jones and Berit Karseth (eds.), Governing Higher Education: National Perspectives on Institutional Governance, 213—234.
© 2002 *Kluwer Academic Publishers. Printed in the Netherlands.*

character of university governance, this approach presumes that the character of decision-making is largely a function of the interactions within the policy network.

The focus of this paper is on institution-level policy networks at Canadian universities with a particular emphasis on the formal structures of university governance and the ways in which faculty and students, both through these formal structures and through the work of associations that represent their interests, participate in these networks. By focusing on universities across Canada I will attempt to provide a broad, national portrait of these governance arrangements, but it is important to recognize that there are differences in these policy networks by institution. Aside from differences in institution-level policy networks by university, it is also important to note that there are policy networks operating at the federal and provincial system levels of authority that significantly influence institution-level arrangements (see, for example, Cameron 1991; Jones 1996; Jones, Shanahan and Goyan 2002; Tudivor 1999), but which are largely excluded from this analysis. At the same time, there are also policy networks at other organisational levels within universities (for example, policy networks within departments, faculties, or service units) that are only briefly discussed in the paper.

My analysis employs data from five different but related studies[1] conducted over a seven-year period. In 1993 and 1994 I conducted 20 in-depth, open-ended interviews with university leaders (including 6 university presidents as well as faculty and student association presidents) in four Canadian provinces. These interviews included questions on institution-level policy networks in order to obtain a preliminary understanding of these arrangements at six Canadian universities. In 1993 I conducted a study of institution-level student associations at Canadian universities and community colleges (Jones 1995). Bilingual questionnaires were sent to the president or senior official of 238 organisations asking for information on the structure and goals of these organisations and the ways in which these organisations attempt to influence institutional and provincial system policy. A total of 100 questionnaires were returned for a response rate of 42%. Barbara Anderson and I conducted a similar study of university faculty associations in 1994 (Anderson and Jones 1998). In this study, bilingual questionnaires were sent to 78 institution-level university faculty associations and we received 44 responses, a response rate of 56%. In 1995 Michael Skolnik and I conducted a two-phase study of Canadian university governing boards (Jones and Skolnik 1997). In the first phase, we obtained data from board secretaries at 45 institutions (75% of provincial government-supported universities in Canada) on board structure, composition, and basic operating arrangements. In the second phase we sent questionnaires to all governing board members at all participating institutions. The response rate for the survey of governing board members was 49% (583 of a population of 1191). Finally, in 1999 Theresa Shanahan, Paul Goyan and I conducted a study of Canadian university senates using the same two-phase approach that had been employed in the governing board study (Jones, Shanahan, and Goyan 2001). We received data on the structure, composition, and basic operating arrangements of the university senate from 42 institutions, and we received questionnaire responses from 890 senate members for a response rate of 40 percent.

The paper has been organised into three major sections. I will begin by reviewing the legislative foundation of Canadian universities and the implications of their legal status and distinct charters. The second section focuses on the university policy networks and analyses the work and role of the university governing boards, senate, central administration, faculty association, student association, and other participants. I conclude the paper with a discussion of key issues concerning university governance in Canada.

2. THE LEGISLATIVE FOUNDATION

In legal terms, Canadian universities have always been created as corporations. Until the creation of the Canadian federation in 1867, the source of this corporate charter varied by region and historical period. Several universities in what is now Quebec were originally created under papal authority, while other institutions were created by colonial legislatures, or Royal (English sovereign) Charter (Cameron 1991; Jones 1996). Under the British North America Act of 1867, the British legislation that created the Canadian federation of several colonies, the responsibility for education was assigned to the provinces, rather than the new federal government, and the provinces became the legislative authority for the creation of new universities[2].

There are several characteristics of the legal foundation of Canadian universities that become extremely important to the discussion of university governance. The first is that Canada's public universities are legally chartered as private not-for-profit corporations. They are private in the sense that they are not owned by the state, though one would suspect that the government's interest in these publicly supported institutions would be clearly established if one of these private corporations were ever dissolved. In terms of the legal status of a corporation, Hatton has noted:

> Once created or sanctioned by the state, the corporation is autonomous, self-sufficient, and self-renovating, governing itself by means of an internal constitution outlined in a set of bylaws. In concert with autonomy and self-sufficiency, a corporation is characterized by perpetual succession. In this sense, members may come and go, directors may die or retire, shareholders may sell their shares or go insane, but the corporation continues (Hatton 1990: 2).

Not-for-profit corporations do not have shareholders and they are subject to different tax and reporting arrangements than for-profit corporations, but their status as a 'fictitious person in law' allows them to hire staff, enter into contracts, sue and be sued, and own property.

The second important characteristic of their legal foundation is that, with a small number of exceptions, each Canadian university was established by a unique legislative charter. Each charter names the university and describes the institution-level governance arrangement through which the decisions of the corporation will be determined. While there are many common elements in terms of these governance arrangements, each charter is unique and there are substantive differences in terms of the composition of governing bodies and the language used to describe the powers and responsibilities of these bodies. Aside from creating the corporation and establishing the basic governance arrangements, these charters assume that the corporation will determine what it will do and how it will administer its affairs. At the same time, a university that determines that its governance arrangement should be substantively reformed must seek provincial government approval, in the form of a legislative amendment to the charter, to do so. A number of the university officials I have interviewed have indicated a reluctance to move in this direction since, in opening a discussion of the charter, there is a concern that the government might decide to make changes above and beyond those requested by the institution.

The formal governance arrangement articulated in most Canadian university corporate charters is bicameral, that is, the legislation creates two university governing bodies and describes the division of responsibilities between these two entities. A number of scholars have reviewed the historical evolution of bicameralism in Canadian university governance (Cameron 1991; Jones 1996) and the origins of this framework are frequently traced to a 1906 Royal Commission on the University of Toronto[3]. The new governance arrangement that emerged following the Commission's report represented an attempt to distance the University from the direct political interference of the provincial government. Rather than view the publicly supported university as an arm of the state, the Commission argued that the university should be an autonomous, self-governing entity where provincial government interests would be delegated to a governing board dominated by government-appointed lay members. The governing board would assume overall responsibility for the administrative affairs of the institution, including the appointment of the president and other staff, and financial matters. The Commission noted that it had been impressed with the governing board arrangements it had observed when visiting a number of new American state universities.

At the same time, the Commission was also aware of the academic oligarchic arrangements associated with elite British universities and argued that a university senate should be assigned authority over academic matters. Bicameralism represented a governance structure that attempted to balance the need for external accountability to the state which financially supported the institution with the need for the participation of the professoriate in decisions that focused on academic standards.

The recommendations of the Commission were quickly adopted by the Government of Ontario through the approval of the University of Toronto Act of 1906. This governance framework influenced the legislation creating new universities in Western provinces and was gradually adopted by other institutions. By the 1950s, bicameralism had become the dominant model for university governance in Canadian universities.

Calls for greater faculty and student participation in university governance in the 1960s let to important governance reforms at most Canadian universities. While a national review led by Sir James Duff and Robert Berdahl provided recommendations on governance reform (1966), the response to local pressures to increase the participation of students on the university senate, allow for greater internal constituency participation on the governing board, and generally create a more open and transparent governance process, was institution-specific. Most university charters were amended by government in response to recommendations from the university, and these reforms to the legislative foundations of these institutions generally took the form of changes to the composition of the board and modifications to the composition and scope of authority of the senate. For most universities, the reform of university governance in the 1960s and 1970s involving tinkering with, rather than abandoning, bicameral governance structures.

Most of the new universities that emerged as a function of the massification of higher education in Canada were also assigned bicameral governance structures though sometimes under omnibus rather than institution-specific legislation[4]. The new University of Quebec was created as a multicampus provincial system with a central governing body but with a bicameral governance arrangements at each constituent university involving an administrative council and an academic council. Bicameral governance structures were also legislated for the new universities that emerged in the province of Ontario, though for several of these institutions the charter legislation abandoned the notion of government-appointed lay members in favour of members appointed by the board itself – an important modification given the assumption that the board plays a role in representing the public interest.

The University of Toronto chose a very different path and consciously abandoned bicameralism in favour of the creation of a single governing council that included representation from both external (including a substantive number of members appointed by government) and internal (including faculty, student, and staff) constituencies. While the reform was designed to avoid the problems of bifurcated decision making through the creation of a single community governing body, faculty leaders soon perceived a loss of faculty influence over traditional academic governance. This concern later was addressed through the delegation of considerable authority to each of three boards. The Academic Board has been assigned a central role in academic policy and has a composition that closely resembles the university senate at other Canadian universities. The Business Board, with lay-members in the majority, deals with financial matters.

In summary, Canadian universities are created as private not-for-profit corporations. The legal foundation for most universities is a unique charter that creates a bicameral governance arrangement with authority delegated between an administrative governing board and an academic senate. In situations of conflict between the bodies, the governing board is regarded as the superior of the two, though it is important to note that at most universities the academic senate is created by the charter legislation; the senate is not a creature of the board as is the case in some jurisdictions. Finally, it is important to note that the charter legislation provides these governing bodies with significant substantive and procedural autonomy, to use Berdahl's terms (1971), to act in the best interests of the university. While there are limitations to this autonomy, especially in terms of government steering through regulations attached to operating grant and targeted funding mechanisms, Canadian universities continue to enjoy relatively high levels of institutional autonomy compared to universities in many other jurisdictions (Jones 1996; McDaniel 1996), and the formal university governance structure is assigned considerable flexibility in terms of determining what the university will do and how it will accomplish its mission.

3. UNIVERSITY POLICY NETWORKS

The charter legislation of most Canadian universities implies at least three sources of decision-making. The governing board is assigned responsibility for administrative matters while the senate is assigned responsibility for academic matters. The third source of decision-making is the central administration of the university. The board is charged with the authority to appoint the university president (sometimes referred to as a principal or rector) who is assigned responsibility for the day-to-day affairs of the university, and who, in turn, often determines or recommends the delegation of administrative authority within a central administrative structure specific to that university. In addition to the governing board, senate, and central administration, the university policy networks at each institution include a number of other influential actors that play an important role in institutional decision making. At all Canadian universities this policy network includes student organisations and faculty associations, and at some universities there are still other participants who play a role in shaping institutional policy. In this section of the paper I will draw on the data sources described above to elaborate on each of these major components of the university policy network.

3.1. The governing board

The national study conducted by Jones and Skolnik (1997) provides a useful overview of the membership and work of Canadian university governing boards[5] and the perceptions of governing board members. Recognizing that there are substantive differences by institution, this study provided a national overview by collecting data from 45 universities and the findings described below represent average or aggregate responses from all participating institutions and board members.

The composition of the governing board is normally stated in the university's legislative charter, and membership is commonly described in terms of specific categories or constituencies. In terms of how individuals become members of the governing board, approximately one quarter are appointed by government, one quarter are elected by a constituency, and one quarter are appointed by the board itself. The remaining members are ex-officio (that is, they are members of the board because of the employment position they hold), appointed by some other organisation (for example, the university alumni association) or appointed to the board by the academic senate. The average size of Canadian university governing boards is 27 members.

Approximately one-third of all board members are from constituencies inside the university. The largest categories of internal members are faculty (17% of all board members), and students (9% of all board members). The university president is a voting member at all universities. In addition, at some institutions, board membership includes other senior university administrators and/or support staff representation.

Two-thirds of all board members are from outside the university community. Approximately half of all board members can be categorized as lay-members, and almost all of these individuals are either appointed by government or by the board. Ninety percent of all governing boards also include representation from the graduates of the university, often selected or elected by the university alumni association.

Board members tend to be mature, well-educated individuals. Two-thirds of all board members are between the ages of 46 and 65 and approximately 25% are between 51 and 55 years of age. In terms of education, over 90% have at least a baccalaureate or professional degree and almost all members have some level of postsecondary education. Slightly less than one-quarter of all members hold a doctorate, and half of all members have completed some level of graduate education. It is interesting to note that the majority (59%) were board members at the same university where they had once been a student.

The majority of board members are male. Approximately 64% of members indicated that they were male and 34% indicated that they were female, and this ratio was the essentially the same for both inside and outside members.

In terms of the occupation of board members, 37% indicated that they were employed in the education sector, a figure that includes most of the board members who are from 'inside' the university community, as well as faculty and administrators from other universities or employees of the school sector. Other common occupational sectors included business (26%, frequently business executives), and professions (13%, with law, accounting and medicine as the most frequent responses). Eleven percent of board members indicated other occupational sectors, with non-profit sector enterprises and government as the largest subcategories, and 11% of board members indicated that they were retired.

Most board members are volunteers who are not remunerated for the time they devote to board activities[6]. The average number of hours per month that board members indicated spending on board and board committee work (including preparing for and attending meetings) was 10.3, with approximately 20% of members indicating that they spend five or less hours per month and another 20% indicating that they work 15 hours or more each month on board business. Over 85% of members indicated that they were active members of the board, with 4% of outside members (and no inside members) strongly indicating that they were not active.

On average, university boards meet eight times each year. All of the boards surveyed in the Jones and Skolnik study had created standing committees that provided recommendations to the board on some area of policy. Most boards had created bylaws that described the composition and terms of reference of standing committees and, in some situations, delegated board authority over certain types of decisions to these committees. Most boards had created an executive committee that created the agenda for board meetings, including determining what matters would go before the board, and routed board business through the standing committee process. Two-thirds of governing boards reported that their meetings are open to the general public, though certain items of business (for example, personnel matters) are conducted in closed session.

The majority of board members indicated that they were able to influence board decisions. Approximately 75% indicated that they receive the information that they need to make decisions with about 21% of outside members (and 9% of inside members) reporting that they receive 'too much' information from the university. While the majority of board members indicated that they 'know the organisational structure of the university,' 80% of inside members and only 40% of outside members agreed strongly with this statement.

The Jones and Skolnik (1997) study found that there was considerable consensus in terms of board member perceptions of the role of the board. Board members believed that the board should act in the best interests of the university, it should be the final authority for approving major institutional policies, it should act as a 'watchdog' on behalf of the public interest, and it should ask 'tough questions' of senior university administrators. Board members indicated that the board could and should do more in terms of reviewing the performance of the university president, lobbying for change in government policy, and periodically reviewing the performance of the board.

The findings of the study suggest that board members believe that these boards are functioning reasonably well. Members believe that they have the information and knowledge necessary to make decisions that are in the best interests of the university, and while they identified areas of weakness, they generally indicated that they were satisfied with the work of the board.

3.2. The senate

Of the 45 institutions that participated in the Jones and Skolnik (1997) study of governing boards, 39 (87%) indicated that they had a bicameral governance structure while 5 indicated that the governance structure of the university was unicameral (that is, with all authority vested in a single body). Even unicameral governing bodies, however, have created some senior academic decision making body to provide recommendations to the board on academic matters. In 1999, Jones, Shanahan, and Goyan (2001) conducted a national study of academic senates[7] and their findings provide a useful overview of this component of Canadian university governance.

The senate is a larger body than the university governing board. The average size of the academic senate in the Jones, Shanahan and Goyan (2001) study was 58, though there was considerable variation in senate size by institution ranging from less than twenty to several hundred members. Senate membership is usually described in terms of different constituencies, and most members are elected to the senate from within a specific constituency. While the majority of board members are from outside the university community, the vast majority of senate members are from internal constituencies, in fact only 5% of all senate members are from specific external constituencies (approximately 3% are lay-members and 2% are alumni representatives). In order to facilitate communication between the board and the senate, approximately 3% of all senate members are appointed by and from the membership of the board.

The largest single category of senate members is faculty (44% of all senate members). All university senates include student members (17% of all senate members). In addition to faculty and students, a significant number of senate members are ex officio in that their senate membership is a function of holding a specific academic administrative appointment within the university. For example, approximately 11% of all senate members are university vice-presidents or deans and an additional 11% of senate members hold other senior positions such as registrars, or directors of academic service units. Including the university president, who is a member of most senates, roughly one-quarter of all senate members hold administrative positions within the university. Since many of these academic administrators hold faculty appointments in the university their participation can be viewed as increasing faculty representation, but their membership also means that there is a substantive administrative presence on the senate and that many of the individuals that will be making recommendations on academic policy are members of the body that is charged with making decisions on these matters. Other senate members may include the university chancellor, representatives of university support staff (3% of all senate members) and representatives of federated colleges (3% of all senate members, and many of these individuals also hold faculty appointments within the university).

On average, senate members reported spending 6.5 hours per month preparing for and attending meetings of the senate and senate committees. Like the boards, senates have created standing committee structures governed by senate-approved bylaws and most have an executive committee that determines the agenda of senate meetings and oversees the movement of policy matters through the committees and to the senate. Most senate members characterize themselves as active members who are able to influence senate decisions, receive the information necessary to make decisions, and are knowledgeable about the structure and organisation of the university.

However, compared to the findings of the governing boards study, senate members indicated less satisfaction with the overall work of the senate and there were indications of discordance between the role that they believed the senate should play and the role that they believe the senate does play within university governance. Less than half of senate members view the senate as an 'effective' decision making body, though 64% indicated that it plays an important role as a forum for discussing issues. There was considerable agreement that the senate is, and should be, the final authority on issues of academic policy, though one interpretation of senate member responses is that there is a degree of ambiguity over the boundaries of the notion of 'academic' matters. Senate members believed that the senate should play a role in university budget matters, in determining the future direction of the university, in research policy, and in determining the priorities for fundraising and development activities. Senate members indicated that the senate does not currently play the role that it should in these policy areas at many universities.

Many senate members also indicated that the university provides little in the way of orientation to new members on the role of the senate and the work of senate members. They also indicated that few senates review their own performance, though most indicated that the senate should periodically review its work and role in university governance.

The findings of this study suggest that senates are large, participatory decision making bodies. The vast majority of members are from constituencies inside the university and there is significant representation from faculty, students, and academic administrators. While most members characterized themselves as active and knowledgeable, many believe that the senate should play a stronger role in a number of important policy areas within university governance. While most members believe that the senate continues to play an important role in university governance, only a minority of senate members believe that the senate is an effective decision making body.

3.3. Administration

Most Canadian universities have a chancellor as the titular head of the institution. While the chancellor is frequently an ex officio member of the governing board (and, in some cases, the senate), this individual's formal responsibilities within the university are largely ceremonial. These ceremonial duties frequently include officiating at the university's convocation ceremonies.

The senior officer of the university is the president, sometimes referred to as the rector or principal. Perhaps as a mechanism for avoiding confusion over the different titles used at different universities, the Association of Universities and Colleges of Canada uses the term 'Chief Executive Officer' to describe this position, though this may also reflect the way in which the role is perceived by this association of university presidents. Regardless of the title, this senior officer is appointed by, and reports to, the board of governors of the university. While the final decision on appointment is assigned to the board under charter legislation[8], it is now common practice for the governing board to create a search committee that includes representation from major university constituencies, including members of the board, members of the senate, faculty, students, and university administration. The search committee, frequently assisted by a private personnel consulting agency employed by the university, reviews the needs of the university, conducts a national search, interviews candidates, and provides the governing board with a recommendation. University presidents are usually former faculty members (frequently faculty who have obtained previous academic administrative experience as department chairs, deans or vice-presidents). The president is a member of the governing board and frequently a member of the senate.

Aside from the fact that all universities have a president, the administrative structure of the university is idiosyncratic to the specific institution based on decisions made by the governing board on the recommendation of the president. Most universities have at least two vice-presidents: an academic vice-president, sometimes called a provost, who plays a leading role in academic policy; and an administrative vice-president who supervises the administrative affairs of the university including finance and budget issues. Department heads or chairs report to the deans of each faculty which, in turn, report to the academic vice-president. It is difficult to generalize, however, beyond the basic notion that there is a central administrative structure unique to the institution[9]. Aside from differences in the organisational arrangements of senior personnel, it is also important to note that there are differences in terms of the ways in which certain types of authority are centralized within the central administration of the university, or decentralized in that departments or faculties are given considerable autonomy over decisions associated with the unit (see, for example, Hardy 1996).

While there are important institutional differences in terms of administrative structure, there are a number of common practices that are important to the discussion of university governance. For example, it is the central administration of the university, often represented by the president, which plays the lead role in terms of the interface between the university and the provincial government. The president articulates the needs and interests of the university within what Clark refers to as the superstructure of the higher education system (1983).

Second, it is important to note that the same participatory processes employed in the appointment of a president are also utilized in the appointment of other senior officers of the university, including academic deans. A search committee, which includes faculty and student representation, will be created to review the needs of the position and make recommendations on the appointment.

Finally, most universities have created committees at almost every level of the institution that provide advice to university officials. There will normally be committee structures at the department and faculty levels, as well as committees dealing with university service units. These committees generally include faculty and student members. In addition, the university will frequently create ad hoc committees to provide recommendations on specific policy issues.

In summary, all universities have a central administrative structure that is approved by the board of governors of the university, usually based on the advice of the president. This administrative structure is responsible for the day-to-day administration of the university as well as providing recommendations on policy to the formal structures of university governance. There are committees that include faculty and student representation at all levels of the university.

3.4. Faculty associations

While a number of institution-based faculty associations were created in the period from 1920 to 1950 as a means of ensuring that the governing board and administration were aware of the interests of the faculty (Nelson 1993), it was the recession of the 1970s that catalysed the emergence of the modern Canadian faculty association and its role in university governance. Following a mammoth expansion of Canadian higher education in the 1960s, the recession of the early 1970s forced many provincial governments to control expenditures. The universities, which had become accustomed to significant annual increases in operating support, suddenly found themselves dealing with grant levels that were lower than anticipated. The universities, in turn, began to look for ways of reducing expenditures, and given that the largest single area of expenditure was faculty salaries, faculty members began to look for mechanisms for ensuring that their interests were dealt with appropriately in the new budgetary environment.

The answer for faculty at many Canadian universities was collective bargaining. As Neil Tudivor has noted, "by the mid-1980s the landscape was transformed, with over 50% of faculty unionised on 29 campuses" (1999: 85). A new group of faculty associations unionised in the 1990s in response to new waves of government cutbacks and corresponding concerns about the impact of these cuts on faculty job security, salary, and other workplace issues.

Unionisation changed the decision-making processes within Canadian universities in a number of important ways. Unionisation meant that the governing board of the university could no longer unilaterally determine faculty salaries. Salaries became a key component of the collective agreement negotiated between the unionised faculty association and the university governing board. The same became true for a range of issues associated with the work of faculty that became part of collective agreements, including: the definition of academic freedom, procedures for new faculty appointments, faculty tenure and promotion; workload; professional development support; and other issues associated with the relationship between the faculty member and the university. The negotiated procedures for decisions concerning faculty appointments (including new appointments, tenure and promotion) not only specify the steps in the process, but also frequently prescribe the membership of relevant committees and the role of academic administrators. Prior to unionisation, many of these issues had been subject to administrative discretion, in fact while many universities had long awarded tenured appointments it was not unusual for this decision to be made based on the recommendation of a department head or dean without a formal review process (see Horn 1999).

Not all Canadian university faculty associations are unionised, but even non-unionised associations have often reached a contractual agreement with their governing board that specifies salary arrangements and many of the appointment and workplace issues that would be found in a collective agreement. This 'special plan bargaining' implies a relationship that is somewhere between consultation and certification (Anderson and Jones 1998; Ponak and Thompson 1984).

Unionised or non-unionised, all Canadian universities have a faculty association that represents its members in discussions or negotiations with the central governance and administrative structures of the university. The way in which membership in the association is defined varies by association, though most include all full-time faculty and many include part-time faculty. Membership may also be extended to other groups such as laboratory instructors or librarians. Faculty members pay a fee to the association, often a percentage of salary, which funds the operating costs of the association. Most faculty associations have paid staff who provide administrative or technical support for the work of the association. The president of the association is either elected by the members (91% of associations) or elected/appointed by an association committee or council (9% of associations) (Anderson and Jones 1998).

National survey responses from faculty leaders suggested that the three greatest priority areas in terms of the activities of faculty associations were "negotiating salaries and benefits" with the university, "assisting members with grievances", and "influencing university policies" (Anderson and Jones 1998). These three areas of activity were ranked highest by both certified and non-certified associations. Other association activities included providing faculty members with information on university policy, attempting to influence government policy, and organising professional development activities or materials for faculty.

Most faculty associations attempt to influence university policy through the certified or special plan bargaining process, through monitoring and participating in the formal governance structures of the university, and through regular interaction with the central administration of the university. Faculty association leaders generally meet weekly or monthly with representatives of the central administration of the university, and university administrators will frequently ask representatives of the association for advice or assistance on certain policy matters.

3.5. Student associations

Student associations have played a role in student life on Canadian university campuses throughout the history of these institutions. While these early associations were primarily focused on the organisation of extra-curricular activities, they frequently played a role in terms of representing the interests of their members through interactions with the central administration of the university. With the reform of university governance in the 1960s and 1970s, the participation of students in university governance increased and student organisations came to play a formal and legitimised role within the decision-making structures of the university (Jones 1995).

Every Canadian university has at least one institution-level student association, and in some cases there are several organisations operating at the institutional level where each represents a specific component of the student population. For example, there may be a single organisation for all students, or all undergraduate students may belong to one organisation and all graduate students belong to a second. Regardless of the organisational arrangements, all students are automatic members of at least one university-level organisation. Student association fees are usually mandatory and collected by the university at the time of registration. These fees are then transferred to the student association, which is frequently charted as an independent, not-for-profit corporation. Student associations have their own internal decision making structures, often led by a president elected by the membership. A 1993 survey of student organisations noted that, on average, Canadian university-level student associations collected over $300,000 in fee revenue and employed seven full-time staff to support the activities of the association.

Student associations are involved in a wide range of activities, including operating service businesses (such as photocopy services, pubs and restaurants), publishing a student newspaper, organising social activities, funding student groups or clubs, and providing students with academic services. However, student leaders ranked "influencing institutional policies," "monitoring institutional policies," and "helping students through 'institutional red-tape'" as the three highest priority activities of these associations.

In the 1993 study, all student associations reported that they attempt to influence university policy. Their participation in university governance includes formal student representation on governing boards and university senates, membership on university advisory committees and task forces, and through regular interaction with the central administration of the university. Student leaders reported that they meet weekly or monthly with university officials to discuss university policy and student issues, and over 80% indicated that representatives of the university frequently ask the association or advice for assistance on policy matters. Approximately 56% of student association respondents reported that the association has "some influence" on university policy, and 27% indicated that the association has a "strong influence" (Jones 1995).

3.6. Other participants

At some universities other groups and organisations play a role in university governance in addition to the parties described above. The university alumni association, whose members are sometimes represented on the university governing board and/or senate, may also play a role in governance through representation on internal committee structures, ongoing interaction with the central administration, and through its direct involvement in and policy influence over fund raising and development activities.

Other employee groups may also play an active role within the university policy network. Unionised support staff associations, for example, may play a role in governance beyond simply representing the interests of their members through collective bargaining. Of increasing importance at some universities has been the rise of unionised associations representing the interests of part-time faculty, that is, the emergence of an association distinct from the traditional faculty association wholly focused on part-time faculty issues, as well as separate associations representing teaching assistants (who are frequently graduate students).

4. CANADIAN UNIVERSITY POLICY NETWORKS

Most of the research literature on university governance in Canada has focused on the evolution and central principles associated with bicameralism, and on the composition of governing boards and senates (Jones and Skolnik 1997). In this paper I have attempted to expand the discussion by moving beyond the basic structural elements of bicameral governance and review the findings of a series of complementary national studies that focus on the work of governing bodies and relevant associations and the perceptions of board and senate members and association leaders.

While the legislative foundation of most Canadian universities created an internal governance structure involving an administrative governing board and an academic senate, the charters also provided institutions with the flexibility to determine in operational terms how these bodies would make decisions, the administrative structure appropriate to the needs of the university, and, within the broad parameters established by legislation, to make decisions on how the university would be governed. Over time these governance arrangements have come to include standing committee structures, administrative appointment procedures focusing on the work of search committees that include representation from a variety of constituencies, complex administrative structures, and the participation of faculty and student organisations. The charter for each institution is unique, but in addition to the differences in governance arrangements prescribed by the charter, institutions have also created idiosyncratic administrative arrangements and found somewhat different answers to the question of how to organise the governance process in order to meet the needs of the institution. While the discussion above has attempted to highlight a number of the common structural elements associated with Canadian university governance, it is important to recognize that each university has a unique policy network.

While the arrangements are unique, there are a number of common issues associated with Canadian university governance. I will focus on three issues, the structure and balance of participation, the boundaries of authority, and the capacity for governance reform, and then conclude the paper with a number of observations on policy networks as a conceptual framework for understanding Canadian university governance.

4.1. The structure and balance of participation

The governance reform process of the 1960s and 1970s shifted the balance of representation in university governance in order to allow for greater student and faculty participation. One of the issues facing university governance is whether the structure and balance of representation that emerged three decades ago is still appropriate.

The governance reform process predated the rise of faculty unionisation. If the level of faculty participation on university senates and boards was designed to ensure that faculty interests were appropriately represented in the governance process, then unionisation clearly shifted this balance further in favour of the faculty. A number of scholars have noted that unionisation probably decreased the authority of the senate (Cameron 1991; Penner 1994).

These governance arrangements also defined constituencies in ways that addressed the needs of the 1970s, but may not address more recent changes within the university. For example, part-time faculty are seldom represented within the formal decision making structures of the university, and yet they play an increasingly important role in university teaching. Faculty and student members are often elected or appointed from constituencies that are defined by traditional discipline boundaries, and yet many of the very difficult policy issues that universities face involve an attempt to move toward the more equitable participation of groups that are defined in quite different ways, such as by gender, race, and sexual orientation. Structures of representation based on traditional discipline boundaries may also fail to address the special interests of interdisciplinary educational programming and research initiatives. Universities have created a wide range of specialized technical, administrative, and support staff positions that simply did not exist at the time when the formal governing structures of the university were debated, positions ranging from sexual harassment officers to information technology specialists. The issue here is not whether every new category of interest should be officially represented within the formal governance structures of the university, but rather whether the structural assumptions that underscored the patterns of representation articulated within the governance structure continue to be appropriate.

Another issue concerns the level of participation. The formal governance structure at all Canadian universities assumes the participation of faculty, students, and other members of the university and external communities. In addition to these formal structures and associated committees, most universities have also created a host of other advisory committees, not to mention issue-specific task forces and policy review processes. However, the fact that the enrolment of Canadian universities has continued to expand while the number of full-time faculty has gradually declined has placed increasing pressure on faculty workloads. Participation in university governance may be regarded as an important service activity, but some believe that the time available for service activities is being squeezed by the much greater professional and institutional rewards associated with research and teaching. Part of the problem may simply be that the committee structure has expanded in response to new policy issues and university activities, and that a review of these arrangements could lead to a consolidation of committee arrangements while maintaining the principle of faculty and student participation. However, it is important to note that Canadian university governance relies heavily on the expertise and judgement of individuals who either work for free or whose contribution represents an opportunity cost in terms of pursuing activities that would bring greater career rewards – a phenomenon that would be unthinkable, and probably unsustainable, in the for-profit corporate sector.

4.2. The boundaries of authority

There are three types of recurring boundary issues in Canadian university governance. The first, assumed by the basic structure of bicameralism, involves the boundary between 'administrative' and 'academic' decisions. Almost all budgetary decisions have an impact on the academic work of the university, and almost all academic decisions have resource implications. At most universities the boundaries of authority between the governing board and the academic senate have been negotiated over time, but while governing board members appear satisfied with the role of the board, senate members believe that the role of the senate should be strengthened to include a greater role in the budget process and in establishing the future direction of the university. Two faculty senate members at Trent University recently initiated a court challenge to a governing board decision to close a university residence facility that had been opposed by the university senate, arguing that the decision involved an academic matter under the authority of the senate. The court sided with the governing board, though this decision is currently being appealed. The boundaries between academic and administrative policy matters are often ambiguous, but given the superior authority of the board, disputes on these boundary issues are often resolved in favour of the 'administrative' perspective. This may be an expedient means of resolving boundary issues, but the findings of the senate study described above suggest that there may also be a need to create a forum for identifying the basic principles that underscore the division of responsibility between these two governing bodies so that both have a clearer understanding of how each contributes to the governance process.

The second type of issue concerns the boundary between the executive authority of the university president (and the central administration) and governing authority of the board and senate. The governing bodies have a responsibility to make decisions that are in the best interests of the university, but the central administration plays a key role in determining the information that these bodies will receive in order to make these decisions. The authors of one Ontario report noted that governing boards do not always receive the information they should receive in order to fulfil their role in terms of public accountability (Task Force 1993). At the same time, some university presidents that I have interviewed have provided examples of governing board members who wanted to move well beyond their role as governors into the day-to-day administration of the university. This boundary issue is being further exacerbated by the increasing complexity of the system-level policy environment in many provinces and new federal government research funding initiatives, changes that frequently require that the executive officers of the university engage in complex negotiations and respond quickly to what are perceived to be fleeting opportunities. These initiatives reinforce the importance of executive authority in the context of issues that may have significant policy implications for universities.

The third type of boundary of authority issue concerns the ways in which academic/administrative and executive/governance boundaries are negotiated for new policy issues. In this complex governance arrangement, who should have authority over a policy issue that the university has never dealt with before? Universities are now dealing with a range of new policy issues, such as issues related to intellectual property, research ethics, new relationships with industry, and new forms of fundraising and development arrangements. Given a governance structure based on a division of authority, who should have authority in a situation where the assignment is far from clear?

4.3. The capacity for governance reform

The high level of institutional autonomy of Canadian universities presumes that these institutions have the capacity for self-government, and the findings of the studies discussed above do not allow one to conclude that there is a 'crisis' in Canadian university governance. These institutions have weathered many storms in the last decade, from increased enrolment to major funding cuts, from new accountability requirements to dramatic changes in research policy, and while it is impossible to determine whether the institutional responses to these external pressures represented the 'best' decisions, the universities clearly demonstrated their capacity to make decisions through their governance structures.

At the same time, the findings do suggest that there may be a need to review the role of senate in the context of bicameral governance, to seek greater clarity on the division of responsibility within university policy networks and the boundaries of authority, and to consider whether the structure and balance of participation in university governance continues to be appropriate. Given that universities operate under unique charters, and that the governance arrangement at each institution has evolved in unique ways, the response to these issues will vary by university.

However, the findings of the studies described above might lead one to question whether most Canadian universities have the capacity to reform their governance arrangements. A key limitation to this capacity is the fact that changes to the basic structure and composition of university governing bodies cannot be made without the approval of government, and some institutions may be reluctant to move in the direction of reforms that require government sanction. Another limitation is that most governing boards and senates do not review their own performance to determine whether there may be ways of improving the current governance arrangements. The absence of any periodic self-assessment or feedback mechanism means that these university governing bodies have a limited capacity to improve themselves. Finally, few universities place much emphasis on orienting new board and senate members to their role as institutional governors, perhaps based on an implicit assumption that new members come to the table with the knowledge and experience necessary to determine what course of action is in the best interests of the university. Orientation programming, where it exists, tends to focus on governing board members and involves a review of institutional regulations and bylaws. In short, senate and boards members, as individuals, have little formal opportunity to learn about the broader principles and organisational assumptions that underscore their work, and the governing bodies seldom take a step back to discuss and evaluate broader governance issues.

4.4. Policy networks

The concept of policy networks provides a useful way of capturing both the formal governing arrangements associated with Canadian universities as well as the role of faculty and student associations and other interest groups that attempt to influence institutional decision-making. This frame allows one to observe the complex range of interactions that underscore the development of institutional policy.

Decision making in Canadian universities cannot be neatly categorized by applying any single governance model involving normative assumptions about process and power relationships. Some decisions may be bureaucratic, while others are the product of collegial consensus, and still others may be the end result of difficult political disputes. In other words, 'how' decisions are made as well as the actual policy outcomes emerge from the complex interactions within the policy network.

These policy communities are also dynamic in that both the process of making decisions and the outcomes of this process change over time. The appointment of a new university president with a less-consultative, more autocratic approach to leadership will obviously lead to changes not only in decision making process, but also in the style or nature of the interactions within the policy network. The same is true for changes in the membership of the governing board or senate, or in the leadership of interest groups. The emergence of new interest groups and voices within these policy networks may lead to significant changes in power and authority relationships. For example, the emergence of a new union representing part-time faculty may not only lead to new policy decisions concerning the working conditions of union members, but the resulting collective agreement may also lead to changes in the responsibility of university administrators, force the governing board to deal with a policy issue that had once been delegated to departments, shift the responsibilities of the senate, and have an impact on the lobbying and/or collective bargaining position of the association representing full-time faculty. While Canadian universities continue to have relatively high levels of institutional autonomy, even minor changes in the external environment can lead to significant changes in the power and authority relationships within the institution-level policy network.

Interest groups play an important role in these policy networks. They obviously play a role in terms of articulating the interests of their members within this network. In some respects, association leaders can be viewed as lobbyists within the university governance process, but they can also be viewed as having specialized policy expertise. Both the student and faculty association studies described above found that association leaders frequently responded to requests for advice from the university administration. Interests groups also play an important role in university governance because of the services that they provide to their membership, especially in terms of communication. At the very least, interest groups have some form of representative structure that facilitates communication between the leadership and those representing specific constituencies within the membership, but almost all student associations provide financial support to student newspapers and faculty associations communicate directly with their membership through newsletters or other media. In other words, interest groups facilitate two-way communication between their members and the university governance process. Their leaders provide input to decisions made within the policy network, but they also play a role in terms of keeping their members informed of policies and policy issues. These associations help members of the university community understand university policy. Student associations help their members work their way through administrative 'red-tape'; faculty associations frequently run workshops that help explain university tenure policies to new faculty, or university pension arrangements to senior faculty. The same communications media can, of course, be used to mobilize dissent in situations where there is conflict between the interests of the membership and the decisions made by the university administration or governance structure.

The core decision-making structures within these policy communities involve the formal bicameral governance structures and the executive authority represented by the university administration. As already noted, these core features are surrounded by a complex web of interactions associated with the formal and informal roles assumed by constituency associations and individual members of the community. The complexity of these policy networks raises interesting questions concerning the transparency of university governance. The transparency issue arises from the complexity of the governance structure and from the plethora of interactions within the related policy networks. While the meetings of most, though not all, university governing bodies are 'open' (at least when they are not addressing personnel matters or other confidential issues), these meetings primarily deal with proposals that arise through a complicated combination of administrative recommendations, advisory bodies, informal and formal consultations with association leaders and other interested parties, and then through the frequently complex subcommittee and standing committee structures of the formal governance bodies. The structure may be transparent in the sense that the final decisions emerging from meetings of the governing board and senate take place in a public forum, but for many faculty, most students, and external observers, the complex combination of formal and informal steps leading up to some of these final decisions are filled with mystery and shadows. In short, the outputs of these policy communities may be 'transparent' but relatively few members of the community have a clear sense of the roadmap of steps that are required to take a new initiative through to a final destination, and governing board and senate secretaries have come to play an interesting role at many institutions as the 'experts' in the routing of decision matters through the required committee structures.

The governance arrangements of Canadian universities have evolved in unique ways. They are unique from a national perspective because they share common characteristics that, in combination, make this approach to university decision-making quite distinct from their American, English, and continental European peers. They are also unique at the institutional level, since institutional autonomy has allowed each institution some degree of flexibility in determining how decisions should be made and who should decide. If we are to understand the implications of these unique elements, scholars of Canadian higher education now need to focus on the analysis of institutional case studies. We need to understand how these policy communities function at different institutions, how these communities are influenced by the external environment of the institution, and how these institutional governance processes are understood and experienced by various policy actors.

NOTES

[1] All of these studies were conducted with support from the Social Sciences and Humanities Research Council of Canada.

[2] There are two important exceptions. Queen's University and the Royal Military College are both chartered by the Government of Canada, the former under unusual historical circumstances in the nineteenth century and the latter because it operates under the federal government's explicit constitutional role for national defence. While both owe their corporate existence to federal legislation, their authority to grant degrees in the province of Ontario is obtained under Ontario (provincial) government legislation.

[3] Several universities had already experimented with bicameral structures. The importance of the Commission was that the final report articulated a clear rationale for this structural arrangement that seemed to address many of the political concerns of the day.

[4] For example, in order to facilitate the timely creation of the new University of Winnipeg and Brandon University out of what had previously been colleges of the University of Manitoba, the Government of Manitoba passed framework legislation that allowed for the approval of new universities by order-in-

council. Given this legislative framework, the Government was later able to modify the composition of the bicameral governing bodies of these institutions in the 1980s by order-in-council (essentially by Cabinet decree).

5   There are minor differences in terminology by institution. While most of these bodies are referred to as 'governing boards' some universities use other terms, such as the board of trustees, the administrative council, or the governing council.

6   Jones and Skolnik (1997) note that two universities reported that they provide honoraria to board members, one of which provides a modest honoraria only to student members of the board.

7   This study focused on the senior academic decision making body at each university. While 'senate' is the most common term, some universities use other names for this body, including general faculty council, academic board, or academic council.

8   In some Quebec universities the appointment is confirmed by community election.

9   For example, while some Canadian universities may have only two vice-presidents, the University of Toronto currently has seven, with specific vice-presidents assigned responsibility for academic policy (Provost), business affairs, human resources, fund-raising and development, government relations, research and international activities, and policy.

REFERENCES

Anderson, B. and G.A. Jones. "Organizational Capacity and Political Activities of Canadian University Faculty Associations." *Interchange* 29.4 (1998): 439 – 361.

Baldridge, J.V. *Power and Conflict in the University: Research in the Sociology of Complex Organizations.* New York: J. Wiley, 1971.

Berdahl, R.O. *Statewide Coordination of Higher Education.* Washington: American Council on Education, 1971.

Birnbaum, R. *How Colleges Work: The Cybernetics of Academic Organization and Leadership.* San Francisco: Jossey Bass, 1988.

Cameron, D. *More Than an Academic Question: Universities, Government, and Public Policy in Canada.* Halifax: Institute for Research on Public Policy, 1991.

Clark, B. R. *The Higher Education System.* Berkeley: University of California Press, 1983.

Cohen, M. D., and J.G. March. *Leadership and Ambiguity: The American College President.* Boston: Harvard Business School Press, 1974.

Coleman, W. D. and G. Skogstad. "Policy Communities and Policy Networks: A Structural Approach." In Coleman, W.D. and G. Skogstad (eds). *Policy Communities and Public Policy in Canada: A Structural Approach.* Mississauga, ON: Copp Clark Pitman, 1990, 14 – 33.

Duff, J. and R.O. Berdahl. *University Government in Canada.* Ottawa: Association of Universities and Colleges of Canada and the Canadian Association of University Teachers, 1966.

Goodman, P. *The Community of Scholars.* New York: Random House, 1962.

Hardy, C. "Putting Power into University Governance." In J.C. Smart (ed). *Higher Education: Handbook of Theory and Research.* Volume VI. New York: Agathon Press, 1990.

Hardy, C. *The Politics of Collegiality: Retrenchment Strategies in Canadian Universities.* Montreal: McGill Queen's University Press, 1996.

Horn, M. *Academic Freedom in Canada: A History.* Toronto: University of Toronto Press, 1999.

Jones, G. A. "Student Pressure: A National Survey of Canadian Student Organization." *Ontario Journal of Higher Education* (1995): 93 – 106.

Jones, G. A. "Governments, Governance, and Canadian Universities." In J.C. Smart (ed). *Higher Education: Handbook of Theory and Research* , Volume XI, New York: Agathon Press, 1996, 337 – 371.

Jones, G.A., T. Shanahan and P. Goyan. "University Governance in Canadian Higher Education." *Tertiary Education and Management* 7 (2001): 135 – 148.

Jones, G. A., T. Shanahan and P. Goyan. "Traditional Governance Structures – Current Policy Pressures: The Academic Senate and Canadian Universities." *Tertiary Education and Management* 8 (2002): 29 – 45.

Jones, G. A. and M.L. Skolnik. "Governing Boards in Canadian Universities." *Review of Higher Education* 20.3 (1997): 277 – 295.

234 GLEN A. JONES

McDaniel, O.C. "The Paradigms of Governance in Higher Education Systems." *Higher Education Policy* 9.2 (1996): 137 – 158.

Millet, J.D. *The Academic Community: An Essay on Organization.* New York: McGraw Hill, 1962.

Mintzberg, H. "The Professional Bureaucracy." In M.W. Peterson (ed). *Organization and Governance of Higher Education.* Lexington, GA: Ginn Press, 1991, 53 – 75.

Nelson, W. T. *The Search for Faculty Power: The History of the University of Toronto Faculty Association, 1942 – 1992.* Toronto: University of Toronto Faculty Association, 1993.

Penner, R. "Unionization, Democracy and the University." *Interchange* 25.1 (1994): 49 – 53.

Ponak, A. and M. Thompson. "Faculty Collective Bargaining: The Voice of Experience." *Relations Industrielles* 39.3 (1984): 449 – 463.

Pusser, B., and I. Ordorika. "Bringing Political Theory to University Governance: A Comparative Analysis of Governing Boards at the Universidad Nacional Autónoma de México and the University of California." In J. C. Smart (ed). *Higher Education: Handbook of Theory and Research,* Volume XVI, New York: Agathon Press, 2001, 147 – 194.

Stroup, H. *Bureaucracy in Higher Education.* New York: Free Press, 1966.

Task Force on University Accountability. *University Accountability: A Strengthened Framework.* Toronto: Task Force on University Accountability, 1993.

Tudivor, N. *Universities for Sale: Resisting Corporate Control over Canadian Higher Education.* Toronto: James Lorimer and Company, 1999.

V. LYNN MEEK

ON THE ROAD TO MEDIOCRITY?
GOVERNANCE AND MANAGEMENT OF
AUSTRALIAN HIGHER EDUCATION IN THE
MARKET PLACE

1. INTRODUCTION

The question of how best to optimise the performance of the higher education sector has generated much debate both at institutional and system levels. In part, the debate has been fuelled by the steep growth in higher education participation rates and the pressures on higher education institutions to find increasing proportions of their operating grants from sources other than the public purse. Concerns regarding the relevance of higher education to the labour market and to economic growth and prosperity have also focused attention on this sector. A common theme in the performance debate has been the adequacy of existing institutional governance and management structures and processes to meet stakeholder expectations. However, neither in Australia nor elsewhere is the debate on how best to govern and manage higher education new.

The issue in the late 1950s and early 1960s concerned the democratisation of departmental management and limiting the power of the so-called 'god-professor'. In 1963 the distinguished Australian historian, Geoffrey Serle, argued for "a system of government which embodies a return towards the traditional idea of a university as a community of scholars and teachers; in which there is a more even gradation of authority and responsibility, according to status and experience, in place of the existing concentration of power in professors' hands ..." (1963: 11). The latter part of the 1960s and early 1970s saw concerted campaigns to increase student representation in university decision making at all levels.

In the 1970s and early 1980s the debate shifted more towards system level issues, such as the federal government assuming full financial responsibility for higher education, the creation of a single national coordinating ('buffer') authority (the Commonwealth Tertiary Education Commission – CTEC) and rationalisation through institutional amalgamation, and the management of higher education in a no growth, steady state environment. By the mid-1980s, participation in higher education was starting to increase dramatically, raising questions about the efficiency and effectiveness of higher education management, culminating in CTEC's 1986 *Review of Efficiency and Effectiveness in Higher Education*. Government intervened in 1987/88 with the Green Paper (*Higher Education: a policy discussion paper*) and White Paper (*Higher Education: a policy statement*) on

235

235

Alberto Amaral, Glen A. Jones and Berit Karseth (eds.), *Governing Higher Education: National Perspectives on Institutional Governance*, 235—260.
© 2002 *Kluwer Academic Publishers. Printed in the Netherlands.*

higher education which abolished CTEC and the binary distinction between universities and colleges of advanced education (CAEs), and created the unified national system (UNS) that would contain a much smaller number of significantly larger institutions. An important aspect of government's reform agenda was the strengthening of management at the institutional level. The White Paper (1988: 101) stated, for example, that "effective management at the institutional level will be the key to achieving many of the Government's objectives for the unified national system: growth in areas of national need; an effective partnership with other parties to the education and training process, including employers; improvements to equity and access to higher education; and efficiency of operation".

The 1987 – 88 reforms, however, did not settle the management debate. The 1993 DEET *National Report on Australia's Higher Education Sector* devoted an entire chapter to management issues, and the reviews of the Committee for Quality Assurance in Higher Education conducted between 1993 and 1995 focused, in part, on management. In June 1995 the Minister for Employment, Education and Training announced a review of higher education management, sparking widespread concern throughout the sector. Interestingly, the review was led not by an educationalist, but by the Bankers Trust Australia Chairman, Mr David Hoare. The review was commissioned to "examine and advise on the management and accountability requirements for ensuring Australia has a high quality, efficient and effective higher education sector" (*Higher Education Management Review* 1995: 104). The more recent Review of Higher Education Financing and Policy also made recommendations with respect to governance and management issues (*Learning for Life* 1998). The Committee commented that:

> The present funding framework does not assist, or provide incentives for, institutions to manage effectively. Governance structures hamper management and there are no incentives for institutions to be aware of their costs or to minimise them. The public support provided to institutions and students is not always delivered in a transparent way (p. 89).

The chair of that review, Mr Roderick West, was not from the higher education community either, but the head of a well known private school in Sydney.

In one sense, the debate about the governance and management of higher education has not changed much since the early 1960s. It is still about governance by a community of scholars versus centralised managerial authority: "Consistent with what John Millett has called the 'dynamic of consensus in a community of scholars', the collegial leader is expected to only facilitate the process of decision making by consensus and not to lead, direct, or manage anything" (Moore and Langknecht 1986: 1).

At an even deeper and more immutable level, the debate concerns the tension between 'the idea of the university' and the institutional form within which that idea is realised: "The institution is simultaneously indispensable and a standing threat to the idea of the university", as Karl Jaspers (1946: 51) pointed out shortly after the second world war. Half a century later, Marginson and Considine (2000: 8) make a similar observation: "It has become all too easy to imagine the university without one or another of the academic disciplines; it is impossible to imagine the academic disciplines without their institutional setting, and its governance". Or, as Jaspers puts it:

> The university exists only to the extent that it is institutionalized. The idea becomes concrete in the institution ... Yet 'institution' necessarily implies compromises. The idea is never perfectly realized. Because of this a permanent state of tension exists at the university between the idea and the shortcomings of the institutional and corporate reality (1946: 83).

Of course, the 'idea' itself has been open to various interpretations and never wholly articulated, although Jaspers' (1946: 20) short definition is difficult to surpass: "The university is the corporate realization of man's basic determination to know". The debates about higher education governance go well beyond questions of management best practice.

While it is questionable whether decision making by consensus ever existed in any significant form, the importance of collegial governance is, if nothing else, evidenced by government policy attacks throughout the 1990s and into the present century on what is perceived to be an over-emphasis on collegial decision making and associated norms within Australian higher education institutions. And, clearly, collegial decision making and the professional authority of the academic has given way to that of the university manager:

> Many see this concentration of nodal power as overdue, as essential to the effective running of universities in the manner of government departments or business firms. Others see it as the primary cause of what they perceive as a crisis of university purposes and values. Either way, governance is critical (Marginson and Considine 2000: 8).

Increasingly, pressure has been placed on universities to institute strong managerial modes of operation, with vice-chancellors being called and assuming the role of chief executive officers, and councils becoming boards of governors. Some vice-chancellors now include the word 'president' in their title to denote a role similar to that of the presidents of North American universities. Most deans of faculties are no longer elected collegial leaders but appointed positions and a part of line-management. Heads of departments have direct supervisory responsibilities for academic staff, and staff in turn are starting to be treated more like employees rather than autonomous professionals. Changes in the governance and management of Australian higher education are not about any ill conceived 'dynamic of consensus in a community of scholars' but directly concern the re-norming of the academic profession and possibly fundamental transformation of the idea of the university itself. Marginson and Considine (2000: 9 – 11) provide a useful summary of major trends and issues in the changing pattern of governance and management of Australian universities:

> • a new kind of executive power, characterised by a will to manage and ... a freedom to act greater than was once the case;
>
> • the remaking or replacement of collegial or democratic forms of governance with structures that operationalise executive power and create selective mechanisms for participation, consultation and internal market research;

- an enhanced flexibility of personnel and resources, of means of communication, and of the very location of power and authority;

- a discernible decline in the role of the academic disciplines in governance;

- new methods of devolution.

The managerial approach in higher education is the culmination of a number of factors: more than a decade of perceived inefficiencies in higher education management by government and some institutional leaders; increasing institutional complexity brought about by growth and the transition from an 'elite' to a 'mass' system of higher education; and labour market priorities. But what is more important than any single factor, is the general climate of public sector reform prevailing in Australia and many other OECD countries and the financial and ideological concerns driving it. It is a reform agenda much influenced by the economic rationalists where market competition and consumer control replace strong government regulatory frameworks, on the one hand, and traditional institutional values on the other.

Little work has been done in Australia to explain changes in higher education governance and management in terms of the broader reform of the Australian public sector and the introduction of new public management. Hence, the first major section of this paper will look at the transformation of the Australian public sector in some detail. The next section of the paper looks specifically at the transformation of higher education, followed by an analysis of achievements and deficits brought about by the reforms. This is followed by an analysis of market steering and the limitation of the use of the market to govern major social/public institutions, including universities. The paper concludes with a discussion which questions the probity of markets and competition to the governance and management of higher education.

2. REFORM OF THE AUSTRALIAN PUBLIC SECTOR

Harman (2001) notes that there has yet to be a serious study of how new public management ideas came to Australia and their influence on the public sector in general and universities in particular. Clearly, Australia adopted ideas and strategies being developed in the 1980s and early 1990s in other countries, England and New Zealand in particular. Also, a number of OECD reports were influential. *Universities Under Scrutiny* (OECD 1987) which argued for greater public accountability and strengthened university governance was referred to in the introduction of the 1987 Green Paper on higher education. Other more general OECD reports were also influential, such as the 1995 *Governance in Transition: Public Sector Management Reforms in OECD Countries.*

Several domestic reviews and reports helped re-shape the management of the public sector (see Hilmer 1993; Industry Commission 1991 and 1995; Scales 1995; Clare and Johnson 1993). The Hilmer report was probably the most influential, though all of them, as Harman (2001: 155) observes, share common assumptions and values, underpinned by the virtues of competition: "Competition was seen as improving performance and productivity, and leading to improved customer service.

According to the Hilmer report, 'enhanced competition' is an unambiguous good that improves efficiency and productivity, reduces the price for services and makes the economy internationally competitive". The virtues of market competition were (and still are) being promoted as the key to good government, a strong economy and better education.

In a number of OECD countries there has been a corporatisation of the public sector brought about by the replacement of principles and values of democratic government with those of managerialism and market discipline. Terms such as contracting-out, re-engineering, mission statements, continuous improvement and performance evaluation, are those of the corporate manager, not the government mandarin of a past era. Moreover, it does not appear to make much difference whether the stimulus for reform comes from the political 'left' or 'right'. While in the United States and the United Kingdom the push towards a smaller, more efficient, client oriented and market conscious public sector came from the conservative right, in Australia much the same was accomplished by the Australian Labor Party (ALP), traditionally based on principles of social democratic government and what Argy (1998) terms progressive liberalism. Castles, Gerritsen and Vowles (1996: 2) maintain that Australia and New Zealand "were the only OECD nations in which Labour/Social Democratic governments sought to actively transform society and economy toward a 'more market' model on a scale comparable with the ambitions of the right".

3. SHAPING THE PRESENT AUSTRALIAN PUBLIC SECTOR

After eight years in opposition, in 1983 the ALP came to power with a mandate to reform the public service and with a strong desire to portray itself as a sound and responsible economic manager. The new government in late 1983 tabled a White Paper entitled *Reforming the Australian Public Service*.

The White Paper stated that "the responsiveness, efficiency and accountability of the Commonwealth administration have a major impact on the quality of Australian democracy" (in McInnes 1990: 108). The paper proposed the abolition of the 'permanent head' classification, a competitive senior career service based on lateral recruitment, contract-based employment and managerial ability (Laffin 1996: 43), and "formalised the employment of ministerial staff and consultants under statute" (McInnes 1990: 109). This started a shift away from bureaucratic assumptions and service ideals, towards generic management, creating what some have maintained is a new breed of managerially oriented cadres at senior career levels (Laffin 1996: 51). The subsequent *Public Service Reform Act* of 1984 increased ministerial control, introduced merit based employment, and created the Senior Executive Service (SES) with an emphasis on managerial competence (Considine and Painter 1997; Considine 1994; Corbett 1996). Somewhat later, the values and ideals of the SES entered the universities.

Clearly, the impetus for a corporate ethos within universities came from the federal government and the SES of the Commonwealth Public Service and the then Hawke Labour government's commitment to public sector reform and the introduction of private sector managerial practices into the public sector (cf. Williams 1988). According to Bezant (1995: 60), universities' SES has become a "formidable and remote authority" which pre-empts the collegial authority of academic/professional boards: "It takes a brave academic to stand up and oppose a united gaggle of mega-Deans, Deputy Vice-Chancellors and a Vice-Chancellor at a board meeting".

Following the 1987 election at which the ALP was returned to office with a substantial majority and in order to exercise more direct stewardship of the economy, the Hawke government substantially reduced the number of statutory authorities in the belief that "for many purposes government departments have the decided advantage of making the relevant Minister directly responsible for the effectiveness and efficiency of administration and of saving costs through the use of long established administrative machinery ..." (Williams 1988: 2). As part of an ideology of 'let the managers manage', the Public Service Board was abolished and personnel responsibilities devolved to departmental heads, and the Treasurer promised to reduce the size of the public service to its 1950s level (McInnes 1990: 112). According to Williams (1988: 7), the analysis in the government's policy discussion paper, *Statutory Authorities and Government Business Enterprises* (1986), "on the relations between Minister and statutory business enterprises does not leave room for a statutory body ... to stand between the Minister and the business enterprises". Or, as McInnes (1990: 115) puts it, "by defining the role of public authorities and enterprises within a business rather than a service framework, the government has clearly argued that there is no place in the public sector for independent agencies that do not have the potential to raise revenue". One such agency that was quickly 'axed' following the 1987 elections was the Commonwealth Tertiary Education Commission, with long term consequences for the higher education sector.

All governments are influenced by both ideological and budgetary factors, and Australia's massive overseas deficit was often mentioned as a motivating factor for many of the Hawke Labour government's policies — as it is now by a government of a different political persuasion and Prime Minister, Mr John Howard, and Treasurer, Mr Peter Costello. By the mid to late 1980s, public sector reform in Australia was caught in the web of economic rationalism, and much of the rhetoric used in defence of policy invoked the fear of national bankruptcy. Public spending, supposedly, had to be geared in an inverse ratio to the size of the overseas debt in order for the country to survive economically. In light of the government's election promise not to increase taxes, it was (and is) said that government instrumentalities must become more economically efficient through such means as greater competition in a more open market-like environment, through the strengthening of public management along the lines employed by major corporations, and through improved public accountability and formal assessment of performance. The adverse balance of payments dominated nearly every aspect of public policy and the public was conditioned to accept, even demand, radical measures that would address the adverse economic situation.

Orchard (1998: 19) argues that there have been three main intellectual catalysts to change in the Australian government and the public sector: "the social democratic, the economic rationalist or public choice, and the managerialist". Though each have different origins, they pushed the public sector reforms of the Hawke and Keating Labour governments throughout the 1980s and early 1990s, and underlie the "more strident reform in the same rationalist and managerialist vein" as is being pursued by the present Liberal-National Coalition government led by Mr John Howard. For nearly two decades now, all "Australian governments have sought to shift their central control mechanisms away from traditional bureaucratic control devices, such as detailed controls over staffing levels, and towards broader financial management controls" (Laffin 1996: 48). For the reformist, this new public sector required a new style of management.

The managerialist push has not only infiltrated nearly every aspect of the way in which public instrumentalities are run, but also has resulted in the private management of many institutions until recently regarded as inherently public, such as prisons. Continuous improvement, mission statements, performance indicators, evaluation, etc., are more than merely new tools of public management. They are part and parcel of a much more intrusive process of replacing ideals of public value and good with managerial imperatives, making the process inherently political. And, while the 'managerial revolution' in Australia has much in common with similar movements elsewhere, "debates on what governments should do inevitably integrate political imperatives with managerial demands" (Weller 1996: 8–9). Or, as the Evatt Foundation (1996: 106) puts it, "Proponents of market outcomes downplay the fact that decisions over the allocation and management of public resources are ultimately questions of political priorities. There is a strong current in conservative ideology that reinterprets public policy in terms of managerialism". Zifcak (1997: 107) summarises some of the main features of new public management in Australia:

> Taken together, the most important components of the new public management appear to be a stress on private sector methods of management practice, a shift to greater competition in the public sector, polycentricity in public sector design, greater emphasis on explicit standards and measures of performance ... The initiative advances a preference for market mechanisms of governance, more business-like management of public agencies, the minimisation of public bureaucracy, a focus on clear responsibility and accountability for results and the empowerment of consumers of governments services.

4. REFORM OF THE AUSTRALIAN HIGHER EDUCATION SECTOR

In line with the reform of the public sector in general and in order to make higher education more relevant to national economic needs and priorities, in the late 1980s, the then federal Labour government initiated a dramatic transformation of Australian higher education. The reforms had several immediate effects, such as extensive consolidation of institutions through amalgamation. But, more importantly, the government set in train a number of long-term trends, that are still helping to shape the system today, such as:

- a shift in the cost of higher education from the state to the individual; the government has curtailed its financial commitment through the introduction

of such mechanisms as the Higher Education Contribution Scheme (HECS – partial tuition payment through the tax system);
- enhanced national and international competition for students and research income;
- greater emphasis on accountability for the government dollar and some movement towards performance based funding;
- greater deregulation within the higher education sector through, for example, collection and retention of student fees, and the right to borrow money for capital works;
- an increased reliance on income gained from sources other than the Commonwealth.

With the change of federal government in March 1996, it became clear that the size of the task to which higher education must adapt had in fact substantially increased. The 1996 budget statement from the newly elected Liberal coalition government regarding higher education placed additional pressures and challenges on this sector. Harman (2001: 161) maintains that "new public management ideas clearly influenced the Coalition's first budget of August 1996 that had an important impact on higher education. Savings targets were set for most areas at painfully high levels and in a number of areas new approaches to public policy were introduced". Key changes announced in the 1996 budget statement included:

- a reduction of operating grants by 5 per cent over three years;
- a lowering of the HECS repayment threshold; an increase in level of HECS payments; and the introduction of differential HECS according to course of study;
- no Commonwealth supplementation of academic salary increases (Since 1996 there have been two rounds of enterprise bargaining resulting in on average a 12% non-government funded salary increase in each round);
- an insistence upon return of funds if enrolment targets are not met;
- a phasing out of postgraduate coursework enrolments from Commonwealth funded load.

The privatisation of public higher education and the introduction of market like relationships to achieve both greater institutional efficiency and adaptability have become national policy goals. A number of factors have influenced government policy and expectations of the higher education sector and include:

- the substantial costs associated with mass higher education which have led to a concern by government to realise more value per dollar committed in this sector;
- a clear expectation by government that the higher education sector is more closely tied to the national economy both in terms of meeting national labour market needs and also through the commercialisation of its research and teaching activities;

- as a larger proportion of the population expresses an interest in participating in higher education, inevitably, higher education also becomes more of a political issue;
- due to an ageing population, the social service burden on the national treasury is rising dramatically, which is coupled with pressures to cut government expenditure and to demand greater efficiencies from public sector institutions;
- as with other industrialised countries, traditional manufacturing industries are being replaced by the so-called 'knowledge processing sector', of which higher education is an integral component.

In Australia, as elsewhere, the last decade has ushered in a new phase in higher education planning and policy development, one characterised by:

- reductions in public expenditure;
- increased emphasis on efficiency of resource utilisation;
- increased emphasis on performance measurement, particularly in terms of outcomes;
- increased emphasis on demonstrable contribution to the economy of the nation; and
- the strengthening of institutional management and of the policy and planning role of individual institutions.

The marketisation of Australian higher education has had mixed results. The decline of government funding per student place has put tremendous pressure on institutional infrastructure and as many are currently arguing, threatened the quality of the educational experience. On the other hand, institutional management has to a considerable extent been successful in finding additional financial resources for their institutions. Some aspects of the performance of the reformed higher education sector are outlined below.

5. PERFORMANCE OF THE REFORMED HIGHER EDUCATION SECTOR

5.1. Participation and equity

As can be seen from table 1, over the last five decades, Australian higher education has experienced tremendous growth in student numbers. It has been transformed from a small, elite, male-dominated system into a mass system catering for nearly 700 000 students, the majority of whom are female. Growth in student numbers in the first half of the 1990s was particularly impressive – growth which the Commonwealth government said could not be funded entirely from the public purse. The leaders of Australia's universities have had to manage substantial growth while at the same time finding new forms of income to maintain that growth.

Table 1. Higher education students by selected characteristics, 1950–2000.

| | | | Proportion | | |
Year	Total Students	Full-time	Part-time	External	% Female
1950 (a)	30,630	62.7	28.1	9.2	21.6
1960 (a)	53,633	58.7	31.1	10.2	23.1
1970 (b)	161,455	57.9	36.1	5.9	27.1
1980 (b)	329,523	54.5	34.7	10.8	45.3
1990	485,066	61.7	27.4	10.9	52.7
2000	695,485	58.6	27.6	13.7	55.2

Source: DETYA 2001a

(a) Figures are for universities only

(b) Figures include universities and colleges of advanced education (CAEs)

All Australian studies, and there have been a number, conclude that the participation rate of a number of equity groups has improved substantially in recent years. For example, women made up 57 per cent of all 1999 non-overseas commencing students, a considerable improvement on their participation a decade ago. Indigenous Australians and persons from non-English speaking backgrounds with respect to overall participation have become over represented. However, these studies also indicate that little or no progress has been made on the relative access by rural and isolated students, or by persons of low socio-economic status. Despite a dramatic increase in student numbers since the mid-1980s, participation in higher education by persons of low socio-economic status has not improved, in fact, evidence suggests that it has worsened.

5.1.1. User pays

Towards the end of the 1980s, though participation in higher education was increasing; the student population continued to be drawn largely from the middle and professional classes. Arguing the benefits of participation in higher education for the individual, it was not difficult for the government to reintroduce student fees in the form of the Higher Education Contribution Scheme (HECS).

HECS was a very clever political device for reintroducing student fees. Though since the 1970s the level of income of graduates relative to non-graduates had fallen, these incomes have still been substantially more than those earned by the rest of the workforce. But, for reasons of equity and access, the then Labour government was not prepared to charge up front fees. Rather, HECS students were to contribute to the cost of their course through a tax levy that would come into effect only when their income reached the average national income. A similar scheme for domestic postgraduate coursework students was introduced in 2001.

The public/private good debate with respect to higher education intensified with the 1996 election of the Liberal coalition government. The new government has substantially increased the HECS charge for all students and lowered the income threshold for commencement of repayment. Based on both the cost of the course and the earning power of graduates, the government has introduced a differential HECS which, for example, resulted in a 92 per cent fee rise for engineering and business students and a 125 per cent rise for law and medicine students. This has made tuition fees for Australian university students on the average amongst some of the highest in OECD countries. In 2000, enrolments of commencing domestic students in Australian universities declined for the first time. This led the Australian Vice-Chancellors Committee (AVCC) (2001: 2) to comment that:

> Australia cannot afford to have rising fee income act as a disincentive to developing the knowledge and skills of its people ... and there is no justification for raising this burden still higher. Moreover, the direct fee income paid by students and their families can never be a complete substitute for investment by the government in the infrastructure and resources (human and capital) that is fundamental for ensuring quality outcomes in teaching and learning.

5.1.2. Full-fee paying overseas students

Up to the mid-1980s, the education of overseas students was seen mainly as a form of foreign aid. Students were subsidised by government aid programs and fees were not paid directly to institutions. But, in the late 1980s, government foreshadowed a more market oriented approach to foreign students – from 'aid' to 'trade' – by indicating that full-fee paying overseas students provided another important source of potential revenue growth.

The deregulation of the foreign student market created an environment of fierce competition amongst institutions for the overseas student dollar. Nearly all institutions regularly send representatives on student recruitment drives throughout South East Asia, and some institutions have established overseas campuses. In 2000 there were 153,372 international students enrolled in Australia with a further 34,905 enrolled with Australian providers operating overseas – a relatively new phenomenon in this area is for Australian universities to enrol overseas students through distance education or at an offshore campus established by a university in collaboration with a foreign partner. In 2000 alone, a total of 188,277 international students at all educational levels contributed about $3.7 billion to the national economy, making the education of overseas students one of the country's largest export earners. Higher education enrolments increased to 107,622 in 2000. In 1999, international students contributed about $805 million in fees to higher education. Australia has a higher proportion of international students in its tertiary education sector than any other major exporter within the OECD. Here is an example of how enhanced competition in a deregulated higher education environment appears to produce the desired outcome.

5.2. Diversification of the funding base

The history of Australian education can be told, in part, by the way in which it has been funded. Figure 1 displays the proportion of university income by major funding source for the period 1939 to 1998.

V. LYNN MEEK

As can be seen, before World War II, the Commonwealth government did not contribute to the running of the universities, while nearly 80 per cent of the income came from state governments and student tuition. In 1981, nearly 90 per cent of the income came from the Commonwealth, and student contributions had effectively disappeared as a source of income, as had money from state governments.

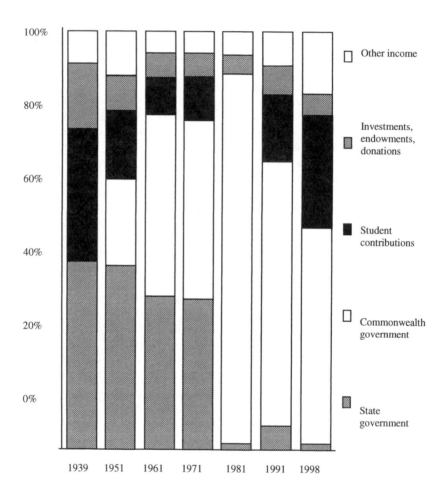

Figure 1. University income by source
Source: Gallagher 2000.

Table 2. Earned income as a percentage of total income.

Grouping	Institution*	State	1992 %	1993 %	1994 %	1995 %	1996 %	1997 %	1998 %	1999 %
Go8	The Australian Nat. Uni.	ACT	21	21	16	33	30	34	27	30
	The Univ. of NSW	NSW	35	36	29	30	31	37	37	39
	The Univ. of Sydney	NSW	30	34	30	28	31	36	34	40
	The Univ. of Queensland	QLD	31	34	35	34	34	37	35	36
	The Univ. of Adelaide	SA	14	16	29	27	28	30	31	30
	Monash University	VIC	25	29	35	38	39	40	43	43
	The Univ. of Melbourne	VIC	23	34	30	32	33	35	29	31
	The University of WA	WA	30	46	28	44	46	47	47	46
ATN	Univ. of Tech., Sydney	NSW	18	17	19	22	22	26	29	36
	QLD Univ. of Tech.	QLD	17	17	19	19	22	23	25	25
	Univ. of South Australia	SA	10	20	11	12	13	18	19	19
	RMIT University	VIC	17	26	26	29	33	35	42	41
	Curtin Univ. of Tech.	WA	25	32	28	31	32	36	38	37
Pre'88 non Go8	Macquarie University	NSW	30	32	28	26	27	34	33	37
	The Uni. of New England	NSW	22	23	25	24	23	25	23	22
	The Univ. of Newcastle	NSW	29	25	21	21	25	26	29	28
	University of Wollongong	NSW	26	28	25	27	29	41	32	28
	Griffith University	QLD	21	22	22	25	26	27	29	30
	James Cook Univ.	QLD	14	24	23	22	22	24	24	26
	The Flinders Univ. of SA	SA	11	26	24	23	26	28	31	19
	University of Tasmania	TAS	18	19	17	17	18	20	19	18
	Deakin University	VIC	17	19	22	24	27	30	37	41
	La Trobe University	VIC	20	19	18	21	25	25	35	29
	Murdoch University	WA	21	18	29	27	28	31	32	32
New universities	University of Canberra	ACT	21	30	29	29	28	32	32	33
	Australian Catholic Univ.	Multi-	10	11	13	14	14	15	13	15
	Charles Sturt University	NSW	24	23	25	25	23	28	31	33
	Southern Cross University	NSW	na	na	11	13	15	19	22	21
	Univ. of Western Sydney	NSW	16	17	17	22	20	20	22	25
	Northern Territory Univ.	NT	6	24	13	21	25	23	25	24
	Central Queensland Univ.	QLD	21	19	20	25	28	29	34	36
	Univ. of Southern QLD	QLD	21	23	25	26	29	31	30	26
	Uni. of the Sunshine Coast	QLD	na	na	na	na	na	na	na	9
	Swinburne Univ. of Tech.	VIC	25	23	25	27	25	26	32	36
	University of Ballarat	VIC	16	19	18	19	24	24	30	27
	Victoria Univ. of Tech.	VIC	12	15	19	19	23	26	28	26
	Edith Cowan University	WA	13	15	17	19	22	26	25	24

Source: adapted from DETYA 2001b
*See the section 'institutional diversity' below, for an explanation of the rationale for grouping universities in this manner.

Currently, it is clear that at least some Australian higher education institutions are successfully meeting the challenge to diversify their funding base. In 1999, the total operating revenue for Australian higher education was $8.7 billion (excluding abnormal items). About 44% ($3,914,264) was from Commonwealth government grants and 19% (or $1,662,425) from HECS. The remaining operating revenue was divided as follows: other Commonwealth government grants − $276,572 or 3.2%; fees and charges − $1,546,589 or 17.7%; investment income − $275,726 or 3.2%; donations and bequests − $11,550 or 1.3%; state government − $93,495 or 1.1%; and other sources − $853,127 or 9.8%. In the early 1980s, non-government sources of funding for higher education were neglible across the sector. Presently, a number of institutions (mostly the older, well established ones) receive over half their operating revenue from non-government sources. On average, about a third of university revenue is from earned income (revenue derived from other than Commonwealth or state grants and HECS). Financially, Australia has moved from being a publicly supported to a publicly subsidized system. It is also clear from table2, that some Australian universities are finding life much more difficult than other universities under the new entrepreneurial funding regime. More will be said about this below. Australia has become one of the world's leaders in terms of the proportion of higher education funding coming from non-government sources.

5.3. Corporate models of management

Market steering of higher education supposedly requires strong corporate style management at the institutional level. And in Australia, as elsewhere, there has been a substantial shift towards a more managerial approach to running universities in recent years, deliberately encouraged by government policy. The push to diversify the funding base has been one of the primary factors making university management so difficult and complex, as Michael Gallagher, Head of DETYA's Higher Education Division recognises (2000: 17):

> With currently a third of university revenue on average dependent on 'earned income' that is hard to win, that can be volatile and uncertain, that costs funds to earn and when earned may be available for use only in designated activities, with little discretion for the university at large, the tasks of university management become more complex and require new skill, systems and cultures.

Within the changed policy context, many responsibilities have been devolved to individual universities. But, at the same time, institutions are held more directly accountable for the effective and efficient use of the funding and other freedoms they enjoy. Moreover, institutions are now placed in a much more highly competitive environment, and considerable pressure has been placed on them to strengthen management, to become more entrepreneurial and corporate like. The large universities with more than 30,000 students and annual budgets that run to hundreds of millions of dollars, rival many private corporations in size and complexity. Institutions must respond quickly and decisively in order to take advantage of market opportunities.

There can be little doubt that the sheer size and complexity of Australian higher education demands strong and expert administration at the institutional level. But the current emphasis on what some have termed 'hard managerialism' (Trow 1994) is creating significant tension between rank and file academic staff and the executive. This tension between the managerial and collegial approaches to running the university is widespread and contributes significantly to staff alienation which, in turn, may undermine commitment to the very corporate planning processes that the managerial approach is intended to accomplish.

In 1995, a survey of executive officers (vice-chancellors, deputy vice-chancellors, pro vice-chancellors), deans of faculty, and heads of departments/schools was carried out in all Australian universities (Meek and Wood 1997). The questionnaire canvassed the appropriateness and effectiveness of management and governance structures and procedures.

The results confirmed that in Australia as elsewhere the perception is that corporate style management practices are replacing more traditional methods of collegial decision making. There was a clear indication that executive management priorities and practices take precedent over collegial decision making. A significant majority of respondents agreed that the trend toward central management is at the expense of collegial processes; that the values of staff and management goals are in conflict; and that executive management takes precedence over collegial decision making in their institutions. A substantial majority of heads also indicated that this should not be the case, while the majority of executive officers seemed more supportive of these shifts in management style. Since the time of that survey, tensions between management and academic staff have increased considerably in many institutions.

But management tensions are not merely focused on internal disputes over power and control between academic staff and the executive branch. Many executive officers too feel defenceless in the face of government wishes and directives – which is curious since the only substantive power the federal government has over the universities is financial. Australia is a federation of six states and two territories and, for the most part, all legislative authority for higher education rests with the states while funding comes from the Commonwealth government. The states have the power of law and the federal government has the power of the purse, with the latter winning hands down every time.

What many may interpret as direct government intervention in institutional affairs may be attributed to the financial reward structures devised by government and the enhanced competitive environment in which institutions compete for such rewards. The relationship between higher education and government is nominally centred on autonomy to respond to government objectives but is actually based on funding rewards to institutions that support government objectives which results in university competition for funding and enforced conformity to government goals: "The 'new' autonomy is then a paradox: it is the autonomy to be free to conform" (Mahony 1994: 125).

Neave (1996: 30) encapsulates this seeming paradox in what he terms as the "law of anticipated results". The law of anticipated results operates at the institutional level, giving the impression of autonomous institutional action to what is in fact an institutional reaction to actual or anticipated external forces, directives or events. Institutions interpret what is or will be required by government policy and act accordingly, making it considerably difficult to determine whether change is bottom driven or top-down imposed. "Thus", according to Neave, "the rhetoric of public policy is often at odds with the institutional behaviour it elicits".

In Australia, as elsewhere, institutions compete with one another in attempting to interpret how best to take advantage of the financial incentives available, and in so doing have been caught in a continuous process of attempting to second guess both the 'market' and government policy. It may be the general competitive environment that government policies help create rather than the policies *per se* which many university managers perceive as unduly infringing on their activities and freedom.

5.4. Institutional diversity

With respect to diversity, there are two possible institutional responses to increased market competition: institutions can diversify in an attempt to capture a specific 'market niche', or they can imitate the activities of their successful competitors. The direction in which institutions respond depends on a number of factors, not the least of which are the history and traditions of particular national systems and the reward structure put in place by policy. It appears that the competitive environment in which the Australian higher education system operates has enforced a degree of uniformity on the sector.

The policy intention was that competition would encourage institutions to find their own particular market niche. However, it seems that institutions have been more prone to copy each others' teaching and research profiles than to consciously diversify.

In attempting to diversify their funding base, for example, the overseas student market has proved a lucrative avenue for many institutions. As indicated above, full-fee paying overseas students are big business for Australian higher education. But the majority of these students are only interested in a fairly narrow range of courses centred around economics and business studies. In attempting to cater to the preferences of the overseas student market, many institutions have engaged in course duplication.

With the abolition of the binary divide, subjects once relegated to the non-university sector (nursing, tourism, lower levels of teacher training, etc.) were suddenly exalted to the level of university degrees. Combined with a process of extensive institutional amalgamation between 'older' universities and former CAEs which occurred immediately after the collapse of the binary system, these subjects were automatically dispersed throughout the system. Looked at from this perspective, programmatic convergence rather than diversification has been the result.

Research policy and the reward structure that it set in place stimulated institutions to imitate, at least to a degree, one another's research profiles. The competitive nature of performance based research funding also encourages institutions to engage in research of a particular type. The newer universities have not done as well in the competition for research dollars as the older universities. But what gains they have made are seen as significant in bringing other rewards in their train. On the other hand, the older and more prestigious universities appear to resent sharing any of the research spoils.

In terms of the type, range and structure of programs offered, Australian higher education institutions do not fall into distinct categories (Huisman, Meek and Wood 1998). Nonetheless, there is a categorisation, of a sort, of Australian universities. The older and more prestigious research universities have formed a cartel with its own secretariat (called the Group of 8 or Go8), as have the universities which were former institutes of technology under the old binary system (called Australian Technology Network universities). The other former ex-CAEs form a 'class' of new universities, while the pre-1988 non-Go8 are much of a mixed-bag.

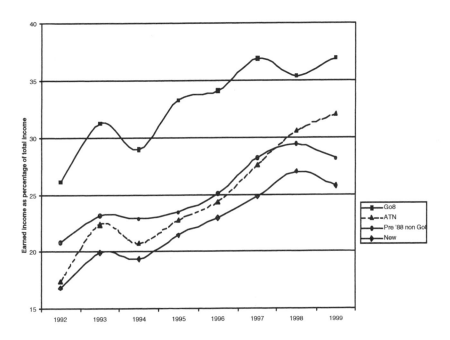

Figure 2. Proportion of earned income by institutional type
Source: Adapted from DETYA 2001b.

If we accept that these categories have some empirical validity, then it is interesting to compare performance across categories. In all such comparisons, the Go8 universities come out on top. For example, figure 2 uses the data in table 2 to compare performance with respect to proportion of earned income.

While this sort of categorisation (Go8, ATN, pre '88 non Go8, new universities (ex-CAEs)) is diversity of a kind, it is not one that can be seen to fulfil any obvious worthwhile policy objective other than one of a rather 'blood-thirsty' competition of the strong against the weak.

Diversity is probably one of the most important issues to face Australian higher education over the next couple of decades. At stake is whether weaker institutions will merely become pale imitations of their more powerful and prestigious brethren, or create their own excellence in different and varied ways. Uniform policy probably stimulates a degree of uniformity in institutional response, as does market competition where institutions are competing for the same clientele, such as full-fee paying overseas students[1]. There is a growing body of evidence in Australia and elsewhere to suggest that formally regulated and separate policy environments better serve the principles of diversity than market competition.

5.5. Market steering and future funding models

Historically, and in contrast to the situation in a number of other OECD countries, the Australian private sector has invested little in public higher education. This is due, in part, to the fact that many Australian companies are multinational corporations which prefer to invest in R&D in the country of their home office, such as the USA or Japan. In the early part of the 1990s, there was some increase in private funding of Australian R&D, but those gains have largely disappeared in more recent years.

The way in which Australian higher education may be funded in the future is presently subject to considerable speculation. There is pressure on government from the scientific community to substantially increase funding for research. In terms of gross expenditure on R&D, Australia is well behind the major industrial countries in its commitment to R&D. In the two-year period from 1996–97 to 1998–99 expenditure had slumped 10% against GDP. These were the worst results in an international comparison of 17 OECD countries (*OECD Education at a Glance –* 2000 edition). Overall, the funding cuts to higher education initiated in 1996 only really started to bite in 1999, and are now culminating in what many observers claim is a funding crisis.

Clearly, since the mid-1990s, there has been a substantial reduction in investment in research and an alarming deterioration of infrastructure. While over the last few years a number of comparable countries, such as Canada and Ireland, have witnessed renewed and substantial investment in research infrastructure, the Australian response so far has mainly been the issuing of a White Paper on research that provides a blueprint for the restructuring of the Australian Research Council and a concentration of research effort within universities all within the current revenue base. Disappointingly, the White Paper makes little reference to the substantial international literature evaluating different research funding models and questioning the degree to which the concentration of research funding should be a goal in itself.

More generally, student centred funding based on a voucher system was the main recommendation of the *Review of Higher Education Financing and Policy* (West Committee) which reported in April 1998. A Cabinet document, prepared by the Minister for Education, Training and Youth Affairs and leaked to the opposition and the press in October 1999, proposed a student demand-driven model for funding higher education where institutions would be allowed to set their own tuition fees and students would be encouraged to obtain loans (replacing HECS) at commercial interest rates. The government and the Minister were embarrassed by the premature publication of the document and quickly denied its intention to implement the new financial arrangements recommended. But the Cabinet submission itself admitted that the funding of Australian higher education had reached crisis point, and this is generally agreed upon by all concerned with the sector. It is clear that the government prefers a further deregulated consumer-driven system, funded largely through student fees.

In January 2001, the federal government announced its $2.9 billion five-year strategy to boost innovation in R&D. The plan, *Backing Australia's Ability*, is built around three concepts: strengthening Australia's ability to generate ideas and undertake research, accelerating the commercial application of these ideas, and developing and retaining Australian skills. In addition to government commitment, the *Backing Australia's Ability* plan also requires the states and business and research institutions to spend $6 billion over the same period to attract its grants and incentives.

Whilst the Innovation Strategy has been welcomed by many in the public and private sector, there is the question of whether the financial commitment will be sufficient to offset the substantial funding cutbacks to the higher education sector since 1996. Despite the claim that this is 'the largest commitment to innovation ever made by an Australian government', it will only spend $159.4 million in its first year of 2001–02. Much of the funding announced will not begin to flow for 2–3 years, with $946.6 million to be outlaid in 2005–06. According to one commentator, the main problem with the plan is that it "merely reclaims opportunities squandered over several years".

According to the AVCC, in total funding terms, public investment in Australian universities peaked in the mid-1990s and then decreased through to 2001. "New specific government initiatives announced in 2001 for science and rural education have arrested but not reversed this decline" (AVCC 2001). The AVCC argues that to ensure internationally competitive quality in teaching and learning, the government component of university operating grants needs to return to the peak reached in the mid-1990s, and then needs to be progressively increased over five years.

6. CORPORATISATION AND MANAGERIALISM IN AUSTRALIAN HIGHER EDUCATION

The argument that public resources to higher education not only have declined, but must decline, should not be accepted unquestionably. In many countries, the absolute amount of public resources provided to higher education has increased, including Australia up to the mid-1990s, although funding per student unit may have declined. The financial predicament is only a part of a larger crisis facing the governance and management of higher education. At the root of this crisis is the corporatisation of the idea of the university, the rise of a managerialist mentality that leaves little room for traditional academic values. At the same time, tremendous pressure is being placed on universities to serve new roles and functions, while simultaneously preserving key traditions and values. The deleterious effects of these pressures are nowhere more apparent than in Australia.

The argument here is not that the governance and management of Australian higher education driven by market competition is all bad. The introduction of market competition into the steering of higher education at both systems and institutional levels has achieved a good deal, particularly with respect to raising revenue outside the public weal. But, when the market becomes an end in itself – an ideological self-proclaimed good, rather than a means of balancing the private and public benefits of higher education for the overall welfare of the society – the distortions are worrying indeed. Some of those distortions outlined in this paper are: educational provision determined more by client demand and profitability than by the long term cultural and educational needs of the nation; a very narrow view of the benefits of higher education in terms of private economic return; a concentrated effort to actually privatise public higher education through fees; and the treatment of universities like any other corporation in terms of industrial legislation (e.g. enterprise bargaining).

One thing that should be made absolutely clear is the distinction between the market as a specific, concrete set of exchange relationships having predictable outcomes, and the market as an ideologically constructed 'black box' that is *presumed* to produce the desirable outcomes and effects. Even in the economic literature, there is a good deal of debate about what is a market (Rosenbaum 2000) and the primacy of the market versus organisation as the coordinating mechanism of human activity (Simon 2000). And, in practice, there is not a one size fits all market, particularly in the public sector:

> a market does not automatically work as it is supposed to. 'Leave it to the market' is usually bad advice. With an ordinary private-sector market, the rules and procedures that govern it have evolved over years of trial and error. A public-sector market, by contrast, is judged by how well it works from its inception. Its rules and procedures therefore must be exhaustively thought through in advance. For a market to deliver on its public-policy promise, the government must design it skilfully (McMillan 2001: 2).

McMillan also makes the point that markets are limited and "can provide only part of the solution to a public problem ... Regulation continues to be needed; the role of the market is to help the regulators do their job more efficiently". He notes that the "very reasons why particular activities have been placed in the public sector – natural monopoly, externalities, common property – make implementing markets for them difficult". Moreover, Simon (2000: 753) maintains that research "shows that, on average, profit-making and governmental organisations that produce the same products, both operating in markets, attain about the same levels of efficiency – the profit motive appears to give no visible competitive edge to private business". The Australian government's approach to higher education management has largely argued the opposite.

Internationally, much of the reform of higher education has involved the creation of accountable governance structures, providing institutions with the autonomy they need to strengthen internal management and diversity their funding base. While achievement of these goals has been much more difficult in some systems of higher education than in others, there has been little questioning of its desirability. On the other hand, enhanced institutional autonomy, strengthened corporate management and diversified funding have not proven to be the panacea for all higher education ills as is commonly assumed. The Australian case demonstrates that these criteria may be necessary though not sufficient conditions for the overall effective management of the sector and individual institutions within it.

Public higher education institutions in few countries would have the degree of autonomy, the extent of corporate management or the lack of dependence on government grants that is the case in Australia. But what we find in Australia is a system in danger of becoming bogged down in its own corporate, market-driven mediocrity. This is not to argue that countries that have inherited centralised bureaucratised systems of higher education have not been paralysed in their capacity to reform in the light of rapid expansion and other environmental pressures. But what can be delivered by the market, public sector reform and the new public sector corporatised management, requires close scrutiny.

Orchard (1998: 28) argues that recent changes to the Australian public sector:

> reflect a much narrower and more circumscribed meaning of democracy and the public interest from that imagined by social democrats at an earlier time. Political rather than public and independent meanings of those terms now dominate ... Such a view reflects not social democracy but the cynical public choice, economic rationalist and post-modernist views that governing is driven by nothing other than specific and narrow interests of an increasingly disparate and chaotic assembly of groups and individuals. The reforms of the Australian public service introduced by the Howard government are simply speeding up the rationalisation and cutback of the role of government and will further undermine the independence of the public service.

Throughout the 1980s and into the 1990s, the theoretical underpinning of the economic rationalist and microeconomics rather than those of social democracy drove the reform agenda. At the same time, the number of critiques of economic rationalism have grown (for an overview, see Barker 1991; Pusey 1991; Argy 1998). In summarising a number of criticisms of economic rationalism and neo-classical economic market theory, Self (1998: 113) writes that:

> (a) The market system is not (nor is it likely to become) a 'level playing field'. There are big differences in effective market power and bargaining strength between capital and labour, big and small business, rich and poor countries .
>
> (b) The rewards of the market system are very unevenly and unequally distributed between people and nations ... these differences are becoming greater, save where effectively modified by political action. The 'trickle down' theory is not working.
>
> (c) The market system is highly unstable, especially in a global economy. It has frequent, destructive effects upon the life and livelihood of local communities ... It never has produced anything like a stable and high level of employment and will not do so in the future.
>
> (d) The directions of economic growth are less generally beneficial and more harmful than used to be the case. They combine a fierce search for sophisticated gadgets and entertainments for the relatively affluent with a failure to meet basic welfare needs ... for large numbers of poorer people. They are in many ways environmentally destructive and perverse.

Critiques of managerialism highlight many of the same issues: the introduction of inappropriate business practices into the public sector; an undue preoccupation with outputs and objective performance criteria; a narrowing of centralised control; a heavy reliance on the measurable; linking management competency almost solely with monetary rewards; stifling of dissent; a marketisation of public services that disenfranchise the poor; and a management environment that is not only highly competitive, but brutal (Orchard 1998; Zifcak 1997; Armstrong 1998).

Criticisms of the direction of public sector reform in Australia should not obscure the fact that change was necessary, that an inward looking public service protected by tenure and rank was entirely unsuited for the modern world of global economic competition, and that there is nothing inherently wrong with making the public sector more efficient, responsive, accountable and flexible. The same could be said of higher education. The purpose here is not to deride all changes to the Australian public sector or higher education. But, nonetheless, it does appear that reform has been largely captured by the intellectual radical right and there are strong indications of long term damage to the social fabric of the nation.

Much of the debate on public sector reform in Australia contains a strong element of inevitability – globalisation and economic imperatives meant that the substance of change to the public sector could not have been otherwise. However, this is not true; the theories of public choice and economic rationalism are strongly deterministic and build almost solely on their own internal logic.

Many if not most of the changes to the Australian public and higher education sectors that have occurred over the past 20 years are probably irreversible. Moreover, few if any who now advocate a change in direction argue for a return to the 'good old days'. It would be absurd to deny, for example, that the new public management reform agenda has not improved many aspects of the way in which the public sector operates in Australia. Moreover, the term 'new public management' itself does not depict a single unified approach to management issues. Nonetheless, Australia increasingly has been intent upon emulating "hard-line free-market policies, backed by a strengthening coalition of free-market interests and a government-inspired stultifying economic correctness" (Argy 1998: 249). Hopefully, the public sector Australia ends up with will be based on political choices on economic and social policy, rather than managerial imperatives.

7. CONCLUSION

It is extremely unlikely that Australia will ever return to the days when government provided nearly all the funds for higher education. Moreover, there are a number of reasons why the sector desires a diversified funding base, institutional autonomy being one of them. On the other hand, viewed comparatively, Australia is probably approaching the limit to which government can abrogate its responsibility to an unquestioning faith in the market and corporate management efficiency for financing public higher education.

Much of the policy in Australia, as elsewhere, has been directed at making higher education more relevant to industry and ensuring a direct contribution to the nation's economic well being. But we are hearing both nationally and internationally an argument that higher education's contribution to the knowledge economy must extend well beyond the parameters of economic growth (Dunkin 2000; OECD 1998).

In the latter half of the 1990s, the managers of Australian higher education institutions substantially increased their skill and capacity to find new markets and methods to at least partially offset the significant and continuing decline in government funding. Also, government resolve that an increasing proportion of the cost of higher education has to be transferred to the consumer has remained steadfast. But government (despite the political persuasion of the party in power) is in danger of becoming captured by its own rhetoric and ideology, reducing one of the nations most important assets to a state of for-profit mediocrity.

Rather than an emphasis on economic efficiency and an immediate return of money invested, what Australian higher education needs now is a very substantial injection of what has been termed as 'patient capital'. However, the sector cannot remain patient for much longer for that to occur, as the President of the AVCC makes clear (Chubb 2001):

> I suggest that we can't afford to wait. Nobody else is waiting for us ... the risk of playing catch-up relies on a dangerous assumption – the assumption that we can in fact do so. But that will prove increasingly difficult. For example, a group of my colleagues collaborated in a paper which shows that to re-establish our position within even OECD terms, we would now need an injection of around $13 – 14 billion for research funding alone. A big gap. But only part of the story. We must add to it the cost of re-investing in the base of our universities – a base that has also been let slip. Australian governments ... have let the per capita investment from the Commonwealth slide ... – let slip the patient capital – and have allowed it to be wholly or partially replaced by what might be called the impatient capital – of fees, tied (or specific) grants and outside earnings.

Over the last decade and particularly since the mid-1990s, it has been the political will of government to shift the funding of higher education from the state to the consumer and to treat higher education more as a private than a public good. It is also clear that little of this could have been accomplished had it not been for the capacity of management within institutions to become much more corporate like and entrepreneurial in the running of individual institutions. But the sector now is in danger of moving so far in the direction of privatising public higher education that government policy and managements' complicity are resulting in an era of higher education mediocrity from which the system may never recover.

In Australia, as elsewhere, a rethinking of the benefits of past strategies of economic and public sector reform is just starting. In the late 1980s and early 1990s there was a feeling of inevitability amongst politicians, practitioners and economists about privatisation, the superiority of the market over other forms of public sector management and the inherent efficiency of such mechanisms of privatisation as outsourcing, downsizing etc. However, it has become apparent with the start of the new millennium that not only is there a questioning of the inevitability regarding these processes but also there is a recognition that many of these processes are based more on ideological precepts than on technical rationale. We are also witnessing a significant social backlash to globalisation and privatisation. It is far from clear at this stage whether the reforms of the past decade will be fundamentally altered or subject merely to incremental adjustments. But what is clear is that an understanding of these processes and their likely future developments is a prerequisite to effective governance and management of the Australian public sector in general and of its higher education institutions in particular.

NOTES

[1] It should be pointed out that Geiger (1996) hypothesises that: "when resources are tight, the market is a much more powerful force for the differentiation of higher education institutions and functions than centralised policy and control". His argument is that in times of prosperity, institutions can afford to duplicate one another's product, but under more austere conditions they must find their individual market niche. While the first half of the 1990s in Australia could not be described as financially prosperous for higher education, there was substantial growth in the system and increasing budgets from all sources, including government. The effects of the severe belt-tightening that commenced in the mid-1990s, and the cost of past growth, are only starting to be felt now throughout the higher education sector. Geiger may well indeed be correct, but it will be several years before we know.

REFERENCES

Argy, F. *Australia at the Crossroads: Radical Free Market or a Progressive Liberalism?* Sydney: Allen & Unwin, 1998.

Armstrong, A. "A Comparative Analysis: New Public Management - The Way Ahead?' *Australian Journal of Public Administration* 57.2 (1998): 12 – 24.

AVCC Public Under Investment in Higher Education, AVCC: Canberra, 2001, www.avcc.edu.au.

Barker, G. "Elegance Without Relevance." *Age* 11 October (1991): 11.

Bessant, B. "Corporate Management and its Penetration of University Administration and Government." *Australian Universities' Review* 38.1 (1995): 59 – 62.

Castles, F., R. Gerritsen and J. Vowles (eds). *The Great Experiment.* Sydney: Allen and Unwin: 1996.

Chubb, I. "A presentation to the National Press Club", Sydney, 14 March, 2001.

Clare, R. and K. Johnston. Education and Training in the 1990s: Background Paper no. 31, Economic Planning Advisory Council, AGPS: Canberra, 1993.

Commonwealth Tertiary Education Commission Review of Efficiency and Effectiveness: Report of the Committee of Enquiry. AGPS: Canberra, 1986.

Considine, M. *Public Policy: A Critical Approach.* Melbourne: MacMillan, 1994.

Considine, M. and M. Painter (eds). *Managerialism: The Great Debate.* Melborne: Melbourne University Press, 1997.

Corbett, D. *Australian Public Sector Management.* 2nd edn. Sydney: Allen & Unwin, 1996.

DEET National Report on Australia's Higher Education Sector. AGPS: Canberra, 1993.

DETYA Higher Education Students Time Series Tables, selected higher education statistics, 2001a, http://www.detya.gov.au/highered/statinfo.htm.

DETYA Finance, selected higher education statistics, 2001b http://www.detya.gov.au/highered/statinfo.htm.

Dunkin, R. "RMIT: The Way Forward, From Entrepreneurial University to Innovative University", Inaugural Address, Melbourne, 30 October, 2000.

Evatt Foundation *The State of Australia.* Sydney: The Evatt Foundation, 1996.

Gallagher, M. "The Emergence of Entrepreneurial Public Universities in Australia." OECD/IMHE General Conference, Paris, 11 - 13 September, 2000.

Geiger, R. "Diversification in American Higher Education: Historical Patterns and Current Trends." In Meek, V.L., L. Goedegebuure, O. Kivinen and R. Rinne (eds). *The Mockers and Mocked: Comparative Perspectives on Diversity, Differentiation and Convergence in Higher Education,* Oxford: Pergamon, 1996, 118 – 203.

Harman, G. "Impact of New Public Management on Higher Education Reform in Australia." In N. Brendan (ed). *Public Sector Reform: An International Perspective*. London: Palgrave: London, 2001: 151 – 166.

Hawke, R.J.L. "Ministerial Statement: Reforming the Australian Public Service." Commonwealth Parliamentary Debates, Canberra, 25 September, 1986.

Higher Education: A Policy Discussion Paper circulated by the Hon J.S. Dawkins, MP. AGPS: Canberra, 1987.

Higher Education: A Policy Statement (1988), circulated by the Hon J.S. Dawkins, MP. AGPS: Canberra, 1988.

Higher Education Management Review Hoare Committee Report, AGPS: Canberra, 1995.

Hilmer, F. *National Competition Policy: Report by the Independent Committee of Inquiry*. Canberra: AGPS, 1993.

Howard, J. *Backing Australia's Ability*. Commonwealth of Australia: January, 2001.

Huisman, J., V.L. Meek, and F.Q. Fiona "Measuring institutional diversity in higher education: A comparison of ten national systems", unpublished manuscript, 1998.

Industry Commission Exports of Education Services, Report No. 12. Canberra: AGPS, 1991.

Industry Commission Research and Development, Report No. 44, Canberra: AGPS, 1995.

Jaspers, K. *The Idea of the University*. London: Beacon Press, [translated from the German Die Idee der Universitiät, 1946], 1960.

Laffin, M. "The Bureaucracies Compared: Past and Future Trends." In Weller, P. and G. Davis (eds). *New Ideas, Better Government*. Sydney: Allen & Unwin, 1996, 38 – 54.

Learning for Life: Final Report, Review of Higher Education Financing and Policy, R. West, Chair of Committee. AGPS: Canberra, 1998.

Mahony, D. "Government and the Universities: The "New" Mutuality in Australian Higher Education - A National Case Study." *Journal of Higher Education* 65.2 (1994): 123 – 46.

Marginson, S. and M. Considine. *The Enterprise University*. Melbourne: Cambridge University Press, 2000.

McInnes, M. "Public Sector Reform Under the Hawke Government: Reconstruction or Deconstruction?" *Australian Quarterly* Winter (1990): 108 – 24.

McMillan, J. "Using Markets to Help Solve Public Problems", Twelfth Annual East Asian Seminar on Economics, Hong Kong, 28–30 June, 2001.

Meek, V.L. "Australian public sector reform." In N. Brendan (ed). *Public Sector Reform: An International Perspective*. London: Palgrave, 2001, 34 – 47.

Meek, V. L. and F. Q. Wood. *Higher Education Governance and Management: An Australian Study*. Canberra: AGPS, 1997.

Moore, J. W. and L.F. Langknecht. "Academic planning in a political system." *Planning for Higher Education* 14.1 (1986): 1 – 5.

Neave, G. "Homogenization, Integration and Convergence: The Cheshire Cats of Higher Education Analysis." In Meek, V.L., L. Goedegebuure, O. Kivinen and R. Rinne (eds). *The Mockers and Mocked: Comparative Perspectives on Diversity, Differentiation and Convergence in Higher Education*. Oxford: Pergamon, 1996, 26 – 41.

OECD Universities Under Scrutiny. OECD: Paris, 1987.

OECD Governance in Transition: Public Sector Management Reforms in OECD Countries. OECD Public Sector Management Committee: Paris, 1995.

OECD Redefining Tertiary Education. OECD Publications: Paris, 1998.

OECD Education at a Glance – 2000 edition. OECD: Paris, 2000.

Orchard, L. "Managerialism, Economic Rationalism and Public Sector Reform in Australia: Connections, Divergences, Alternatives." *Australian Journal of Public Administration* 57.1 (1998): 19 – 32.

Phillips, D. "Competition, Contestability and Market Forces." In J. Sharpman and G. Harman (eds). *Australia's Future Universities*. Armidale: UNE Press, 1997, 221 – 237.

Pusey, M. *Economic Rationalism in Canberra*. Melbourne: Cambridge University Press, 1991.

Reforming the Australian Public Service. Canberra: AGPS, 1983.

Rosenbaum, E. "What is a Market? On the Methodology of a Contested Concept." *Review of Social Economy* 58.4 (2000).

Scales, B. *Report on Government Service Provision: Steering Committee for the Review of Commonwealth/State Service Provision*. Canberra: AGPS, 1993.

Self, P. "Public Choice and Public Benefit: Politics, Public Service and Markets." *Canberra Bulletin of Public Administration* 90 (December 1998): 113 – 14.

Serle, G. "God-Professors and Their Juniors." *Vestes* 6 (1963): 11 – 17.

Simon, H. "Public Administration in Today's World of Organizations and Markets", 2000 John Gaus Distinguished Lecture, Political Science, December (2000): 749 – 756.

Trow, M. "Manageralism and the Academic Profession: The Case of England." *Higher Education Policy* 7.2 (1994): 11 – 18.

Wagner, L. "So Who Owns Our Universities Then?" *Times Higher Education Supplement* 22 December (1995): 10.

Weller, P. "The Universality of Public Sector Reform: Ideas, Meanings, Strategies." In Weller, P. and G. Davis (eds). *New Ideas, Better Government*. Sydney: Allen & Unwin, 1996, 1 – 10.

Williams, B. "The 1988 White Paper on Higher Education." *Australian Universities' Review* 2 (1988): 2 – 8.

Zifcak, S. "Managerialism, Accountability and Democracy: A Victorian Case Study." *Australian Journal of Public Administration* 56.3 (1997): 106 – 119.

ELAINE EL-KHAWAS

GOVERNANCE IN US UNIVERSITIES

Aligning Internal Dynamics with Today's Needs

1. INTRODUCTION

In the United States, as in most countries, universities confronted increasing social demands throughout the twentieth century. As higher education expanded, universities and colleges repeatedly took steps to serve a more diverse clientele, to deepen their research engagements, and to extend their public service and outreach activities. By the early 1980s, the term 'multi-university' came into use in order to describe the multiple roles and wide range of activities of major US universities (Kerr 1982). By that time, many universities enrolled 25,000 and more students, offered degrees in 40 or more subject areas, and supported research efforts that accounted for hundreds of millions in annual expenditures (Glenny 1980; National Center for Education Statistics 1989). Today, size and complexity have reached further dimensions, as more than 4,000 institutions of higher education enrol almost 15 million students (The Chronicle of Higher Education 2001: 7, 9).

It appears that universities have made a remarkably successful response to changing demands. Participation rates among high-school leavers have grown significantly, to the point that most of those eligible for university study pursue a post-high-school degree program of some kind (National Center for Education Statistics 2000). Universities have absorbed vastly increased enrolments, in some instances repeatedly doubling their enrolment totals every decade. New institutions have been founded, largely fulfilling the hope that some form of post-high school study could be available to American citizens throughout the country. Community colleges have become a ubiquitous presence on the American landscape; collectively, over 1,700 two-year institutions serve vital roles as a point of initial entry for members of previously underserved populations and as a transfer mechanism opening up opportunity for further study. New research centres and new forms of collaboration between academia and industry have emerged; entrepreneurial ventures and collaboration with local and regional partners have become a hallmark of university operations, sometimes in the form of applied research partnerships and in other instances in expanded study opportunities for employed workers.

Several questions can be raised about how universities have been affected by their responses to changing environmental conditions and demands. What structural adaptations have been made to accommodate an expanded scope of activity, both educational and entrepreneurial? Have relationships among the core units of

Alberto Amaral, Glen A. Jones and Berit Karseth (eds.), Governing Higher Education:
National Perspectives on Institutional Governance, 261—278.
© 2002 *Kluwer Academic Publishers. Printed in the Netherlands.*

academic organisation changed? How has the distribution of power changed, as schools and departments have taken on new roles and as university structures have been modified to respond to more assertive external constituencies? Have the long-standing relationships between academics and administrators been changed within the university?

Numerous studies suggest that many internal changes have occurred among academic institutions (Brinkman and Morgan 1997; Dill 1997; Gumport and Pusser 1997; Kerr and Gade 1986; Massy 1996; Massy and Wilger 1998; O'Neil, Bensimon, Diamond and Moore 1999). Of particular interest for purposes here are several analyses showing that universities have modified their mechanisms of governance during the last few decades (Gumport 1993: 2000; Gumport and Pusser 1997; Lee 1991; Marcus 1997; Schuster et al., 1989, 1994). Special concern has been raised as to whether members of the professoriate have sufficient voice under the new arrangements that have emerged.

It must be acknowledged, however, that the available research is limited in scope. At best, studies have been exploratory, examining specific issues or the in-depth experience of a few institutions. Such work has provided largely descriptive evidence and interpretive commentary. These studies have yielded helpful insights but they do not offer firm conclusions about the overall direction of change. Moreover, scholarly analysis has given limited attention to broader questions about the impact of recent changes in governance patterns or the purposes they serve. Studies are needed that will help assess whether lasting gains have been achieved in terms of organisational adaptation and vitality (cf. Kezar 2001; Sporn 1999).

This paper is designed to encourage the pursuit of such broader research questions. Its purposes are, first, to assess some of the major changes that have taken place in governance and decision-making at US universities and, second, to offer a conceptual perspective that may guide needed research on the impact of recent changes. The larger question is whether these changes can be seen as examples of successful organisational adaptation, that is, whether recent changes will help universities and colleges to be stronger and more effective in dealing with the challenges they face in the years ahead.

The paper begins with an overview of the governance structures found at most US universities and colleges. Several aspects reflect the unique history of US higher education and, despite similar vocabulary, are different from what is found in many other countries (cf. Clark 1983; Goedegebuure and De Boer 1996; Van Vught 1995). A review is then offered of major changes over the last few decades that have had an important effect on university governance. This review is interpretive, bringing together a wide range of developments and assessing their effect on the prerogatives traditionally accorded to academics in university governance. The focus of the review is on institutions that offer at least a bachelor's degree and, usually, master's and doctoral degrees as well.

The paper then turns to some conceptual perspectives that might help create a research agenda to evaluate whether today's style of university governance offers a stronger, more adaptive university structure. The work of John Kotter is given special attention because of its potential relevance in gauging the adaptiveness of recent changes. A particular focus is a distinction Kotter has drawn between the organisational tasks required for coping with complexity and the different tasks required for coping with change (Kotter 1990; 1996).

2. UNDERSTANDING GOVERNANCE IN US UNIVERSITIES

Bearing in mind that variations occur in specific university or college settings (Clark 1983), the general structure of governance in US universities is hierarchical, and includes the elements shown in Figure 1.

In most US institutions, these basic structures have been in existence throughout the institution's history. So too, there have long been sharp, broadly understood demarcations of function among these structures, including a clear recognition of the primary role of academic authority in making decisions on academic matters (Floyd 1985).

- A board of trustees
- A president and administration
- Major subunits (mainly, schools or colleges, each devoted to a subset of academic subjects); and
- Academic departments, other centres, and institutes
- An academic senate (university-wide)

Figure 1. The General Structure of Governance at US Universities.

Governing boards – also called boards of trustees – are responsible for making the overall decisions about the policies and long-term directions to be taken by academic institutions. Board members are elected or appointed, and serve limited terms. They typically are well-regarded business persons or other professionals in the community, with some chosen on a national basis. They offer their services and advice in support of the institution's goals and may also be critics of the institution's activities. In many instances, they make financial contributions to the institution. In all of these respects, board members act in their capacity as individuals, not as official representatives of a specific 'stakeholder' group or organisation (Fisher 1991; Association of Governing Boards 1992).

Most US universities and colleges do not include students as members of governing boards, although some members of the board may be alumni, including recent graduates of the institution. So too, university staff and academics are not generally represented on university governing boards. At most, individuals holding academic or professional positions at other universities may serve on the board but they serve in an individual capacity, not as formal representatives of academic interests.

The role and structure of governing boards have remained largely the same for decades. A long-standing differentiation exists between public and private institutions in how board members view the institution and perceive their own role. At public institutions, governing boards generally reflect external perspectives; they offer assistance and guidance, but also play a strong oversight role, ensuring that the university serves public interests. At private universities, boards generally emphasize assistance and guidance, seeking to help the institution carry out its own plans.

Public and private institutions also differ in how board members are chosen. At public institutions, members are appointed, usually by a state official such as the governor. In a few instances, board members are elected to public university boards by a direct, popular vote. At private institutions, in contrast, the formal system is that boards are self-perpetuating. That is, the entire board votes to approve and appoint new members, usually relying on preliminary choices made by a board subcommittee.

Formally speaking, the president and other administrative officers of the university are not members of the board, except in an *ex officio* role. The president (and, sometimes, senior administrators) work directly with boards, but these relationships may range from being cordial, informal and collaborative to formal, tense and adversarial (Kerr and Gade 1986; Fisher 1991). In general practice, effective presidents work very closely with their boards and, because of their greater knowledge and perspective on most matters, the board often defers to the president for determining the final direction of actions that a board may take.

One way that this informal relationship can be observed is found in the process of developing an agenda for board meetings. Technically, the board – that is, the board chairperson or the board's executive committee – sets the agenda. Typically, however, the board chair and the president jointly confer and develop an agenda, both for each board meeting and for the board's role over the long term.

The university president is the chief executive officer, with direct authority for making decisions on almost all aspects of university operations. Much has been written about the wide scope of responsibility held by today's university presidents (Kerr and Gade 1986; Rosovsky 1990). They have demanding institutional roles, as both the symbolic and functional head of their universities. In this internal capacity, they handle a wide range of day-to-day matters while also helping the university community understand and support the university's larger purposes and potential. They also have a demanding external role, working in their city or community on important problems and representing the university in its efforts to secure new projects, research funding or donations. The external role is becoming more important, and many observers have argued that it has become the dominant part of a president's role.

Typically, the president has a cabinet, or administrative management team, that includes several vice presidents and a general counsel (who addresses legal matters). Presidents work very closely with members of their cabinet, meeting at least weekly as a group and in numerous other meetings as well. Vice presidents generally include vice presidents for finance, for administration, for academic affairs, and for student affairs. Collectively, the senior officers and the president are the major locus of decision-making for many universities. Day-to-day matters are settled informally in meetings among members of this group, and general strategy on most long-term issues is initially discussed by this group (Fisher 1991; Gumport 2000; Rhoades 1995; Rosovsky 1990).

The person in charge of academic matters is the vice president for academic affairs, sometimes called a provost, an academic dean (especially at smaller institutions) or a director of educational services (especially at community colleges). The provost is the senior officer with direct responsibility for all matters related to the academic role of the university, including academic staffing, development of new teaching or research programs as well as decisions to cut back on or reorganise those programs.

Deans are the heads of the major academic subunits within a university (equivalent to faculties in many other countries, but called schools or colleges in US universities). Deans report to the academic vice president (or provost) and, at most institutions, they meet regularly with the provost to discuss issues and new directions being proposed. In formal terms, these meetings are informational and advisory, and thus not part of the governance structure. In practice, however, much of what is discussed and agreed upon in these meetings becomes the operating practice of the institution (Gumport 2000; Rhoades 1995; Wolverton, Gmelch, Montez and Nies 2001).

It is important to recognize that deans have an unusual status in the organisational hierarchy of universities. They are not part of the president's 'cabinet' or top administrative team, yet each dean serves as the chief administrative officer for his or her school. Furthermore, although the academic vice president and the school deans typically have academic training and often join academic departments when they resign from administrative duties, the deans and the academic vice president are nonetheless considered to be part of the university's administration.

Although many policies and practices of universities are settled on a university-wide basis, a significant number of decisions are made by each school within the university. Most universities are organised into several schools, which may include schools of law, medicine, education, engineering, and arts and sciences. School-level decisions reflect the special needs and concerns relevant to the subset of academic subjects and research arenas found within each school. Such decisions are subject to the final agreement of the provost and/or president, but often are accepted without revision.

Academic departments and institutes represent the 'basic unit' level within a university, where teaching and research is actually conducted (Walvoord, Carey, Smith, Soled, Way and Zorn 2000; Hecht, Higgerson, Gmelch, and Tucker 1999). Persons serving as the chairperson of academic departments often are significant players in university governance. In the last decade, they have taken on greater administrative responsibility, moving from a role of handling routine academic decisions (when courses will be taught, how courses might be revised, etc) to one of making administrative decisions about planning and budgeting, and about faculty hiring and workload.

Most universities also have a large number of institutes, with varying patterns of linkage between the institutes and the departments. At some universities, institutes report to a school dean; at other universities, they report to the provost's office. Some are closely affiliated with one academic department; others are linked to several departments. Members of academic staff generally hold an appointment in a specific department, even when their responsibilities are taken up entirely with the work of an institute.

The academic senate has long been the principal decision-making body that represents the views of academics on university matters. The terms used to refer to this body, and its rules for eligibility, vary among universities. A general pattern is that the senate is made up of those who hold regular, full-time academic positions at the university (Lee 1991; Gumport 2000). In some cases, only tenured academics, or only those with full professor status, are members of the senate. Frequently, especially at very large universities, the senate is a representative body, and includes only a small number of academics elected for limited terms. Each member of the faculty senate, under these arrangements, is elected by a voting procedure undertaken within his or her own school, with voting typically limited to those academics who would be eligible for membership in the senate (i.e., usually, regular full-time faculty). Practice varies but, at a few institutions, the academic vice president or the president is a member of the academic senate and may preside over its deliberations (Gumport 2000; Jordan 2001).

Faculty unions have become another voice for academic staff at many universities and colleges (Kemerer and Baldridge 1981; Rhoades 1998). Generally, unions participate in a limited range of matters, focused on the 'terms and conditions' of academic employment and the preservation of procedural rights accorded to academic staff. Even so, many universities find that they have two organisations that speak for academics on many matters, and thus two organisations that are to be contacted on matters affecting academic staff (Rhoades 1998).

3. RECENT TRENDS IN GOVERNANCE AND MANAGEMENT

The last few decades have seen relatively little change in university governance structures. Although most universities have become larger, and may have more subunits, their governance structures are much the same. Changes have occurred, however, in the internal dynamics of decision-making, that is, in a shifting distribution of influence across these structures.

Of particular interest are the internal changes that have affected the participation of academic staff in university decisions (cf. Kezar 2001; Jordan 2001; Rhoades 1993). Some universities have taken steps to establish new opportunities for academics to participate in decisions, especially some of the 'big' decisions that need to be made (Dill and Helm 1988). As Schuster et al. (1994) have documented, several institutions have established university-wide planning councils to accomplish this objective. This structure operates in addition to the regular governance and decision-making structures that have long been a part of university life.

The issues in allowing effective academic participation in university decisions are far from settled. If anything, they are made more difficult by other trends affecting academics. Full academic participation in university deliberations has become impossible at large universities, for example, where the number of academics at the university might well exceed 2,000. The changing nature of the teaching staff is another factor, as a larger proportion of teaching duties is carried out by teaching assistants – doctoral students who also serve as instructors – or by contracted, part-time instructors who are not eligible to be members of the academic senate. Research institutes often operate with a small nucleus of regularly appointed academic staff and a large number of contracted research associates. As a consequence of these trends, the formal decision bodies in which academics do participate are able to represent the views of an increasingly small and privileged component of those who teach and carry out research under the university's auspices.

To review the significant changes occurring over the last few decades in university management and governance, this paper considers three important changes:

- Strengthened administrative steering
- New university-wide decision bodies, and
- Internal shifts in authority

The paper argues that these changes in the internal dynamics of universities have had significant effects on governance. Some have been very consequential, although they have not received much attention. One such change, stronger central 'steering', is evidenced by a broad pattern of new management rules that are implemented on a university-wide basis and that constrain the areas that traditionally were the prerogative of academics. Other important changes include some shifts in internal patterns of authority, especially in ways that strengthen the administrator perspective at the cost of academic perspectives.

3.1. Strengthening administrative steering

Both administrators and academics would agree that the degree of purposeful 'steering' at most US universities has increased over the last few decades. This parallels the pattern in Europe, reflected in Clark's focus (1998) on a strengthened 'steering core' for entrepreneurial universities. A more generalized wording better describes the US pattern, however, which has taken a wider variety of forms.

One manifestation is an enlarged professional capacity at the level of the 'top' administration. More vice presidents have been appointed in administrative areas, including vice presidents for university advancement (that is, fund-raising), for planning, for external affairs, and for continuing or distance education. A large university may have seven or eight vice presidents, each with several assistant or associate vice presidents. Their backgrounds are generally not in academic disciplines but, instead, may be in business management, law, or finance. Collectively, such top officers are viewed within the university as administrators who are loyal to the president. Further, as Kezar has noted (2001), there is an increased sense that divergent institutional cultures are developing on many campuses, as an 'administrative' subculture gains ground in relation to the traditional academic culture.

Some analysts have reported a tendency for administrators to pay less attention to academic views when making decisions. Gumport and Pusser, for example, identified a pattern in which quick changes are called for, with purported urgency being the reason for bypassing traditional academic governance (Gumport 1993; Gumport and Pusser 1997). The inclination to bypass academic governance also may be related to the increased size of the administrative ranks. Thus, as more senior administrators meet to work out new initiatives, they may feel more comfortable with what they've developed and less inclined to extend their internal deliberative process to academic groups. The administrator view, generally, is that academic deliberations are slow and inefficient (Jordan 2001; Chabotar 1995).

Another aspect of strengthened administrative steering is a broadened use of mechanisms that represent 'steering by regulation'. Thus, most universities have introduced new rule-based systems for performance monitoring and resource allocation that, together, represent a significantly different and stronger 'steering' of university activities by the administration. Under this approach, centralized administrative rules operate as constraints that 'steer' decisions and actions taking place throughout the university. Academic senates generally have had a limited role in setting such rules. Strictly speaking, these are administrative, not academic matters. Yet, they usually have significant effects on the work of academics.

The most significant examples of this approach are found in rules designed to improve productivity and accountability, which have become a widespread phenomenon in US universities over the last few decades (Brinkman and Morgan 1997; Massy 1996). Models for cost-effectiveness have been developed and implemented on an institution-wide basis. Automatic, multi-year budget cuts have been implemented at some universities, with the explicit rationale that they are to be offset by 'productivity gains'. Responsibility centre budgeting, a widespread form of formula-based rules (sometimes referred to by its initials, RCB), involves guidelines and formulas that allocate university resources, in principle by allocating to each 'unit' the income that it actually earns. Under RCB strictures, for example, new ideas can be pursued only if the unit can first identify and obtain income that will cover any expenses the new initiatives might require. Such rules are prudent and sensible, but one of their 'costs' is that they constrain initiative and creativity.

A different layer of institutional steering has appeared as institutions have introduced rules that specifically govern academic matters. Examples include tighter rules about course sizes, limits on faculty sabbatical leaves, or data-based monitoring of faculty productivity, workload and outside activity. Such rules, which set guidelines designed to promote greater efficiency on matters that traditionally were left to academic decision-making, represent new constraints on academic planning at both the school level and at the level of academic departments (Gumport 1993; Tucker and Bryan 1988).

Some universities, as part of their response to external, state-agency pressures for quality assurance, have developed systems of performance indicators (El-Khawas 1995, 1998; Seymour 1992). Other approaches focus on specific aspects of university operations, as with planning systems for space usage or growth models for library acquisitions. Decision support systems, increasingly widespread and sophisticated, are also part of this strengthened steering approach that relies on data analysis, objectively defined goals, and resource-allocation rules (Brinkman and Morgan 1997; Massy and Wilger 1998).

3.2. New university-wide decision bodies

Although academic senates have long been the key mechanism by which academics formally participate in deliberations over new policies and practices, there has also been a history of administration frustration with the inefficiencies of senates. Their agendas are often narrowly academic, their deliberative process quite slow. While many university presidents recognize the value of such deliberative bodies, many have also established other mechanisms, usually ad hoc committees or task forces, to obtain academic perspectives on important matters (Jordan 2000; Birnbaum 1989b).

At some universities, a formal structural change has been to develop university-wide strategic planning committees (Schuster et al., 1994). A distinctive feature of such committees is that they include a mixture of senior administrative personnel as well as academics, often with academic representation from each of the constituent schools or colleges within the university. Another distinctive feature is that they typically are charged with a special role: to address long-term planning for the university. David Dill (e.g., 1997) has given us insightful analyses of the ways that such strategic planning committees have addressed their responsibilities. These committees collectively gather and evaluate a wide range of information on the university's performance. Often, they hold public hearings, at which testimony and evidence are presented on specific matters under review. The committees typically conduct a formal process for sharing their ideas and for seeking comments from a wide range of university constituencies about their emerging recommendations.

This strategic planning role, by its nature, falls outside the activities of university administration (Keller 1983). It also requires the participation of academics, partly to obtain their special insights into needs and opportunities but also to give the planning exercise a sense of academic legitimacy. Although most universities follow procedures in which their normal, ongoing governance structures – especially, the academic senate – have a chance to consider the strategic plans that the committee is developing, it is the strategic planning committee itself that has the greatest influence on the shape of the plans that emerge.

These 'big decision' strategic planning bodies have complex and ambiguous purposes. As a result, failures are to be expected. Many of these committees fail to arrive at clear agendas or consistent priorities and plans (Schuster et al., 1994). Despite the best efforts of these committees, a university's plan often seems to be a lengthy compilation of vague but laudatory purposes. At times, the committees operate without sufficient structure and solutions seem to be offered almost randomly by a changing set of actors. It should be recognized, too, that only a few academics serve as members of such committees, and they are usually appointed by top administrators rather than elected. They are often thought of as being 'hand-picked' to match administrative views and perspectives (Jordan 2001). As a practical matter, these academics are not representing the views of other academics, nor are their views properly considered to be anyone's views other than their own.

Their role on such committees is mainly to offer information and opinion. They are a minority of the membership and, generally, are not able to influence or control committee decisions.

If reliance on such strategic planning committees becomes widespread, this could mark a significant new departure in the mechanisms of university decision-making. Even now, because of the attention such committees have received within several universities, this new mechanism needs to be understood and analysed.

3.3. Internal shifts in authority

Another consequential set of changes can be found in a shifting distribution of authority among various parts of the university. As one component of this change, a devolution of authority can be described, as deans of the constituent schools within the university have gained greater responsibility. This change has been gradual but most observers agree that, compared to a few decades ago, deans today have greater ability to take autonomous action without relying on specific instructions from higher authorities (Tucker and Bryan 1988; Wolverton and others 2001). It must be acknowledged, however, that what has increased is, in part, their authority to carry out activities that will meet university-wide planning goals or that will conform to university-wide rules for resource allocation.

Nevertheless, a significant nexus of university decision-making today resides in the role of the dean. As the head of one of the university's constituent schools, the dean will necessarily be a strong advocate for its needs and prerogatives. Yet, the dean is also, in certain respects, a member of the central administration, having participated in processes that have developed new university-wide rules and monitoring systems, for example, with respect to productivity or resource allocation. Each dean is consequently expected to abide by the centralized rules (Gumport 1993; 2000).

Deans have also benefited from another shift in authority and responsibility that has occurred within the university. They have gained power from the lower ranks of the academic hierarchy, that is, from the academic departments that are found within each school or college. In the US, the traditional model was one in which academic departments were the locus of most academic decisions – about curriculum, about degree offerings, and, especially, about the hiring and promotion of academic personnel. Increasingly, university rules have been modified and decision authority is located in the dean's office.

One of the most striking examples of this shift in authority is found when a vacancy occurs in an academic position, due to the retirement or resignation of a professor. In the past, the prerogative for decisions to fill the vacancy rested with academic departments. Today, the widespread pattern is that the position vacancy 'reverts' to the dean's authority. At best, the department has some ability to make a recommendation for reclaiming the position.

Other influences are also at work to expand the scope and significance of the dean's role (cf. Wolverton and others 2001). An increased level of research and other, 'third-stream' income – which Clark (1998) described in terms of an "expanded developmental periphery" – has also occurred within US universities. However, these activities – and funds – are generally linked with a specific college or school within the university. This pattern (which provides the practical basis for Responsibility Centred Budgeting, mentioned earlier) obviously favours certain schools, such as business or engineering, more than others, but it also prevents the central administration from having its own control over a significant flow of funds. A related development is that deans have begun to take an active role in fund-raising, working to increase such external support for initiatives that will be conducted within their own schools (Hall 1993; Mercer 1997). Here, too, the dean's position is strengthened.

4. THE RELEVANCE OF ORGANISATIONAL THEORIES

In light of these changes in university governance over the last few decades, there is reason to consider their general impact on universities. It might be argued, for example, that an overall effect of the various trends – strengthened administrative steering, the development of university-wide planning bodies, and internal shifts in authority – has been to introduce a much stronger degree of rationality to university functioning. Whether we call it corporatist or managerial, the evidence summarized above and, in more extended treatments elsewhere, does suggest that more orderly and comprehensive planning and decision processes have become a prevalent mode of university functioning.

To evaluate these changes in a systematic and comprehensive way, it may be fruitful to assess them in light of scholarly work on organisational structures and dynamics. One area of inquiry would be to question how these new steering processes and expanded administrative activities have changed the internal dynamics of academic decision-making. A larger question can also be raised: have such changes strengthened universities and given them greater capacity to adapt to changes they face in their external circumstances?

The work of many organisational theorists in the 1970s and 1980s stressed the weak capacity for decision-making in universities (e.g., Birnbaum 1989a; Cohen and March 1974; Weick 1976). Universities were not very effective in resolving problems, they argued, as "choices are made only when the shifting combinations of problems, solutions, and decision-makers happen to make action possible" (Cohen and March 1974: 90).

This view certainly poses a contrast with the strengthened steering and other changes that have just been described. Have universities therefore increased their capacity for decision-making? This is not clear, although it certainly can be said that universities have strengthened their general capabilities for understanding, monitoring and controlling their own internal processes. Although important gaps are readily apparent, it is no longer true that universities have a 'weak information base'. So too, as a result of formula-based resource allocation models, presidents and the central administration of many universities can influence many more areas than they could in the past, including academic personnel decisions and matters of educational policy.

Another question should be addressed: have the administration's gains caused an erosion of academic influence? On matters of academic tenure, for example, some universities have introduced centralized mandates that limit the proportion of academic personnel who can hold tenure. Other administrative decisions limit the ability of academic departments to make tenure-eligible appointments. Although decisions about the academic curriculum remain the province of academics, these decisions are also constrained by central administration rules, especially with regard to the likely 'market demand' for a curricular subject or degree option. Aside from these changes, significant new areas of university decision-making – from fund-raising to decisions about auxiliary enterprises – are sometimes made almost entirely without academic consultation and influence.

Some concepts from Robert Birnbaum's work on university management and decision processes (Birnbaum 1989a) offer the basis for several observations about recent changes in university management and governance. His perspective on subunits within the university, for example, may help to interpret how deans handle their conflicting decision pressures. For deans, the specific rules may have changed but they have always operated on a 'subsystem' basis, monitoring their own operations and making adjustments in response to the limited number of inputs that directly affect their school (Birnbaum 1989a: 183 – 184). So too, deans maintain a considerable degree of autonomy as long as they operate within the boundaries set by the university's new rules and regulations.

Birnbaum's insight into the role of social controls – that is, implicit controls and shared attitudes that are embedded in university culture and that have built up over time – also suggests that there may be some limits to the effectiveness of the new university-wide decision bodies at some universities. When these new committees are compared across several campuses, substantial differences emerge in the issues they address, in the solutions they offer and, even in the specificity of their recommendations (Schuster et al., 1994). It seems that the new 'big decision' committees are showing respect for implicit norms at their institutions and thus, it might be predicted that their results may not be so threatening to long-term organisational functioning (Birnbaum 1989a: 182).

What can be said about the larger question, whether these changes are adaptive and strengthen the university? An initial judgment can be made on the basis of work by John Kotter, who has written extensively on organisational behaviour in the context of changing environmental conditions. Much of Kotter's work makes a critical distinction between the organisational tasks required for coping with complexity and the different organisational tasks required for coping with change (Kotter 1978; 1990; 1996). Thus, although universities may be continuing a long-term evolution from traditional forms of administration and governance, Kotter's work suggests that they may be concentrating too much on the more visible and immediate problems created by growing organisational complexity. As a result, they may be giving too little attention to the challenges of addressing a rapidly changing environment. In other words, they may have become more effective in dealing with complexity but have not adapted to the different needs of rapid change (Kotter 1996).

This concern can be illustrated in terms of three comparisons Kotter has offered, as outlined in Figure 2. As this outline suggests, the indicators of coping with complexity seem to be more descriptive of recent trends in university governance than those indicators that focus on external change.

Three Decision Areas	*To cope with complexity*	*To cope with change*
What actions are needed?	Plan and set goals; Decide on actions and budget to meet goals	Set a direction with a vision of the future
How can these actions be achieved?	Organize structures and jobs; delegate; monitor implementation	Align people by new coalitions committed to change
What will ensure that results are achieved?	Control by monitoring and corrective actions	Motivate and inspire toward change

Figure 2. Needed Organisational Actions to Fit Different Environmental Challenges,
(Kotter, 1990).

The first major decision to be made by university leaders regards the nature of the planning task. In Kotter's model, planning differs according to whether the imperative is to cope with how a complex organisation can achieve its long-standing goals or, instead, whether the imperative is to cope with significant environmental change. If a plan to address rapid external change is needed, Kotter posits that the key task is to identify the right direction for future effort. An organisation needs to gather and analyse a broad range of data, looking for patterns that help understand the organisation and its changing context. The organisation also needs to create a vision that describes what it should become over the long term, along with some broad-based strategies for realistically reaching that vision. The vision need not be lofty or even original, but it must match the interests of the university's various constituencies and must fit with what the university can realistically accomplish (Kotter 1990).

The trends reviewed in Part 2 offer some contrast to Kotter's model for change. Those trends – for example, to develop detailed long-range plans and to establish formula-based rules that monitor both administrative and academic activities of the university – resemble the aspects of the Kotter model that adjust operations to increased internal complexity, not to greater environmental change. Kotter's work also offers some ways to gauge whether planning efforts have the wrong focus. One sign is when formal plans need to be revised frequently because of continuing changes in external conditions. Another sign is when planning seems to be endless, as sub-issues get explored at great length and the process gets politicised. Still another sign is when the plan gets put on a shelf and forgotten because it did not provide a practical sense of direction.

Kotter outlined two other imperatives: deciding what should be done and deciding how to monitor whether results are being achieved (Figure 2). These are among the fundamental 'design' questions for any formal organisation. Under his first model, directed inwardly to help an organisation cope with its own complexity, these questions become matters of deciding, first, how an organisation will structure its work (for example, through reporting relationships and authority hierarchies, job descriptions, and plans for financial compensation) and, secondly, how it will implement adequate monitoring procedures.

In Kotter's model, these two questions require a different response if the organisation believes that its greatest need is to adapt to a changing environment. To cope with external change, decisions on what needs to be done must be made by many individuals, with each making appropriate adjustments to fit new needs. The organisation 'directs' this change by communicating to individuals throughout the organisation. Individuals then 're-align' their actions once they have a chance to understand the new realities and their implications. This view assumes that, under conditions of rapid external change, formal controls and centralized regulations are not able to respond quickly enough to the specific changes facing each organisational unit.

Similarly, monitoring of results is handled differently in organisations that give priority to coping with external change. Rather than 'pushing' people to comply, the goal becomes one of motivating them. The organisation explains its vision and helps its staff gain a sense of how they can be involved and take initiative. The work of many units is 'coordinated' through strong staff networks and informal relationships that transmit information and resolve potential conflicts more effectively than formal mechanisms could (Kotter 1990).

Again, it is sobering to compare Kotter's model for coping with rapid change and recent trends in university actions. It seems that US universities have adapted well to yesterday's governance challenges, adapting their organisational structure to large size and its consequent complexity. However, in their preoccupation with complexity, these universities may have neglected the emerging challenge – already faced by many profit-directed business organisations – of adjusting to rapid change.

5. TOWARD A BETTER UNDERSTANDING OF TODAY'S GOVERNANCE PATTERNS

These preliminary conclusions offer a basis for developing a new research agenda on universities as organisations. Three new directions for research will be identified; each raises questions that could increase our understanding of the adaptiveness of organisational decisions.

First, Kotter's work suggests several specific, and testable, research questions that could clarify the actual effects of recent changes in university governance. He has argued, for example, that increased attention to long-range planning and to management controls may not be productive if the university is facing rapid change in its environment. Some practical research questions emerge from this proposition, including:

- To what extent have recent governance activities to develop strategic plans been productive? Are they seen as time-consuming and wasteful? Have they found active use once they were formally completed?
- To what extent have recent activities to manage universities been productive? How have they changed the behaviour of academic staff?
- Under what conditions, or in what parts of the university, have planning committees and management controls been effective?
- What is the relative extent of academic versus administrative influence over specific university decisions? How constraining, for example, are formulas and other decision rules to the actual operating decisions of academic departments?

Secondly, the Kotter model suggests some theoretical considerations. How can we understand the nature of the organisational structure of universities today? Does it still resemble the 'organised anarchy' model described by theorists during the 1970s and 1980s, or has it evolved to match more closely the characteristics of other large organisations, including the business firms that have been the basis for much of Kotter's conceptualisations? An intensive research inquiry would be needed to address this fundamental but important question. Is it appropriate to think of universities as another type of formal, complex organisation, comparable to other organisations of similar size? Do certain universities fit this characterisation and, if so, what distinguishes them from other academic institutions? In terms of the potential criteria for organisational adaptiveness, do universities continue to have any distinctive organisational characteristics or strengths?

A third set of questions follows from this rethinking about whether universities continue to have important distinctive characteristics. It would be timely to conduct a new inquiry into the nature of university structures and processes, an inquiry conducted without the assumptions derived from earlier analyses and, perhaps, an inquiry conducted in a variety of university settings. An unbiased inquiry might, for instance, find evidence that a 'mixed' organisational form is viable. For example, certain subparts of universities may still be distinctively 'academic' in organisational terms, even though the universities as a whole exhibit many general features that 'look like' business corporations. As an alternative hypothesis, certain parts of the university – and especially those subunits most strongly linked with external circumstances – may have positioned themselves to 'look like' business entities even though the overall university still honours significant aspects of traditional academic organisation. Supporting this hybrid view, perhaps, is the evidence indicating that, as universities become more 'business-like', they continue to acknowledge the legitimacy of academic involvement in decision-making. Academics participate in bodies that address broad issues of policy and purpose. They continue to make decisions about teaching, learning and the shape of academic programs. Thus, academic voices still seem to matter, even in organisational settings where the overall influence of academics has been attenuated.

To conclude, one can certainly argue that the changes in university governance and decision-making that have been reviewed in this paper need to be better understood. They may be 'hollow' changes that will not change the fundamental nature of universities as they have long been understood. Instead, they may presage a fundamental redirection of universities as organisations. This paper has attempted to identify issues that may advance a research agenda designed to clarify these issues. Above all, we need to challenge our own assumptions about the organisational life and adaptiveness of universities in the early years of the twenty-first century.

REFERENCES

Association of Governing Boards of Universities and Colleges. *Trustees and Troubled Times in Higher Education*. Washington, D.C.: Association of Governing Boards of Universities and Colleges, 1992.
Birnbaum, R. *How Colleges Work: The Cybernetics of Academic Organization and Leadership*. San Francisco: Jossey-Bass, 1989a.
Birnbaum, R. "The Latent Organizational Functions of the Academic Senate: Why Senates do not Work but will not Go Away." *Journal of Higher Education* 60.4 (1989b): 423 – 443.
Birnbaum, R. (ed). *Faculty in Governance: The Role of Senates and Joint Committees in Academic Decision-Making*. New Directions for Higher Education, no. 75, San Francisco: Jossey-Bass, 1991.
Brinkman, P. T. and A. W. Morgan. "Changing Fiscal Strategies for Planning." In Peterson, M. W., D.D. Dill, L.A. Mets and associates. *Planning and Management for a Changing Environment*. San Francisco: Jossey-Bass, 1997, 288 – 306.
Chabotar, K. J. "Managing Participative Budgeting in Higher Education." *Change* (September-October 1995): 21 – 29.
Clark, B. R. *The Higher Education System: Academic Organization in Cross-National Perspective*. Berkeley: University of California Press, 1983.
Clark, B. R. *Creating Entrepreneurial Universities*. Oxford: Elsevier Science Ltd, 1998.
Cohen, M. D. and J. G. March. *Leadership and Ambiguity: The American College President*. New York: McGraw-Hill/Carnegie Commission on Higher Education, 1974.
Cohen, M. D. and J. G. March. *Leadership and Ambiguity: The American College President*. 2nd edition. Boston: Harvard Business School Press, 1986.
Dill, D. D. and K. P. Helm. "Faculty Participation in Strategic Policy-making." In Smart, J. C. (ed). *Higher Education: Handbook of Theory and Research*, vol. 4. New York: Agathon Press, 1988, 319 – 55.
Dill, D.D. "Focusing Institutional Mission to Provide Coherence and Integration." In Peterson, M. W., D.D. Dill, L. A. Mets, and associates. *Planning and Management for a Changing Environment*. San Francisco: Jossey-Bass, 1997, 171 – 190.
El-Khawas, E. "External Review: Alternative Models based on US Experience." *Higher Education Management* 7.1 (1995): 39 – 48.
El-Khawas, E. "Strong State Action but Limited Results: Perspectives on University Resistance." *European Journal of Education* 33.3 (1998): 317 – 330.
Fisher, J.L., *The Board and the President*. Washington, D.C.: American Council on Education/Macmillan 1991.
Floyd, C. *Faculty Participation in Decision-Making*. ASHE-ERIC Report No. 8. Washington, D.C.: Association for the Study of Higher Education/George Washington University, 1985.
Goedegebuure, L. and H. de Boer. "Governance and Decision-making in Higher Education: Comparative Aspects." *Tertiary Education and Management* 2.2 (1996): 160 – 169.
Glenny, L. A. "Demographics and Related Issues for Higher Education in the 1980s." *Journal of Higher Education* 51.4 (1980): 376 – 389.
Gumport, P. J. "Contested Terrain of Academic Program Reduction." *Journal of Higher Education* 64.3 (1993): 283 – 311.
Gumport, P. J. *Academic Governance: New Light on Old Issues*. AGB Occasional Paper. Washington, D.C.: Association of Governing Boards of Universities and Colleges, 2000.

Gumport, P. J. and B. Pusser. "Restructuring the Academic Environment." In Peterson, M. W., D. D.Dill, L.A. Mets and associates, *Planning and Management for a Changing Environment*. San Francisco: Jossey-Bass, 1997, 453 – 478.

Hall, M. R. *The Dean's Role in Fund Raising*. Baltimore: Johns Hopkins University Press, 1993.

Hecht, I.W.D., M.L. Higgerson, W.H. Gmelch, and A. Tucker. *The Department Chair as Academic Leader*. Phoenix, Arizona: Oryx/American Council on Education, 1999.

Jordan, R. "The Faculty-Senate Minuet." *Trusteeship*, Washington, D.C.: Association of Governing Boards of Universities and Colleges (September/October 2001): 18 – 22.

Keller, G. *Academic Strategy: The Management Revolution in American Higher Education*. Baltimore: Johns Hopkins University Press, 1983.

Kemerer, F. and V. Baldridge. "Senates and Unions: Unexpected Peaceful Coexistence." *Journal of Higher Education* 52.3 (1981): 256 – 64.

Kerr, C. *The Uses of the University*. Cambridge, Massachusetts; Harvard University Press, 1982.

Kerr, C., and M. Gade. *The Many Lives of Academic Presidents: Time, Place and Character*. Washington, D.C.: Association of Governing Boards, 1986.

Kezar, A.J. *Understanding and Facilitating Organizational Change in the Twenty-First Century*. ASHE-ERIC Higher Education Report, 28.4. San Francisco: Jossey-Bass, 2001.

Kotter, J. P. *Organizational Dynamics: Diagnosis and Intervention*. Reading, Massachusetts: Addison-Wesley Publishing Co., 1978.

Kotter, J. P. *A Force for Change*. New York: Free Press; London: Collier Macmillan, 1990.

Kotter, J. P. *Leading Change*. Boston, Massachusetts: Harvard Business School Press, 1996.

Lee, B. A. "Campus Leaders and Campus Senates." In Birnbaum, R. (ed). *Faculty in Governance: The Role of Senates and Joint Committees in Academic Decision-Making*. New Directions for Higher Education, no. 75. San Francisco: Jossey-Bass, 1991, 41 – 61.

Marcus, L. R. "Restructuring Higher Education Governance Patterns." *Review of Higher Education* 20.4 (1997): 399 – 418.

Massy, W.F., (ed). *Resource Allocation in Higher Education*. Ann Arbor: University of Michigan Press, 1996.

Massy, W.F. and A.K. Wilger. "A Cost-Effectiveness Model for the Assessment of Educational Productivity." In Groccia, J.E. and J.E. Miller (eds). *Enhancing Productivity: Administrative Instructional and Technological Strategies*. San Francisco: Jossey-Bass, 1998, 49 – 59.

Mercer, J. "Fund Raising has become a Job Requirement for Many Deans." *The Chronicle of Higher Education* 43.45 (1997): A31 – 32.

National Center for Education Statistics. *Digest of Educational Statistics, 1989*. Washington, D.C: U.S. Dept. of Education, 1989.

National Center for Education Statistics. *Digest of Educational Statistics, 2000*. Washington, D.C: U.S. Dept. of Education, 2000.

O'Neil, H.F., Jr., E. M. Bensimon, M.A.Diamond and M.R. Moore. "Designing and Implementing an Academic Scorecard." *Change* 31.6 (1999): 32 – 40.

Rhoades, G. "Rethinking and restructuring Universities." *Journal of Higher Education Management* 10.2 (1995): 17 – 23.

Rhoades, G. *Managed professionals: Unionized Faculty and Restructuring Academic Labor*. Albany, New York: State University of New York Press, 1998.

Rosovsky, H. *The University: An Owner's Manual*. New York: Norton, 1990.

Schuster, J.H. and associates. *Governing Tomorrow's Campus: Perspectives and Agendas*. New York: American Council on Education/Macmillan, 1989.

Schuster, J.H. and associates. *Strategic Governance: How to Make Big Decisions Better*. Phoenix, Arizona: Oryx/American Council on Education, 1994.

Seymour, D. *On Q: Causing Quality in Higher Education*. Phonenix, Arizona: Oryx/American Council on Education, 1992.

Sporn, B. *Adaptive University Structures: An Analysis of Adaptation to Socioeconomic Environments of US and European Universities*. London: Jessica Kingsley, 1999.

The Chronicle of Higher Education. *Almanac Issue, 2001-2002*, (August 31, 2001): 7, 9.

Tucker, A. and R.A. Bryan. *The Dean: Dove, Dragon and Diplomat*. New York: Macmillan, 1988.

Van Vught, F. A. "Autonomy and Accountability in Government-University Relationships." In Salmi, J. and A. M.Verspoor (eds). *Revitalizing Higher Education*. Oxford: Pergamon Press, 1995, 322 – 364.

Walvoord, B.E., A.K. Carey, H.L. Smith, S.W. Soled, P. K. Way and D. Zorn. *Academic Departments: How They Work, How They Change*. ASHE-ERIC Higher Education Report, 27.8. San Francisco: Jossey-Bass, 2000.

Weick, K.E. "Educational Organizations as Loosely Coupled Systems." *Administrative Science Quarterly* 21.1 (1976): 1 – 19.

Wolverton, M., W.H. Gmelch, J. Montez, and C.T. Nies. *The Changing Nature of the Academic Deanship*. ASHE-ERIC Higher Education Reports, 28.1. San Francisco: Jossey-Bass, 2001.

ALBERTO AMARAL, GLEN A. JONES AND BERIT KARSETH

GOVERNING HIGHER EDUCATION: COMPARING NATIONAL PERSPECTIVES

1. INTRODUCTION

The authors of the thirteen core essays in this volume share a common belief that issues of governance are central to our understanding of higher education and the evolution of these extraordinarily complex institutions and systems. Each chapter frames the analysis of higher education governance in a somewhat different way, in part because our authors are attempting to understand governance issues in quite different contexts and they are exploring issues at different levels of the higher education system. While the operational definition of governance varies somewhat by author, the contributors to this volume share a common understanding that governance focuses on a series of questions related to the determination of what higher education is or should be in a specific context: Who decides? How do they decide? What do they decide? As Michael Reed, V. Lynn Meek and Glen Jones note in their introductory chapter, another common element in how our contributors have conceptualised governance "is the notion of the relationship or dynamic interaction of bodies and groups operating at different levels of a higher education system."

The objective of this essay is to look across these jurisdiction-specific perspectives in order to compare and contrast the different stories of higher education governance that emerge from this collection. We attempt to locate these national studies within a broader conceptual map and, in doing so, explore common issues and findings as well as unique observations.

We have used Clark's (1983) basic notion of levels of authority within a higher education system as an organisational tool. What one sees in higher education depends on where one looks, and higher education governance is frequently understood and defined in different ways at different levels of the higher education system. We therefore begin our analysis by looking at the superstructure or system level of higher education, and then turn to review the findings of our authors that relate to the institutional or enterprise level of authority, and then focus on the understructure or basic academic unit. We then discuss the complex interrelationships between these levels. We conclude the essay by reviewing major findings and suggesting some important areas for future research.

There are a number of limitations associated with our approach that should be noted at the outset. First, our cross-national analysis of higher education governance draws primarily on the research findings and observations of the contributing authors. While we attempt to locate this work within the broader

Alberto Amaral, Glen A. Jones and Berit Karseth (eds.), Governing Higher Education:
National Perspectives on Institutional Governance, 279—298.
© 2002 *Kluwer Academic Publishers. Printed in the Netherlands.*

international/comparative literature on higher education, we cannot pretend to be experts on higher education governance in each of the nine jurisdictions covered in this volume. One of the dangers of cross-national or comparative analysis is that the experience of different systems and cultures are frequently reinterpreted through the eyes of a single observer who operates from a particular, often implicit, frame of reference, though our decision to write this essay as a collaborative effort involving three researchers from three quite different jurisdictions was designed to at least partly address this methodological concern[1]. Second, there are obvious limitations associated with the jurisdictions represented in this compilation. Our emphasis is obviously on institutional governance in nine specific countries, and it is important to note that all of these countries are rooted in western cultural experience and have highly developed economic systems. In other words, our observations are based on the reported experience of a sample of developed countries in Europe, North America and Australia, and there is little doubt that different issues and theoretical perspectives might have emerged from the inclusion of different countries with different cultural foundations and quite different economic circumstances. Finally, it is important to note that most of our contributors focus on a single institutional form or sector within what are frequently complex multi-sectoral higher education systems. Little attention is devoted to inter or intra-sectoral governance arrangements, those these structures or practices may play an important role in system and institution-level governance (see, for example, Jones, Skolnik and Soren 1998).

Despite these limitations, the research papers presented in this volume provide a rich foundation for looking at issues of higher education governance across different systems. There is much that can be learned by stepping outside national boundaries in order to look at common issues and contrasting experiences through cross-national analyses.

2. SYSTEM-LEVEL GOVERNANCE

The superstructure of the higher education system includes the complex web of interactions, structures and regulatory mechanisms above the level of the individual institution. A central issue in system-level governance is the nature of the relationship between the state and the institution of higher education, but in multi-institutional systems this level of authority frequently includes differential regulatory arrangements for different sectors or institutional types and mechanisms to relate component parts of the system to each other.

A number of scholars of higher education have noted that system-level governance arrangements can be broadly categorized into different models corresponding to quite different assumptions about the relationship between the state and higher education (for example, see Clark 1983; Harman 1992). As Alberto Amaral and António Magalhães[2] note in their paper, the model of system-level governance that emerged in Continental Europe was premised on the assumption that the university was a state institution. The university was viewed as a key social and cultural instrument for the development of the modern nation state, and the state assumed a central role in regulating and controlling these institutions. Higher education was simply too important to be left in the hands of independent institutions. The development of a 'whole' nation with a common identity often implied the need for common standards and homogeneous institutional forms, and the state frequently mandated national curricula and program standards. At the same time, the interests of the state were served by providing individual scholars with academic freedom so that they could explore truth without interference from the surrounding civil order. The modern state required modern ideas that could contribute to the national identity in social, cultural, political, and economic terms, and the state protected the freedom of scholars to pursue those ideas in their search for truth. Authority was shared between the state and academic guilds.

The Anglo-Saxon model, in contrast, was premised on the belief that higher education was too important to be left to the political whims of the nation state. The Oxbridge archetype focused on the college as the primary organisational entity. Instead of state control, this model emphasized the importance of institutional autonomy and self-government. The basic tenants of this model were exported to the colonies and national variations began to occur. The system level governance arrangements in the United Kingdom, the United States, Australia and Canada were founded on a common belief that institutional autonomy should be protected, but the assumptions underscoring the ways decisions were made within these autonomous institutions varied by jurisdiction. In the United Kingdom, authority was shared between a strong academic oligarchy and institutional administrators and trustees, while in the United States authority was shared between a much stronger institutional administration and a weaker academic oligarchy. Arrangements in Australia and Canada fell somewhere in between these two variations on a common theme.

It is now commonplace to conclude that both of these models have been revised as a function of government reforms of higher education during the last few decades. There is now a substantive body of international/comparative literature that describes these reforms in detail (see, for example, Neave and Van Vught 1994), but the common observation is that many continental European nations have abandoned the state-control model in favour of steering higher education from a distance and providing local institutions with increased autonomy. In contrast, the United Kingdom, the United States, Australia and Canada have all experienced increased government intervention and regulation. A number of the papers in this collection contribute to our understanding of these changes in the context of higher education governance, and a number of key themes emerge from these contributions.

The first theme is that shifts in the relationship between the university and the state have led to important, and sometimes revolutionary, changes in system-level governance. While there are significant differences by jurisdiction, the authors provide clear evidence that all of these systems are subject to external pressure to adopt management approaches that favour responsiveness to the economic needs of the nation and the incorporation of the ideas and values of business. There is considerable variation in the nature of this pressure, ranging from increasing 'market rhetoric' to the introduction of significant changes in the mechanisms and structures of system-level governance, including the use of performance funding, state-university contracts, and system/institutional rationalization.

Perhaps the most dramatic reforms have taken place in countries associated with what we have called the Anglo-Saxon model of system-level governance. For Australia and the United Kingdom, these reforms are not isolated to a particular public sector but are a component of a much broader rethinking and restructuring of the role and function of government. The core ideological assumptions that underscored the modern welfare state are being challenged, and in some jurisdictions conquered, by neo liberal discourse. Common tenets of this new approach include a preoccupation with the market as a mechanism for improving public sector productivity and efficiency and the closely related emphasis on managerialism, including the introduction of new forms of performance accountability and other approaches designed to increase the management capacity of public sector institutions. In short, the language of government, and of the state, has shifted in favour of the discourse of the marketplace. Neo liberal ideology also implies a diminution of the role of the state based on the belief that anything 'public' is inherently inefficient and less productive than any corresponding activity assigned to the 'private' sphere. Good government is less government, especially if less government can be accomplished by restructuring public sector responsibility into private industry.

The trends associated with the Australian and United Kingdom reforms described by Oliver Fulton, Meek, and Reed are not unique to these countries and similar changes have been identified in both the United States and Canada. Slaughter and Leslie (1997), in their comparative analysis of higher education policy in Australia, Canada, the United Kingdom and the United States, noted common pressures in all four countries but they also observed that the impact and implications of these common trends appeared to vary by jurisdiction. Changes in the United States were viewed as less dramatic and more gradual that in Australia and the United Kingdom, but this may be a function of the fact that the market has long been regarded as a legitimate force in American higher education and, as Elaine El-Khawas notes in her chapter, universities in the United States generally assign a strong role to central administrators and recent changes in governance include 'strengthened administrative steering.' Slaughter and Leslie concluded that Canada was an exception in that "higher education did not undergo the same degree of change as the other countries," though this conclusion may have been a function of the timing of their study. More recent analyses suggest that neo liberal policies are beginning to have a significant impact on Canadian higher education (Currie and Newson 1998; Jones 2000; Magnusson 2000) including shifting the boundaries of authority, and the balance of power, associated with administrative and academic decision making (Jones, this volume; Jones, Shanahan and Goyan 2002). In short, there appear to be common policy trends in all four countries, with jurisdictional variations in terms of the magnitude and implications of these changes.

It is rather surprising that the changes taking place in all four jurisdictions seem to be rather independent of the political party in power (Slaughter and Leslie 1997: 37), and while Castle, Gerritsen and Wolves (1996: 2) argue that Australia and New Zealand "were the only OECD countries in which Labour/Social Democratic governments sought to actively transform society and the economy toward a 'more market' mode on a scale comparable with the ambitions of the right," it is also true the Mr. Blair's 'third way', while employing a different rhetoric than the previous Conservative governments, has continued and extended 'new managerialism' in the public sector through the privatisation of public services, and, in the higher education sector, through tuition fee policies and the increased movement towards quasi-market approaches. Major reforms in the United States occurred under the presidency of a Democrat, while major Canadian federal government reforms occurred under a Liberal government that portrays itself as being in the centre of the political spectrum.

All of these reforms are associated with broader public sector transformations, and, as both Meek and Reed note in their papers, these broader public sector changes have received much more attention in the research literature than the specific implications of these changes for the higher education sector. In this vein, it is interesting to speculate whether the assumptions underscoring the Anglo-Saxon model of system-level governance described above have made these higher education systems particularly vulnerable to neo liberal reforms. Trow (1996: 312) considers that Britain paid the price "for 70 years or more of elite university politics, involving informal discussions at the Athenaeum between the great and good on one side and ministers and civil servants on the other, many of whom on both sides had gone to school and university together ... universities did not quite know what to do when they got a Prime Minister who was no gentleman..." The notion of institutional autonomy, rooted in independence from the state, was often operationalised by distancing the system-level governance of higher education from the public sphere. It may be easier to privatise and steer autonomous institutions than those that are innately associated with more statist traditions. In the end, the notion of institutional autonomy, whether protected by Royal or legislative charter (as in the United Kingdom or Canada) or constitutional law (as in Portugal), does not mean much when the government decides to intervene to make universities fall in line with what are considered to be the supreme interests of the nation.

The changes reported by our Western European colleagues are qualitatively different. The general trend in these countries has been for the government to step back from detailed, centralized regulation in favour of steering institutions that are provided with greater levels of autonomy. However, as our authors note, there are dramatic differences in terms of the nature and magnitude of these changes by jurisdiction.

Peter Maassen argues that The Netherlands "was the first Continental European country to translate the changing social expectations with respect to higher education into reform initiatives." The long list of substantive reforms associated with the early 1980s included "a new government steering approach, a new comprehensive higher education law, new quality assessment mechanisms, a new structure for the teaching programmes of the universities [and] a new landscape for the higher vocational sector." Maassen and Harry de Boer focus on the recent government reforms of the governance structure of the increasingly autonomous 'managed' universities.

In Portugal, the main political goals following the 1974 Revolution were ideological, aiming at a complete transformation of an educational system tainted by the former dictatorial regime. This was clearly evident in the first Programme of the Socialist Party (Congresso do Partido Socialista 1974: 39), the winner of the first general elections after the revolution, which stated that "the school will no longer be used as an instrument for diffusing the ideology of a society divided into classes, by means of a teacher-student relationship following the model of dominator-dominated. Education will no longer develop young people's behaviours and reflexes leading to acceptance of the aggressions of an oppressive system."

All this has changed with time, and successive Ministers of Education have assumed an increasing economic role for education. For instance, Minister Victor Crespo (who was in office from 1980 until 1982) considers that "there is no member of the EU that is not considering its educational, professional training and research systems, in order to create the best conditions to compete, to face the new reality created by free circulation of people, where jobs are obtained according to the levels of educational training" (Crespo 1993), while Roberto Carneiro states that "the successive transformations postulated to the highest level of education aim at anticipating the big challenge of the preparation of the Portuguese manager for the third millennium" (Carneiro 1988: 19 – 20). The Portuguese higher education system has followed the Continental European trend of increased institutional autonomy, and Autonomy Acts were approved by Parliament in 1998 for public universities and in 1990 for public Polytechnics.

Jef Verhoeven and Geert Devos describe the substantial reforms associated with the rationalization of the college sector in Flanders, Belgium. Government policies created an environment where small institutions were essentially forced to merge to create larger colleges. The new institutions were granted higher levels of autonomy within the restructured system-level governance arrangement.

Sectoral rationalization through institutional mergers was also a major component of higher education reforms in Norway analysed by Ingvild Larsen and Berit Karseth. Both authors focus on the implications of the increased level of autonomy provided to these new institutions. Larsen notes that recent changes in Norwegian higher education have been marked "by the introduction of market-type solutions and quasi markets, increased decentralization of public control and a more competitive mentality" leading to the incorporation of elements of private sector practice in public management. At the same time, both authors note that the state has retained centralized control over several important areas of policy, including the establishment of national curricula in certain professional programme areas.

The French case reminds us that it is important to not over-generalize about European higher education reforms. France is a country of deep-rooted republican traditions with a government (with Prime Minister Lionel Jospin as head of a left-wing coalition) that, so far, has not bowed to the pressure to adopt the values of the market. A long tradition of strong and centralized state control has left little room for institutional autonomy. Thierry Chevaillier and Christine Musselin and Stéphanie Mignot-Gérard consider the role of public contracts negotiated by universities with the government as a tool that is changing the nature of leadership in French universities. However, French universities are still strongly in the public domain and are likely to remain so for the near future. In fact, it remains to be seen whether the planning contracts (or negotiated public rules, to use Chevaillier's phrase that takes into account the blatant asymmetry of power in these agreements) will lead to increased institutional autonomy or whether the "overall control of the ministry has increased when the focus shifted from detailed administration to strategic management".

In many parts of Western Europe, where the state continues to be the primary source of university operating support – and, when it comes to the bottom line, institutional autonomy depends on funding – the state seems to experience certain 'moral' qualms towards the market and privatisation. In much of Western Europe the 'market' continues to be primarily a rhetorical construction and an ideological concept within the higher education sector. As Trow noted:

> Markets are still a relatively minor factor in Europe, which on the whole does not provide a market for education, and whose governments rather dislike the idea of a market for higher education and it potential effects on quality and status (Trow 1996: 310).

A second, closely related theme that runs through the core papers of this volume is that changes in system-level governance reflect direct challenges to, and conflict over, the 'traditional' objectives and goals of the university. Changes in system-level governance arrangements are not value neutral; they represent an attempt to replace one set of assumptions concerning the role and function of higher education with another. The 'new' objectives reported by our authors include such values as 'responsiveness', 'adaptability' (Amaral and Magalhães) and 'competitiveness' (Larsen). In short, changes in system-level governance are not just a function of changes in the relationship between the university and the state; they imply significant modifications to the traditional view of the relationship between the university and society.

The Portuguese sociologist Santos (1996: 165 – 166) argues that the contemporary university is living a crisis of hegemony and of legitimacy, as well as an institutional crisis. While each of these three components was initiated in different periods during the development of the capitalist mode of production, they only assumed a virulent role over the last two or three decades.

The university's crisis of hegemony is related to the loss of its former exclusive role in society, due to the fact that the university was unable to fully perform the diverse and sometimes contradictory roles imposed by society. The establishment of the polytechnics as a means of offering vocational training more adapted to the immediate demands of economic development, or the establishment of large research organisations outside the realm of the university, are examples of the university's loss of hegemony. Even the university's exclusive role of awarding degrees is being challenged.

The legitimacy crisis is mainly the result of the success of the fight for social and economic rights, such as the right to education (Santos 1989: 10) that unmasked higher education and higher culture as a prerogative of better-off social classes and led to the massification of higher education. It is also the result of demands that the university's programmes become relevant, as the right to employment consecrated in many national constitutions is being inescapably replaced by the concept of employability (Neave 2001). The traditional pact between the university and society has clearly changed, with the balance of expectations on the socio-economic role of universities shifting away from the social and cultural towards the economic function of the university.

The institutional crisis centres on the autonomy and organisational specificity of higher education institutions. This crisis is evident in the fact that the relative increased autonomy given to universities in the mode of state supervision functions in the context of subordination to stringent efficiency and productivity criteria associated with managerialism.

While many of our authors focus directly on issues associated with the institutional aspects of this crisis, all three of these notions underscore the broad transformations in system-level governance described in this volume. System reforms frequently imply significant changes in the understanding of whether higher education is a 'public' or 'private' area of activity, of whether academic research should be viewed as the search for truth in whatever form that journey may take or whether it should be focused on addressing the economic needs of the state, and whether faculty should be viewed as playing a special/elite/professional role within these institutions or as ground-floor workers in a knowledge industry..

With this in mind, it is particularly interesting to note that the communiqué of the Ministers assembled in Prague on May 19th 2001 clearly stated that higher education is a public good and should remain so, and an important recommendation issued by the Minister's Committee of the Council of Europe (2000) makes an eloquent re-statement of the Humboldtian university and "most interesting amongst this re-statement of the neo Humboldtian credo is the plea for governments to restore the research role to those establishments from which it has been withdrawn" (Neave 2001).

3. GOVERNANCE AT THE LEVEL OF THE INSTITUTION

Most of our authors focus on institutional governance and the volume includes a rich analysis of changes at this level of authority within these nine jurisdictions. Before describing a number of common themes that emerge from these analyses, it is important to note the tremendous differences in the organisational and structural assumptions that underscore these institution-level governance arrangements, recognizing that these organisational characteristics provide the background for recent changes.

Perhaps the most extreme differences represented in this volume are found in France and the United States. As Musselin and Mignot-Gérard note, the French university sector was largely characterized by strong state-control and strong academic guilds represented in structural terms by the deans and the academic units. The governance arrangements at the institutional level were viewed as weak and university-level participatory councils were seen as indecisive and ineffectual. Recent changes, largely initiated by government, have resulted in a somewhat strengthened university-level governance structure with presidential teams and participatory bodies that are now making strategic decisions. While these changes imply an increased capacity for university-level governance and administration, it is important to recognize that these are 'evolutionary' modifications within a sector where the state continues to exercise centralized system-level control over such policy areas as the opening of competitions for faculty appointments and programme approval. In contrast, the governance structure of universities in the United States involves a strong, centralized approach to decision-making focusing on the institutional president (the chief executive officer), and her or his cabinet, functioning under the supervision of a governing board composed of elected or appointed external members. El-Khawas suggests that recent trends involve a movement towards even stronger central 'steering', evidenced by a broad pattern of new management rules. There has been a general reluctance to include faculty representation on university governing boards, senates are generally regarded as weak, and there is a concern as to whether "the professoriate have sufficient voice under the new arrangements that have emerged." In contrast to their French peers, these are relatively autonomous institutions vis-à-vis government, though they are subject to state regulation and accountability requirements.

A second caveat is that recent changes should not be regarded as the restructuring of ancient or timeless traditions of institutional governance. As Reed, Meek, and Jones note in the Introduction, a number of our authors report governance reforms in the 1950s, 1960s and 1970s that predate the current debate on institutional management in the context of new managerialism/public management. Governance has been a recurring issue in higher education, and while recent changes in some jurisdictions signal radical reforms, there has never been a 'golden age' of university governance or a 'utopian model' that satisfied the often conflicting interests and visions of higher education.

A common theme running through many of the chapters of this volume is that recent changes in institution-level governance have shifted the balance of power and authority within these institutions through the development of new central governance structures, changes in participatory governance arrangements, and strengthening the role of the central administration. In terms of new governing structures, the governing board now plays a prominent role. While some form of institution-level board or council has long been a component of universities in Australia, Canada, and the United Kingdom, there is a sense that there has been a increase in the authority and responsibility associated with these bodies relative to academic councils or senates. Under the rubric of managerialism, the internal logic that led to the creation of bicameral governance arrangements appears to have shifted in favour of strengthening the administrative capacity of the university (Fulton; Jones). In the case of the Norwegian colleges, system restructuring led to the creation of ostensibly strong, institution-level governing boards that now fulfil a variety of complex roles within these organisations (Larsen), and similar structures were created in the newly merged colleges of Flanders, Belgium (Verhoeven and Devos). Governing boards were an important component in the governance reforms associated with the development of 'managed universities' in The Netherlands (De Boer, Maassen).

At the same time that a number of systems have adopted 'corporate-like' governance arrangements, these is evidence that this 'private-sector' approach is frequently subject to inflexible 'public-sector' regulation. Larsen reports that while the new Norwegian college boards have been assigned broad responsibilities under legislation, the members of these boards view state rules and regulations as restrictive. Jones suggests that the creation of bicameral governance structures in Canada was based on the assumption of a delegation of state interests to a governing board composed of individuals appointed by government, and one might assume that a somewhat similar logic underscored the creation of governing board structures in other jurisdictions. The new governance environment is one in which the state continues to appoint 'respected citizens' to ensure that 'wise' decisions are made in the best interests of the university, while the state increasingly narrows the range of 'wise' choices available to the board through regulation and/or establishes the acceptable parameters of performance through the use of accountability and performance funding mechanisms.

In addition to the creation of new structures, chapter authors also describe important changes in terms of participation on governing bodies and councils. To make universities more relevant and responsive to the demands of society – economic demands, not cultural and social – external stakeholders are assuming an increased role in governance and in several cases they are members of the equivalent of boards of trustees (Amaral and Magalhães, Meek, De Boer, Maassen, Jones, Fulton, Reed). A similar trend is observed in Belgium (De Wit and Verhoeven, 2000). In some European countries (Spain, Italy, France) a stronger role for local authorities is emerging. For many of these countries, the participation of external stakeholders or 'external personalities' represents a substantive change to the traditional assumptions underscoring university governance. Amaral and Magalhães identify a number of serious concerns with both the role and reality of external stakeholder participation in university governance, while Larsen suggests that the introduction of external members on Norwegian college boards has been generally well received.

There have also been changes in the level and form of participation of internal constituencies. The most dramatic example described by our authors is associated with the governance reforms in The Netherlands, where the internal, representative councils have essentially become advisory bodies and where central executive authority rests with the new boards that are wholly composed of external members. As both De Boer and Maassen note, the reform signals a significant change in terms of role of university community members in institution-level governance.

A closely related trend is a repositioning of the rector (or vice-chancellor, or president) as a chief executive officer in many, though not all, of these systems. In some jurisdictions these are now 'appointed' rather than 'elected' positions, and in many the 'job description' includes responsibility for the overall administration of the university as well as institutional spokesperson, lobbyist, and a plethora of other leadership roles.

All of these points combine to suggest a general trend towards the centralization of authority in institution-level governing structures and administrators and a decline in the 'academic voice' in institutional decision-making. Traditional forms of academic governance, with a strong reliance on collegiality, became the target of fierce criticism, being diversely, or simultaneously, branded as inefficient, corporative, non-responsive to society's needs and unable to avoid declining quality standards of teaching and research (Amaral and Magalhães). Philip Altbach (2000: 9) has observed that "Worldwide, the traditional control of the central elements of the university by the faculty is being diminished. In the name of efficiency and accountability, business practices imported from the corporate sector are coming to dominate the universities."

On the issue of centralisation, Verhoeven and Devos' analysis of the consequences of the merger process that has changed the panorama of college education in Flanders is particularly relevant. Despite the legal definition of an integrated college as a democratic organisation recognising the right of participation of all its members in decision-making, the authors observed that there is tendency for centralisation of decision-making in the hands of the managers as a tool to promote integration of the different units into the new college structure. It remains to be seen if this will remain as a more managerial approach or if, on the other hand, once the integration process is solidified there will be a move towards a more decentralised management structure.

4. GOVERNANCE AT THE UNDERSTRUCTURE LEVEL

While most of our authors focused on governance issues at the system and institution levels, they also acknowledge that the 'real work' of higher education takes place in the classrooms, libraries, and laboratories and not in the board room or council chambers. The central question raised by a number of our authors related to the understructure level of authority concerns the impact of system-level and institution-level governance on the basic discipline unit. Three major themes arise from the papers.

The first is that the movement towards greater centralization of decision-making authority through strengthened governing board and central administrative structures has reduced the level of authority associated with local collegial governance arrangements. In other words, authority over some policy issues has moved up within the institution in order to allow universities to develop cohesive strategies and policies. In France, for example, the evolutionary changes associated with the development of university-level strategic capacity has come at the expense of the previously strong discipline-based decision-making structures. Similar changes have taken place in the Netherlands, through the changes in the role assigned to local councils.

A second, closely-related theme concerns the reconstruction of local academic administrative positions as 'middle-managers' within the more hierarchical, managerial organisational culture. In many instances deans of faculties are no longer elected by their peers but appointed by the rector or the board of governors (Meek, Maassen, De Boer). In some systems deans are now regarded as faculty-level chief executive officers. Some authors note that there is considerable tension associated with the repositioning of local academic leadership. In some cases the presidential team at the institution-level excludes deans and other local representatives, perhaps based on the assumption that central institutional strategic decision-making can only occur if these processes rise above the frequently conflicting issues and perspectives associated with the institutional understructure. De Boer notes that the new deans working under the 'managed' university structure of the Netherlands find themselves in the untenable position of balancing between local interests and ambitions and university-level administrative mandates and priorities. What is clear is that in many systems deans are no longer viewed as senior academics who are willing to devote attention to facilitating the collegial development of their unit. They are increasingly viewed as administrative professionals.

A third theme is that the shift in power and authority relations associated with increased managerialism and governance restructuring has serious implications for the work that is taking place at the understructure level of the higher education. Some of these implications are obviously related to broader system-level changes, for example the notion of 'relevance' and the prioritisation of the economic functions of higher education are creating a new hierarchy of knowledge that privileges research and academic programs that are more directly related to the market. All university faculty may search for truth, but those who are involved in fields that are viewed as more closely addressing the economic needs of the nation may have access to greater research support, salaries, and other professional rewards.

At the same time, there is a sense that the magnitude of complexity and diversity associated with the understructure level is such that some of the implications of these changes are ambiguous and unanticipated. We will return this point below, but it is important to note here that the impact of changes that appear rational at the institutional level may lead to extremely complex, multidimensional changes at the local level. Karseth's case study of changes in nursing education in Norway provides an excellent example of how system reforms led to the repositioning of this area of professional education and dramatic changes in the power and authority relationships associated with academic work and the construction of professional curricula. A surprising outcome from these complex changes is that the relative influence of the profession, as represented by the professional organisation, has declined relative to other actors as a function of sectoral and programmatic restructuring, and professional educators have shifted away from their traditional emphasis on practice in favour of the new values and cultural elements associated with their new organisational location. Others note the importance of local-level resistance to broader organisational change, and strategies to obscure or mediate the effects of the new pressures of managerialism on the institutional understructure.

Finally, it is important to note that there are frequently both horizontal and vertical dimensions to system-level reforms that may add yet another layer of complexity to changes taking place at the understructure level. Higher education restructuring has frequently resulted in shifts in the relationships between component parts of the higher education system, often leading to the academic drift of institutional forms that had previously been primarily associated with vocational, tertiary or further education. In some systems the definition of 'higher education' has expanded to include programmes and institutional forms that had once been regarded as 'beneath' the plane of elite university-level education. Looking across the system, this implies that the understructure level now includes faculty and programmes that not only represent different academic cultures, but dramatically different historic traditions and cultures related to practice, vocationalism, and conceptions of knowledge. New people and programmes have moved into the 'higher education neighbourhood' and this may suggest tensions in the understructure community as the traditional tenants find themselves living alongside new peers with different values, cultures, relationships and priorities. There are also important governance issues concerning the relationships at the understructure level between local units in different institutions focusing on programme standards, credit recognition, transfer and articulation (see Jones 2001).

5. ACROSS THE LEVELS OF AUTHORITY

Many of the most important issues raised by our authors cannot be neatly categorized by level of authority because they involve the interactions between component parts of the higher education system or issues that transcend these levels. We will focus on two of these issues: trust, and the complex interactions between the institutional centre and what Clark (1998) refers to as the academic heartland.

One of the main concerns that runs through many of the papers in this volume concerns the issue of trust. Trow (1996) suggests that trust is visible in the provision of support, by either public or private bodies, without the requirement that the institutions either provide specific goods and services in return for that support, or account specifically and in detail for the use of those funds. The laws of autonomy or envelope budgeting are examples of trust. Over the last decades, trust has been replaced by increased demands for accountability. Trow (1996: 311) argues that accountability can be viewed as "an alternative to trust, and efforts to strengthen it usually involve parallel efforts to weaken trust" and he adds that "accountability and cynicism about human behaviour go hand in hand". The United Kingdom under the leadership of Margaret Thatcher provides a classical example of the withdrawal of trust from the universities as a matter of government policy rather than of changes of attitudes in the broader society. Trow argues that in United Kingdom the universities did not know how to develop and then translate support in the society at large into political support so as to be able to defend themselves through the ordinary devices of real politics in democratic society. This same idea is restated by Fulton: "government has made very clear that it has largely withdrawn whatever trust it previously placed in professional norms and standards."

The loss of trust in public institutions has led to what Neave (1996: 37) calls the evaluative state "which appears to be more effective in enforcing systems of accountability (the other face of institutional autonomy) and control directed at the main activities of academe – teaching, learning, researching and spending". Most of the countries addressed in the core chapters of this volume have national systems of quality assessment that, with differing degrees of intrusiveness, impact on the traditions of local self-government associated with local academic communities.

The loss of trust has also impinged upon the professions. Slaughter and Leslie (1997: 4 – 5) consider that "the very concept of a professional turned on the practitioner eschewing market rewards in return for a monopoly of practice. Professionals made the case that they were guided by ideals of service and altruism. They did not seek to maximize profits; they claimed to put the interests of client and community first" and they add that academics constitute a profession that has been especially insulated from the market as "they have worked for institutions that were non-profit and often state funded, they have not become fee-for-service practitioners, whether solo or in group practice."

No ideal could be more alien to the present movements towards market values, relevance to the labour market, operational efficiency and entrepreneurship. Market mechanisms would destroy, or at least weaken, the sclerotic professional monopolies and corporate bureaucracies that continued to dominate public life (Reed). According to Freidson (2001: 34) the right of expert autonomy and discretion "implies being trusted, being committed, even being morally involved in one's work". And this contrasts with Reed's findings of "a generalised perception of increasing managerial and bureaucratic control with declining levels of trust in and discretion afforded to professional academic mores and practices." The attack on the academic's probity and altruism took several roads. In the United Kingdom, the Conservative discourse of derision (Stephen Ball as cited by Fulton) included allegations that universities were full of incompetent or inefficient academic staff protected by tenure (a point that has been articulated in many other countries) and the accusation that universities were 'producer-dominated' with the implication that producers, unlike professionals, are of course by definition self-interested (Fulton). And also that (*ibid*) "Jarratt and Dearing were making – and promoting – value judgements: alongside relatively innocent comments about speed there are accusations of inertia … conservatism … and even malign self-interest." According to Ball (1998: 125) "part of the attraction of a new policy often rests on the specific allocation of 'blame'". And "blame may either be located in the malfunctions or heresies embedded in the policies it replaces and/or is redistributed within the education system itself and is often personified", leading to what Thrupp (1998) calls the "populist 'tough on schools' discourses of recent governments in both countries (UK and New Zealand), pursuing 'failing' schools and 'incompetent' teachers with uncommon vigour."

The issue of trust, or more accurately mistrust, transcends level of authority in the discussion of higher education governance in this volume. In terms of the new 'managed' universities in the Netherlands, De Boer argues that the absence of trust may have serious implications in terms of the interactions between organisational members and in terms of overall tenor of change within these institution, especially since one can argue that 'efficient' organisations are built on trust. Jones notes that a lack of trust in the degree to which faculty interests were addressed within institutional governance led to the rise of faculty unionisation in Canadian universities, and has more recently led to the unionisation of other groups that feel marginalized in an environment of increasing economic uncertainty, such as part-time faculty and teaching assistants. Many of the significant changes associated with the reforms in Australia and the United Kingdom can be viewed not only in terms of changes in the level of trust in the relationship between the university and state, but also in terms of the relationships within these institutions.

One might also note that the new higher education governance environment that is emerging in some jurisdictions places considerable trust, or faith, in governance structures that are primarily associated with private-sector industry. Recent events suggest that there are issues of trust emerging in corporate governance as well. Over the last few years, shareholders have raised serious concerns on the efficacy of senior administrative remuneration plans that reward short-sighted management decisions over the long-terms of interests of the corporation, and the recent Enron failure does little to boost confidence in the conclusion that private sector corporate-style arrangements represent some sort of panacea for the ails of public-sector governance.

The second core issue concerns the relationship between central institutional governance arrangements and activities and work at the local or understructure level. On the one hand, institutions are increasingly under pressure to reprioritise their activities to focus on the economic objectives of higher education, and to adopt managerialist approaches that presume the existence of hierarchical structures and power relationships. On the other hand, the 'real' work of higher education takes place through the activities of extraordinarily specialized, expert academics who engage in complex interactions with students and local and national intellectual networks. Taken together, these two points create a core conundrum in the quest to regulate and strengthen the efficiency of what is increasingly viewed as an expert-driven knowledge industry. How do you manage genius? To what extent can the energies of the university be harnessed by managerialist approaches that are, by their very nature, designed to apply to all of the public sector? Beyond the aggregate, to what extent to do we truly understand the implications of these changes on the real work of the university?

6. MOVING FORWARD: AREAS FOR FUTURE RESEARCH

This book concentrates mainly on changes that occurred in the relationships between higher education institutions and governments, and corresponding changes in power and authority relations at the institutional level. Some questions remain open for further discussion, or even to the divinatory powers of political prophets, and this includes guessing whether the present trend towards neo-liberal politics and market values will continue or if, on the contrary, the pendulum will begin to swing back in the opposite direction. In countries where the logic of market values was imposed to solve problems of public sector management and efficiency it is now apparent that the results have not met the expectations or have even produced disaster. Telling examples are the privatisation of British Railways, the supply of water and energy in California or the costs and quality of the privatisation of health services in Australia and the United Kingdom. Instead of a growing faith in the virtues and superiority of the market, Meek considers that "it has become apparent with the start of the new millennium that not only is there a questioning of the inevitability regarding these processes but also there is a recognition that many of these processes are based more on ideological precepts than on technical rationale. We are also witnessing a significant social backlash to globalisation and privatisation. It is far from clear at this stage whether the reforms of the past decade will be fundamentally altered or subject merely to incremental adjustments". In those countries where free-market policies have been most virulent, it remains to be seen if many (or even most) of the changes to the public and higher education sectors that have occurred over the past two decades are irreversible (Meek).

Many of the questions for future research raised by our authors are, however, linked to the internal changes of higher education institutions. El-Khawas offers a new research agenda on universities as organisations by listing three main proposals. The first proposal starts from the premise that the present changes in university governance – management controls and long-range planning – aim at dealing with the increasing complexity of the university as an organisation in order to analyse how far the new arrangements are appropriate to a situation of permanent external change. The second proposal deals with changes in the organisational structure of universities; are they still an 'organised anarchy' or have they become similar to other large organisations such as business firms? The last proposal considers whether universities have kept some characteristics that are inherent to the university enterprise, and suggests that universities might adopt a 'mixed' or 'hybrid' organisational form combining distinctively academic components with business-like components?

Both Fulton and Reed refer to the intriguing behaviour of academic managers and governors that so far have resisted to become the fully fledged champions of new managerialism, and El-Khawas agrees that in United States the "new 'big-decision' committees are showing respect for implicit norms at their institutions" and that "academic voices still seem to matter, even in organisational settings where the overall influence of academics has been attenuated." This is another question open to research: can we understand better the behaviour of the new academic managers? Is the survival of academic values a tribute to the persistence of collegial values, or to the deeper functionality of collegial practices for the survival of the institution? (Fulton).

Trow (1996) has raised the problem of the loss of trust and increasing demands for accountability. De Boer raises the problem of trust in university governance as an important topic for further research and considers that "in times of uncertainty, unpredictability, insecurity and instability, trust is needed but scarce. Trust may reduce these negative feelings, but at the same time it is extremely hard to establish and maintain it under these circumstances." And Reed asks the question: "the extent to which the control ideology and practice that defines new managerialism as a strategic discourse and programme for transforming university life can facilitate, indeed permit, the necessary levels of trust-based autonomy for 'delivering the goods' may be the underlying conundrum that our manager-academics remain fated to confront?" If this lack of trust is characteristic of times of uncertainty and unpredictability, how can universities cope with change? How can the academic-manager 'motivate and inspire toward change' or align people by new coalitions committed to change? (see El-Khawas). What are the institutional conditions that promote trust or distrust? Why were the reforms in the Netherlands more easily implemented in some institutions than in others (De Boer and Maassen)?

Other authors (Amaral and Magalhães, Meek, De Boer, Maassen, Fulton, Larsen, Reed and El-Khawas) refer to the emergence of external stakeholders in university governance. Amaral and Magalhães distinguish between Form 1 stakeholders (the control function prevails) and Form 2 stakeholders (the advisory function prevails). While El-Khawas considers that in the US stakeholders in governing boards of public universities "also play a strong oversight role, ensuring that the university serves public interests" while at "private universities, boards generally emphasize assistance and guidance, seeking to help the institution carry out its own plans", Larsen refers to the tension that arises in college boards as their "ambition to be a policy-forming board with importance attached to strategic tasks" is lost to the easier and more obvious task of control, sometimes even yielding to the temptation of exercising comprehensive control. The papers by Amaral and Magalhães and Larsen refer to some characteristics of stakeholder behaviour, such as absenteeism. More research will be necessary to understand the different roles and modes of behaviour of external stakeholders and how effective they are in promoting the social or economic relevance of universities.

Glen Jones describes the unique situation in Canada where universities have some degree of flexibility in determining how decisions should be made and who should decide. The author uses the concept of policy network as a way of looking at 'how' decisions are made as well as 'how' the actual policy outcomes emerge from the complex interactions within the policy network. However, despite "a number of the common structural elements associated with Canadian university governance, it is important to recognize that each university has a unique policy network", and if we are to understand the implications of these unique elements, we need to focus on the analysis of institutional case studies.

Chevaillier and Musselin and Mignot-Gérard concentrate on the French national case; while Chevaillier speaks of a new generation of university presidents and the emergence of a strong centre composed of a small group of academics and administrators working closely with the president, Musselin and Mignot-Gérard still see many obstacles and difficulties in the development of more cohesive institutions. The authors agree that there is increasing diversity within the French university system despite some homogenising factors such as national laws, implementation of similar management software, and routinisation of the management of contracts within the central state administration) but while Musselin and Mignot-Gérard see a shift in the balance between ministry and university-level policy development, Chevaillier considers that changes did not translate into a loss of state power. All three authors would agree with El-Khawas' assertion that universities no longer have a 'weak information base.' Musselin and Mignot-Gérard suggest a need for further theoretical research returning to some of the early models and theories that have been used to characterize and explain the organisation of higher education.

Finally, Karseth and Verhoeven and Devos deal with the consequences of college mergers or re-structuring and they focus on the behaviour of internal institutional actors. Karseth considers that while the power of the professional body declined, individual faculty members acquired increased freedom from the norms and values of the profession but she also suggests that more data are necessary in order to analyse individual strategies and behaviour. On the other hand, Verhoeven and Devos consider that the "challenge to create some sense of cohesion among what had previously been separate, independent units" has resulted in centralisation being assigned a more prominent role in the opinion of institutional actors. The authors believe, however, that "over time, these colleges will move towards greater decentralisation in decision-making as they become more functionally integrated" and this may provide the basis for additional research.

All the previous questions are the starting point to a number of research projects. The first Douro River seminar, held in October 2001, was concerned with the changing governance of higher education, set in the context of changing state-society-university relationships. In essence, the seminar and this book set out to track changes in the wider environment for higher education and corresponding changes in power and authority relations internally. Following this stage, it now seems appropriate to focus in more closely on the internal governance of higher education institutions (HEIs): in particular, on questions related to the rise of management as an activity and managerialism as a set of practices and their accompanying ideologies. The key question will be how management and managerialism have affected the basic institutional functions of higher education teaching and relations with students, research and the generation of knowledge, and relationships with external stakeholders

A number of trends have conspired, albeit in different balances across various higher education systems, to bring questions of institutional and sub-institutional management to the fore. First, the stepping back of state ministries in many European countries from direct control and detailed regulation has in effect left a vacuum which institutions have been expected to fill. However, we have to emphasise that this trend is generally linked to a shift in focus from input to output in governmental steering of higher education. One consequence of this shift is the introduction of contracts between the government and individual universities. In other words, institutional autonomy has increased, but at the same time has become more conditional.

Second throughout the last two decades the traditional pact between the university and society has been seriously questioned leading to different expectations with respect to the socio-economic role of the university, i.e. the emphasis has clearly shifted away from the social and cultural towards the economic function of the university.

Third in a number of countries public investment in higher education has decreased with the accompanying requirement that universities find new, non-governmental sources of income.

In some countries this has been a relatively gradual and by now well-established process. In others, historically the institution level decision-making apparatus has been notably weak and neither structures nor cultures appear to have been prepared for the change. Comparative work, drawing on papers that analyse institutional development in response to these new expectations, should reveal whether it makes sense to draw general or differentiated conclusions about the emergence of managerialism across national settings.

As indicated, the aims and expectations that underlie the rise of institutional management are not entirely coherent. There have been, and are, attempts to reorient higher education towards greater external economic effectiveness by increasing the entrepreneurial spirit of institutions in a more competitive environment, and by linking teaching programmes and research activities directly to economic needs. In addition, there are national concerns with greater internal effectiveness and efficiency through cost saving and performance monitoring; and with increasing accountability to a greater range of stakeholders than in the past. In tension with these pressures are the expectations of securing academic standards and assuring or enhancing academic quality.

Each of these trends or factors appears to have led in a variety of different contexts to a new or increased emphasis on the institution as a locus of power; on strategic decision-making at the institutional and sub-institutional levels; on the generation of non-state income; and on resource management, including the management of staff as human resources and on the management of academic work. The consequence in a number of countries has been the rise of managerialism, albeit in a number of forms, sometimes categorised as soft and hard, old and new, etc. In other countries this rise of managerialism has been called the professionalisation of institutional administration, referring to the changing nature of the administrative structures, the administrative work, as well as the administrators themselves.

The aim of the next seminar and book will be to bring together researchers who have addressed the questions outlined above in their work. This offers an opportunity for discussing ways to further the knowledge on the rise of management and managerialism in higher education. In addition, the seminar will provide a forum for documenting the range of forms across different national and institutional settings, and to tease out the aims and expectations of new management approaches, on the basis of the empirical material included in the papers prepared for the seminar. Evidence will also be sought on the ways in which these new approaches have in fact, or in discourse, penetrated the core business of higher education, assuming that they do not remain relatively insulated from everyday practice at the level of a management cadre.

NOTES

[1] A draft of this essay was circulated to all of the authors that contributed to this volume and we would like to gratefully acknowledge the helpful comments and suggestions that we received.

[2] Unless otherwise noted through citation, author references refer to chapters in this volume.

REFERENCES

Altbach, P. "Academic Freedom in Hong Kong – Threats Inside and Out." *International Higher Education* 21 (Fall 2000): 9 – 10.

Ball, S.J. "Big Policies/Small World; an introduction to international perspectives in educational policy." *Comparative Education* 34.2 (1998): 119 – 130.

Carneiro, R., *Educação e Emprego em Portugal: Uma Leitura da Modernização*, Lisboa: Fundação Calouste Gulbenkian, 1988.

Castles, F., R. Gerritsen and J. Wolves (eds). *The Great Experiment,* Sidney: Allen and Unwin, 1996.

Clark, B. R. *The Higher Education System.* Berkeley: University of California Press, 1983.

Congresso do Partido Socialista. *Programa e Estatutos do Partido Socialista.* Lisboa: Partido Socialista, 1974.

Conseil de l'Europe. Recommendation no (2000) 8 du comité des Ministres aux Etats Membres sur la mission de recherché de l'université. Strasbourg: Conseil de l'Europe, 2000 (download from cm.coe.int/ta/rec/2000/f2ooor8.htm).

Crespo, V. *Uma Universidade para os Anos 2000: O Ensino Superior numa Perspectiva de Futuro,* Mem Martins: Editorial Inquérito, 1993.

Currie, J. and J. Newson. *Universities and Globalization: Critical Perspectives.* Thousand Oakes: Sage, 1998.

De Wit, K. and J.C.Verhoeven. "Stakeholders in universities and colleges in Flanders." *European Journal of Education* 35.4 (2000): 421 – 437.

European Council of Education Ministers. *Towards the European Higher Education Area,* Communiqué of the Meeting of European Ministers in charge of higher education assembled in Prague on May 19th 2001.

Freidson, E. *Professionalism: The Third Logic.* Cambridge: Polity Press, 2001.

Harman, G. "Governance, Administration and Finance." In *The Encyclopedia of Higher Education.* Oxford, Pergamon (CD-ROM version), 1992, 1 – 16.

Jones, G.A. "Islands and Bridges: Lifelong Learning and Complex Systems of Higher Education in Canada." In Aspin, D., J. Chapman, M. Hatton and Y. Sawano (eds). *International Handbook of Lifelong Learning,* Volume 2. Dordrecht, The Netherlands: Kluwer Academic Publishers, 2001, 545 – 560.

Jones, G.A., "The Canada Research Chairs Program." *International Higher Education* 21 (2000): 22 – 23.

Jones, G.A., T. Shanahan, and P. Goyan. "Traditional Governance Structures – Current Policy Pressures: The Academic Senate and Canadian Universities." *Tertiary Education and Management* 8 (2002): 29 – 45.

Jones, G.A., M. Skolnik and B. Soren. "Arrangements for Coordination Between University and College Sectors in Canadian Provinces: 1990-1996." *Higher Education Policy* 11.1 (1998): 15 – 27.

Magnusson, J. L., "Canadian Higher Education and Citizenship in the Context of State Restructuring and Globalization." *Encounters on Education* (Special Issue: Building Common Spaces: Citizenship and Education in Canada and Spain), 1 (2000).

Neave, G., "Anything Goes: Or, How the Accommodation of Europe's Universities to European Integration Integrates – An Inspiring Number of Contradictions", Paper presented at the EAIR Conference, 8-12 September, Porto, Portugal, 2001.

Neave, G., "Homogeneization, integration and convergence: The Cheshire Cats of Higher Education Analysis." In Meek, V.L., L. Goedegebuure, O. Kivinen and R. Rinne (eds). *The Mockers and Mocked: Comparative Perspectives on Differentiation, Convergence and Diversity in Higher Education.* London: Pergamon, 1996, 26 – 41.

Neave, G., and Van Vught, F., "Conclusion." In Neave, G. and Van Vught, F. (eds). *Government and Higher Education Relationships Across Three Continents: The Winds of Change,* London: Pergamon Press, 1994, 264 – 319.

Santos, B.S. *Os Direitos Humanos na Pós-Modernidade.* Coimbra: Oficina do Centro de Estudos Sociais, 1989.

Santos, B.S. *Pela Mão de Alice. O Social e o Político na Pós-modernidade.* 5th edition, Porto: Edições Afrontamento, 1996.

Slaughter, S. and L. Leslie. *Capitalism: Politics, Policies and the Entrepreneurial University.* Baltimore: Johns Hopkins, 1997.

Thrupp, M. "Exploring the Politics of Blame: school inspection and its contestation in New Zeeland and England." *Comparative Education* 34.2. (1998): 195 – 209.

Trow, M., "Trust, Markets and Accountability in Higher Education: a Comparative Perspective." *Higher Education Policy* 9.4 (1996): 309 – 324.

Higher Education Dynamics

1. J. Enders and O. Fulton (eds.): *Higher Education in a Globalising World.* 2002
    ISBN 1-4020-0863-5; Pb ISBN 1-4020-0864-3
2. A. Amaral, G.A. Jones and B. Karseth (eds.): *Governing Higher Education: National Perspectives on Institutional Governance.* 2002   ISBN 1-4020-1078-8

KLUWER ACADEMIC PUBLISHERS – DORDRECHT / BOSTON / LONDON